In Search
of Life

A Motorcycle Odyssey
Leon Pang

Copyright Leon Pang 2009©

Iron Hand
Publishing

In Search of Life
A Motorcycle Odyssey
Copyright Leon Pang 2009©
Published by Iron Hand Publishing
4th Edition
Reprinted in 2009 and 2010
ISBN 978-0-9564765-0-0

A CIP catalogue record of this book is available from the British Library

For all those who believed in me

ACKNOWLEDGEMENTS AND PREFACE

I wrote this book by myself using my limited powers and resources despite general pressures and general busyness elsewhere. Though this book came out by accident, how on earth do you write a 158000-word book by accident? Well typing up my travel diaries in quiet moments all of this was going to be published online, then some copyright 'issues' occurred regarding my old articles. Which meant I felt that it was unsafe to put it online in my usual manner. These have been resolved currently at the time of writing. I'm not a millionaire rock star who can afford a bit of piracy on the side lines so I formatted it properly and sent it out to various publishes trying my dumb luck. If you are reading this then my dumb luck hit gold I feel that it is only correct to give acknowledgement where it is due as without it would be almost cheating. This is the 4th edition by the way as my first run was rather more successful than I anticipated and it was incredibly poorly edited, this has had some professional editing. Although it is not perfect little can be it is better than the first editions!

This book is primarily a comedy attached to a biking adventure above anything else; I'm not quite a die-hard adventuring type. As my accounting ex colleagues will recant, if you can't compete with people directly you differentiate so that's what is done here. I formatted and edited it properly and gave it a long edit and my touch that was completely missing from my blog. My blog was a bit too realistic, gritty, harsh and downright too down to earth for many people. This is only possible in the way you can only do when you sit back after the event and look back upon it

Pictures are in black and white as colour photos and binding are bloody expensive, so visit my website for my photo albums which are unfortunately rather thin due to camera issues explained later. I hope to leave this as a monument to something I did in life during a long summer of 2009, something I am uncertain if will ever be repeated if the economic woes continue as they are.

Although this is not an exhaustive list I would like to thank the following people for their help during my trip without which this would have been impossible.

First and foremost David Lambeth the XT supreme mechanic who supplied me with parts when needed and uncompromising advice at any time of the day. Tiffany Coates for generally being an all round nice person and provider of uplifting email motivators at all the right times. Riders 'Blue88', Walter and Tony for being great guys also providing motivation at my low ebbs. Wendy Choi for helping get the XT home (where unfortunately it was stolen almost immediately upon its return). Jason for providing armour upgrades which saved me more than once.

Mostly though a massive thanks to all of Russians and Siberians, the people who I met on this trip who helped me out for no reason other than out of the kindness of their hearts and that I asked. Hongjin Park for being such a gracious host in Seoul resolving all the problems that I had in Korea. Doug P for being so entertaining and helping pick my morale off the floor in Mongolia again at low ebb and showing me that life doesn't have to be the way it is portrayed.

Simon E for restoring my faith in German people and for being an excellent friend for my time in Seoul. I would also like to thank all of the people I met on my trip, the French, Belgians, Italians, Greeks, Bulgarians, Turkish, Georgians, Russians, Mongolians, Koreans, Japanese, Chinese and anybody else who helped me out. The Russians and in particular the bikers deserve a special mention that without their kind help and company. I would be still in Siberia wondering how to get out.

I hope you enjoy the book and I hope it inspires you to go upon your own adventures, remember life is short and time waits for nobody thanks also of course to my parents, and sister who were always there for me.

Thank you everybody.

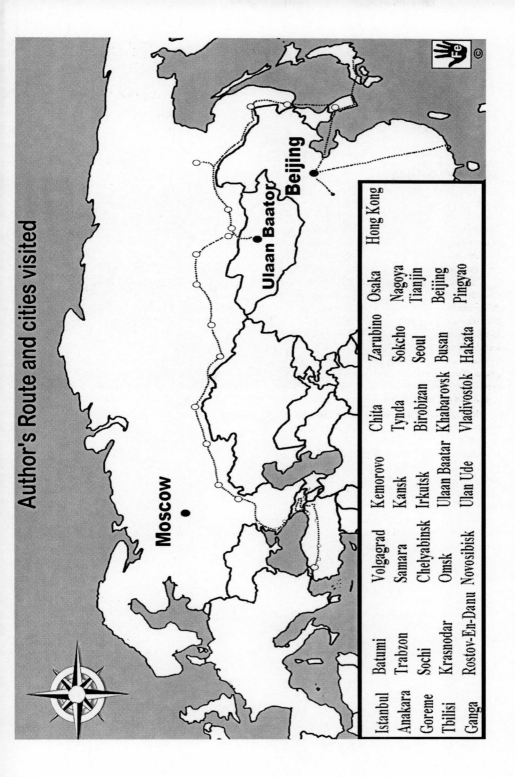

Author's Route and cities visited

Moscow

Ulaan Baator

Beijing

Istanbul	Batumi	Volgagrad	Kemorovo	Chita	Zarubino	Osaka	Hong Kong
Anakara	Trabzon	Samara	Kansk	Tynda	Sokcho	Nagoya	
Goreme	Sochi	Chelyabinsk	Irkutsk	Birobizan	Seoul	Tianjin	
Tbilisi	Krasnodar	Omsk	Ulaan Baatar	Khabarovsk	Busan	Beijing	
Ganga	Rostov-En-Danu	Novosibisk	Ulan Ude	Vladivostok	Hakata	Pingyao	

Horses can climb mountains (Mongolia Terej National park) a few minutes into our horse trek; Salar looks on in the background.

1 : ORIGINS

At the end of the 1970s a woman called Wong gave birth to a healthy baby boy. 6lbs zero ounces. Wong shortly after delivering her baby took this child to the local fortune teller as some Asian parents will. Though not completely believing it. It's one of those things people do just in case. Somewhat like the fictional Suzie Wong, who went to see fortune-tellers out of tradition. Not really believing it sometimes but to go through the motions to sooth her fears regardless. However as an indicator that they were willing to accept the prognosis by the act of actually going to see such a fortune-teller was telling.

Unfortunately the fortune-teller did not have the best of news. Rather than the usual wealthy, happy, lots of grandchildren sort of prediction this was different.

Instead the fortune teller suggested that the life of this child would be unconventional and different. Almost but not quite like the old Chinese curse of may you live in interesting times. I've never been that big of a believer of such things either. In this modern day and age as fortune-tellers are considered to be entertainment and hence must hold entertainment licences.

Modern day entertainers, which you may see on TV, use camera tricks or insinuate and force decisions on people. Sort of like Hobson's choice situation, where people think they have a choice but really do not at all. Although without the confidence trick and money this usually involves. Though Chinese people are incredibly superstitious of even the most ridiculous things, although you may think I am portraying this in jest but it is completely true, such as always closing the toilet lid in case their wealth escapes down the toilet. Or an even stranger one where if a woman gets a Brazilian trim down there it is unlucky for any lucky men who manage to bed her. Such that a super model could be pulled but when it came to the actual act once the knickers were off it would be a case of:

"Erm, no thanks luv but I'll just have to pass."

Or whatever they would say in Chinese. This sounds ridiculous but it is true, it is called white tiger if you are interested or wish to raise a smirk from asking a Chinese person. I wonder if dental floss sells well there.

Fast forward nearly 30 years and those interesting things started to happen and would change my life forever.

2: EACH JOURNEY BEGINS WITH THE FIRST....

The start of 2008 I'd been feeling low for a while. I'd been looking online for reasons for my existence. Two prior motorbike tours were a sort of reason for living. I would put up with the drudgery of daily life to look forward to tearing up the tarmac in Europe. Europe would be a nice distraction but somehow it didn't feel enough it felt like a tease. There is an old saying in Chinese, "A single glass of wine is best spilt." My tours were like one of those addictive foods, when you pop, you can't stop!

However Europe itself had become a bit samey after a couple of visits you realised it was another version of clone town. Each French of Italian or Spanish city had the same chains. Much like the British malaise of clone towns but to a lesser extent. My 3rd and 4th visits to Europe via motorbike I didn't feel inspired enough upon my return to write about them in much depth.

I also felt that I lacked a decent number of biker stories. A couple of biker acquaintances John and Scott had always managed to tell long lively interesting often-hilarious tales of being on the road. My own tales of the road would last maybe an hour tops. Telling my biker stories while John and Scott could tell stories for hours if not days with everybody listening glued to their every word. My own offerings were less than impressive with just the odd bike catching fire, which was memorable.

I had just taken it for an MOT where it had passed with flying colours; this was much to the surprise to the MOT station owner. However once I had wheeled it out and turned the ignition key it burst into flames causing the MOT man to dive for cover. In addition to this a few cases of breaking un-official world records, which can never be claimed as prison would be the only outcome. My best story being in Spain. Where while riding along we were stopped by the police. The policemen acted like tough guys puffing out their chests as if to prove it.

"Only good riders, like us can ride so fast on roads!" They would proclaim after giving us a short lecture in Spanish we did not understand. They got on their bikes and rode off not paying attention to the road. With one of the cops putting his bike

8

into the side of a passing car. You could feel the tomato red glow of embarrassment through their darkened helmet visors. Of course I didn't want to take this to the extreme though. As in the past in country pubs stopping for lunch on ride outs there were always people who saw your bikes and would use it to start a boring conversation. Usually they cornered you in the pub and not letting you escape. Being the boring old fart that occupied each and every pub in the land was not something I wanted to be. Instead a nice smattering of stories was needed. Another less interesting method for attaining stories and far more risky was to sign up as a dispatch rider. A certain dispatch rider who shall be named only as James has an incredible number of stories to tell from the job of dispatch riding. Though dispatch riding is dangerous with the average life expectancy being a little over 2 years ask me to go riding in downtown Beirut or Kinshasa the capital of the Congo I'd jump at the chance. Ask me to be a dispatch rider I'd have to think about it for a very long time.

Many websites offered religious solutions or pay £100 and we will tell you the meaning of life. That is not to say that I did not find interesting diversions on the Internet though. However there are too many to list here some of the discussions got fairly engrossing and amusing. Most notably however the worst way to die threads on forums or how to dispose of a dead body. Although the dead body disposal threads never got very far as they were deleted for potential illegality. Pigs came up top trumps though. Darker themed threads such as what is the worst death you can think of ones never ceased to raise a smile. The most popular ones mentioned were scaphism that you can read about on wikipedia. Being picked apart by fire ants, burnt alive, being buried alive or pure loneliness in a hospital bed or simply helplessness. There were some comical suggestions so it wasn't all dark. Live vivisection, or being dry-bummed to death by an elephant that fingers you first or being trapped in a lift with a certain people. All were great for short-term laughs and comedy but were mere snacks in my desire for a big hearty meal of life. Though youtube proved to be more entertaining where self-styled professional backpackers would explore the planet with abandon. Hmm, I thought this might be a plan. I have never done a **REALLY** big trip my life of working in the office restricting my adventures to flying from civilisation to civilisation. Or tourist traps these barely count as travel I suppose. Nothing in particular answered my thought of there must be more to life than this. Ironically on the bottom of my CV I had always put liked to travel but my travels had abruptly come to a halt nearly a decade ago and hence it felt like a fraud to put it there.

So I continued my day in day out job as an accountant-feeling empty inside. My dad had often said it all seems to have gone so quickly life. He says this a lot when he is in Hong Kong namely as the development is so fast each time he returns to his home it doesn't look the same anymore. One day he stood in the middle of a square in Hong Kong just off Central and said, "When I was a boy I used to fish here." It seemed that even the sea has moved. Which was a warning in disguise as life passes you by quickly if you don't change.

I had a certain fear one day I would wake up and that my life would have passed me by. My own personal theory into the fast passage of time is that if there are no significant landmarks in your memory, i.e. the drudgery of day to day life simply isn't worth remembering most of the time then the passage of time is hard to gauge. Much like navigating in a featureless environment you can't tell how fast you are going or not going. Hence time feels to be going quickly. You're born you live and you die. I'd hoped to put something notable in the bit filed under live. Almost like stasis in fiction because you do not remember anything of the passing of decades you think you just got in the stasis booth. Then again life is full of fears. Fears of not meeting deadlines, fears of not living up to expectations at work, fear of being disliked by colleagues at work, fear of upsetting the boss. Fear of losing your job all of which is the normal status quo in the corporate workplace. There are plenty of other fears in a wider context. There is a fear of losing your home, being hurt, being a victim of crime worst of all a fear of fear. I decided to let all this go just to conquer my other fears. That is not to say that I am fearless but I now I am afraid of a whole lot less.

Of course a normal accountant type would have taken a short vacation, shrugged and gotten on with it. Perhaps learnt to play a musical instrument to let the creative demons out or in an extreme case have gone to a psychiatrist. I don't think this is really a solution to be made happy, happy joy, joy on Prozac or that particular drug that makes people even more suicidal as a side effect and I'm not talking about beer! However I am not a normal accountant and being sat in an office with the boss at the time being told, "You are not different or special you have to do this and that." In almost a sick parody of the scene in the 1999 film The Matrix. Where the boss for being late was telling off Neo as Mr Anderson. Though I cannot say it was a bad place to work actually. The bosses did seem human at the very least and were civil and would speak to you and be frank. I have worked in places where the boss didn't even talk to you and all communication was done by post-it note. A meat packing place I spent a few months working at in between decent jobs in Plymouth I never saw the boss and after doing a ton of overtime for him I left him a note on his desk saying:

"Can I have a pay rise?"

The next day when I came into work, there was a similar note on my desk, it read:

"No, you can't."

You'd have thought he'd be able to spell properly as the boss of such a company, wouldn't you? I'm just relieved I had a relatively easy escape to be honest. I owned and still own very little, no mortgage, no children, no spouse nothing much.

The lack of children though might be attributable to being an accountant. Like a bad personality being an accountant has some perks if you can call them that. In that it seems to be an excellent 100% effective form of contraception. I feel almost pained when I hear of others who tell me they have bought houses over the years. In that prices of houses are insane. It is bizarre. People love high house prices and yet when there is the high price of other things they do not like it. It's not ok to have high cost of food, petrol, transport and day-to-day expenses such as insurance and such like. But hey high house prices are suddenly a good thing. It pains me because you know the people who have bought have effectively put a ball and chain around their ankles. They are suddenly stuck in jobs they probably hate, are broke from paying off the mortgage, generally have a fear of losing their homes no matter what amount of equity paid. They have to cut down on their spending, having their evenings watching DVDs or manufactured pop like pop idol or X factor. Closing their minds to new ideas. Gaining weight and becoming set into their ways. It is utterly depressing. The worst part of all this is that people who bought in the 2005-2008 ultra pyramid scheme of house prices don't even like where they live as it was the only place they could afford. I'm not saying it's a bad choice as you make your own choices and some things make people happy while others make others happy. It's just that I'm not yet ready to sign my name on the dotted line and want to see the alternative instead if only for a while.

I don't know perhaps I am one of the Generation X with no incentives to join this seemingly rigged game. I know I was born in the right years to be considered part of this group.

This was life for me my everyday life. Until one day this all changed. An acquaintance online on a motorbike forum made a call to ride in the middle of 2008. It would be the spark on the blue touch paper that would change things beyond all recognition.

3: PREPARATIONS

It was normally me in 2007 making the calls to ride and this ended up in the forging of the Northern Clan from humble beginnings. This had been credited to myself personally. Nothing lasts forever though and the group had started to splinter off into their separate ways. Groups always did over time. I had seen the Northern group crumble twice previously and the Southern group of which I was once a part of diminish to nearly nothing. But again of course nothing lasts forever and that includes your time on the earth.

This forum had a plucky guy self styled Nathan wanting to do a big trip to Kazakhstan and central Asia and back. For a few months this was forgotten and we had separate trips planned out. But my wingman was unable to come and so had his. A few exchanged emails, which led to phone calls and a meeting was arranged this meeting consisted of beers and we hasty decision making to combine our plans around the world. I was a bit bowled over when he turned up on a rat bike. It seemed more hammerite than bike and the tales told about him of being rather feral in my opinion seemed to seem apt.

Central Asia and Russia were in our minds. It was fresh and untamed few people went there. In comparison to Europe which ten maybe twenty posts a year regarding European tours Central Asia, Mongolia and Russia were rarities. A few people here and there popped over to Moscow but never far, far away into the depths of the unknown and the track less well travelled. I had doubts I would find clone malls and chains in central Asia and Russia, not the places I was going anyway.

The next few months I was giddy inside looking forward to the departure date of this trip. I kept it totally secret from everybody bar the forum and trying to hide the look of delight at work as the leaving date drew ever closer.

On top of this I also had an ulterior motive. LWR (Long Way Round) had bought to light the adventure riding community and allowed people a glimpse into this world. But they did it in such a way I felt that it discouraged other people to just go out there. They made people think such a trip was only possible if you had money and lots of it. People have been doing this lark for years without support crews and tons of money. I set out as an ulterior motive to do my trip on a meagre £20-25 a day.

If you are reading this I was a tight wad at the end of my reign of terror to save for this trip. Although socialising for lunch now and again was pleasant this trip took absolute priority over everything. I had dropped everything for this as this was a once in a lifetime event do or die now or never.

Though this posed some problems as I had limited off road experience and I had at the time two completely unsuitable bikes for continent crossing. A CBR600F and an NTV650(P). Both are excellent bikes but only for the tarmac. One is a sports touring bike the other being a bit of a cross between a cruiser and a street bike. Being a bit of a short arse and off road bikes being tall posed a big problem. I'd watched people waddle their bikes both feet down across rivers and deep sand if I can't do that there will be big problems!

But firstly why a motorbike? Motorbikes are uncomfortable with off road bikes being doubly so. With their cheese wire narrow seats and your head far into the wind. They are slow, needing lots of maintenance compared to cars. You can fall off hurting yourself. They smell bad and you get rained on, sun burnt when hot and get everything thrown at you. But I suppose that's why bikers love motorbikes. It's one of those hard things to explain to a non-biker, cars are just boxes that insulate you with some degree of comfort so that you don't REALLY get to taste everything. It seems a much rawer experience to be had from riding and it is an excuse to kick up conversations with random people as well. Some people might compare it to meditation as well. When riding skilfully around a challenging part of the road all thoughts other than how to ride round this corner what line to take what gear to be in would blot out other thoughts from your mind. In effect it was road meditation with less closing of eyes and sitting cross leggedness. Additionally motorbikes are effectively a go anywhere technology, places where cars even 4x4s would struggle motorbikes have been there probably. Perhaps the biggest factor was I don't actually own a car capable enough to do such a ride and would not be able to afford the shipping of a 4 wheeler on some of the legs where shipping is the only option that is open to you.

The first bike I considered was what the ADV rider crew would consider a beast, a 1989 XLV750RD04 Honda Africa twin. A tough as boots massive machine it *seemed* to tick all the boxes. It was in effect like an accountant with a fellowship. To non-accountants this means 3 years of work experience to get full accountancy body membership (ACCA or ACA) and seven years post qualification of working to get their fellowship kudos and to change the first A to an F. If you can get it great but it is not for me. The Africa Twin was completely ible, i.e. dependable, reliable, good mpg, had massive cargo carrying capacity and a nice tall screen to boot which was useful as I wanted my shirts to fit when I got back. If a nuclear war occurred and there were super radioactive zombies and roving gangs the Mad Max type riders of the apocalypse would ride an Africa Twin. It would survive along with cockroaches. Honda has never built a bike as tough as the Africa Twin since. Probably a good business move in that if they were so tough nobody would ever buy a new bike, as they would seldom break.

My Africa Twin arrived in December and I'd realised I'd made a huge mistake. This Africa Twin had actually been taken to South Africa twice and back. But when Greg pulled up outside to sell me the bike I could see it wasn't good it was way too big. Laying it down on its side and attempting to lift the bike was also impossible for somebody of my small build and it was a case of back to the drawing board.

I redid my spec and asked on ADV rider and BCF as to what the answer was to my dilemma. Maciek Swinarski recommended the answer. The answer came in the form of a single cylinder bike a DR perhaps. Maybe an XT Yamaha (XT stands for cross trail). I very nearly went for a husquvarna TE610E, as this seemed perfect, low weight 60 bhp, kick-starter excellent brakes and handling. This turned out again to be problematic since the TE was effectively a race bike converted to have some road manners and had a reputation for reliability problems and I would effectively be live testing it. Sure people have ridden across the US on TE610s but in Americana spares and mechanics are common and you are never far away from a mechanic or parts supplier. I had doubts the same things could be said about Siberia and Mongolia. The same problem with the KTM640 the KTM was also a 'too' bike, i.e. too bad vibration, too tall, too high compression and too fragile before 2004. Post 2004 bikes had all these things corrected; problem was I couldn't afford a post 2004 bike.

Another nasty problem was all off road bikes are obscenely tall, and I am short very. Every bike I tried was way too tall for me leaving my legs dangling in the air and probably unable to do the mud/sand waddle i.e. both feet down pushing the bike forward when you get stuck.

The solution came to me in a pile of scrap. A big pile of scrap. Digging round I found in an open top crate under a ton of scrap an old 1997 XT600E or rather the parts to build a complete working XT600E perfect! This bike had a low seat and has been proven more than once in crossing deserts and it is THE choice of bike for any plucky rider who wanted to do a big trip. Also because the bike did not cost much I could spend the money on fixing it up modifications and other equipment that might take my fancy.

The parts were put in the back of a car and ferried into a local friendly workshop. It took 2 weeks to put everything back on the frame a week to get the wheels rebuilt onto the front and rear hub and a few days to check everything was ok. It had to be ok my life would depend on it in a matter of weeks. Finally she was ready. Another scrap yard produced a 26-litre tank that had been modified at the bottom to accept 3 more litres 29 litres of fuel total. The XT ticked all of the boxes I had wanted and I took her out for a spin down a spoil tip and she handled nicely.

The XT however was a bit of a hodgepodge of parts. The cylinder head was taken off a 3AJ, the frame was a 3TB, the forks came off a 3AJ and the electrics came off a 4PT bike. David Lambeth the XT supremo was shocked at the monster of

Frankenstein I had created and effectively said in no uncertain terms that my trip was as he put it lightly, "Utterly fucked." Though he did appreciate my choice of bike though the XT engine would probably outlive the Africa Twin. All in all it still looked like a pile of scrap with rust here and there. It was just the look I was actually looking for. A couple of riders went across Russia last year and had trouble with corrupt police as they had ridden across Russia with brand new Triumph tigers. An expensive bike in the UK, never mind Russia. This meant to the police of all flavours that they had money even if they didn't. I played the odds here in that a corrupt police officer would see my bike and think, "By eck," (or whatever they say in Russian) if he is riding that pile of scrap across Russia he probably doesn't have any money anyway. Soft luggage and bin bags were used to enhance this effect greatly. Though this was more to do with the fact metal boxes and a few rods of steel, which comprise the mounting racks, cost £1000. Additionally to boot there were many reports many expensive well-known brands had jumped onto the fashion bandwagon. Such that many boxes just were not tough enough to handle a real trip and had been manufactured with people who wanted to look the look. But these boxes from certain companies wouldn't walk the walk. This was somewhat similar to SUV owners who get a machine that looks like an off road machine but would sink to the bottom of the first pool of mud they ever encountered. The issue on many of them was they used cheap manufacturing methods and stupid short cuts. For instance they would bang a tube flat for a convenient mounting point. This short cut reduced the manufacturing process significantly but suddenly made a big weak point on the bike. While myself I just drilled through solid pieces of tube and bolted the tube onto the frame these were fine and cost me less than £50 in total to make my entire luggage assembly.

The XT would go for one last journey; it had been offered a reprieve from the scrappers.

Maps, GPS, guide books what are those? The problem with maps and guidebooks is that they are often wrong, hideously out of date and take up weight and space. Taking a guidebook is takes away some of the adventure and hence I didn't take any. My general experience with people who used guidebooks such as the Lonely Planet and even the Rough Guides was that they were essentially on a slightly cheaper less guided package tour. Yet were not really willing to admit to this fact. The irony is that the Lonely Planet does not live up to its namesake. The guidebook carriers would go to the same hotels or hostels. They would go on the same tours and the same buses same ferries and would bump into other guidebook carrying tourists, which seemed to me to be a perversion of independent travel. The second a guesthouse a hotel or a hostel got into the Lonely Planet guide book the quality can fall and the owner has a licence to print money, sack that. It went against adventure biking in that adventure biking IS different you have a go anywhere you want technology. Hence you can go where you want, you can see what you want you can go on the beaten track or as off it as you like. Without sitting with people who are essentially on a vacation on rails guided by their guidebooks.

Sure, guidebooks are useful sometimes. But should not be over relied upon. They can often be useful for hints toilet paper or even to cover a bored moment by reading some history or some interesting curiosity of the place you are at. Even if the book is accurate it takes away some of the reason why you went out there to meet people. A bloke who lives there 365 days a year is going to know a hell of a lot more than some bloke who passed through there to write a book who knows how many years or decades ago. Locals can and do help sometimes they don't but that in itself is an experience too. The more you mix and talk with local people the more you get out of your travels. It's a damned shame to go on such a big trip generally to only live vicariously other peoples' adventures when I was out there to make my own.

As soon as you check into a hostel or hotel from the Lonely Planet, you will surrounded by gap year students from Germany, Holland, England, Scotland, Australia, Canada etc. What was the point of doing that when you are there to meet the locals? That is not to say that such people can't be fun in that they can be incredibly fun as they are often no longer constrained by their day to day lives. The inner selves normally suppressed for everyday living can come out (or perhaps even demons), and such people maybe out for a voyage of discovery or something like that. However this can also be just like a big Friday night out on the town and again it proves some sort of insulation against meeting others.

Finally quite simply I like going out into the unknown, perhaps this is why I like mysteries so much. My prior trips out to France, Italy and Spain were barely planned it was a case of lets go out there and see what there is to see. Many people do not like this and over plan but this in itself is a barrier to going out. On top of all that guidebooks were just another cost to soak up my ever-diminishing funds. I thought that petrol and food would be a better way to spend the money as there were potentially so many countries to pass through it was a substantial amount of money to spend.

I felt the same way with maps. Bah! Just wake up each morning and look at the direction the sun rose. Although this wasn't a particularly smart plan, again maps cost money! The alternative i.e. swallowing your pride and asking local people standing around or finding an Internet café was cheaper and more convenient or so I told myself. You could always change your mindset, i.e. I am not lost I am just exploring uncharted territory.

GPS was a similar choice namely as it cost a lot of money and the problem with GPS is that it removes the skill of navigation from you. The biggest issue was that with GPS you rarely get lost. I said rarely since it is not infallible. Far too many stories of people putting total reliance into GPS putting total blind faith into it driving into the sea over cliffs and such malarkey. Most famously was a guy I know who put Andorra into his GPS and ended up in the south of Spain instead of Andorra the country. Rarely getting lost you may think is a bad thing especially in say Mongolia and Kazakhstan where there are no road signs, but when you do get lost you may find a beautiful scenic spot to camp which might be undiscovered country. In my previous trips to Europe I had deemed it unnecessary which led to excellent encounters with local people, places I would never have seen, so GPS directions on screen and following the arrows was out. In comparison however GPS felt a bit like painting by numbers. I think when people have accidents from too much faith in GPS it just shows the absolute lack of awareness there is in many road users. How can people drive off cliffs or think there isn't something wrong when you are on a dirt track or drive into the sea, the mind boggles. I did buy a £5 GPS bluetooth module so I could track my location on a map in the future. Though it must have been an omen as it was broken before I even got the bike sorted out.

In the weeks pending before my departure I spent much of my free time before going generally giving things away. Mostly old books magazines and clothing even my old computer hardware. Free cycle proved very useful for this purpose. I also sold an awful lot of my junk I had accumulated over years. Generally to help pay for this trip as the budget for this trip was tight more money = more comfort a £20-25 a day budget generally didn't get very far. Having no sponsors or freebies given to me meant everything had to be carefully planned and pennies pinched everywhere. However having sold nearly everything I owned of value it felt oddly liberating I could literally walk away and leave very little behind.

The penny pinching meant carrying tyres which are a bulky problem, full camping equipment, food, water and enough clothing and spares to see me through. There were no advance tyre drops, no free hotels and no mechanics to look after us. The preparation involved using cheap solutions would have made utter tight wads look generous but this was not through choice. I still haven't found a proper money tree yet.

The XT loaded up looked bad very bad, getting on the thing the XT felt unstable immediately. With a top box crammed full of stuff above the recommended maximum 15-kilos maximum, although the top box was bolted on to the rack negating this. It was stuffed with food, water filter and tools nothing could be left behind if there was to be true independence of exploration. Two enormous side panniers 45 litres each. Spare tyres strapped to the side panniers. The passenger part of the seat with various bags tent and sleeping bag attached. It was a mock parody of the commercial in the 1980s where men are loading Castle Maine XXXX onto the back of a pickup truck. Where the tyres sit nicely in the wheel arches whereby it collapses and they think they have too many drinks for the ladies.

However quite simply there was no way around it or so I thought at the time, as the adventure motorcycling guide book stated I needed all this stuff. My impressions of Siberia and Mongolia were typical of somebody who has never been there. My impressions were that there is nothing there but small villages and the odd big town with massive shortages of everything so you have to bring the kitchen sink as a matter of survival.

4: UNCERTAIN BEGINNING

I slipped away quietly without any fanfare without anybody more than my parents to see me off. I had set off to Nathan's place where we repacked up our things putting on the spare front tyre Nathan had given me making the bike sag even more, or in my case reorganised them. It was one helluva big trip we each needed a lot of equipment and we had duplicated our equipment so that we could split up if needed without leaving each other in the lurch. He did seem particularly impressed with my tool tube, which was in actual fact an ASDA 99p water jug with lid jubilee clipped to the sub frame. While his own ammunition boxes and soft satchel luggage was equally thrifty and impressive. His clothing seemed to be devil may care, the only protective gear being helmet, leather jacket and army boots, no leg protection, not even eye protection which I thought was a bit insane.

We set off down the A1 / M1 motorway quite late that afternoon with perfect clear sunny weather it looked like a perfect beginning to our little trek. We managed to get all the way down to the coast just outside Dover. Absolutely nothing of note happened on the way down. We stayed at a pub and were to camp for the night in the garden of a pub Nathan's wing often stopped in before a cross channel trip. En-route I had a minor crash where a strap had come undone and locked the rear wheel causing me to skid a few yards and drop the bike unable to put my foot down. A lucky escape as if it had happened on the motorway moments before I'd have been toast. Of course it would have been luckier not to have happened but in light of it happening without much damage was pure luck. A watery eyed Nathan from travelling down the motorway without any eye protection and me had beers a-plenty attracting a minor crowd. Everybody asked where we were off to probably expecting an answer about Europe.

I said, "Korea."

Nathan said, "Siberia."

There were audible gasps in the pub we were semi treated like heroes that evening and everybody came to talk to us and wish us good luck. I slept in the big Wendy house while Nathan slept in his bivvy bag outside on the grass and he instantly fell asleep while I was relegated to the wind constantly banging the shutters keeping me up all night.

The ferry was uneventful but quite a nice new one where we pored over map fragments of the route to take. Nathan decided on Belgium and down via Switzerland and Italy to Brindisi as we had been delayed over a week by Nathan's engine troubles. We had clocks ticking down on our visas and had to get to Azerbaijan quickly in case our visas ran out.

I've been to France before on a motorbike and it is a great place to be riding, in 2007 I had a tour out there on a sports bike and it felt similar to before. Though the speed was slower this time as knobbly tyres you can feel horribly step out when cornering too hot.

My aim was generally to get out of Europe as soon as possible. Europe was incredibly expensive to do anything, eat, sleep, buy fuel and drink beer. France epitomises how to build a road system, being at the heart of Europe and a method to avoid Austria and Switzerland an awful lot of traffic passes through France. Snooker table smooth and flat roads everywhere. They have wide roads to accommodate traffic and a sparse speed camera system that actually alerts you to where the cameras are. A bikers nirvana in its current state, I do not know how long this will last.

This is where it all started to go wrong. The ferry docked at Calais and all of a sudden the XT refused to start. We rolled it out to the dock and attempted to bump start it down the ramp, no joy. Nathan then tied some rope around his DR and towed me around with me taking him off twice. Finally diagnosing a flat battery. This didn't make any sense at all as the battery was new and it was impossible to have ridden total loss down the A1. Nathan gave me a tow outside the ferry port and left to go find a new battery for me in Calais town centre while I set about finding the wiring problem. I had the bike side panel off and started to run my fingers along each of the wires looking for a bad connection but could find none. Eventually I considered a problem mentioned to me back home that the starter relay on the XT was weak and burnt out every 8000 or so miles sometimes and so I replaced it with my spare one. Thankfully I had a spare one and replaced it in minutes.

The day before Nathan had scoffed at me for bringing a starter relay with me, as it would be unlikely to be ever used. I had thought about dumping it but kept it anyway tossing the old starter relay away but grabbing it back just in case. Finally with two working bikes we rolled out of Calais and onto the autoroute towards Belgium when all of a sudden he stopped at the side of the road. I went past him and wondered what was going on and had to turn back. His carb had broken and needed to be fixed. So here we are on the shoulder of the autoroute fixing his carb something to do with a bolt coming lose which he didn't have the allen key for. On we went on our merry way until we got to the outskirts of Belgium where his bike started to smoke, smoke really badly...

In the petrol station we stopped at I could see why. It was leaking a few drops of oil onto the forecourt, a bad sign. The next news was even worse he topped up an entire bottle of engine oil and tightened a nut. All seemed fine and we continued our way deeper into Belgium. We were passing Mons and towards the Swiss border when it happened.

A huge bang and an almighty cloud of smoke came out the back of his bike and he stopped in a bus stop and surveyed the damage. He had over tightened the bolt and stripped the threads. He had effectively run the top end of the bike without oil for the past 40km. For the non-technical types the head is where the cams which press open the valves are situated the valves, which let in air fuel and open to expunge exhaust gas out the cylinder. Here we were stranded with a broken bike middle of Belgium on day two the XT was fine, his bike wasn't. We pondered what to do and had dinner by the side of the road couscous and chicken curry.

The decision was made that I would tow him back to Mons where we would find a mechanic. I have never towed anybody properly on a bike. Years ago I saved a guy on a fireblade by towing him a few miles but this was something else. This was unfamiliar territory a very heavily over laden bike towing another heavily laden bike. We slowly made it to Mons with him taking me off a few times, and parking up next to a church. Where we were to look for an Internet café. Nathan found a campsite and at an Internet café and we prepared to tow again. But the rope snapped (the rope didn't snap I found it snapped a piece of steel on my sub frame). I was riding around with a loose rope that got caught in the wheels of a car taking me off again.

Somewhat annoyed I went back to find him and started to tow again, where he took me off again. One final time we re-attached the rope where finally he took me off one last time. I had enough of it, and rode off leaving him by the side of the road. I calmed down and went back offering to tow him to the campground, but he refused.

We went to the campsite and he immediately started to pull his bike engine apart while I set up my tent and got in. It had been a very, very long day. In the morning it felt different immediately the start of the friendship that had formed before was broken and it felt as if it would never be the same again. Harsh words were exchanged the night before and he had not forgiven me. A line had been crossed which could not be undone.

Though I see it slightly differently if he had prepared his bike properly none of this would have happened. What you are going to read would have been markedly different to what it is now. The rest of the morning he spent he sat with his back to me as I went to various Suzuki dealers to source parts. A Fazer pilot was leading me there. He was good enough to take me miles out of town to a motors district. Some rooting around I found a complete DR350 engine but Nathan declined it for some unknown reason. I called David Lambeth for some help and he could post parts to me and he also managed to call Austin Vince to see if he had a spare engine in his lock up. Unfortunately this turned out to be a dead end though. David was fairly

21

sure that the DR350 engine was unsalvageable. Running it low enough on oil to ruin the top end would half ruin the bottom end. As the bearing shells the big bit that goes round and round at the bottom of the piston would also have been starved of oil. Staying one more night I thought this won't do and made the decision to head back home and re-equip my bike do some repairs and get some rest. Partly because we had broken down in possibly the most expensive town in Europe and really I didn't particularly warm to the prospect of being stuck there awkwardly not speaking to each other for the next week. While he fixed his bike or rather waited for the parts to arrive.

I left the spare front tyre and rode off into the sunset back home to catch the last ferry of the day and ride back up North. This was nothing major other than a puncture on the rear and the discovery my front tyre valve was damaged. It was leaking a small amount of air that was easily fixed and the collapse of my shock absorber. Nathan had commented that it was pretty badly sagged by the time I was in Belgium and felt hot to touch. It failed 220 miles from Manchester though the bike was still ridable it just had to be wrestled and ridden at 40mph on the motorway but seeing as it was the middle of the night this wasn't much of an issue.

5: LETS TRY THAT AGAIN

I got back home and felt disappointed that I had in effect failed even the customs bloke wasn't great about it.

"Oh so you came back and failed eh?"

"No I didn't," I protested weakly to the customs officer, "I'm going to have another crack at this soon," I replied.

"Oh right good luck with that I might see you on your way out then," he replied. This immediately gave me thoughts of failure and I felt crushed and defeated at this prospect. Immediately upon my arrival back to stop these thoughts of failure, which could spiral out of control in the way only failure can. I set a new time on target to leave in 5 days do or die time sort of.

I phoned up David Lambeth to provide me with a new shock and heavier spring. I re-soldiered up the electrical connections and decided to leave behind 70% of my stuff and reduce the weight of the XT. I figured I should travel lighter as the XT was essentially problematic in handling and that was just on the tarmac road. How I would ride this on dirt tracks and sand in its current condition I didn't know so I did the old lets lighten it as much as possible. The XT would have to go on a crash diet as a bonus this would save some fuel and give me some more ground clearance for the rough stuff.

I managed to strip 6 Kilos off the XT in removing various unnecessary bits, one mirror indicators replaced with smaller ones various holes drilled here and there handles replaced with lighter plastic ones that sort of thing. I replaced all of the wheel bearings packing the insides with happy meal levels of grease meaning I didn't have to carry them. As well as this I replaced the bearings in the headstock again removing the need for me to carry them. I didn't find anyway to make the fuel hoses secure though as they seemed really vulnerable. In essence somebody could walk up to the XT yank a pipe and steal all of my petrol but I didn't have any solution, as it was plastic onto plastic fuel line.

I also managed to strip 17 kilos out of my luggage most of the spare clothing went along with trainers and sleeping mat. Effectively all I had was a bike tool kit, one change of clothes (which were worn) a few spare pairs of underpants two pairs of socks and three t-shirts one for cooking pan a small stove and a water bottle and a set of Swiss army knife type things. As a precaution I carried a fairly basic medical kit including a ton of anti chafe stick. It might sound rather girly to bring that sort of thing but your face is being dehydrated by wind 8 hours a day. My prior visit to

France I had made the mistake of not bringing any such thing and I spent a week with my lips stuck together. Three spare inner tubes down from the original eight although tubes can be mended they can also be destroyed and those Russians use 18-inch wheels front and back, not compatible with the XT. My tent and sleeping bag nothing else bar my helmet gloves boots had been down graded to army boots, back protector and waterproofs.

A week had allowed me to make peace with some acquaintances I had left in the middle of things and generally built up my confidence. It also allowed me to research a few alternative routes just in case.

I slipped out in the middle of the night escorted by my sister who took me round the M60 before finally waving farewell and I was off down the M6. The M6 was uneventful other than two punctures on the way down and a front puncture on the M25. I nearly missed the ferry. The ferry again uneventful bar a couple of ex bikers asking where I was going, they didn't expect me to say Japan. They wished me luck and even bought me a pint at the ship bar as a measure of respect for going so far out there. When the time came I went down to the car deck and noticed the bag containing my unused Coleman stove had gone missing. This was a bit of a pain, as I would not find another stove until Istanbul.

I'd actually made a diversion to Belgium to the campsite at Mons to attempt to make peace with Nathan to see if at the very least we could patch things up. This was not to be however as I rode into the street where the campsite was and Nathan rode past me either ignoring me or not seeing me. I had no idea as to which it was. I forgot about it and thus my fate was sealed to ride this trek alone.

"Who wants to live forever?" I said to myself and remembered I promised myself not to fail and started the bike heading south towards Reims.

En-route to Reims I stopped to help out a Frenchman on a Honda firestorm who had run out of fuel. I gave him a litre; he commented that my tyres looked a bit flat. My French is passable and he led me to a mechanic with a compressor who fixed me right up. They went inside got me some bread some ham and a small bottle of wine when they heard of where I was going. They were stunned that I was to attempt to get to Japan (not knowing the French for Korea it is unsurprisingly Corea) on this ratty old XT600. A huge big welcome from France the first of many as one of the men went in and got me a couple bottles of wine, they offered me a, "Bon Chance!" Which sounded better than the one I had heard in France 2 years prior. Which sounded almost as if it was a good luck but I don't think you will make it. French people are always excellent to me because they see that I am Chinese looking they forgive me for speaking to them in English or poor imitation of French.

My first night in France on the second attempt was however quite cheap. I had managed to get to Reims without the use of the autoroute (which costs money) and had been unable to find a campsite or a hotel two years ago I had stayed in the Hotel formula 1. But Reims had some serious road works going on that I found it very, very late, which meant it was full.

The F1 hotel in Reims had grown bigger in my absence. Almost every rider who goes there without a booking had been turned away for the past two years as most riders blaze out of England to France and Reims is the first big city and is a good resting place. Having ridden close to 700 miles this session (360 from Manchester to Dover, 110 to Mons in Belgium, then 220 to Reims). I was utterly exhausted that my limbs started to shake from exhaustion. On a twin a triple or a four-cylinder machine the machine is tuned to cancel out the vibrations. But on a big single all there is to cancel out the vibrations is a counter shaft, which doesn't work that well. I was in no real mood to look for another hotel but went in anyway and took a shower, hotel F1 is great for this in that many of them have a staff of zero, before 9pm when the gate locks the doors and the facilities are effectively open.

A burning hot shower felt heavenly after being wind cooled for hours on end.... I slunked out of the hotel and checked my chain tension. Oiled my chain sticking my hammer under the swing arm to lift the rear and spinning the rear wheel to oil the chain with a bottle of oil. It was fine looked like new, though without my earplugs the bike sounded strange as if there were a grinding knocking sound I couldn't identify. Revving the bike would make the sound indistinct, and letting it die down made it sound like there was some sort of rubbing. I spent half an hour undoing the washing I had done for free and eventually came to the conclusion that I would have to ignore it. The oil level was fine, the chain was fine, and the bearings were fine, nothing seemed to be out of place. Perhaps it was the dry sump of the bike as all my other bikes have been wet sump bikes. For those who don't know a wet sump is where the oil is stored. On the XT and many trail bikes the oil is stored in a completely separate tank in the frame which makes it easy to plumb in oil coolers and such like.

After all these mechanical shenanigans I jumped on the bike and had to look for somewhere to stay. Round and round an industrial estate nothing. I was just about to consider the 66 Euro hotels but then saw a perfect camping spot.... in the middle of the city. I'd been going round in circles and had repeatedly passed a medium roundabout, which had a fairly high hedge and for some unknown reason a sunken middle. I looked around until the coast was semi clear then rode into the middle of it, most cars even fairly tall ones couldn't see into the middle. I could but only standing on the pegs. And the tent was used for the first time where I fell into sleep having a strange dream about being a child riding my bicycle into a field with my friend Jamie, who I lost contact with about two decades ago. We were playing with a boomerang type thing but it was a cool at the time pink aero orb triangle thing. We could never get it right and one successful throw the plastic boomerang thing came back and was about to hit me on the head. I woke up completely surprised that I was considerably older fatter in the middle of a French round about illegally camped in an unfamiliar place. Getting out was troublesome however the traffic was silly around this round about and I was stuck in a hedge waiting for a gap to cruise out. A gap did appear and plop straight out into horn bashing and I scooted away into the traffic south.

The next day was spent getting to Grenoble. I really have mixed memories about Grenoble having been here 2 years previously on another motorbike trip. Namely being severely lost score +1 to GPS. Grenoble is hard to navigate there are no landmarks to navigate and the inner city is horrendously samey so that one place looks like another. The road signs are also somewhat less than helpful disobeying the general conventions set about through the rest of France. I managed to get lost and stay lost in Grenoble for about 3 hours. To anybody who wants to know the secret, it is the Rocade Sud. Do not turn off it at all just go straight through. Although if you really want to visit the best idea is to stay on the edge at the university district perhaps at the hotel F1 and take the tram into the city. Though in truth I do not know what there is to see. There are nice campsites to the South before you get to Gap.

I found a perfect campsite just south of Grenoble and stayed there, the campsite owner pulled up on his 640KTM adventure. We had a chat swapped some stories. One of his best stories as he spoke excellent English was a story about a visit to the legendary Ténéré tree. He had seen it sometime in the 70s before a lorry driver hit the tree and killed it while it actually was a tree rather than a steel monument to the tree it is today.

This I felt was a good sign a very good sign since the XT600 is the son of the Ténéré named after a particularly gruelling part of the Dakar Rally. I found a place for dinner consisting of Kebab and pizza managed to find a sign for WIFI so I had myself some free WIFI usage to update others of my progress and to inform them I was good and OK. I crawled into my tent and fell into a dreamless sleep.

Only to be woken hours later by a woman screaming.

6 : SLEEPLESS IN FRANCE & ITALIA

This made me panic and make a grab for my hammer. I generally worried about hammer gangs on my trip. During my trip preparations somebody tried to talk me out of riding this trip and showed me a video nasty of a couple of teenagers torturing a man to death. Or rather beating him to death with hammers, which didn't look out of place in a medieval torture chamber. It wasn't the best thing to see before a trip. It got worse when he turned the sound up and it turned out to be a bunch of Russians who had done this. The original hammer gang were caught last year and, I think they said it was because they were bored… so that makes it ok then? Unfortunately I thought about copycat hammer gang types instead who had not been caught.

The screaming was in a sort of a regular pattern however and soon turned to moaning the moaning got louder and louder faster and faster until it culminated in a scream. She whoever she was evidently practicing her vowels in a rather unorthodox manner. I think she missed the 'i's' and the 'u's' so her fella was obviously a rather poor English teacher. I pondered comically if they wanted any help for a moment but I turned over and tried to sleep. Life isn't like a porn film where when you are in the throes of shall we say lovemaking. An additional gentleman into the proceedings is not generally welcomed as some films may portray. The moaning started again then stopped shortly afterwards then started again then stopped driving me to despair. I thought it had finally stopped then it started again. I was instantly reminded of an old golfing joke which I cannot repeat here in its entirety as I'll probably get sued, not that I play golf though the punch line ends like this: "No! I'm calling to find out what's par for this damned hole!" The par for that particular hole was unusually high it seemed, as the screaming continued throughout the night and well into the next morning.

The next day was spent getting to Gap down the N85 a road every biker once in his or her lives must ride on a sports bike. The route was different to that I had taken in 2007. In 2007 part of the N85 had been closed leading to a diversion up and around a large part of the N85. Today oddly was somewhat devoid of bikers. Two years ago I had met a huge group of unfriendly Germans on their big BMWs who didn't even say hello back to me, which was more exciting it went a bit like this:

27

I stopped and waved and said Hallo, they all ignored me on their K1200S and GS1150/GS1200 BMWs, catching up with the pack of BMWs they saw me and I unmistakably saw them change down a couple cogs to pick up the pace a bit. I thought I'd have some fun and decided to show what a British biker can do, Japanese IL4 (inline four cylinder engine) vs. German IL4 and Boxer twins, needless to say I had some fun destroying £140,000 of German bikes on an old £1850 Japanese IL4. Treat bikers like brothers my arse.... not representative of the entire German biker population of course!

Today the N85 was deserted there were not even very many cars. I wished I were on a sports bike in reality. Although a trail bike can be ridden quickly it just doesn't feel right. The tyres step out on corners making it feel horrible and the soft suspension meaning it wobbles and needs to be hustled back to a good line making it hard work. While a sports bike would be a quantum leap of performance almost glued to the ground going faster is so much easier and enjoyable. On a sports bike I would be going round the corners sideways almost cranked over as far as possible. Extra emphasised by my non-hanging off riding style. After going absolutely nuts in Spain last year on some phenomenal roads I could easily go to the limits of the CBR I wasn't so sure about the limits of the XT. The empty road implied that it might have been a Sunday for all I knew.

Later I managed to meet a British couple in a big camper van type thing who gave me a packet of biscuits and a good luck. They themselves were heading down to Italy and crossing over to Tunisia but were astounded by the magnitude of my trip.

I pulled into the rest area part way down the N85 a few miles north of Castellane. Two years prior I had met Bill and we spent 2 days together buzzing around the Alps. Alas there was nobody there and when I phoned down to Nice to see if Ugenie was there I was told she was on holiday by her flat mate, darn nobody to couch surf in France.

Down the N202 it had changed since 2007. In 2007 I accidentally went down this road and it was glorious though in the opposite direction. The landscape looked different much drier and much harsher than the last time I saw this. With very little greenery and very few cars I supposed that I had romanticised this section of road to an extent that the memory in my mind no longer represented the reality. With the deep blue of the med on my right I crossed over into Italy and promptly ran out of petrol at San Remo just outside a campsite.

Thankfully a German couple gave me a litre, which was enough to go back into France fill up and come back. I had a few beers at an extortionate price for a very small beer making a prat of myself as per usual.

"*Cerveza*?" I asked.

"No! No, this is Italia my friend in Italia it is *Biro* in South Italia it is *Bira*," he replied. A note for future travellers, and myself you should learn the name of beer or whatever your poison is in each and every country you are to pass through along with the name for petrol. Supper was all I could see i.e. things I could point at in shop windows. Although I know the names of lots of Italian food an awful lot of Italian food we know of originates from the South. Northern Italians apparently don't do pizza or lasagne they did have some incredibly meaty 135% meat salami sausages though. Along with a stick of bread made my day. Not to mention the battalions of ants which feasted off the crumbs and eventually on my soft flesh.

The next day I arrived at Pisa. An easy ride keeping the water on my right through narrow roads winding along the mountains saddling the coast. Warm sunshine, a nice onshore breeze a perfect riding day. The only fly in the ointment was a bicycle race over the mountains which was impossible to get round hence the short distance I rode today 300km. I filtered up and down goat tracks on the side of the mountain passing through narrow alleyways between houses got to the top of the mountain and saw the racers I had seen earlier at the bottom of the hill pass by. I waited it out and approached Pisa.

The road to Pisa was abnormally hot and even 50mph average did not keep me cool. In Spain in a previous trip any speed above 40mph would keep you cool enough to remain in full biking leathers, but this heat was something else. Such was the intensity of the heat I had to remove my fuel filter to stop it from vapour locking regularly. This is when petrol vaporises in the fuel filter from heat off the engine and blocks the fuel flow. Also twist my hand guards downwards to get some airflow onto my hands and up my sleeve. This proved to be an incredible mistake though in that the birds must have been suicidal that day and I received not one but TWO bird impacts on my hands. Luckily I was wearing good quality gloves as they exploded in a puff of feathers, though the bloody meaty smell however was more difficult to get out.

In biking and in biking groups suicidal birds are always a problem. A few years back one of my mates crashed his bike after being hit on the visor by a bird. It disintegrated into feathers blood and meat. In the process he dropped his bike sliding down the road on his rear end and for the most part was ok, all that was hurt was his ego. But he reached up to open his visor and saw a huge amount of blood and immediately thought he was dying and was distraught at this.

Another incident was at a local burger bar famous in Plymouth where one rider clipped a sea bird, which wandered around, dazed for a few minutes. We were rewarded by a few weeks of bird guano in retaliation for clipping that bird oh happy days.

The approach to Pisa was full of diversions and I saw an ever-increasing number of chair ladies (prostitutes) sitting by the side of the road looking for business. By the time I got into Pisa I must have passed 2 maybe 300 of them. Pisa was terrifically expensive tourist trap going into the campground it was 35 Euros to camp for one night. Seeing as I had paid 6 in France for just about the same quality I declined.

So did Nathan an American who was had rejected his lawyer life style and decided to pack it in for a big trip backpacking, he ended up sleeping on a bench in town last I saw. I cruised back out to the forests just outside Pisa and thought hmm this will make a good rough camping location. Turning off onto a tough and rutted gravel road passing a few chair ladies, about half a mile into the forest following two tracks left by cars. I came upon a beautifully secluded pond. It looked perfect; far enough away from the main road not to hear the cars yet near enough for a quick getaway and to walk back if there was a pub nearby. I guess a few people had the same idea as there were other tents popped up here and there though a noticeable absence of people like you would find at other campsites.

I stopped and undid the straps tying the tent onto the bike and sleeping bag when something hit me on my shoulder. Something big and heavy and I fell to the ground and jumped up instantly lashing out with a quick few swings and suddenly stopped as they fell unconscious to the ground. The assailants were a huge black man and an equally large tanned man. But there was something wrong very wrong as usually people get up and fight back or pull a knife on you in a robbery. They were dressed in women's clothing with incredibly obvious fake blonde wigs. I grabbed my tent and sleeping bag strapped it to the back of the bike and rode off, and thought it over....

I think what had happened is that I had gone to camp in an area full of chair ladies and they thought that me putting up a tent or attempting to was muscling in on their territory. The added twist was that the chair ladies turned out not to be ladies after all. It is not exactly as if I had stopped and gone over them with a fine tooth comb or anything you'd see them out the corner of your eye as you buzzed past them.

I grudgingly went back to the campsite paid up and found several bikers around the campsite. Mostly BMW riders on big 1000cc+ bikes who had been to Sicily and an XTZ pilot from Switzerland who had been around the Black sea and wasn't talkative. I went to get something to eat. Italy is notorious as a tourist trap, and I ordered a pizza of some kind and a burger. Let me ask you this dear reader what do you think of when you have a pizza and a burger?

A pizza with a thick crust with generous toppings? But no they gave me authentic Italian pizza. a thin piece of bread that looked more like a wrap thing with some tomato paste and three yes three pieces of salami. The burger was worse. I had imagined well at least the burger will make up for this. What came was a large plate with a patty of beef no bigger than a two pence piece. Absolutely MOST insulting was the bill that came to 40 Euro for a bit of bread and a tiny piece of beef, suffice to say they didn't get a tip. Disgusted I returned to the pool area for a cocktail, at least the cocktails were reasonable. About 3 Euro each I figured that they were that cheap, as the manly men would drink beer at 7 Euro for a quarter pint and not drink cocktails for fear of being seen as a poof.

En-route back I met a girl from Beijing who spoke virtually zero English who didn't have a place to stay. Naturally I offered to share my tent. Share meant to me we both sleep inside. Share to her meant I slept outside under the XT while she slept inside with my sleeping bag while I slept in my clothes outside. And yet people say chivalry is dead. At least she bought, well... said she would buy me breakfast, which incidentally I ended up paying for. Though it was admittedly a nice enough night to sleep under the stars, as it was surprisingly warm and slightly cloudy evening.

I stopped to take a few typical touristy type photos in Pisa of the leaning tower and the chapel nearby. Which in real life looked much smaller than it did in pictures or in films something, which I term the porn star effect. In that it's the camera that makes it look bigger than it really is. A bit like mobile phone adverts to emphasise the small size of phones they always find somebody with massive hands. To emphasise how big something is like a burger or some other sort of meat, they always find somebody with tiny hands.

I headed down south to Rome. Entering Rome I had that big city feeling again where I was immediately lost. But I somehow managed to get to the big coliseum take a few photos buy some postcards and scarper South to Rome moving inland it grew warmer and down into Rome.

Rome even though I pretty much passed through was a mad place. Scooters buzzing left and right traffic jams that you could easily starve to death in. I decided to stay somewhere outside Rome as it would likely cost less. This is a motorbike trip. Rome is a 2-hour flight away from England there isn't any reason to hang about when it is virtually on your doorstep. I did manage to see the coliseum though this was by accident passing through the city more than deliberate it would have made a pretty neat picture to have somebody take a photo of me riding around it though when riding solo this isn't possible.

I found much to my amusement that Romans are a relaxed bunch terribly expressive and emotive to the outsider. People could be discussing something as mundane as last night's football game. Yet it looked from the waving of arms touching of each other's chests and wild flinging of hands here and there as if this was a life or death argument. Or that somebody had ran over their mother or something.

In Rome traffic lights appeared to be optional. Same deal with zebra crossings, it's YOU that has to move not the cars. I had a particularly horrible moment when stuck in the middle of a 4 lane junction which merged roads from four directions. When ever you made a mistake here people would permanently attach their hands to the horn. I think in Italy they must have a special accessory designed for this. Much like in Sweden where official accessories probably include exhaust pipe to front window accessory straight from Volvo. In that it would be like cruise control where people just set the horn on and don't have to be even troubled by the need to depress the horn or worry about making the airbag inflate accidentally. It reminded me of an old Joke that goes a little like this.

Q: What does FIAT stand for?
A: Frenzied Italian At Traffic lights.

However bad the driving though the parking was worse having lived in the UK most of my life where there are fines for bad parking. Particularly the park more than 2ft away from the kerb equates a hefty fine Italy and Rome has no such laws. People would park in the tiniest of spaces at all sorts of angles with half the car jutting out from the street. Such parking would give a British parking attendant a squeal of orgasmic delight. I witnessed a man performing 50-point parallel parking manoeuvre bumping into the car in front and behind each time just to get in. Russ Swift the bloke who does the cool hand brake parking manoeuvres would be hard pressed to park into some of the spaces you see in Rome. Bumpers, hubcaps would be strewn over the streets I passed through and when they fell off from such manoeuvres the drivers would get out and look at them as if it were a meteorite from space shrug their shoulders and sling the offending car part into the back of their cars.

If the space wasn't big enough to fit a car it would be filled with scooters, where triple quadruple and even quintuple parking was the norm. I wondered how the bloke who parked next to the wall would get out as any space between scooters cars and walls was piled high with rubbish of every kind. Half eaten food, even defecate in towering piles that would collapse if the car it leant against moved away.

I think that somebody should make a video game of Rome to rival the Grand Theft Auto series, something like Italian driver where you have 10 minutes to find a parking space in Rome.

I quickly figured the way out of the city and rode out quickly to keep myself cool. An hour or so later I made it south to a town called Latina. I guessed that there would be a campsite here. There was and it was idyllic. Giovanni the campsite owner led me in by bicycle and I followed him to the pitches as he rode his little fold up bicycle. This was a highlight so far of my trip as the place was empty except for a couple of static caravans and a few day-trippers using the beach. The campsite was less than 10 metres from the sea front. It felt nice to sit on the edge of your tent sipping cheap beers and watching the sun go down. It felt even better when I got one of my portable barbecue packs out of my bag and cooked up some fantastic skewer kebabs, all in all today was a nice day.

I had wondered why nobody was camping on these particular pitches as those who did have tents seemed to pitch a bit farther back for some reason. No worries all the more for me. Although all by myself on the pitches and everybody being somewhat insular ignoring my hellos and even my, "Bon journo!" I felt kind of isolated with this magnified more as a couple of times I turned to a non existent Nathan and before I uttered a word I remembered we had parted company. So this is what the trip will be like by myself I thought to myself for a moment. It is in such situations like this that make you get up and go find somebody to chat to which is exactly what I did.

The campsite manager Giovanni had closed up and had a drink in the bar with me to practice his English along with the barman and we sat drinking a brand of red star beer. Giovanni ended up shouting the beers for me as a gesture of good luck for my journey.

A little later he invited me into his home a small cottage to one side of the campsite. We ate possibly the most delicious fiery pasta dishes and salad I have ever tasted. I think karma must have been on my side after yesterday being ripped off in Pisa badly. I had an incredibly awkward moment here as they said a prayer before the meal, at the best of times I consider myself to be agnostic, the fact that I had already scooped a generous amount onto my plate while everybody else went quiet was an uh oh moment. I don't know what was redder the pasta sauce or my face that evening. I bid them farewell but not before many photos were taken and Giovanni's wife (who I didn't get the name of) said a prayer for my safety. I slunked off to my tent and fell asleep quite quickly.

Only to be woken by the feeling that I had wet myself badly, waking up in the dark it was wet everywhere, I unzipped the tent and the tide had come in right to the lip of my tent and waves have crashed over the small lip on the ground sheet. I jumped out and tore the tent up and realised why nobody pitched their tents on the first few rows. I didn't get any more sleep that night though thankfully the hazy Italian sunshine quickly dried everything out other than everything feeling a bit salty but there was no major damage.

Naples was the next destination. It was crowded and surprisingly industrial as I passed through and onto the Autostrada to Brindisi. All I really remember of Naples was horrendous traffic, slippery cobble streets that were rutted beyond belief and lots of underpasses and over passes on a complicated road system.

On exiting Naples the landscape turned to spaghetti western style desert where the odd cactus would not have gone amiss. I think I was near the place where the Clint Eastwood spaghetti westerns were filmed after a few miles the scenery changing to green forests, farmland and eventually green foothills enveloping the road. What struck me was how much litter there was everywhere here, as well in the city it seemed quite normal I suppose. In each lay by I stopped in piles and piles of rubbish were strewn over every space possible. It wasn't tourists throwing it out it was the Italians themselves. I wondered why they took so little pride in keeping their country tidy.

I arrived at Brindisi fairly late and found the ferry port even later. The ride into Brindisi proved to be through an industrial area that was grey, grey and more grey. Towering dirty industrial plants surrounded me as I weaved my way through them before a short hop on an Autostrada. Conveniently they provided a sign from way outside the city for the ferry port following these are for a fair distance.

The ferry ticket office staff said to me, "Sorry ferry left 3 minutes ago."

"Will there be another ferry tonight?" I asked in vain hope.

"No I'm sorry not till tomorrow." I received in reply I had wanted to catch the night ferry to save on one night's accommodation but would have to catch the 2pm ferry tomorrow instead. As I turned to go one of the guys working for the ferry company told me to wait and he would find me a place to stay, result! He finished work 10 minutes later and handed me a ticket and told to pay tomorrow no problem. Here was me following him through Brindisi with him on his little vespa weaving in and out of traffic and we stopped outside a workers pub and Antonio started the drinking shouting me drinks for a couple hours until he had to go home.

Drunk I saw a sign **youth hostel** and followed it pushing the bike along which a short distance was the Carpe Diem. A fairly large hostel run by a huge guy called Maurizio. Maurizio was an ex NATO peacekeeper who was also a biker and hostel owner at this point. The hostel was somewhat empty with Maurizio and his two Polish staff who happened to be asleep. I pushed the bike through the gate and he asked me, "Do you need any spare parts?" motioning to all the stuff I was carrying.

"You should have seen it before," I told him. He laughed and we spent the next few hours getting drunk surrounded by Canadian memorabilia. This hostel it seemed was very, very popular with Canadians. This place would have been nice had there been more people there but as fate would have it I ended up staying there alone in a 10-bed dorm by myself of which the hostel had 5 such dorms. As Maurizio's other guests failed to materialise, the mosquitoes that night got incredibly fat on my blood and flew around bloated at 3am and I couldn't sleep spending the time smashing the mosquitoes.

The next day was an absolute scorcher and I was up by 6am, and checked out his bike collection. Maurizio had an impressive collection of wrecked bikes about 30 of them Yamahas of various types and an ultra rare RC30 I have no idea how he got his hands on that bike. He came down stairs in his dressing gown and asked me if I needed any bits and I nearly asked for a reg/rec (a regulator / rectifier which converts the bike alternating current to direct current) but declined thinking it would be ok. I didn't know it at the time but I would regret this.

I made my way to the ferry port and told Antonio the guy who had been out drinking with me that I hadn't paid for the ticket yet he said, "No problem this is gift to you, for good luck to get to Japan."

"Thanks," I said. As he put a big sticker on the side of my petrol tank that said Athens it would give me an awful lot of trouble as everybody thought I wanted to go to Athens much later on and went to get on the boat.

The waiting was the only fly in the ointment here in that there was lots of waiting in a rather basic ferry terminal. A coffee shop or two and a few benches with overpriced ice cream. There were also rather a lot of touts selling bags, socks and underwear. For some reason all of them kept trying to sell me underpants. Big Y fronts with pirated David Hasselhoff pictures on the front of them. Fake watches, cigarettes, bum bags money belts and wallets. Not that I condone it as it encourages them but I bought a couple of cheapo wallets to act as extra decoys and some shock cord to keep the bike luggage attached as it was falling apart already.

The ferry to Greece was uneventful and was punctuated by a rather expensive and rotten shin stew dumplings with chips. I met a couple of Mormon missionaries who were en-route to Africa. I half expected for them to attempt to convert me. However as we got chatting it turned out that they were believers but generally did this missionary work for a sneaky reason. In that they were missionaries because it allowed them to travel far and wide on somebody else's dollar. Why can I never think of these sorts of scams to get other people to pay for my treks? They did however state that they would pray for me and pray for my journey to go well though. This combined with the prayers at Latina seemed to make the journey seem more dangerous as they obviously thought I would need God on my side.

7: GREECE & BULGARIA

I had tried to avoid this but I arrived in the middle of the night at Igoumenista 11.45pm type late, with no map and no guide I came off the ferry and into the port I realised that I was lost almost immediately. The other English tourists onboard had decided to sleep in their cars in the ferry port itself. My Greek isn't great I knew oh two words 'humus' and 'feta,'. The names of a chickpea based dish and a cheese were not going to get me very far however optimistic I was.

Even worse was that the road signs where spray-painted black all over and also unlit. It meant I had no idea where I was and managed to take the relief road around Igoumenista instead of into the town where I would have probably found somewhere to stay. I rode around looking for hotels but found none, then started looking for places to rough camp. I found some likely spots but often had rock solid ground which wasn't flat so there was no possibility to put the tent up. I finally found a bench seemingly in the middle of nowhere and put my sleeping bag on it and crawled in.

I was having a strange dream about using a stick of cheese to fight a shark until I was woken by the sound of an engine trying to turn over. Waking up some bugger had hot-wired my bike and was attempting to turn it over. I jumped out of my sleeping bag semi naked and the blokes did a runner. The sight of a half naked man running towards them would have scared anybody off I suppose. I got back on the bike conducted a very rough repair. I always turn the fuel taps off before I leave my bike and this had saved it luckily enough. I rode around looking for another place to stay. I managed somehow to find the town and found that all the hotels were shut but found a bloke who would let me sleep in his shop, which was undergoing renovations.

With no cars I rode directly up the kerb and into the high steps into the shop, damn I love this bike it can do anything it seemed. Where he found a soldering iron and some wire and helped me do some repairs and fitted a small metal plate across some of the wires to make them less vulnerable to hot wiring before wishing me goodnight.

I woke up to find I was locked in but after an hour the kind man opened the front door and I noticed I was blocked in by cars and the narrow pavement preventing me from getting out. He didn't know who the cars belonged to and I wanted to get going. On the 4th pass looking around I saw the stairs. I had a walk up and they went to a small terrace with a fire escape on the back street wide

36

enough to get out. I thought well this is a bit more interesting that it normally would be and rode the bike up the steps at the top of the stairs we twisted the bike on the side stand and rode towards the fire escape. Twisting it again I got down the fire escape and into a narrow street to my escape.

The next day was spent cruising up the E90 in Greece watching the magnificent view from the mountains down to the valley that Greece sits in on. A completely deserted road bar a few masochistic cyclists and a few donkeys wandering around, it reminded me greatly of Spain. The road surface was reasonably good and smooth and the day went by without incident taken at 60mph I was across most of Greece in a very short time and Thessalonica came up in no time at all.

Thessalonica was huge hilly and devoid of Internet cafés. I had a tactic now sorted out. In that when visiting a big city the first thing to do was to find an Internet café. As with that you can print out maps, find addresses of hostels and generally get directions when you are completely lost. It's apparently the new age of backpacking. Previously travellers would research which cities to visit and where to stay in each city first. Although it didn't work this time as there were no Internet cafés I could find or campsites or hotels.

Though I may well have passed a ton of hotels or campsites I cannot read Greek I don't know what comes after beta is it gamma or epsilon? Who knows? So after riding round in circles over and over in the blazing heat and dropping the XT more than once (though this was due to the very steep hills around Thessalonica). I called it a day and decided to head out and find somewhere else to stay the night. This was easier said than done as I was still lost and the XT had developed an annoying electrical problem.

I was cruising nicely out of the city and the bike would cough choke a few times and continue as if nothing was wrong. It was fine until I got to the worst possible place for there to be a break down and it happened in the outside lane of a 4-lane motorway north of Thessalonica. Great I'm causing a massive traffic jam with Greeks leaning out their windows shouting Greek obscenities at me, which I thankfully do not understand and realised it is the fuse. The fuse kept vibrating out when the engine got up to speed. A length of gaffer tape cured this and I set off again into the throng of traffic, which slowly petered out as I went northeast towards Drama.

Bulgaria was never on my initial itinerary it was supposed to be a gun run down to Istanbul through the fastest possible route. Thus preventing too many interesting things from happening. As Europe from experiences of the tourist traps in Italy had proven expensive. I'd gotten as far as I could in one day in Greece and was stuck in a town called Drama with no hotels, nowhere remotely safe to camp no guesthouses or hostels, just an Internet café and bars. The Bulgarian border was just 40km north so I thought meh why not go into Bulgaria? Ok so there was a hotel called the King Solomon. King Solomon I hear is apparently famous for his gold lust and they wanted enough to buy a brick of gold to stay a night in that hotel....

"But sir we have a pool, showers a video room, sauna and gym," claimed the receptionist.

"But I don't want that I just want to sleep!" I replied alas I did not stay at the hotel King Solomon. Ged had specifically warned me not to go to Bulgaria. Ged the man who taught me how to ride years ago had heard of my plan to cross through the Balkans while I went to MOT the bike.

"Oh you don't want to go there you'll get your throat cut in the middle of the night and you'll just vanish forever, you'll end up in a fuckin' kebab you will!"

"Erm, Ged, have you actually been there?"

"Fuck no why the fuck would fuckin' want to go to fuckin' Bulgaria for it's a dump!".... Ged seemingly has an amazing talent to be able to use the word fuck as an adjective, noun or verb in each and every sentence at least twice. I remember a particular fondness when I dropped the bike I was training on. A pink and purple GS500e one of his training bikes and he used it as every second word. Have a try it's quite difficult trust me if he ever got on to a radio show you might wonder why you have suddenly tuned into an emergency Morse code channel or something with the number of beeps. This is not to say that he is a bad guy he is a great guy but would make tourettes sufferers blush with his indiscretions. But it was Ged who years ago who started the ball rolling in biking and without him this trip would never have happened I am forever in his debt for this.

Of course due to the need to return back home for repairs and reconfiguration and the clock on two visas had started already. This meant I needed to make up some time and the Balkans were swapped with Italy instead.

As a country with low GDP and thus low costs I thought why not. The road was good dual carriage way but very poorly lit and the kind of asphalt that is smooth to touch and thus on a trail bike unpleasantly slippery. It also seemed to be insect night or something as thousands upon thousands of insects attracted to my headlamp squished onto my helmet, causing all sorts of streaks on my visor.

Crossing into Bulgaria was painless enough EU passport and all. I ended up in the first town after the border crossing which seemed a bit dead to be honest. Though around a truck stop appeared to be at least a hundred working-women plying their trade at passing lorry drivers. It just showed the amount of poverty that Bulgaria had compared to wealthier nations.

The first town after the border was somewhat dead. It was more like a Cornish town with the main road running from one end to the other. The number of houses could be counted on your extremities if you took off your shoes happened to be male and naked. Granted I had arrived in town at 10.30pm I started to look for a guesthouse and failed miserably. Running into countryside 50 metres out of town I turned back and found what looked like a guesthouse and knocked on the door. An old man invited me in, he said things in Bulgarian or what ever they speak and showed me to a room a nice cosy place where he fed me beer and some sort of chicken dish that was delicious. We chatted for a while over an enormous number of glasses of *rakia*. Or rather he spoke to me in Bulgarian with the odd English word thrown in while pouring himself more and more whiskey before I washed and went to bed.

In the morning the place looked very different and it dawned on me that I was the only person staying there. I hadn't stayed in a hotel at all this was a private farmhouse and the old man had invited me in out of the kindness of his heart. He utterly refused payment for a very long time. Instead I reached into my pannier and pulled out a bottle of wine given to me in France. It was good for both of us really he thought he got a very special exotic gift. I saved some weight in my panniers and some bulk good for both of us. I suppose the bottle of wine from Reims really did bring me some good luck that night. I discretely slipped 10 Euro into his pocket and set off for the border.

Bulgaria if you were somehow kidnapped and dropped by helicopter into the middle of Bulgaria could well be mistaken for Cornwall. Rolling green hills, hedge lined roads double white lines everywhere. If somehow I could find a real Cornish pasty this would have completed the illusion that this was Cornwall and not Bulgaria. Crossing back into Greece I had to retrace my path back into Drama and found a campsite 2km down from where I had decided to go to Bulgaria, tsk always the way of things... Live and learn. I passed through a few forgettable generic cities down towards Turkey. Where every few hundred metres I would see lorries and jeeps full of heavily armed soldiers on a perfect new sealed road that could put a few motorways in the UK to shame. But all that mattered was that I had gotten to the Turkish border.

Turkey was effectively 1/3 of my trip over and although it had only been just over a week I had come a very long way from home. Essentially I felt as what is described in hitchhikers guide to the galaxy. Where when you are far from home you have a huge longing to be there. Turkey was the start of Asia and beyond that laid the caucuses somewhere, which to me was unknown. Nobody I knew had been there and thus nobody had any recent prior information as to what it would be like over there. Although the actual feeling of being in one place or another is the same, you never know who you may meet or what you might see over the border. I had felt pretty low in having to return and thought once I got to Greece I would reconsider my options, as it was a convenient place to turn back if needed.

Greece had turned out to be mostly forgettable other than the scenic mountain route that I had taken to get where I was now.

I suppose this was related to the fact I didn't really talk to many people virtually blazing the entire country in less than a day. As it was a small narrow country with very little in the way of traffic outside the main cities. Though this was a conscious choice in choosing instead to get to Turkey soon as possible, a shame really.

On the other hand Greece again is one of the European countries, which is easy to get to. An Easy Jet flight out, and there you are. However the temptation to keep on going was enormous, as I had caught some serious white line fever. I thought to myself in a small border town a few miles from Turkey I WILL NOT FAIL. I stopped off at a small bakery in this town sat back and relaxed for a moment enjoying a coffee and some of the food and answering questions of curious locals. The town seemed to have rather a lot of soldiers sat in the back of lorries driving around endlessly around the edge of town for some reason. Though this was normal outside Europe I was to discover, it just felt a little unsettling that there was such a need for this. Then again borders again are a place where similar people draw an imaginary line and then fight over the perceived differences of those next door.

I finished off my crusty bacon pie thing going back for another as well as another small bag of pies just in case, nothing to do with my greed. I dusted the crumbs off mounted the XT and thumbed the starter. The engine span over momentarily, grunting into life. I kicked the side stand up in an almost reflexive motion and trundled off down the dual carriageway towards the Turkish border point.

8: TURKISH DELIGHT

I have never been to Turkey before namely as the only holidays out there were to the massive touristy spots which would give Ibiza, Kos (Greece) and Magaluff a run for their money. Thus it never entertained my thoughts to go to such a place other than off the beaten track. But since Turkey was en-route to Georgia I had no choice, and with my own transport it was different. I would have the freedom to really see what it was like away from even hardcore backpacker locations. It was also an awful lot of miles as Turkey is as wide as Europe itself and I was informed (wrongly) it had to be taken slow.

I crossed the border with ease, other than a £10 sticker to go in my passport and 15 Turkish Lira for insurance for a month it was no trouble and out into Turkey. Welcome to Turkey the sign said to me. The road looked like an American desert road from my memories. Long and straight, red sandy soil to the left and right of the road. Heat haze in the distance obscuring the vanishing point of the road a big blue sky where you could see to the horizon in all directions and a heat haze each direction you looked. A darkly tanned man riding a donkey, people with carts sitting in the shade, besides the buildings every now and again. It was totally barren with small copse of trees here and there and the odd poorly looking patch of grass being assaulted by cows.

I had been told that in Turkey the speed limit was 60kmh and rolled in slowly towards Istanbul for fear of being fined. My budget was fairly small for this trip and I didn't really want it reduced even more. The slow riding wasn't doing me or the XT any good as we were both air cooled creatures and the low air flow meant literally cooking on the bike with no reprieve. The old tested trick I learnt in Spain was to approach a petrol station water tap and just completely drench myself head to toe to keep cool. This trick in Turkey worked for about 30 minutes as the heat blazed down and dried me up in next to no time.

Well I had to do something to get my money's worth from the incredibly expensive petrol. Petrol in Turkey is expensive very expensive in fact. Monopolies and high taxes make UK petrol seem cheap at the time. Stopping with amazement at the sign in that nowhere has petrol quite as expensive as the UK, or so I thought. It turned out to be £1.70 per litre of 95-octane petrol. I put some fuel into my small 3-litre can just in case and noticed the petrol was absolutely filthy full of black bits and dust. I started to worry a bit since I had removed my fuel filter in Italy by the side of the road and not put it back in. I had been informed by Alex to bring along a pair of tights to act as a fuel filter. I wondered how I would get a pair of tights or stocking in Istanbul without being seen as a pervert. Thoughts being in a shop trying to explain, "No really it's for a fuel filter!" Would be met with cynical stares and muffled giggles I thought. The only woman biker Tiffany was already in Georgia so I couldn't ask her to buy me a pair so I was stuck for now.

Pootling into Turkey partly to save fuel I stopped by a cop and asked him what the speed limit really was. He told me that with green card insurance speed limit is the same as cars 110kmh! He smiled and asked where I was going.

"Georgia," I said.

"Then where?"

"Azerbaijan."

"Then where?"

"Kazakhstan," I said he then twirled his finger around as in around the world.

"Almost," I replied. I found his name was Akhun and that he didn't like his job that seemed to revolve around sitting by the side of the road in the blazing heat watching tumble weed drift by. He fumbled in the back of his car and produced a *chai* making set and in the burning hot sun that didn't seem to faze Akhun he wasn't even sweating even a little bit. I gracefully accepted the burningly hot shot glass of *chai* with a ton of sugar in it. They put an awful lot of sugar in it as the tea in Turkey is somewhat bitter unlike your Tetley brew and I was glad for the refreshment and somebody to talk to.

I don't understand this in that my grandma has always said if it's hot drink something hot it'll cool you down. Who thought of that? Some so and so while utterly cooking in the heat thought I know it's hot so I'll drink something hot to make me hotter genius! One of my old bosses, my sister and assorted people say this. Surely if you are hot drinking something cold will cool you down right? I've never managed to get it to work and after this burning hot *chai* sweat cascaded down my face and back and I couldn't stand it anymore. I bid farewell to the cop who shouted at me.

"*Ili Sanslar!*" Which meant good luck. I had learnt a couple of Turkish phrases so I wasn't too much of a tourist.

I continued on my merry way towards Istanbul on the E90 next to the coast. The coast was a bit drab to be honest there was almost continuous beach going all along the coast. It seemed kind of polluted and smelt wrong not a normal sea smell kind of oily in a way. I rode through to a big town north called Corlu and met some road works. The first of many I would see in Turkey, this was now trial by fire. I have barely any experience of riding off road. There was deep gravel all along the now dug up road and my speed dropped markedly. And slowed even more when I got to the wet slippery patches. Most insulting was that a CBR600FX the other bike I have at home over took me as if there was nothing wrong.

The scenery from here on in became very urban very urban and there were grey concrete parades of shops either side of the sealed road enclosed by crash barriers. The sky had closed into a sullen sort of grey colour and the air became thicker with pollution. There also seemed to be an awful lot of people on the verges of the road cars and mini buses would swerve and pick them up. Huge families with huge red, blue and white striped nylon bags waiting. The buses all seemed to run incredibly badly they seemed to constantly be belching black diesel smoke constantly. I suppose the greyness all around in part was due to the diesel fumes being spewed out everywhere.

The heat had died down a bit by now and it had actually started to rain. The scenery became dark and uninviting. Although the cool wind was refreshing after the desert section I had recently done and the XT was sounding a lot better too with moist cool air going across its cooling fins. It sounded happy and contented as far as a lump of metal can be happy and contented. I made a few wrong turns managing to get onto completely deserted new roads leading to literally nowhere. The road would peter out after a few km making me turn round a few times. Turning round was easier said that done however. To turn round I had to get out my biggest spanner, undo the Armco crash barrier. Bend it to one side push the bike through and do it up again.

A few hours easy ride on sealed roads I came over a hill and saw Istanbul. It was absolutely enormous sprawling all the way to the coast over the hills as far as the eye could see. I've always had trouble in navigating cities and this proved to be no exception. I managed to ride around in circles for half an hour looking for an Internet café. My destination was the Mavi guesthouse where Russ a fellow biker on a BMW had set out before me. I had been chasing him through Europe ever since.

I managed to get lost in the wrong section of town for a while until I was directed to an Internet café hidden in a back alleyway that didn't look like an Internet café at all. I printed out a few maps and decided the best solution was to keep the sea on the right it had worked in Italy right what could go wrong?

At the Internet café I lost a dummy wallet one of many I was carrying and my forever sunglasses. Somebody dipped me while I was preoccupied looking for the Mavi on google maps. I had a theory about these sunglasses I have never crashed or been hurt while wearing these lucky sunglasses. They have followed me for the past 13 years that's how old they were. Although they looked battered they were still my lucky sunglasses. I almost got annoyed but thought well crying wont get them back and proceeded through the suburbia of Istanbul. This could have almost been the south of France with white washed stone buildings. The old mixed in with the new. Expensive speedboats and yachts moored to the piers that dotted the coastline. What felt like an hour I arrived at the correct peninsula in the centre of old

Istanbul outside the Aya Sofia and into the guesthouse. The Mavi guesthouse and asked for Russ another rider going out to see the world on a bike.

Russ (as I write this) is still out there in India somewhere as his destination was to be Australia via Kazakhstan and China. We had totally different schedules as I was running for the Russian visa and he did not even intend to visit Russia. Russ is an easy going BMW riding chap who had only passed his test 3 months prior but did have an awful lot of nice kit and equipment. Russ was a cheeky chap who was like an older version of Simon Pegg in looks but had led an alternative life style. He had effectively done a few well-paid jobs bought a house and had been utterly addicted to life travelling. He had met Tiffany in Cornwall before all of us had left and I had effectively been chasing him all the way through Europe. We had a few beers together and Kebap (as they call them in Turkey). It turned out Russ was waiting on some tyres and a few tools to arrive before he left so would be stuck there for another week.

The Mavi guesthouse isn't too bad although comparatively expensive at 10 Euro a night to sleep in the roof terrace dorm type arrangement. It was vaguely clean and very central and after 2 days without a wash the shower was delightful. Ali the owner knew how to stack beds though three high in some places and arranged right up to the edge of the balcony. Unfortunately the Mavi is located nearby a Mosque directly opposite in fact. Ok so I was in Turkey everything is near a Mosque, which meant that every 5 or 6 hours there would be a Muezzin making a call to prayer. That in Turkey everybody ignored but would ring out around the streets it went a bit like this:

"Allllllllllllaaaaaaaaaaaaaaaarrrrrr aaaaaaakkaahhhaaaaru!" Turkey might be a Muslim country but the Muslims there are like people who put down on census forms that they are Christians. They declare themselves Christians but don't really follow Christianity. They don't even go to church or pray or take communion and such like. Muslims in Turkey drink alcohol smoke and don't fast either, if only the fundies could be like that. An excuse I heard often was Allah loves every Muslim and understands they do not pray as proscribed.

I had a walk down the coast and managed to get multiple photocopies of my documents. V5C, driving licence and passport for a few Lira before making my way back to the hostel to put my photocopies in a safe place and thought of what I could do next. Dinner consisted of Shami Kebap and I spent the evening drinking Effes beer in the tiny common area of the Mavi guesthouse. Checking our emails, writing blogs and postcards for the people back home.

The next morning everybody was woken by the Muezzin call to prayer at 4am. Everybody turned over and ignored it and went back to sleep. The call to prayer I don't understand at all. But sometimes they got synchronised with the other Mosques and formed a semi cool almost techno like reverb. Other times one

Muezzin would make the call to prayer first, and the other Mosque would escalate and make a louder call to prayer. Since the verses all had breaks between them, they got to ear bleeding levels as each one ramped up the volume to out do the other one.

I had a goal today to get myself a new camping stove and found a suitable shop selling one of those red bottle stove type things. Nobody had even heard of the brand Coleman, which is what I wanted, but beggars can't be choosers. This involved a harrowing taxi ride through Istanbul whereby the taxi driver seemed to have a desire to meet Allah as quickly as possible braking at the last possible moment and filtering like a motorbike in a car. I bought the stove at the shop and the guy behind the counter seemed to have at least 7 credit card machines. Not thinking about it much I paid him via card, which was a massive mistake.

He seemed to have trouble in getting it to work and fiddled with something underneath the machine. I thought nothing of it and got back into another taxi to go back to the Aya Sofia to encounter an appalling traffic jam and a taxi driver who was clearly taking the piss. I'm suspicious of taxi drivers at the best of times as I always think they have a hidden add fare button and add to the fare when you aren't looking at the meter. This one positively took the piss as he took on other passengers took them to their destination in the opposite direction before half heartedly making his way to the Aya Sofia where the Mavi was. I got out and tried not to leave a tip but then he just refused to give me change and three guys approached me.

"Are you a Soldier?" They asked.

"Erm no I'm not," I replied.

"Your boots and green clothing make you look like soldier be very careful PPK may shoot you," they said. I looked myself up and down and thought hmm as I was wearing a military green T-shirt, military green shorts and army boots. I assured them I was not as we made some small chit chat about life in the UK and they guided me back to the hostel.

It was still fairly early so I went for a walk and as I passed the Aya Sofia. I heard a really rough buzzing noise. Nathan on his DR popped out of a side street onto the street and asked me where the Mavi hostel was. I pointed it out to him and he vanished off while I went to visit the Grand Mosque. I returned to find him unloading the bike; amazingly the DR had made it against the odds and the dire predictions of David Lambeth. David knows his shit and had said that if the DR engine is half knackered the bearing shells at the bottom end will have been starved of oil. And they will fail at the worst possible place they can possibly fail. Yet here he was having made it through the passes of Switzerland but having burnt 4 bottles of oil and done some more damage to his bike. I wasn't confident of his chances. But the three of us went out to the market to check for Russ's DHL parcels and to have a look around. We sat in the square eating kebabs and parted company with me getting severely lost in the souks of Istanbul and making the foolish decision to visit a big market. The big market was incredibly unpleasant, they instantly saw me as not being a Turk and the first man moved to block me and grabbed my wrist.

"Sahib! Special, special price on carpet just for you!"

"No thank you," I said.

"Please, please big discount!" And punched in more figures to his calculator showing me the figures on the calculator.

"Erm I can't carry a carpet on my motorbike."

"Ah, no problem I can FedEx for you!"

"Turkey carpet finest in world! No allergic finest materials."

"NO I don't want a carpet damnit!" Eventually getting to harsher words, "NO I DONT WANT A FUCKING CARPET PISS OFF!" At which the carpet seller would lose heart and let go of my hand. At which you would pass the carpet seller next to him who completely failed to notice you had made it clear to the previous carpet seller you didn't want a carpet. You would go through the exact same process again. What felt like 100 more carpet sellers later I finally made it to the other end. Where the last carpet seller had witnessed the fact that I didn't want a carpet and said just give me your money. I grinned at his directness and walked right past him dodging his cobra like hand snaking out towards my wrist. Performing a bullet time dodge Indiana Jones or Neo would have felt proud of. It felt great leaving the carpet market and unfortunately into a spice market. Where I could suddenly see the faces of 100s of merchants light up at my appearance. Although they were less aggressive as they had their hands full most of the time. I managed to escape rather easily by just walking down the middle so that other tourists buffered me. Though on insistent merchant blocked my final escape.

"Turmeric?"

"No."

"This is best turmeric you will ever buy, never in your life will you buy such fine turmeric my friend!" He insisted. His mobile phone rang and I impolitely scooted off while he was distracted.

I felt something was wrong really wrong somehow and ran back to the hostel to check my bank statements online. My suspicions were confirmed and I had £1000 missing from my account with more pending transactions. I immediately got on my bike and went back to the shop and complained to them. They utterly denied any responsibility phoning their credit card company and confirming nothing had been taken.

I returned to the hostel and got Ali to make another call to them and a very expensive phone call £40 later my bank reversed these transactions and put a harsh £150 limit for withdrawals on my card. The woman said to me pleasantly if anymore than £150 gets taken out on your card it will be automatically stopped. This did of course cause a long sleepless night of worry. All this while Nathan and Russ chatted and watched the England football match and emptied the fridge of the Effess beer it needed to be refilled twice. It was a quiet match, no, 'oooohley oooohley oooohley,' type chanting I've experienced in pubs when football is on the TV. Which was just as well as the hostel was occupied by a large number of French girls from Paris and the Champagne area we were getting friendly with (i.e. we were buying the beers for). I think it would have confused them greatly if old style soccer chanting went on. A large group of English people would apparently be chanting, "With milk, with milk, with milk, with milk!" Enthusiastically. I suppose it's not as bad as an old Eurovision song I think by ABBA which goes "La-la-la-la-la-la," To French people it would be, "the the the the."

The morning couldn't come soon enough a phone call to my bank in the UK at extreme cost of £12. My bank stated everything was now fine and the money had been returned. I considered staying another day but I have itchy feet and decided not to after breakfast. Though breakfast was amusing we met a girl called Leanne who had an unpleasant experience in another hostel. So bad that she moved to the Mavi in the middle of the night. She did have a few more pleasant tales to tell of her travels in Turkey.

Her best story was when her boy friend went to get a Turkish massage. A huge bloke a veritable mountain of muscle exfoliated him all over. Even his sack and crack while being held down by another beefy bloke using crushed walnut shells his cries of agony ignored. The other story was when she went for a Turkish bath, being massaged and the masseuse started to massage her back with one hand for a while she turned round and saw him whacking one off at her.

A few people put suggestions up of a Turkish bath and I thought why not? I had to have a go. Armed with a few phrases, no exfoliation to avoid being rubbed all over by crushed walnut shells or sand or whatever people used to exfoliate. I always force myself into such situations with the phrase. Why not? When is the next time you are going to be here? Considering the end of my trip essentially meant I would be utterly broke. I thought not for a very very long time and thought meh ok lets go for one then.

I asked Ali where I could find such a bath and he directed me to the oldest bathhouse in Istanbul built apparently in 1500. Something I had no idea where it was located. Ali wrote down the address in Turkish and gave me fairly good directions. I passed a non descript building several times until I realised that these were the baths. Parking up and chaining the bike and giving the parking attendant a few Lira I would have ignored as maybe residential or even derelict. I was gently shoved through the men's entrance by an old man sitting at the entrance who gave me a wide sparkling smile as I entered.

47

An earthy smell mixed with spices enveloped my nose and the warm tropical air enveloped me. An exotic sensation charged through me. I thought for a moment wondering what I had gotten myself into and nearly turned back but thought again when is the next time and went in deeper.

The small door led to a very large chamber. Encompassing the room were small wooded cubicles with worn shuttered doors. Three generations of men were lounging on an old threadbare sofa. They were watching a rabbit eared television which seemed to crackle and fizz at the slightest vibration of my steps.

Faded and curled pictures adorned the peeling walls. One of the younger men stood up to greet me with, *"Salem alikum."* On the other side of the room someone was rubbing the back of another man with what looked like a wire brush and steel scourers. The kind you use on baked on food from baking dishes from the oven. Strips of flesh seemed to fly off his back he seemed to be in pain but didn't utter a whisper to betray this to retain his masculinity. I suppose as Turkey is supposed to be a very macho culture. I thought that people would pay good money for that in certain circumstances. I was reminded of this BDSM video I saw a few years ago where a woman used a cheese grater of man's penis and he enjoyed it. It looked like something similar with the amount of flesh that had fallen to the floor.

I fumbled in my pockets for the useful phrases and blurted out no exfoliation when the old man pointed towards that bit and was spared having my skin peeled off. I was directed to a booth and told to remove my clothes and was passed a towel bag carefully tucking my stuff into the folds and trying to imagine what might happen. I was given a tiny towel type thing that left a Balinese dancer gap in the side and was motioned to follow the old man. I was alone in a huge warm marble tiled room. The only light provided were from rays of sun that beamed through stained glass ceiling tiles. A low ledge surrounded the room. Beautifully carved marble basins emerging from the wall were evenly positioned around the ledge. Lion head brass taps dribbled warm water into the basins. The sounds echoed throughout the room. A red plastic bowl floated in each basin. The walls were traditional plaster but you could see shadows of classic frescos etched into them. In the centre of the room was a large circular slab of raised marble.

I was signalled to go to a basin. The towel removed I grabbed a plastic bowl full of water and poured it over my head it felt good so far and I was told to sit. He smiled a metallic grin and motioned to me to wait a moment. Alone and butt naked I wondered what I was supposed to do next. Beginning to feel chilled, it was then that I finally clued in and realised what the red basin was for. I started pouring the warm water over my head and arms. The water was soothing and was making me relax. The room was absolutely enchanting.

A huge mountain of a man entered and took a place opposite to me across the room. Nudging my shoulder, snapping me back to the marble slab. The man was naked except for a sort of towel type thing with a washcloth pattern you see on Arabic headdress. This man would put Swartzenegger to shame. I was motioned to lie down on the marble slab. I felt incredibly vulnerable at this point but thought what's the worse that can happen? I just hoped he tried not to show me a magic trick as I'd heard off a mate. Where from behind somebody sticks a thumb in your butt and shows you both his hands and goes ta da!

The marble felt warm as I lay down on my stomach. His strong hands were all over my body, scrubbing with a loafer and what smelled vaguely like soap. Another man came in and started the massage. I was being held down by one of them as one would massage, although massage was a loose term. It was more like grab and crack every joint possible on my body. He would grab my leg and crack what I thought was not possible to crack. My hip, my knees, my ankle each toe on each joint making me wince in pain each and every time. I'm pretty sure I saw both my ankles in front of my face at one point he was twisting in all these positions. Though with each crack came a sudden warmness to it. I was given a final wash down buckets of warm water then cold thrown over me and given a towel to change in the first room and leave. I felt exhausted had experienced pain lots of pain but felt human again after the long ride through Europe. I was clean for a day or so and it would be the last wash for a couple of days. At least I'm clean leaving Europe I thought. As over the Bridge was the start of Asia and effectively the Middle East.

Leaving Istanbul is harder than it sounds. I had to find the Bosporus Bridge that marked the political end of Europe and the start of Asia. I thought I would follow the coast until I got to the bridge and ended up in some suburb completely lost. I stopped to ask for directions when a big van reversed into me knocking me over and pushing the bike along the ground sparks could be seen. He stopped before the bike ended up crushing me asked if I was ok and drove off. This I suppose was a good thing. As when overseas no matter whose fault it really was you are the one who ends up paying as you are considered to be rich all tourists are considered to be rich as I found out later.

The crossing of the Bosporus Bridge was uneventful other than there being automatic pay barriers in place. As I crossed over into Asia I had no map and I also didn't have a motorway pass card either. A biker stopped to let me use his card to get through the barrier. Although strictly speaking this was un-needed as somebody before me had crashed through the barrier. It seemed that people made a career out of this by parking their bikes or cars next to the barriers taking 50% on top of the fee to go through the barrier.

The ride through to Ankara on the motorway was completely uneventful other than the falling temperature necessitating me to put my fleece and waterproofs on to keep warm. Turkey seems to be a hot country for all the touristy coastal regions. It is hot often painfully so but once you got into the middle of the country where everything was mountainous it started to get cold. You could stop for a minute or two to warm up from the sun but the heat would be robbed from you the moment you started the bike and continued on your journey. Passing through craggy gorges long viaducts over tranquil valleys that looked untouched. With small groups of people sitting by the edge of lakes and riversides that looked idyllic and would have made an excellent if somewhat visible rough camping spot.

I fuelled up with offers of more *chai*, which were gratefully received due to the cold and managed to get to the outskirts of Ankara without any trouble. Other than the incident at the tollbooth just outside Ankara. This I was not expecting and managed to create a huge queue of cars behind me smashing their fists into their horns as I fumbled in my pockets for change. Normally when you do this in Europe to speed things up the booth operator will let you through and let you in for free. I finally handed over a 50 and the booth operator shot me one helluva dirty look as if I had slept with her father or something.

Ankara is huge absolutely massive. I always underestimate the size of cities and this was no exception. I'd gotten off the motorway and into this city and as per usual had gotten very, very lost. I kept stopping and asking people for the city centre and they kept saying 20km over there. In Turkey the land is dirt-cheap as they have lots of it. Turkey a country much bigger than France means they can use as much land as they pleased. I rolled around the suburbs wondering where the city centre was and getting increasingly lost and considered camping in a building site I had passed. But I had no matches and no food to cook for that night and had to find something to eat before sleeping.

I had gotten even more lost if that is possible until I found a Yamaha Fazer rider by the side of the road. This was Giary. I asked him about a cheapo hotel and he said no problem follow me. He spoke excellent English and we ended up sitting at a café drinking *chai* chatting about bikes. Bikes in Turkey other than scooters are expensive he had paid £300 for his tyres alone. He led me to a couple of hotels, which were way out of my budget being $155 and $122 a night and eventually suggested to me to sleep in the park.

I said goodbye and thanks to him and rolled into the park putting up my tent hanging it on a tree and crawled into my sleeping bag. A few minutes later a man came up to me and said no camp here! You go now...

11pm and nowhere to stay, I cruised around for another rough camp spot but found nothing. I'd noticed lots of pickup trucks cruising around with people waiving Turkish flags around jumping up and down honking their horns. I was cruising quite slowly until I was suddenly caught in the middle of the throng of pickup trucks. I reached for my camera and started filming which encouraged them even more to go nuts and flag wave some more. Horns blaring, young women and men jumping up and down all waiving flags and hanging out the sides of their cars singing songs. I wondered what was going on and was led by this convoy for a few miles until they stopped at the outskirts of Ankara at a petrol station and piled out all coming out to shake my hand *chai* was produced from nowhere...

In fact while I am on the subject of *chai*. In Turkey people there love their *chai* (tea) pronounced *cay* that is offered anywhere and everywhere always with enormous amounts of sugar. Such that you will stop and ask for directions, they may not know the way or even understand you but will still offer you *chai*. I have no idea where they get it from. More than once I asked a man wearing flip-flops a T-shirt and shorts. Somehow out of nowhere he magicked out 2 shot glasses of burning hot *chai* and we were in the middle of nowhere. I slightly wondered if Turks kept a flask of emergency *chai* on the slight off chance a visitor would come so that they could offer it.

Food and snacks were served out the back of another car and there was much dancing and jubilation. I worked out that this was a farewell party. The men the sons of the older women were being conscripted for their 2 years service and they wanted to show them off with a bang. I was dragged in to the foray of whirling circles holding hands flag waving and singing. Although I couldn't understand a word everybody seemed happy and glowing and treated me as if I were one of their own such was their hospitality. I do often wonder if this would have been reciprocated if a Turk went to the UK.

At 2am the music stopped there was much hugging shaking of hands the cars all sped off leaving me alone in the petrol station needing to find a place to stay. I cruised down a few villages found a derelict house down a narrow street and slept under the XT using my stove to generate a bit of heat and fell into a dreamless sleep.

The next morning I awoke to the sound of the Muezzin. He was making the daily regular early morning call to prayer again.

"Allllllllllllllllllaaaaaaaaaaaaaaaarrrrrr aaaaaaakkaaabbbaaaaru!" But sleeping on the ground made me unable to turn over and ignore it. I stood up and looked around headstones lots of headstones all around me I had inadvertently camped in a cemetery, oops this is a big no-no in Muslim societies. But I'm not Muslim so there and strained myself to get up. With total irony yet again within 5km of setting off I found a big truckers hostel, live and learn I suppose.

The morning was cold at 5am and I stopped to make coffee with my stove. Although the stresses of buying the stove and being subjected to fraud were harrowing I was muchly glad to be having hot coffee out of little Nescafé tubes on such a cold morning. It was cold enough to see my breath in the air and with the wind chill combined with this it felt colder. I had to stop every half hour until 10am to warm myself up with the stove and some coffee.

The landscape changed yet again. It was somewhat colourless grey within grey against dusty grey foothills and a gravel track leading off into the distance. There were no cars nobody by the side of the road and a hollow silence surrounding the whole valley I was passing through. Everything seemed to be dormant no signs of life and the buzz of the XT could be heard echoing against the mountainsides.

At 10am the scenery changed as I entered a sort of plateau and the temperatures increased markedly. With bored cops sitting by the side of the road ignoring me. The scenery turned into farmland with row after row of identically ploughed fields of cabbages and aubergines. The road got better for a while turning almost into a road you might find in Europe sealed generally flat and straight. It was an uneventful ride to Goreme though not very interesting as it was just farmland repeated over and over. The odd tree would poke out of the farmland but this was a rarity.

I opened up the throttle and sped towards Goreme a little faster and arrived in a small village neighbouring Goreme and Capadocia. Stopping for lunch and asking for directions at a small café, which was just a window out of a stone house for kebab lunch and onwards to Goreme.

I Capadocia

I had been advised by Russ to come here but he was at least a week behind me waiting on his tyres and drinking with Nathan. I had absolutely no idea where to stay. Cruising into Capadocia, en-route I immediately stopped and took in the incredible view of the Capadocia valley. It looked like nothing I have seen before small caves cut into the rocks in every direction as far as the eye could see. It was a lunar landscape of strange rock towers and stone cliffs. The original arrivals the trilobites burrowed in to the rock towers and cliffs to create their simple dwellings.

The heart of the area is a now tourist town called Goreme which became my home for a couple of days. Here I met Jim, Matt Damon, the New Yorker, Arfan, the Two American girls, a weird Canadian, a Texan, Eircon, Airfan his wife child and Ali who made kebabs.

Jim was a road train driver from Australia who turned out to be a stroke of luck for Russ who arrived a few days later. Russ was ultimately heading out to Australia. Jim was THE life of a party and would have the most outrageous stories to tell. For some strange reason he had decided to up sticks and move to London and get a job there. It's just that he had decided to travel overland and had gotten stuck at various places and had been stuck in Turkey for well over a month.

Matt Damon (not his full name) was a semi hippy with an impressive beard that he wrapped around his head like a turban. He was from California who had come to Europe and beyond to drink. We labelled him the porcelain queen due to his drinking habits.

The New Yorker was a strange guy Jim tagged the virgin as he was totally socially awkward and unable to tell a single joke over the 3 days he stayed with us.

The Two American girls Jane and Lisa were finalist law graduates who Eircon attempted to knobble. The weird Canadian was well…. Weird. He had quit his high paid job in Ottawa and come out to Turkey to work in a carpet shop earning $2 a day he tended to avoid us completely namely as he had to work.

The Texan was kind of quiet but wanted to try everything. Eircon was the Internet café owner who hung about the hostel more than he did the shop. Airfan was the owner who vanished quite often and used to juggle knives, poorly very poorly.

I walked into the hostel to be greeted by. "Oh God not a Japanese guy, they are really reserved and shit he'll be no fun!" They were all saying thinking I wouldn't understand. Once they found I was from England it got worse, "Oh God a bloody Pom!" I'm not sure which is worse.

This hostel was the nomad cave hostel 10 Lira a night for a bed in a hostel, compared to the burning sun outside it was nicely cool but smelt of mildew and felt kind of wet everywhere. The first night we had one hell of a party as the hostel was good enough to let us buy our own beers and drink them in the common area of the hostel. Although where we bought them from it was a contradiction the Muslim shop owner disapproved of us buying alcohol, especially as it was a Friday during the most important prayers. Ironically he would enjoy our business though as we completely emptied his fridge and his shelves of snacks. The party was a typical drink yourself stupid tell jokes and play the odd game of circular give a name for sex, penis, vagina with the winner being my suggestion of a badly packed kebab.

As the sun set over Goreme on the first night the lunar landscape turned to a soft golden red colour and to deeper browns as the sun drifted down below the horizon.

As the Muezzin made out the call to prayer the echo and reverb against the hills was almost majestic as we made a quick climb for a nearby hill to watch the sunset. A postcard moment of absolute bliss as the sun sunk below the horizon we made out way back and started drinking some more. We sat chatted told jokes, stories and watched the stars poke through the shroud of the deep velvet night sky. Goreme didn't have a light pollution problem and they keep the lights low anyway as they are solar powered and it was like a sea of diamonds above us while we had our little party. We moved inside when it began to get cold and continued to have a little club experience as Youtube provided the music. Youtube incidentally in Turkey is banned.

Jim had a day off and the evening was spent recovering from the night before. Everybody was recovering from the night before. Even Eircon he too had ignored to Friday prayers to party with us. Of course the Muezzin call to prayer wasn't appreciated as much when it woke everybody up at 4am.

I decided to explore a little, great places abound in the area with a visit to the underground city and the Ihlara valley. A stunningly lush green canyon, cutting through the dusty surrounding hillside. and some great off roading opportunities. The town of Gorome already had plenty of places to rent off roaders jeeps, quads and dirt bikes. However I had not ridden the best part of 2300 miles to rent a bike. Although tempted with the thought of renting a bike as if you wreck it, it is less important. This however served as a bit of encouragement i.e. don't wreck the bike else your trip is over. I set out to improve my non-existent off roading skills. Since the only off roading skills I had currently was to let the front end find itself by giving it a loose grip. Also to fight the urge to slow down. Many drivers and riders when in trouble slam on the brakes, on a two-wheeled machine the opposite is true.

In that certain situations this seems absolutely insane i.e. during a corner if you so called tank slap by pouring on the power too soon after or before the apex of a corner the bike will go nuts. The wheels with uneven grip fight to regain traction the front wheel wobbles and oscillates as if it is trying to buck you off on a buckaroo ride to hell. If you act on the instinct to brake or slow down you will die, you have to fight every instinct in your mind and pour on the gas steadily. It was like sex when you call out a different woman's name, you can get bucked off just like that and the danger is immense! The off road riding was utterly fantastic, with no luggage on the bike (not that I had bought much in the first place) a loose surface, I was buzzing around the arid barren landscape as if I were an enduro racer. I had a few close calls but my confidence riding off road increased massively, it's not so hard I thought. I returned after a whole day of riding and decided to go spring a few of the tourist traps while it was still light.

One of the major traps was the underground city at Derinkuyu; this was probably the peak of the Troglodytes burrowing activity. 75 meters deep spread over 8 stories it's a veritable warren of passageways and rooms. It is said that several other underground cities in the surrounding area where all linked by 100's of kilometres of connecting passageways. A true navigation feat in itself, through overhearing a guide I could walk to the next underground city. With the heat and stuffiness of the confined tunnels that felt claustrophobic even in their widened state I felt I should take his word for it. I wasn't going to go there just to prove him wrong I wanted out.

One of new guests Anjelica from Colombia turned up. She demanded with quite forceful insistence that we called her An-hellica. She was only there for a day but ended up handing out passes to an unknown Red bull party a few miles away in Urgip. What a party it was, as we all crammed into a single taxi to get there. Laser shows people taking photos of us dancing to the hard techno. Everybody getting extremely wired on the champagne flutes full of Red Bull. Seeing as there were barely any of us there less than 50 people and they had prepared for over 3000 we ate like savages the prepared food and each drank our own weight in Red bull and *Raki*. The Red bull promo party had been a disaster for Red bull as only a few people turned up and we ruthlessly exploited this. Though the photographers often called us around to gather in a corner to make it look like it was incredibly busy even going as far as asking us all to don different coloured T-shirts so it looked like there were a huge number of people there. Though photoshop can do wonders I suppose and it would have to have been used extensively. In a manner not dissimilar to one of the Miracles of Jesus to turn 50 people into 3000.

The next day was spent nursing my incredibly bad hangover and watching people twitch nervously from overdosing on Red bull. We said goodbye to many of the hostel guests as they left that night on a dreary long distance bus with various horror stories to tell regarding these buses. Though I learnt at least these buses stopped now and again for toilets and food was included in the quite reasonable fares. I also spent the day with Jim and Ali at a local kebab place making kebabs. We were told to stop though halfway through as we were making a mess of it. These kebabs were real meat real chicken breasts cut in a certain way and interlocked with other chicken breasts on the spit. Somehow Jim and myself missed kebabs from home. Although the kebaps here were delicious it's just that they missed something. Back home kebabs are generally a disgusting greasy thing you eat after 10 pints on the lash. But when you are drunk off your rocker it is something you want. The combination of the greasiness and chilli sauce that was completely absent in Turkey just seemed to make them seem not right and we strangely enough missed them.

Though food from foreign climes is always Anglicised, Americanised or made more Australian. When you ask for something you find in an ethnic food shop in the UK it is highly probably that those dishes do not exist in their home ethnic countries. For example fortune cookies only exist in the US and UK, people in China and Hong Kong are surprised at pieces of paper inside them. As fortune cookies are a western invention.

The next day Russ arrived and we went back into party mode but with a more subdued crowd. The American girls had left, we had the weird New Yorker, Matt Damon, Russ and two absolutely gorgeous Korean girls who kept to themselves ignoring our advances but still having a beer or two. Eirfan had come back as there were horses outside, Eirfan was supposed to be the hostel owner but we hadn't seen him for days. Eirfan thought himself as a bit of an expert knife thrower and would regularly throw knives into the furniture. He was pretty good until he threw a knife into the balcony to the little terrace the handle hit the wood and it bounced back into his shoulder. He even tried to hide it as it nothing had gone wrong, acting all Mr Cool but with him wearing a white shirt and blood gushing out his shoulder he had little hope of this and eventually made his way to the local hospital once his white shirt became a red one.

Something I had noticed in Capadocia that applied to a lot of Turkey was the apparent infidelity in married men. I chatted to several hostel owners and despite most of them being long time married with young sons and daughters they would still chase the women tourists. Sometimes aggressively sometimes subtlety like Aircon who would take them on long walks up lonely passes and invite them home. I spoke to some of the wives and they seemed indifferent to it and it was almost accepted. They didn't like it but thought that it was something men do and something they couldn't change and therefore didn't try to attempt the impossible.

The next morning everybody was leaving the hostel even Jim. I thought I'd better make tracks too and headed east. Eastern Turkey is something completely unknown. The wealth of the country is all in the western parts and the southern coast. By enlarge the area east of Capadocia is not visited often by tourists with them heading south to Olympus or west to Istanbul instead.

II Eastern Turkey

The roads out of Capadocia changed from decent sealed to poor to gravel tracks to motorway to sports bike country all in the space of a day as I headed eastwards. Erizumcan turned out to be a massive military base. The military bases with high sand coloured walls and soldiers marching inside back and forth. It was quite a sight but I generally did not want to hang around as a few years ago some people were arrested as terrorists for watching and taking photos of Turkish military things. Effectively being an anorak outside Europe is potentially dangerous!

The route there did have some wonderful gorges passing through dusty towns full of barefoot children. The road and the gorges almost replicating my experience in Spain. Spain the year before on the N220 from Bilbao to Barcelona, high cliffs on each side of the road with the road actually being cut into the space just next to the river. The river looked like a chocolate milkshake with froth and brown murky waters rushing down at considerable speed following sometimes going to the left and right of the road snaking its way through the mountains. An awful lot of construction was going on at the roadside for some un-discernable reason huge lorries laden with equally huge rocks and sand kicking up great clouds of choking dust.

It was a sunny blindly hot day the only massive note of interest was when a bunch of men in a truck passed by me too closely. They caught my left pannier and nearly pushed me off. But I wobbled went into the lane opposite and rebalanced it back fairly easily.

In Spain a year before a cop car hit me in a similar manner sending me into a nasty wobble into a gravel trap. No gravel traps here fortunately enough. The driver in his car managed to tear one of the zips on my bag but otherwise there was little damage. Well to me anyway as he came off much worse, as he rolled up to the traffic lights, in the shadow of a great ancient ruined castle. He rolled down his window and apologised. I looked at him and gave him a thumbs up gesture. He didn't notice the huge deep gash in the side of his car where he had hit me as I kept my hammer in that pannier which I've cut myself on the badly burred handle more than once. I think he came off worse truthfully. It just annoyed me a little that my luggage was falling apart so easily when I still had the majority of my journey to ride and probably had nowhere for replacements either which was worse.

I arrived shortly at Erizum, which turned out to be the centre of carpet manufacture. On stopping and asking for directions the obligatory *chai* was offered and I met another man who knew Ali from the Mavi. Thankfully he didn't try to sell me a carpet. It was a fairly large town with hotels expensive ones mind and went out to eat and found a mechanic at a scooter shop who didn't have one in the shop but understood what I said:

"Benzene filter?" I enquired.

"Benzene filter! OK, OK!" he responded. He motioned for me to sit on the back of his 50cc bike. Now here I was wearing no helmet on the back of a 50cc bike with no hand grabs as he jumped the bike off the pavement. In Turkey they seem to love to partition the road with big concrete blocks and high kerbs. It was quite a jump. We were then going against the traffic until he found a small pedestrian crossing he slipped through and took me into a back alleyway to a local mechanic. The mechanic spoke to the other mechanic and said, "Benzene filter."

"Ok, ishallah," a mechanic said. He told me to come round on the bike and he'd stick it in for free (Ishallah) bonza. I went to get my bike and my spare tyre to save myself the trouble of changing it over myself. He said he would change the tyre over (Ishallah). He changed my tyre over to the trellebourg also for free. While looking over the bike he found several worrisome cracks to the rear sub frame and the rack where Nathan a week before had attached the rope. The mechanic said he could fix it (Ishallah). He jumped on a 50cc bike of his own and came back 20 minutes later with several tanks of gas and a welding mask. I was starting to get a bit worried now he kept saying Ishallah, which means God willing. I had started to

57

imagine this mechanic was a cowboy and was doing repairs by luck and had so far gotten away with it by the grace of Allah.

My friend had taken a flight to Morocco once and the pilot would add Ishallah to the end of every sentence he said. "We shall be taking off at 8am Ishallah, we shall be landing at 6pm Ishallah." That kind of thing even though it is cultural and perhaps said as often as out generation say various buzz words. But on a flight would kind of make me lose confidence in the pilot thinking he was incapable.

"God willing the engines won't burn out."

"God willing we won't crash." The human mind being the human mind doesn't process negatives and if you tell somebody something they will think about it. Try it yourself don't think about an orange it is impossible. Just saying the God willing automatically introduces a sort of doubt that he can actually do the repair.

While I was waiting with lightning cobalt blue flashes against the wall from the welding, the mechanic happily doing his welding magic an odd thing happened. The local press were called and another adventure rider who had gone into Iraq and Syria showed me his photos and I showed him mine. This sort of escalated when another man came and started to poke a TV camera in my face. I am very wary of cameras as I had a nasty run in with a TV reporter years ago. Where there was this smarmy get who was wandering around town poking a microphone in peoples' faces. He asked me what APR was and equivalent APR. I told him what it was. The reporter looked disappointed in my response in knowing what they were. He then asked me, "Do you think other people know what APR and equiv APR are?"

"I have no idea," I said. On the evening news they ran a banks are ripping us off as the UK public is retarded feature. It showed numerous apparent numpties saying they did not know what APR was. I was waiting for me to show up to blow them away, at which a cut of me saying, "I have no idea." Making me look like a numpty and the feature ended. They cut it to support the story they had decided to cover. After the programme my phone started buzzing with SMS messages, from my work colleagues taking the mick as I was working as an accountant at the time and appeared not to know these simple things, the shame of it all. In his defence I suppose I had cornered him as he had ducked in from the side and was cornered by me into answering my question. I had given him a very detailed explanation and his eyes seemed to glaze over in a kill me now look.

Accountants I suppose tend to have that effect on people when discussing accountancy. But I'm not a normal every day vanilla accountant I suppose. I was 1/3 of the way round the world on a motorbike. Considering I didn't speak Turkish and would never see the footage I have no idea as to what the reporter cut the video into and what impression people would have gotten from seeing that on their TV screens. Maybe I will return in a few years time and be treated like a hero, I can imagine the headlines in the papers now.

"First Muslim biker to cross the world,"

Though I'm not Muslim though the TV viewers don't know that do they? Anyway the first Muslim biker to ride round the world is Emilio Scotto and he didn't actually start off as a Muslim either. Or more likely:

"Numpty biker attempts to cross the world and is unable to change his own tyres,"

In fact it rather likely that this is what was reported as I was filmed jumping up and down on the edge of the wheel. I was trying to break the bead on the tyre forgetting to let all the air out my tyres causing more than a few laughs this technique was proven it worked on the road plenty of times but just not this time. But then again the mechanic did not use tyre levers anyway. He employed a couple of blokes called another bloke in who was passing by to stand on the edge of the tyre and pulled the tyre off the rim just like that. Probably useful if you are travelling in a big group I suppose. But not me as a bunch of men to stand on the edge of your tyre take up a fair bit of space and probably wouldn't fit into my panniers.

We parted company with him selling my old tyre a part worn TKC80 on immediately for a few quid making him very happy. Strictly speaking the tyre would have last another 1000km but I didn't want to be carrying more weight than needed. Happy all round I returned to my hostel come hotel. I went out for dinner and something nasty happened. As I sat eating my kebab a very large man sat in front of me and started to chat to me. He invited me upstairs to drink *chai*, then beer then *raki*. With Ali's sign fresh in my mind stating I should never go have drinks of any kind in Turkey with strangers, and the desire not to wake up robbed of all my belongings in a bathtub full of ice missing a kidney I declined.

"No thanks." I said and was insistent I wouldn't go off with him. Another large man stood behind me and put his hands on both my shoulders absolutely insisting that I go with him or bad things would happen. I yanked myself free and he cornered me trying to intimidate me into leaving with him. I feigned a kick then pummelled his face as he covered his groin. He did get me on the shoulder with a chair leg but this didn't hurt as I was wearing an upgraded jacket. My IDF friend the kind of guy who has lived in Tel Aviv for far too long and slept with a Uzi under his pillow had told me never to take the jacket off. I returned a few streets down to my hotel and was promptly thrown out I didn't get my 25 lira back unfortunately. In the lobby leading all the way up the stairs I had left a big greasy

59

black stain of various things engine oil, petrol all sorts. I packed up my bags rode out of town 4km and found an abandoned hamlet sans mosque to camp out under the stars. Sleep was not forthcoming due to the cold. I moved into a sort of dilapidated cabin but decided to put my tent up inside the house that gained some extra warmth and put my stove on through part of the night.

The next day was a transit day again I made it to Kars which seemed totally desolate and almost another world from the colourful green Turkey I had been crossing over the past few days. Curiously inside the town the roads turned to gravel. Outside the road was sealed but badly worn with ruts from where all the car wheels had been. A pleasant moment was when I stopped outside a school and the Muslim children inside stood in an orderly fashion to watch what I was doing as motorbikes are rare in this part of the world. I felt almost famous but had to push on as I had no more Turkish money left. I was stopped by a small convoy blocking the road and much singing and dancing up ahead but mostly obscured by a small traffic jam. I considered riding up and around on the edge of the road to get out of the city quickly but had sort of gate crashed a Turkish wedding after a few yards.

The lucky couple were dressed in immaculately and positively shone against the drab background of the environment. I could see them not far away and decided to have a look curiosity wouldn't kill the cat. I just about caught the end of it where the bride and husband were leaving. They were about to leave when they spotted me and were gracious in inviting me in *chai* as customary was offered. I was offered a seat around the edge of the reception type area. They looked genuinely happy at the prospect of their future. The mother was unhappy however as they were to move west as she wouldn't see them often.

Gauging by the way it had taken me two days of hard riding over unstable road surfaces, across hills and through gorges. I had over taken hundreds of slow buses kicking up dust milling their way through the landscape that an off road bike could cut through with ease I sort of saw her point. I had wanted to get away quickly due to bank and border issues, but each time I tried to make my excuses I was told that there is plenty of time my friend. The party dissipated with much song and dance that I didn't understand and I had my picture taken many, many times before every man shook my hand and told me good luck. I said I'd make it Ishallah.

The reason for this rush was the bank, which I bank with, is silly. In that it had only allowed me to input two different countries and dates to be allowed to draw out money in Capadocia I had put I would be in Georgia in 3 days and this was the 3rd day. I was to head north to Aktas Lake, a huge lake the size of Wales. It felt like a loch in Scotland as if I had time travelled back 150 years into the past as rounding corners sheep and goats would be hanging around on the rocks all over the place. Though it was seriously cold and the lake had taken a very long time to traverse. With powerful cold wind drawn off the lake and exposed shore I felt that if I had been here maybe a month later it would have been an idyllic summer camping spot next to the lake.

My aim here was to get to Aktas town and cross into Georgia. Although Turkey was very good with its people who had a kind of spark in their lives that you just don't see wandering around the towns in the UK. They had a sort of zest for life and a giddy humour I wanted to experience something different. The Turks are a fantastic people with an almost child like curiosity who will say hello to anybody who looks different. Although in the east many of them were incredibly poor they would still serve you *chai* at any given opportunity. I could have stayed in Turkey for a very long time but with visas running out of time and the fact that Turkey was virtually on my doorstep compared to the central Asian / Caucus regions I was about to enter I pushed on.

The Lonely Planet indestructible map I had gotten off Ali showed clearly that Aktas was an open border and I put all my faith into it. I had taken all day from a very early start to get to Aktas. I was keen to get over into Georgia and headed to the Aktas border point. Here something felt wrong, I asked the soldier manning a checkpoint.

"Aktas?" I asked pointing towards the hills. He nodded and opened the barrier for me letting me through. Riding up the hill and around the gravel road I noticed lots of brilliant red signs warning of something then signs of men with guns hmm. I don't read Turkish and they had no real effect on me. Passing a few one horse towns I noticed lots of helicopters flying around also and more signs but signs of men with guns. Nah can't be important must be something to do with the Kurds or something. Though I was in the North of Turkey and the Kurds are in the South near the Iraq border. I rounded one final hill and noticed in the distance on the edge of a lake a sort of chain link fenced gunmetal grey building and headed towards it.

Passing a couple of tipped over barrels thoughtlessly left by the side of the road I thought this border point isn't very good. The road to the border point became challenging off road now necessitating me standing on the foot pegs, as it was a sort of combination of mud and gravel. The road took a dip and curve to the right where the road straightened up with the buildings and I could see two soldiers standing in the distance. They put their hands up palm down and waved at me. I thought they were beckoning me on towards them and I thought shit it's late! The border must be closing soon and rode towards them faster. They waved their hands faster; I went towards them faster until.

I was shot at.

9: BOOM BOOM!

The gravel here was a funny colour not funny as in comical or humorous but in that it was a shade of brown I'd never seen before. When I think of gravel I think of yellow or grey from far too many driveways it also hurt my knees a fair bit I had a fairly good view as I was on my knees looking down at it.

I was looking at the gravel to take my mind off the soldiers surrounding me weapons pointing at me shouting things I didn't understand in Turkish, I did hear:

"Ich Spreken Deustche?" which I felt incredibly strange thing to be hearing.

"Kurd?" Another soldier spat out roughly as if it were a swear word. An awful lot of things ran through my mind at that point, better than a bullet I suppose. I entertained thoughts that I would die or at the very least get arrested and deported end of journey after only 3 weeks. So here I was looking at the gravel and thinking about the colour and texture to keep my mind off it. The soldiers milled about a bit while I was on my knees, hands on my head still with my helmet on. I waited for what seemed to be a lifetime probably 2-3 minutes until I heard a jeep pulling up behind me as I was facing away from the military base. I heard a couple of doors open and the crunch of boots against gravel. Oh crap, a man with handcuffs? A man with a revolver for special occasions such as this? My imagination ran wilder than a bag of snakes. Out walked in front of me a Ray Ban wearing big cheese he motioned for me to stand up and for the soldiers to stand down, which they did to my relief. I stood up and he said in almost perfect English:

"What are you doing here? This border is closed, how did you get past the guard?" He demanded in a rather harsh tone I felt.

"What guard?" I replied cautiously.

"The guard at the town! Did you come from the main road?"

"Yes I did but he let me through I'm very sorry very, very sorry." And I went to pick up my map that showed Aktas as an open border crossing.

"Ah this map is wrong, I apologise for this but my soldiers they have nothing to do, and they think you are Kurdistan PPK. We will have to look at passport and search your belongings." He said almost apologetically. To which everybody seemed to lighten up. The big cheese asked me what I was doing in Turkey I told him of my big plan to cross Russia.

"Are you crazy?" He asked.

"Maybe," I replied.

"Why do you do this to ride across Russia is there no good road in England?"

"I ride for Children's charity," I lied, "Children who are very ill." On my return I did actually donate a fair amount of money to Bernados.

"I see, I am most surprised at your presence here everybody crosses at Batumi this border post has been closed since 1999." Pointing Batumi out on my map. "Please you must inform who make this map not to make this mistake again." They proceeded to search through my bags packing them neatly back into my panniers, offered me some *chai* which I have no idea where it came from as we were stood on a remote hill side with no obvious sources of *chai*. Everybody had a look at my passport checking out the various stamps I had collected from my prior travels.

"I am afraid you must leave immediately," said the big cheese. He motioned to a guard, "soldier should not have let you through to here, it is fortunate that you did not come too close as bad things could have happened. I will send an escort with you to ensure you do not get lost," which meant I don't want you poking around here I suppose.

"You cannot cross here, you must go to Turkozu here he pointed on my map, goodbye." Marking a small x and circling it in big wide marker on my map just so I wouldn't forget. He shook my hand and motioned me to go, while barking out an order in Turkish to the soldiers around me. The XT had a bit of a tantrum and wouldn't start, probably as it had been on its side for a while. I could feel the soldiers rolling their eyes as they piled out of their jeeps and gave me a push start. The XT grunted into life giving its usual roaring hum. At which two jeeps with big mean looking machine guns (can a machine gun possibly look cute?) escorted me to the main road and pointed towards a worn away sealed road with huge corrugations and waved me good-bye. I thought I would not make it in time to cross over tonight but would go to the border and wait anyway; playing it through my mind I figured this is what had happened.

I had been riding towards the border point that was actually a military base / border point and the guards had signalled to me to go away. I had mistaken this gesture. In central Asia palm down waving is a sign to go away or stop. I had thought of it in a European way as if it were a beckoning sign. Much like Japanese lucky cats that beckon downwards it was a cultural misunderstanding I was lucky to escape maybe those guidebooks are useful after all to avoid cultural *faux pas*. Except it was a guidebook map which had led me here in the first place!

Hence the soldiers had been telling me to go away and I was riding to them even faster they thought I was some sort of nut and fired a warning shot at me. I'd seen the warning shot, stopped quickly dropping the bike and been surrounded by soldiers who thought I was some sort of terrorist. The soldier 20km ago had let me through the barrier thinking I was going to a petrol station just beyond the ridge and had wondered why I hadn't come back after a long time as it was the only petrol station in the whole area north of Aktas lake.

I had to stop and make myself a fairly strong coffee to get over it, but shit happens. On the bright side I thought hell this will make one helluva story to tell in the future. In that things are often not funny when they are happening but after time has passed you look back and laugh at them. Apparently something identical happened to the Mondo Enduro team in 1995. I wondered for a while if this was the same border crossing as they wanted to minimise their time in Georgia hearing bad things. In wanting to do this they would have attempted to cross somewhere in the middle, i.e. Aktas or Turkozu. I remember seeing on their Mondo promotional video that they rode across patches of ice in Turkey and I had been passing lots of permafrost en-route to Aktas. En-route to Turkozu there was no permafrost except in a few small patches you couldn't ride over like the Mondo group did.... intriguing... Being shot at is a little bit too much adventure if you ask me but we live and learn I suppose. The road to Turkozu was cold and unexciting though the sunset at altitude was beautiful and yet at the same time bad. The high altitude I was at where permafrost never melted it was impossible to camp, as you would freeze to death. A couple days earlier I had nearly frozen to death on the foothills outside Ankara and pressed on, as it got dark breaking the rule of never ride in the dark. After 40km I finally began to descend into a valley where the temperature rose slightly around some twisty roads, which intermittently turned to gravel through some farms through some dirt tracks and around the bottom of a valley. I reached the border point. The border point was closed. I pulled up to the gate and a man popped out and said, "It's closed, come back 9am tomorrow."

I asked him about a hotel he said, "15km back where you came from." Which wasn't good as it was too cold to ride anymore and I was exhausted and cold to the extent I couldn't keep my hands from shaking. I could barely stand still. But with no choice I cruised back to the junction and asked some passing men where a hotel was and they pointed to a big derelict building I had passed. A dishevelled emaciated man came on the back of a flat bed truck and let me in.

I was invited in and the hotel was absolutely rotten and had obviously seen better times, mould was everywhere. A huge unwashed pile of dishes occupied a corner and the windows had a thick cake of mud from the outside and dirt from the inside. Evidently nobody had been here for a while. There was no running water, no electricity for 15 Lira a night. It would have to do as I was too tired to do anything else, with the XT parked in his lobby come kitchen shed thing and me slept in bare bed upstairs in my sleeping bag. It was basic, somewhat rough and unpleasant but after the previous night felt just fine. Except for a few things that go bump in the night and me waking up in panic in a completely black room wondering where I was for a few moments. Even in such clandestine conditions he still managed to make me several cups of *chai*, which I was glad for. It had been one of those long, long days. But I felt encouraged, as just a few hundred metres away was Georgia seemingly remote, apparently dangerous and yet irresistible.

10: GORGEOUS GEORGIA

Do not visit Georgia says the home office website, gangster activity is so bad they state that visitors should stay away entirely. Unfortunately for them I went and visited Georgia since it was the only route to Azerbaijan. And hell if you listen to the FCO and everything the government says you'll never leave the house let alone the country.

I had heard markedly bad things about Georgia in the early 90s I had seen a TV programme called Lost! Which for older Americans may remember as the amazing journey. The plot is teams of two and a cameraman were dumped somewhere and had to make their way home with no money at all. There was an episode where the teams were dumped on a hillside in Azerbaijan. Of course barely anybody saw this TV programme as it was on late night Channel4 and was canned.

It pains me when I say Lost and people immediately think of the American TV show about a plane crash survivors where more and more implausible things happen. Lost! was unique and unlike the myriad of reality shows seen in the past 10 years since it has been broadcast. The people in 'Lost!' shine, achieving things they never thought or realised was possible or in many cases that they were capable of such things. It along with Mondo Enduro had shown what could be accomplished through determination and a bit of blagging as this was proven more than once by the contestants blagging the most ridiculous things. Such as pretending to be Michael Jordan, blagging free flights and getting help from total strangers even getting on the TV. Of course this wasn't all good stuff as bad things did happen to one team in Azerbaijan who had a very hard time and if I recall correctly gave up as she was mistaken for an Indian Illegal immigrant and had left her passport behind at one stage. There was a moment in Baku where she borrowed a mobile phone and was extorted of all the money she had. Ironically the prize in Lost! was incredibly dubious honour if you won you got to participate in the next game. I recall it vaguely but the man who pretended to be Michael Jordan in Iran and his companion were abandoned three times. It's kind of something you don't want to win and if you win you lose. Kind of sounds like the British tax system to be honest.

Even Mondo Enduro in 1995 had no problems many people had stated that Georgia is a bad place to be. Added to the fact that they had just fairly recently had a war with Russia in the North added to the concerns I should get in and out soon as possible.

66

I had gotten up fairly late for me as I usually got up 7am or there abouts but today felt special. There was a brilliant sunrise bringing radiance in contrast to the late dark riding I had encountered the previous night. The sunlight was so brilliant that it made everything seem to glow like a cheap digital camera. Even the most mundane things like the toilet block just outside the border post on the Turkish side seemed to glow. Warmth gently trickled into the valley and made the whole border crossing almost pleasant. Waiting for the border to open I met an Iranian who made everybody *chai* with a big gas stove strapped where the spare tyre of his 4x4 should have been. We chatted idly waiting for the border post to open.

I had considered going to Iran on the route back, and he gave me some good advice and told me matter of fact that a carnet is not needed for Iran. Though I may have trouble buying petrol in Iran as I would need a petrol card else have to buy it on the black-market. Iran may float on a sea of oil but due to an embargo for decades their refining capacity is very limited such that they have to import oil to meet local demand. Much later I found out that China would be upgrading their refining capacity so such problems may not exist in the future. He told me the border point on the Southern tip of Azerbaijan is very bad that it would take him days to cross which is why he carried the gas stove and a large amount of supplies.

All of the home office's concerns were unfounded and the place was pleasant and civilised. Meaning that it didn't need a pre-arranged visa, a stamp into the passport and away you went. Though away you went wasn't quite as simple as that as the border with Turkoza is little more than a goat track. Steep twisty hills with deep gravel and sand invited me to the main road. It was as if I had stepped back in time wooden houses, creaky old Ladas rumbling through the gorge I was riding through along side the river that flowed through the length of Georgia. Rusty buildings vehicles dotted over the landscape it was as if I had stepped into the Lord of the Rings with steam punk culture thrown in.

I managed to get to the main road a few miles short of Borjomi (although I didn't know it at the time as I had no map). I drew out some cash and realised I hadn't seen a single other motorbike since Istanbul strange that. I did however know that Tiffany was here who had gone via Odessa in the Ukraine to Georgia on the Odessa ferry and thus avoided Turkey completely. The whole place seemed nice very nice. Georgians are apparently renowned for their hospitality. With the currency having an excellent exchange rate with the pound I felt it would be a nice place to rest for a few days.

I stopped for lunch of some strange sandwich type thing and jumped on the XT headed for Tbilisi. I stopped at a small café by the side of the road; two heavily armed cops came in each welding an M4 with a grenade launcher attached. I had read about Georgia being terribly corrupt and thought the cops might see a UK number plate bike and try extort me. But they didn't they chatted merrily away to each other and ate their lunch. I found out somewhat later that Georgia has cleaned up its police service massively since the 90s. Signs were stuck on cars saying cops cannot take payment from you in any shape or form the corruption had been wiped out completely. I tried my best at Russian as I supposed Georgians would still understand Russian being ex USSR. The girl in the café giggled at my poor pronunciation and I ended up using the universal backup of pointing at things. I managed to have cold hamburgers, an aubergine salad and black beans all delicious costing me less than 3 Lari (about 60pence). The cops did finally talk to me when I had finished but they were more interested in the CC, top speed and getting a photo. It wasn't everyday that they saw a motorbike, let alone a motorbike with an odd looking fellow doing something they considered to be insane.

As I left the café I was flagged over to stop and allow a huge convoy of vans past all identical to each other. I was there for quite some time and counted at least 70 of them before I was allowed to do leave. The road towards the main road was pleasant and freshly laid in many places with small bits of bitumen sticking to my tyres. Though at the side of the roads fields to the mountains and pipelines reminiscent of the old USSR doctrine of combined heat and power. Children happily playing unsupervised in the fields beside the roads, green and red orchards punctuating the scenery. I managed to get to the main road quite quickly as I had entered via an unusual entry point with everybody entering and leaving through Batumi instead of Turkozu and thus had come in via a small pleasant twisty almost sports bike country road. Passing old rusted signs, which arched gracefully over the road even with the distance to Baku. I fuelled up again more out of paranoia than anything else at a fuel station on the road to Tbilisi and was pleasantly surprised that the petrol was 45p a litre for the good stuff. It wasn't self-serve either with the attendant careful not to spill any on your tank. I passed through a village which seemed to make hammocks and beds lots of wooden pine sort of like an open air Ikea.

After this short stretch the road turned into a modern 3-lane motorway, which had harrowing overtakes. In the UK sometimes you will see double overtaking where a car is overtaking and another car is overtaking the overtaking car, if that makes any sense. In Georgia you needled a steely nerve to drive and I'm not saying that out of bragging even the guidebooks and tourist information websites say this. Quadruple overtaking was quite normal; people would be desperate to overtake you even if this gave them seconds of advantage. The railway constantly shadowed the road so even though the signs were in Georgian it was impossible to get lost you just followed it.

It was getting late in the afternoon so I headed out towards Tbilisi and managed to have a look at Guri where Josef Stalin was born. The museum at Guri tends to gloss over the atrocities of Stalin. Atonement won't bring back the dead it tends to focus on the good aspects of Stalin's rule. In the period of 20 years he transformed a sectarian country into an industrial powerhouse and raised the most powerful army on earth, which remained so for 30 years. It was like what Italians say about Mussolini ok so he was a prat who did some really bad things, but at least he got the trains running on time. Less can be said of current leaders. I read upon my return probably somewhere on wikipedia that 32% of former USSR citizens would still vote for him. Make of this what you will you makes your choice you live with the consequences similar decisions have been made closer to home.

I made my way into Tbilisi and promptly got lost, a taxi driver however saw my predicament and led me into the centre of Tbilisi where I did my old trick of riding round in circles for a couple of hours. I found myself an Internet café after many laps of the city and found out that google maps does not have maps of Georgia at all for some reason, doh! Tbilisi is a strip town it is built along the river so it is long rather than circular like London. There is an upper and lower road on either bank with ramps that go up and down to each deck. The best navigation technique I found was to use the TV tower, which is terrifically ugly but useful as a landmark for navigation. This along with the horrible cubist hotel thing on the hill on the opposite bank that was also a useful aid would be used thus. If it was directly to my left one of the three nearby junctions lead to where all the hostels and cheap accommodation. Old gated mansions split now into flats and tenements. Old stained stone buildings occupied most of the town with only the odd token modern piece of architecture being the Hilton in the middle of the town where the British Embassy takes its residence. The cube building and the TV tower.

I was about to leave the city and camp in the countryside until I lapped a city block several times and some teenagers who had never seen a motorbike before stopped me and asked all sorts of questions. They agreed to show me where a guesthouse was and we made our merry way three up on the bike to a non-descript building, which was the hostel. Where I logged on and agreed to meet Tiffany the next day as I had actually passed her in Borjomi. I thought I might as well stay here a couple of days, as Georgia was indeed a nice place.

Tbilisi is strange in fact much of Georgia is strange, you see many street vendors selling things such as fruits vegetables even *kbac* (pronounced kvass) which is a gingery beer type thing. These people look incredibly emaciated and poor. Yet at the end of the trading day around 9-10pm an expensive car often some sort of SUV would come along. They would load their wares into the back of them and get in the passenger seat.

I stopped for a few supplies mostly emergency supplies, as I hadn't found anywhere decent to eat in Tbilisi. Generally fruit from vendors in the streets surrounding the hostel as the closest thing to fruit I had eaten were some fruit pastilles I had bought in Greece. I found in the bottom of my bag (you can't buy them in Turkey as they are made of pork gelatine). They were friendly enough, though they had a poor sales pitch and would usually try to sell me whatever seemed to be oldest off their cart. I stopped by a haggard old Georgian lady who had the command of a little English.

"Ah welcome to you! Apples very good for you, you eat 2... no 4 a day and you are never ill!" I was after apples and bought some and picked over some Garlic.

"Ah garlic very good, very good for your heart and belly sir!"

"What about vampires?" I cheekily asked.

"Ah yes very good for people with vampires too!" Suffice to say I only bought some apples and a bag of cherries from her. I wasn't in the mood for hunting vampires that night. Also stranger was that the streets were full of people way after dark. Just hanging around but not in a menacing manner, though I couldn't help but feel a bit hmm about it probably from a life time of being raised in the UK we are told not to walk down dark alleyways. Which is precisely what I did walk down dark alleyways to signs that said Internet café. Well a poorly lit one anyway. However there were some really dodgy alleyways that stated Internet café 24h that were completely blacked out. I didn't want to wake up minus a kidney in a bathtub of ice.

Though it didn't exactly work out that way I didn't want to hang around a hostel full of Lonely Planet wielding backpackers and decided to go out and explore a bit. I managed to walk fairly far and get to a place called Vake (pronounced *vakkiee*) Park. Vake Park was notorious for its muggings and stabbings but this is long gone though the place is built on a mass grave to boot. Instead what I saw was lots of middle-aged women sitting around on park benches idly passing the beautiful warm evening at sunset. When I approached as an obvious outsider being that you don't get many Chinese type people around these parts, they called out to me in a friendly sort of manner. Until I thought something was wrong about all of this in that these women were lounging around on benches and corners were a bit too frequent. In addition to this they seemed to be dressed in how I should say risqué fashion. They were soliciting me as prostitutes and they were possibly the most unattractive prostitutes you could imagine. Forty maybe fifty-year-old women attempting to give added credibility that it was the oldest profession in the world. In net stockings, miniskirts, too high heels and hot pink lipstick that was universally poorly applied with tits that went down to their waist. I wondered where on earth they got their clients. But walking through the end of the park that was gated and closed I had no choice but to turn back. Equally old men sashayed through the park doing a bit of punting.

Time again for the mind bleach and I returned to the hostel the top floor of what would have been a mansion and spent the evening chatting to some Israeli tourists who had just come off military service. Also the large number of Americans who had come here to set-up businesses teaching English, some of the Americans even lived in the hostel. Though they did have some more interesting tales to tell, as Tbilisi and Georgia in general are not exactly tourism hotspots. Having recently been a war zone and the foreign offices the world over warning people against coming to this place. The evening ended nicely as there was a firework display for an unknown reason from the top of the TV tower. Quite a number of us had huddled on the balcony to watch it would have been nice to be travelling with somebody at that point.

11 : TIFFANY

Exploring Borjomi the place looked as if it had been bombed out. High-rise flats had visible holes missing balconies and even completely missing stairwells that rose up and ended in a mishmash of rusted steel webbing and concrete. I very much later found out that Borjomi had actually been bombed by helicopter by the Russians in the Georgian / Russian conflict. I did not think that it had come so far south as Borjomi is on the southern edge of Georgia...

As I passed through town I saw a big black and yellow crash barred BMW and thought that can only be Tiffany's bike. Motorbikes are a rarity in Georgia in fact in all of the Caucuses as I had witnessed being the only bike around since entering via Turkey. I parked behind it and was greeted by a small crowd. It was probably like lightening striking twice, and people there perhaps never having seen a motorbike now had two come along at once. If Russ had ridden into Borjomi a bit faster we could have made a classical three.

"Tsk you wait for decades and never see a bike and all of a sudden 3 come along at once, typical!" I found where Tiffany had been hiding in the local Internet café and realised I had absolutely no idea what she looked like. Picking a likely brown haired thin woman in the corner.

"Hello," I said.

"Oh hello who are you?" came a reply from the thin red haired woman sitting two seats down. Let me say this Tiffany is a legend amongst the biking community, and yet almost nobody has heard of her as she has minimal publicity and fanfare tending just to go with the flow this was a refreshing change.

Tiffany yet again reminded me of somebody else having sporting an identical look though her waist length red hair was unique. I found that her hair changed colours on a daily basis depending on who takes a photo of it. She was incredibly chirpy and upbeat about everything, broken camera no problem, worn disc brake? "It'll come soon in Tbilisi," she said. I loved her infectious upbeat nature. I think she embodied what Lois Pryce had said about Austin Vince. Austin had once told Lois that overland travel is not about running from destination to destination but instead it was more a case of moving for a bit. Then stopping for a problem, rest or whatever, then moving on a bit, overland travel was not constant moving.

Tiffany Coates had been almost everywhere the Sahara, South America, India, Australia but not central Asia and Russia. I also found out that she was a good friend of Lois Pryce, Lois Pryce is the wife of Austin Vince. The Mondo Enduro connection again popped up the world of adventure riders though I don't really count myself as an adventure rider as my trip was relatively modest compared to others. Though as I would learn later from riders I met farther down the road the

72

adventure biking community is exceptionally small. There is no more than three maybe four degrees of separation between most adventure bikers. I had a think of it myself, through Tiffany I knew Lois, who knew Austin who knew all of the Mondo Enduro team. I sort of knew a rider with the call sign Clanger who had met Sjaak Lucassen, who had met Emilo Scotto. Who had met the LWRers who had met Ted Simon, all famous names in the biking community though not always for good things.

Tiffany has balls and learnt everything the hard way. Her first trip in 1997 there were no guidebooks or a community online to share advice and experiences with. In 1997-she set off with her best friend and came back 2 years later having gotten to India and deciding to keep on going. It is an experience I felt myself.

She showed me a place to stay Marina's home stay and we piddled the rest of the day exploring the derelict mineral water park. And the rest of the evening chatting to Tiff away drinking and ordering *kinkale*, which I ate 100% of as I found out she didn't eat meat. I discovered that Georgian was somewhat like Welsh to say some words you had to hack them. I.e. *kinkale* to you and me we would say it like it looks Kin-Kal-e but you had to hack the words else it would not sound right. The funny thing about Borjomi is that it has funny water, in the vein of. (Sic) "The worta in Ma jorka don't taste like it ourta."

The water would come out the taps brown or grey, apparently this made it taste nice, Tiffany being a hardened traveller immune to everything under the sun drank it as if there was nothing wrong with it. I felt kind of uneasy watching her drink water that was the colour of the water when I unblock drains it is supposed to taste delicious. I did actually have a try much later it wasn't delicious it tasted like Evian but with a deeper lasting taste. And before anybody says it mineral water DOES have a taste you try drinking some distilled water, tastes foul. People in Georgia and Russia held the water in Borjomi with a mythical quality with healing powers and everybody seemed to know about this place. Georgians and Russians would come from afar to swim in the healing waters. I declined when I went to have a look and found that Speedos and their associated Speedo Afros' were somewhat commonplace.

The next day we decided to go to Vardisia near the Armenian border a cave complex and monastery in the valley wall. I had first hand experience of her riding ability she utterly wasted me. Granted I was on a single and she was on a twin with 200cc on me and with slick more road biased tyres while I was on proper knobblies, which would step out horribly on corners. I had only recently come off sports bikes and the XT was pretty new to me only having it 4 weeks before I had set off.

As Ross had said to me it is a completely different experience to riding a twin or a sports bike. Nor had I bonded with the XT yet, after a while of riding a particular bike you don't have to think about it as much riding it. On my CBR due to the sheer number of miles I put on it the CBR felt familiar and easy to ride (although in the time I spent away I actually de-bonded with the CBR). Though in my defence also she has been riding her BMW affectedly named Thelma for the past 13 years and has effectively put on so many miles she has been to the moon and back mostly on unsealed roads. Though at 280 kilos un-laden I was glad to be on the XT as the XT although not as light as some bikes is comparatively featherweight at 153 kilos stock, while mine was about 143kilos after some aggressive cutting of bits off it.

The ride into Vardisia was ok the road disintegrated at various points to gravel track which was also ok. Though en-route my tool bag vanished due to the straps snapping on the rough road leaving me with absolutely minimal tools a couple of spanners some mole grips and that was it.

Clambering around inside the caves quite fun and our arrival sparked many children to gaze at us, as again motorbikes are virtually mythical beasts in the Caucuses. But leaving was a totally different experience, it started to rain the kind of rain that hits the ground and bounces up to your waist. We decided to wait and waited but it got heavier and heavier until we had no choice and decided to go for it. Tiffany found an utterly disgusting toilet, which overflowed into the car park, and we had to get out of there lest we ride through ankle deep pee or worse.

We got back and had dinner with me prepping to leave the next day. We had more *kinkale* and Nathan lost his bet, sorry Nathan but you lost. On my last day in Istanbul I remember that you and Russ had made a bet for a large quantity of beer. But had discussed at length as I watched the England football match in the Mavi common area how you would find this out. It turned out it was going to be ME who would be doing the dirty work.

Nathan had always insisted that Tiffany as he put it was, "A Man hating lesbian." I generally didn't poke around her website much before departure namely as it was broken in various parts and did not get fixed until our clandestine meeting in Borjomi. I had seen her picture on the beach of Rio and thought she looked like an American. An American that looked an awful lot like one of my old teachers at university. Russ may well have cheated as he had apparently met her fella in Cornwall weeks before but had not realised as 30 people had decided to pack into her house for her meet and greet.

Tiffany was well aware of her reputation as being mistaken as a dyke on a bike, as the only people who had travelled with her were women no men zilch zero. But this was because men don't like being on the back and no men have ever offered to come on the back with her. I offered to be the token male some day to get rid of this reputation. I fit the criteria nicely, as I like to lay women too! All in all it probably made Nathan dislike me even more. Not that I particularly cared, as it was a relationship that could not be reconciled anyway so why worry about it?

We left after much wine and *ludi* that was fine Kazbegi beer (*Ludi* is the word for beer in Georgian) as this place was closing up shop and wandered outside. We heard from a nearby building the unmistakable theme of Hotel California.

I thought back to Spain where an acquaintance had a bar close on him fairly early in the evening so he wandered off somewhere else. The trick in motorbike touring cheaply is to never go to a touristy bar. You should always start your drinking at 6pm or later depending on when the working day ends in the country you are in. Since workers bars you actually meet real people of that country rather than other tourists and you get cheaper beer too. The problem with this little tactic was that workers bars close early since obviously they serve workers who have to go to work early next morning. In his sliding into venues of private parties he had ended up meeting corrupt chief of police, pop stars and even ended up in a dancing contest where his partner was a woman in an electric wheel chair. Where he ended up operating her joystick while they danced. It is these sorts of encounters that make your trip and Tiffany and myself were about to have just such an encounter.

We wondered in and were dragged to a seat by a large bunch of Georgian men who plastered me with wine, vodka and something Georgian. I would slot in the odd Russian word I remembered and they would make an Ah! Expression and speak to me in Russian all going over my head. Tiffany did something rotten to me; she whispered that in Georgia women generally don't speak at parties. This left me to take slug after slug after slug of Georgian wine. Playing the part of humble wife. I did of course blame it all on Tiffany that we had to leave, trying to say.

"Well lads I would love to stay, but the wife here wants to go home sorry." I barely escaped with my liver barely intact. At least I didn't have to make a porcelain phone call that night. For her sins she got a tick off the cat at Marina's. In Siberia they have these lots of these tick things; they bury their head under your skin, releasing a local aesthetic and gorge on your blood. Siberia is said to be full of the damned things and I had bought tick hooks just for this purpose twisting the head in a certain direction and pulling them out. If you pull it out wrong, the head snaps off and continues to burrow in causing massive infection. There are horror stories of people losing feet because of an infected bite probably why people just don't camp in Siberia.

The next day I left to make a break for the Azerbaijan border. As I had decided to go via Uzbekistan. If I got to Baku I could go via Kazakhstan into Uzbekistan applying for a visa in Baku. Attempting to shuffle a letter of invitation en-route and not die on the northern sandy route around the Aral Sea.

Many people in the hostel had had problems getting into Azerbaijan none of them had letters of invitation and the process had changed since I had gotten my letter and visa. The letter of invitation is just money which goes into their treasury it costs money for both the visa AND the letter. Hence probably feeling that people won't pay $200US for a visa they would instead make you pay $100 for the letter and $100 for the visa. Hence they could effectively put the price on their websites as $100. The Uzbek visa didn't come cheap and Tiffany had actually had problems getting it herself.

I got to the border and couldn't find the actual border post. Asking locals where is Azerbaijan they pointed and I followed. The road turned into a dusty gravel track and I thought uh oh on account of my previous experience. Through a dense copse of trees and to a sort of river with a rickety falling apart bridge crossing it. I crossed over it and out of the tree line and noticed mosques...Hmm Georgia is Orthodox what is that Mosque doing there? It dawned on me that I had crossed illegally into Azerbaijan and I turned back and retraced my steps to the real border crossing.

There was real poverty here tiny one donkey villages, bedraggled children and old men staring into emptiness but lush green fields as far as the eye could see. There were an awful lot of sheep on the climb to the border, which seemed to be a good road that curved through each valley and between semi mountainous regions.

I got to the border and was turned back. "This visa is OLD, you must go get a new one!" they said, "You go back to Tbilisi and get tomorrow." I skulked back to the Tbilisi and to the hostel where everybody else was having visa problems. I alerted every biker of this trouble that caused everybody to make a beeline for the border. Next morning I went to the embassy in a taxi, which was scary, as the driver was totally suicidal traffic lights were optional. I suppose it was my fault since the car didn't have any conventional seats just some chairs in it with the legs sawn down. And was told by the embassy staff that my visa was indeed valid. I set off the next morning to find out if my journey would end in 100 miles.

12: AZERBAIJAN

The Azeri border was slow and painful childbirth would be a good word to describe it. It was a case of go to one office fill in some forms. Then cross the road to another office then go back to another office and get something else signed pay the odd bribe here and there (optional as many other riders managed to play dumb and avoid it). It took me 3 hours to get through and at the border point people having rarely seen motorbikes would try my helmet on which was very bad. I'm not saying I have a small head but people with an even bigger heads than me say melon on a toothpick no exaggeration, would cram their heads into it distorting the liner and making the helmet feel terribly loose. If you said no they got terrifically angry about it since I didn't want to get deported before I even got in I acted indifferent towards it.

It took a 20 Lari bribe to get them to get off their rear end to bother to deal with me. Form after form after form and warned not to take the bike into the country for more than 3 days. So in essence I had 3 days to get to Baku. This was fine or so it seemed, as it was only 600km away. 600km something I can do in my sleep without much trouble. What I didn't count on was the immense number of road works and road building that was going on and this was supposed to be the main road to Baku. To add to my woes it had rained while I was in the border post turning the hard pack soil, which formed the foundation of the road into deep sticky mud. I mean you don't expect a red line on the edge of your map to have a small river flowing across it do you?

This was tricky to ride over and I managed by using momentum to effectively skid over the deep parts before the front tyre regained its grip on a gravelly patch. This wasn't so scary as I practiced at home using manholes in the wet. You would ride over a manhole partially leaned over and the front wheel would slide one direction and virtually instantly regain grip the moment you hit the tarmac. This continued for about 30km worrying me deeply about punctures. I even went as far as to stop by the side of the road and ask a farmer who had an old Russian bike sidecar outfit if he would sell me some tools.

The landscape seemed to turn into a wide valley where you could see plains up to about ¾ of the way to the horizon which was they abruptly cut off by mountains to the North and the South. The landscape seemed totally desolate with only the odd police checkpoint to break up the monotony. It seemed that they didn't even cultivate the land and left it as barren scrubland. Though I suppose Azerbaijan has oil and they can import anything they can't grow as the land is supposed to be badly polluted. As night fell and I was riding past red sandy soil fields on a route

"You want passport back, fifty dollar."

"Can't you see I'm hurt and been robbed?"

"Fifty dollar." He repeated. At which he started to pick through my bags and helped himself to a torch an MP3 player and some Euros I was still holding onto... I had been told in such a situation wait them out they will soon get bored.

"I said no," I asserted to him.

"You say yes soon," he said confidently. The cop got into his car and started a to snooze. I had no choice in such situations you are supposed to complain to your embassy but this wasn't really an option. I grudgingly gave him a $50 note I had hidden on my 2nd money belt strapped to my leg. He gave me my passport back and drove off not even helping me pick up my bags and my bike. I sorted everything out and two men from Beijing stopped to ask if I was ok. These guys were part of a work gang sent by the government in exchange for Azeri oil it turned out. They watched my bike for me not that there was anything left to steal anymore as I went into a nearby pharmacy to get some water.

Inside this shop clearly marked 3 Manat items were sold to me for 15 Manat. I think they said take it or leave it. I was disgusted and the Beijing men led me to a rotten Soviet era hotel for 15 Manat a night. This hotel was the pits and then some it was no more than a derelict office block with beds put in it. I had no choice though they did let me park the bike in the lobby. This was possibly THE worse hotel I have stayed in ever. Utterly derelict with only one floor for guests and only me a guest. With idiots optimism I thought I would take a shower looked in the bathroom. I lifted the toilet lid and quickly shut it again. This place hadn't been cleaned since the fall of the USSR in 1990 with cockroaches from the same era too, big ones you could hear scuttling about.

I put my bags in the room and wandered out looking for a beer and noticed my light in my room was on and shadows moving about in my room. It looked like the floor manager was going through my things. Again disgusted I had my beer and went back to the room and slept with my hammer in my hand. I left fairly late on account of being hurt and sleeping in. Though the light showed the true grot of the hotel made me leave sharpish. I rode to the nearest Internet café and attracted a crowd of children around me who said the Internet café would open in an hour. I wanted to talk to somebody maybe Tiffany would still be in Tbilisi a familiar voice as my morale was low and I was utterly hating Azerbaijan.

The Internet café never opened the children who said it would open in an hour had only said that to pick my pockets, which they managed to get a dummy wallet and a few wads of tissue. Again absolutely disgusted for the 3rd time in 24 hours I decided to ride back to the border and see how I felt. The original plan saw me ride to Baku take a ferry to Aktau and ride North to the Russian border where there were decent sealed roads. Or if I could get the Uzbek visa in time to follow Tiffany to the desert crossing. Plan C had been to go into Russia via Sochi by turning back.

As I rode out of town a cop stopped me and said passport, this time I grabbed a hold of it not letting him have it but he yanked it out my hands and did the old $50 demand yet again. This was getting exceptionally tiresome now and I headed back towards the border with Georgia. En-route I was stopped by yet another police man and played the same game again with him. Despondent I was beaten psychologically I utterly hated Azerbaijan totally utterly and completely the people I had met were all terrible and found me nothing more than somebody to steal from. As rode slowly towards the border I stopped for petrol and put in 15 litres. The huge big sign said it would cost £4. I was charged 40 Manat. That was the final straw and I was incredibly glad to see the border point. Where they were surprised to see me as I had said I wanted to go to Baku, no way José am I going into your corrupt country. Pedro a BMW rider came up and was also dismayed at the forms and bribery needed to get in and decided upon following me to Tbilisi. As I was part way through the process of getting out of the country Tiffany pulled up and we chatted about my experiences. I told her to be very careful in Azerbaijan. Tiffany as I have said before is made from sterner stuff and I was pretty sure she could look after herself. I suppose these things happen and somebody has to be the victim. It suddenly struck me that Tiffany was the only woman I had seen in Azerbaijan, although I had not been very far or deep into Azerbaijan I had not actually seen a single Azeri woman at all they must keep them hidden away or something. In supposedly strict Muslim countries like Pakistan and Iran woman are seen going about their daily business but not once in Azerbaijan that was very strange.

14 : GEORGIA

I was back in Georgia and decided to head to see Russ. Russ had been alerted the previous day by the border shenanigans and like everybody else had made a beeline for the border. He said there was nothing I really missed in Azerbaijan as he handed me his Lonely Planet guide. The guidebook said something to the effect of:

> "Baku, where you can see the baby cemetery where the babies have visibly suffered birth defects from the appalling pollution Azerbaijan has suffered and nobody wants to do anything about, or you can see the Peninsula where oil spills occur regularly and cover the land so that nothing grows there ever,"

What a cheerful place. I supposed I didn't really miss anything at all en-route back through Georgia. I did meet an American who said it was probably for the best I go around, as central Asia was even more corrupt than Azerbaijan. The other guests at the hostel said the same things as they had come the other way via train. An American from Houston said he saw it from an airplane from Almatay to Tbilisi and you could see the entire country in 20 minutes from a flight and it looked no better from the ground that it did the air.

Crossing the border had closed my options. It had crossed my mind to follow Tiffany out to Baku as bikers in groups are harder to subdue and her experience in travelling to worse places would be invaluable. But I lacked an Uzbekistan visa and would be stuck alone on the Kazakhstan side. The horror stories I heard though did not turn out to be true about Kazakhstan as Walter whom I met later on and Serge said there is a sealed road from Aktau to the Aral Sea. And North to Aktau that then turns into a gravel road. Though of course I would meet Walter and Serge in the far future I didn't have the benefit of seeing the future.

I didn't fancy staying another night in Tbilisi after Dodos was full and I didn't want to go to Jardine's for another night of Georgian partying and trekked out the 100km towards Borjomi to Marina's to recover a bit.

Marina was totally shocked to see me back and wondered why I was back. I changed upstairs and came down in shorts and she saw the enormous number of bruises and cuts on me. Through passing my phrase book back and forth realised what had happened. Georgians by enlarge utterly hate Azeris for many reasons, wealth oil, differences of religion kinds of things.

She had a huge rant about it and her husband came in and covered me in some sort of healing cream. At the end surprised me by saying he was going to see his second wife. Although it seems strange to us in the western world in Georgia it is completely normal for a husband to visit prostitutes the wife knows all about it but doesn't seem to care and Marina seemed to be glad of the time she would have to herself. I found him in the tunnel restaurant I had been eating in previously.

This restaurant is great absolutely everything they make is from raw ingredients *kinkale* pastry rolled out in front of you the meat chopped up and herbs added. Although it took a very long time from ordering to being served it was delicious made all the more so by the first bit of civil civilisation I had come to. As in my hurry to get to Baku and not wanting to stop at dodgy looking shops which were probably dodgy (though I of course am prejudiced against Azerbaijan but what do you expect from a visitor who went there with best intentions and received a beating). In my haste to sort out the visa problem and apparently closed border of Azerbaijan I had not actually eaten for the best part of 3 days. It turned out that the women who cooked at this fine restaurant were the town's cathouse employees. I'd wondered why they always sat oppositely smiling obscenely like a Cheshire cat that got the cream. They had wondered if I had wanted 'desert' in that they dressed somewhat below their apparent age and would lean forward suggestively to try to give me a better view of their assets, or would go and talk to each other while bending over a table which spoilt my dinner that night. A good occasion for some mental bleach yet again. Strangely though the bill increased each time I went there, I think to be honest that they were ripping me off too, but at least they didn't utterly take the piss as they did in Azerbaijan. Put it this way I will happily revisit Georgia willingly. The only way I would visit Azerbaijan would be to cross the Caspian Sea to get to Kazakhstan or Turkmenistan. But seeing as I now qualify for the multiple entry (more than 2) visa for Russia I have no reason to go that way ever again as I can get the ferry from Georgia to Russia and cross via land into Kazakhstan. Call me a moaner but what do those people hope to expect by cheating people? They may get a tiny bit more profit ONCE. While I go back home and tell everybody to avoid the place like the plague.... seems to be self-defeating to be honest.

So the morning came and the bruises faded a little, and I told Marina I was to go to Batumi to go to the Ukraine and ride across Russia all the way well not quite all the way. She bode me farewell and good luck with a warning to take care of myself or that is what her demeanour suggested as I can't speak Georgian and only a little Russian.

I went to the convenient tourist office and asked them which way to go and they recommended that I go towards Tbilisi and about halfway there nearby Guri turn North and use the middle route instead. Russ had warned me that the road West to Batumi was terrible, with streams, sharp rocks and deep mud and I had seen part of it already and it wasn't pretty so I avoided it.

I set off towards Guri and turned North where I was advised, passing into the greenest of green narrow valleys, up and over the top of a rather rutted pot holed road apparently was no longer maintained as they had dug a tunnel under it. I could have been in a hillier version of Cornwall. Lush green rolling hills with the odd bit of chemical orange gravel here and there and lorry parking stops cut out of the trees to the side now and again. I went over a small landslide towards Kazbegi to see the mountains as I had loved going through the lower Alps previously but was greeted by a mountain shrouded in fog.

I headed west along the northern roads that were in quite bad condition. Bits of metal everywhere and potholes presumably caused by bombs and artillery shells. Some of the buildings here and there were pock marked with scars of the conflict and the streets seemed rather emptier than other Georgian villages I had passed through down south. The few people I did see were mostly old women wrapped up tightly in faded headscarves who gave me the odd toothy smile.

I crossed pretty close to the Russian border and met lots of serious looking paramilitary types who never put their guns down. They would say hello take my postcards but not be very talkative. This I suppose was understandable, as the Northern part of Georgia had been engaged in a war with Russia less than 5 months prior to this. It was kind of frustrating not being able to cross into Russia even though I could see Chechnya and Dagestan just over the border if I climbed a small hill. As I went northwest the roads became fairly rocky and steep and I took the first opportunity to curve down to the main road through to the heartlands of Georgia. This area had a road that was in a worn state with deep ruts where lorries had been through. It followed a railway line and occasionally crossed over from side to side time-to-time. This seemed to be almost the 1950s as if time had stood still, people with donkey drawn carts, very old styled trucks that would not look out of place in a Marilyn Munroe movie. Bright sunshine made this look idealist passing roads lined with old wooden plank board houses. With gardens full of daffodils or pink flowers sometimes even poppies. I cursed myself for not having a camera more than once as a cow was turned into burger meat by a lorry on the downward slope of a particularly big hill and crossed through several valleys to the coast.

The sea looked somewhat grey and the beachfront seemed to sprawl from north to south of Georgia, with small villages built onto the grainy sands. Once in Batumi the usual things check in at an Internet café print out a map find directions.

I did chance upon a policeman on a white XJ900 who led me to a home stay. His bike was the first Georgian bike I had ever seen and it was fairly worn. You could see the steel radial belts poking out of his tyres. With tired yellowing plastics that had been covered in flaking house paint in a vain attempt to hide this. A small crowd gathered and I felt safe and at ease. A crowd in Georgia is nothing to fear and they were only curious and I could feel that there was no malice. Which was a completely different feeling to that I had in Azerbaijan. To me it felt in Azerbaijan as if there was a fight about to break out at any moment in time and that people wanted to hurt me, which felt worse as I had actually been hurt. The eyes of the people in Azerbaijan seemed almost empty devoid of a certain spark and childish charm that the Turks and Georgians seemed to have. Though I had only taken the smallest of glimpses into Azerbaijan so this may have changed later on as western Azerbaijan is poor compared to the Caspian Sea coast where the oil is. The crowd however did comment that I was in a very dirty state. I looked myself in the mirror and they were right. The beat down I received had left big dirty marks on my jeans, which had remained unwashed since Istanbul.

Kulnasi Miqeladze's home stay was neat and comfortable, and if only for Sofo her daughter was well worth staying there to meet some long termer Georgians. A walk around after dark however made me realise why it was so cheap. In that it was essentially in a slum and after dark there seemed to spill 100s of streetwalkers around the whole district. Never mind as I was leaving tomorrow so I went to Batumi beach that was pleasant enough though still with quite an awful lot of Speedo Afros' showing. I didn't really want to swim in the water, as it looked oily and polluted with rainbow patterns floating on the surface.

It is kind of like the Mediterranean. The Black Sea only has a small outlet into the Mediterranean which itself was a virtually an enclosed sea. The bigger problem I'd read was that the Black Sea had been used as a dumping ground for radioactive waste. I'm not usually fearful of such things as short-term exposure does you no harm. Government propaganda aside about dirty bombs, which again are harmless generally, sticks in your mind about this though.

But considering my original plan involved going to Vozrozhdeniya Island (rebirth island) in Kazakhstan on the Aral Sea which is now a peninsula due to the Aral Sea drying up where open air tests of anthrax were conducted in the USSR's time. Although in 1991 the US government sent a team to clean the place up it was never properly cleaned up. When British tests with anthrax on outlying islands of the UK, the UK government left those islands uninhabited for 50 years before going back even then were cautious. I had also planned on going through Semipalantinsk where the USSR tested 456 nuclear bombs. I figured that if you went in you would gain a nice healthy glow but generally I do not like to swim at all. Too many visits to the beach where you would find condoms and turds floating past you as you swam had generally put me off forever. Some of the beaches in the UK you put your foot into the water and took it out all the flesh would be stripped away by the incredible pollution. But I thought you could exploit the radiation in the water if you exposed a certain body part to the water you could play light sabre without novelty glow in the dark condoms.

I found myself a cheap bar, which charged 1 Lari for a pint of watered down Kazbegi beer and drowned my sorrows and gorged myself on the cakes found next door. It pleased me no end when Sofo came back and said yes when I asked her if she would like some cake as we strolled off together to the bar next to the cake shop. Though the cakes seemed to be rather hard and unappetising reminding me of a story my friend told me about his dad in Egypt once at a buffet restaurant.

They had been walking around the pyramids all day and had returned to the restaurant at the hotel. They had eaten quite well at the buffet until his dad sliced one of the cakes and bought it back to the table and began to tuck into the 'cake'. A waiter immediately appeared and asked him if he would like something else, his dad said, "No thanks," and kept digging into the cake, the waiter returned and lifted the cake away. His dad annoyed at this said, "What do you think you are doing!" The waiter apologised and said the cakes were decoration only and were carved out of lard for display purposes only.

Sofo is something out of a dream, pale thin taller than me with the cutest of cute faces. And wore possibly the shortest skirt I have ever seen. Nothing really happened between us though as she was more contented to listen to my stories of the past few days and was interested in where I was going and why. She dropped the bombshell that the ferry no longer runs to Russia anymore due to the recent war that meant I had to go to the Ukraine via an expensive 2-day ferry or go to Trabzon instead. She also was fascinated by Manchester for some reason as her brother had gone to study in Manchester and she had wanted to go there too. I said what for? It's a dump!

15 : TURKISH DELIGHT II

The next day I ended up en-route to Trabzon and met up with a English cyclist doing who had just come back from Kazbegi recently and had missed Azerbaijan due to lack of time.

"Where are you going old boy?" he said.

"Japan probably," I replied.

"Well I'm terribly sorry to inform you that Japan is the other way."

"It's ok I'm trying to get the ferry from Trabzon," I replied. His name was Terry and he was retired and had some amazing stories to tell, in effect he was Tiffany but had done it on a bicycle over the past 15 years.

We parted company and I got to Trabzon via a nice coastal road with cool summery breezes and the bright blue sea to my right. Trabzon was a fairly compact town with the road passing over the airport and high flyovers leading into town. The town was also fairly compact with lots of narrow streets and extremely high kerbs making parking quite difficult. A couple of curious Turks took photos and gave me directions to an Internet café to find a hostel or a hotel and I found a small one on the opposite side of town.

While looking for a hotel / hostel I found a bike shop down a steep set of stairs, where I changed my oil at a local shop who sold me the oil and were happy to let me use their tools and have a general look over the XT for me. With my almost total loss of tools they kindly walked me around the local motor mart buying replacements. I replaced my tool kit around various hardware stores. I was quite pleased with this other than maybe the size of the tools some of them were enormous, with 1 metre long tyre levers you'd get an awful lot of leverage. Shame they are kind of difficult to pack on a motorbike some huge tyre patches and a small set of allen keys and a nice set of mole grips and of course the obligatory *chai*. They yet again fixed my rack that had collapsed so badly the indicator was in the exhaust flow and melted it and asked me where I was going. Japan I told them. While at the same time a couple of mechanics were making a big pizza box to go on the back of a scooter of some kind. I had a quick glance at the odometer and saw it was due to a valve check. This is probably why people like the flat twin airhead design of the BMW twins. In that valve checks are easy on those bikes undo a couple of bolts slip the feeler gauges in adjust with a small spanner and tighten it all up. Singles like the XT are a bit more difficult, tank off then undo the cylinder head bolts then get your hands into the small space measure, adjust measure then adjust, then measure again. Thankfully the XT600E had only a few valves and it was quickly done. It wasn't like the monster NR750 with 8 valves per cylinder, or the more common Yamaha Thunder Ace with its 5 valves per cylinder. So many valves would have taken me all day not to mention the fact that you need a handful of shims to do the job. I hate shimmed engines a mate of mine did his valves and dropped one into the engine case he had to tear the engine apart to find it and ruined the compression somehow.

"Wow that is a very long way!" And all the mechanics lined up to shake my hand. I very nearly got a hard box put on the back of the bike as a couple of guys were in the workshop hammering one together.

"So how you go to Japan?" asked an old man who watched us fixing the bike.

"Oh I'm going to Sochi," I replied.

"Ferry to Sochi leaves once a week today! Hurry!" he proclaimed at which the old man sitting in the corner gets himself a 50cc scooter and leads me on a chase around town. The XT looked like it was on fire as oil had dropped onto the hot pipes, and we make it. He ran in said a few words for me and I get myself a ticket for $200 all in. After having to run around and find a cash machine to get me $200 which would stop my bankcard. Meaning I have to stop off at an Internet café just up the road to get it unlocked via a Skype phone call this is just so troublesome!

I glide through customs and a leathery-faced stocky Kojak look alike in big ray ban sunglasses approaches me this happens to be the captain Gorge. A Georgian with a mouth full of gold teeth and a shaved head approaches me and asks the usual questions.

"When are we going to leave?" I asked.

"When all the cars come," he replied.

"Where are you going in Russia? Moscow?"

"No Vladivostok, maybe Magadan, maybe Sakhalin."

"Are you crazy?" looking around at the others, "this man is crazy, fly to Vladivostok 10 hours, train 2 weeks you want to ride to Vladivostok?!"

"Yes." Again lots of hand shaking on discovery I was to ride to Vladivostok, and lots of test rides on the XT. It took 13 hours to load the ferry with pallet after pallet after pallet of tomatoes before the loading door closed.

The boat was full of Russians who knew Russia. A large Russian man called Mikhail and Serge chatted to me about this and they were stunned. Again listing each and every town, which I had to pass through to get to Vladivostok, when I corrected them with, "I have to go to Ulan Baataar too." Which widened their eyes even more and made them buy me a bottle of beer as a token of good luck. The voyage was unpleasant the cabins insufferably hot that you would gasp for air and everybody slept with their doors open. The food again terrible. The journey was quick as we approached Sochi after only 13 hours. Unfortunately we were not allowed to dock for another 12 hours. On a ship with precious little entertainment it was an incredibly frustrating wait with nothing to do other than sit and watch the sea go by and the sun set on the Black Sea.

This was not alleviated when we were allowed to dock as I was stamped in they searched my bags and found my medical kit and took some of my antibiotics and said they would need to carry out tests on it. I would have to stay onboard for another 36 hours in the insufferable heat. I then had to wait another 18 hours for the insurance sales man to sell me some insurance before I could be off.

The customs man in Sochi is known to be nasty. I was assured I could have at least a month entry on my visa for the bike. He had given me 12 days, I begged him to increase it. He said no, I begged and begged until he lost his rag.

"You take this **NOW** and sign or go back to Trabzon!" He screamed at me turning a bright shade of purple at his anger. I had a look at it and nearly signed it; he pulled it away and got a new one out the office. I thought wow it worked, looked at it and it was now 8 days. He had given me 8 days to cross Russia; nearly impossible it was too far. Working it out in my head I would have to cross nigh on 12000 miles in less than 8 days and the first day was virtually over 1780 miles per day is impossible. He grunted and laughed and while I walked away.

"Fuck you English," he said as a parting shot. I was tempted to say something nasty back but I was in a foreign country and had just annoyed the hell out of one of its border police/customs types. He also had a gun it didn't make the best sense to talk back to him.

I was finally in Russia the biggest part of my journey.

16: ROTTEN GREEN TOMATOES AT THE PRINCESS VICTORIA CARGO BAY CAFE

I suddenly realised I had no map, as the original plan had called for entering Russia via Semipalantinsk in Kazakhstan. Where it would be a simple matter of going to Barnaul and South into Mongolia and to exit Mongolia at Altanbulag where there was only one road out East towards Vladivostok. As I rolled along the sea front the Captain of the Princess Victoria Gorge the Georgian, having seen me still sitting on the dock with my bike, had come to me and with his huge beaming face alight with life had clasped his arms around me.

"Leon, .. Russian vodka I love, … Russian Girls I Love, Russian Women I Love, … but Russian laws are shit I'm glad you got past the customs, Welcome to Russia Comrade!" He proceeded to take me out to dinner with his secret police friend who let me have a look at his pistol. We went for some sort of fish and consumed a bottle of vodka all by himself, as I had to ride. And told me that the customs officer in Sochi was a nasty piece of work he would always find some reason to hold Gorge's delivery of tomatoes for a couple of days letting them rot and keeping the lorry drivers waiting queued up outside the dock area.

Gorge's secret police friend told me, "Russia is very safe, there are no thief in Russia. There is nothing worth stealing, in Russia!" And let out a loud howl of laughter. His friend turned out to be an Armenian who had little love for Russian law too and Gorge and his friend spent plenty of time bitching about Russian law.

I managed to find an Internet café and plot a route. Only this route was wrong really wrong at first I thought Hania who I used to work with was right that Russian roads were absolutely terrible as they became unsealed and turned into a potato rocky road with me ending up under my bike only mildly hurt when attempting to speed up on the rocks. I made my way back to the main road and lent down to bend my rear brake lever back into place I was then hit by all things a Lada....

The Lada drove off the driver seemingly oblivious to what he had just done and I was left clutching my shoulder in severe pain, and making a fairly deep cut on my knee. The trip seemed to be over as I couldn't even lift my arm to horizontal and the bleeding seemed to be quite nasty from the cut. I sat by the side of the road chewing as many painkillers as I had and trying to stop the bleeding on my knee. The bleeding did not stop for a while, and I very nearly seared it shut to stop the bleeding. But psychologically my body was thinking bloody hell he's gone nuts, he's going to burn it shut, best stop bleeding now. I had fixed myself up and the bike best I could, but very gingerly rode on the choke back to the main road. The rain seemed to sweep in and I pulled into a small village and asked a kindly Russian if I could camp on his land. He let me camp in his workshop, which was full of cockroaches. You could hear the tip tap of them crawling about which was disgusting. I woke up middle of the night and noticed for the first time in my life fire flies lots and lots of them. I have never seen them before but there were so many of them the workshop had an eerie glow to it.

The morning came after a sleepless night and so did the rain the heavy rain. I made a choice and thought I can't ride this anymore I'm too badly hurt. Sochi has no airport; Trabzon does though and thought about returning to Turkey to fly home. The rain started to get heavier and I'm subdued in my morale, nothing can be helped I've ridden in lightning before and it doesn't phase me. But then the unbelievable happens a brilliant bright line illuminates up the darkened sky for a moment that seemed to last forever which passed a loud crack shook my body and made my hairs stand up. From thinking back about 100 metres away a lighting bolt struck a pylon that stood to the side of the narrow mountain road. Everything happened within a second, less than that but I had a moment where time seemed to stop.

My enthusiasm and wow factor of this experience can't be properly described in that you had to be there. Although lightening storms I've seen in the UK the crack of the thunder is always a few seconds away meaning it is far way and harmless inside a house or building. But here completely vulnerable with everything I owned in a couple of bags behind me I felt like an ant or less compared to the magnificent power of nature. Humans tangle with nature and twist it to do our bidding; humans seemed to have the upper hand in their relentless conquering of nature. For a moment I wasn't sure who was winning the battle. And that this had been a highlight so far of my Russian adventure. In my dishevelled state every cop in town wanted to look at my passport and the port officials when asking for passage to Trabzon told me to get lost with the guard being totally infuriated at me even attempting to ask a question.

I finally found the ticket office and asked for a ticket back to Trabzon with the XT. Turkey would let me abandon the bike Russia would not. He looked at my passport a 90-day double entry visa in it and asked why I was leaving so soon. No reason I replied. He looked at me and saw the large blood stain on my jeans along with my difficulty in walking. He then thought he could be an absolute arsehole to me. The ticket initially started at $300, $100 more than I had paid in Turkey. I produced this from my stash and the ticket price suddenly jumped to $350, until it got to $1000, when I think he was about to say here you go for the ticket. Then I snapped. I grabbed the money off the table and told him I would rather ride home through the Ukraine than to give any money to that corrupt bastard. He was very displeased about this and threw a fit of rage at me that I only caught a bit of while I made my way out of the tiny little office that was little more than a broom cupboard.

I painfully and slowly retraced my steps, as I knew I had passed a hospital or clinic thing en-route as I had seen the international sign for medicine being the Red Cross. I had imagined that this was an injury bad enough to warrant a medical evacuation. A ride in a helicopter home maybe. Alternatively at the very least some cute nurses in erotic starched sexy uniforms, cute paper hats and some thick black-rimmed glasses. They would coo all over me over me and my extreme trek and bravery which wasn't turning out as extreme as I had initially imagined.

Reality however has a way of disappointing people and today I was no different I was disappointed in a big way. Entering the clinic a huge mountain of a babushka wearing a stained white headdress in a plain white dress suit that wouldn't look out of place in an abattoir and greeted me as if I were some kind of vagrant (though my appearance did give off this impression very well). Initially ignoring me even though the turquoise walled clinic with peeling paint was empty. I approached the desk and spoke to her in broken Russian and she didn't understand. I tried again in English and her eyes widened and she warmed to me immediately. I think there was an association between English speaking and money. She even smiled at me with a steely grin that would have made Jaws the killer from James Bond incredibly jealous. Richard Keil, the actor who plays Jaws could well have been related. The nurse who seemed to be the only other employee in the place asked for my insurance documents which were not accepted as they were in English $100 had to be produced first immediately and I was put on a crude X-ray machine. This machine looked like it had come from World War One. The nurse came in and replaced my crude dressing on my knee and put some sort of glue and white strips to hold the cut closed. Meanwhile the Doc took great pleasure in yanking my arm asking if it hurt. It did and I very nearly passed out at the pain.

"Hurt here?" He would ask again and again.

"Owww!" I would reply to him, "da!" would be my feeble replies.

"No ride for 6 weeks," the doctor said.

"Ok," I lied.

"Dos vit danya!" I was told and let go. Being that means till I see you again I hoped most definitely not to be seeing them again, although the nurse was remarkably pleased to receive one of my postcards from England and a Hong Kong flag patch. I wondered if she realised where that was from actually. I had no broken bones only muscle injury (my shoulder still hurts to this day) but on the bright side I had gotten what I paid for my medical and travel insurance back, though I would have preferred not to use it in the first place.

I had a think about it and decided to head to Rostov which is north quite near the Ukrainian border to make the long trek home. I asked somebody and they told me that I would need to follow the coast to Krasnodar then north to Rostov before being able to cross Russia on the main route. Two bikers at the side of the road just a few miles out of Sochi also gave me some good directions. One actually looked like an acquaintance I know called Keith except with his face kicked in. This road here was a gloriously twisty sports bike country and road there were sports bikes absolutely tearing up the road giving me a friendly wave as they passed. Oddly enough none of them actually had number plates attached to the back of them I thought was strange.

I had run low on petrol and been warned about filling up with petrol, essentially you have to guess how much petrol you need pay for it point at the octane you want and then the babushka behind the armoured glass will start the pump. The Promised Land had come! After the heinous price of petrol in Turkey Russian petrol was 20 roubles a litre, and this wasn't low quality petrol either 93-octane stuff. I opted for the 89 Octane stuff at 18 Roubles per litre that for a bike like the XT with its low compression is fine. Except that motoring in Russia actually costs more in Russia than it does in the UK due to distance. Petrol may well be half the price but when the distances were 10-20 times bigger you spent even more in petrol travelling from town to town. When I think of the next big city over I think of say Birmingham, Liverpool or maybe Leeds. Birmingham is 95 miles away, Liverpool 35 miles Leeds 42 miles. I used to regularly go to such cities. In Russia especially Siberia they would talk about going over to the next town 5-2000km away as if it was just going to the next town over.

The road along the coast improved, almost sports bike country near coastal resorts and what looked like incredibly well developed campsites. What was bad was the traffic this was possibly the biggest traffic jam I have ever seen. Cars and bikes travelled along the verge in the pouring rain crawling forward. I even got knocked off twice into other bikers who would get up and go mad at the car driver who knocked me off. It was at least 150miles of riding on the gravel verge. Although the road generally deteriorated, as I got inland with cracks and corrugations that appeared snaking their way through the glimpses of the road I received every now and again.

Quite amusingly it was often a free for all Russians and me alike riding on verges, on small bits of pavement even on the opposite side of the road that was suspiciously empty for some unknown reason. This all changed in the presence of a police car when everybody suddenly got back into their lanes as if they had been waiting patiently. Nothing to see here officer!

I have no idea as to what this traffic jam was but it lasted to the outskirts of Krasnodar. Not particularly difficult just frustrating as there seemed to be no rhyme or reason for the traffic jam. On the way I started to notice the enormous number of police everywhere in Russia every few hundred metres was another car with two officers sometimes waving money sticks to stop cars. It was effectively a stick with mini stop sign on the end. However more often just standing by the side of the road looking bored almost as if they were cardboard cut out police officers that had a floppy bit of card for the hand. As their hands usually motioned go on keep on going right down at their waist as if a slight flicker of the wind had caught it. I was stopped a few times for a cursory document check, passport, IDP ~ international driving permit, insurance, V5C. I suppose I stood out in Russia the bikers usually preferred sports bikes or enormous cruisers even on the rough stuff. Dual-purpose bikes being somewhat of a rarity.

This was more of an inconvenience than annoying but I often wondered what the police officers thought. For security purposes I strapped my documents around my waist in a money belt and to my leg walking around like a normal tourist this is fine and safe. Riding a motorbike it was also fine until you have to retrieve the said documents. On a motorbike the money belt would migrate in a southerly direction. I would be motioned to stop at a police checkpoint and when asked for my passport it would appear to the police officer that I was going to show them my penis. A few of them were visibly saucer eyed, as I sometimes had to undo my jeans to get at the money belt. Some of them putting their hands worryingly close to their holsters on seeing this unbelievable act unfolding before them.

In Russia being LGTB (Lesbian, gay, bisexual, and transgender) isn't illegal but it is generally taboo and was only decriminalised 10 years ago in Russia. But judging by what some of the shop stands sold, with the top shelf being general eye level this was totally disregarded for tipping the velvet. Double standards everywhere I suppose.

17: RUSSIAN RUSSIA

Once in Krasnodar (Краснода́р), I was exhausted and fell into the first hotel more of a motel really I could find. They refused to register my visa, which sort of defeated the point of staying in that hotel in the first place. But it gave me time to heal up a bit more. Immediately on pulling up two large Russian men approached me.

"Give me five hundred American dollars or we take your moto," they demanded.

"No get lost I'm not paying $500," I responded.

"$450."

"No!" This went on for a while until it got down to $100 which I still said no to, the hotel manager came out seeing what was going on told me to park the XT round the back where I chained it to a huge steel post. The Russians did return later that night while I was watching some kind of game show on Russian TV. I pounced and went outside catching them with a huge pair of bolt croppers. I had my hammer ready they slowly backed off and didn't return.

I felt a lot better a hot shower and half a night's sleep and my arm felt better, but I had been in Russia for 3 days already and needed to get my visa registered and fast. Help came in the form of an airport worker. I thought surely you must be able to register it at the airport right?

I managed to wander around security for about 15 minutes with people wondering who I was and what I was doing there, and eventually managed to accost the an officious looking Russian man. This was Vladimir, completely unable to communicate with me. He called his friend over to speak to me. His friend was Anna an extremely tall thin woman who spoke perfect English. She had a chat with Vladimir who turned out to be her boyfriend.

"Ah you must wait till dinner time and Vladimir here will help you get papers in post office, da?" She spoke to me softly.

"Da da! Spasiba!" I replied immediately. It seemed to me that she was doing the typical thing in pleading her boyfriend to do something he just didn't want to do as she gave him a sly coy look. From the looks exchanged it looked as if Vladimir was going to use this to attempt to get into her pants. As Anna was pale tall thin and sexy but with the tied back hair and thick rimmed glasses while wearing an incredibly flattering blue skirt suit of some kind with a gorgeous smile which would have lit up your world. I think Vladimir had worked out that running this

95

little errand was worth his time, turn the tables and I probably would have done the same thing.

I waited around until lunch and out came Vladimir who realised I was parked in completely the wrong section, which necessitated a mini jump over a fence into the airport car park. It wasn't anything stunt worthy about a metre tall and we scooted off around the airport pay barrier with Vladimir in his Lada Samara going up over the kerb to avoid paying also. We went around a few blocks and found a small post office. He showed me the forms and left me alone as he had to get back to work. Phoning Anna up and confirming what he had done, I do not understand what he was saying in Russian but it sounded dirty. While Vladimir wrote on the side of the form what things were like name address little things like that, but unfortunately he had to get back to work soon and bid me farewell.

I filled in the form best I could over the course of an hour got photocopies and posted it off, pulling in a random Russian off the street to use his ID card number in exchange for 100 roubles. I had done it I had registered my visa by myself a task that is deemed to be impossible to do. Things were looking up already and my most urgent paperwork issue had been resolved so half a headache was resolved. I found out sometime later than nobody actually cares about visa registration anymore it harks back to the old days but nobody seems to care anymore. Though a police officer may use this to extract some money out of you.

I left town quite early but the roads had turned excellent sealed flat and straight I headed towards Moscow and got to Rostov-en-Danu in plenty of time just in time to encounter yet another immense traffic jam.

Rostov-en-Danu (Росто́в-на-Дону) is a westernised Russian city everything looked modern. They even had all the fast junk food places you could see in any western city lots of them. I even found a Yamaha dealer who told me the XT was the bike of choice and many people crossing Russia came in to say hello. Over the next evening I met an Aeroflot pilot and his co-pilot and went out on the lash bar hopping where they kept paying the bill saying you pay the next one. I managed to have drinks shouted for me all night and could barely wake up the next day.

I still had the motorbike import document to worry about, but the hotel staff told me to go to the customs building nearby who directed me to another building next door. The guy with the Ak47 directed me to the airport. I thought the airport I might strike lucky again like yesterday. It wasn't to be as I was directed to the customs point near a police checkpoint and they couldn't help me. Though I did meet a bunch of Ukrainian lorry drivers who were camped by the side of the road waiting for their cargo to be checked who were having some sort of barbecue. These guys were a highlight of my day as we sat on a grassy verge in the nice warm sunshine they shared with me their *Pyrih* dumplings and bread though I had to refuse their vodka I had to drive.

Inside a kindly woman here called Eva wrote down another address for me and after a few laps of the city streets I held a customs import document, which had the life the same as my visa. Result! for 150 roubles. I had done the impossible twice in two days register my own visa and extend my bike import document both are considered to be absolutely impossible to do without a Russian speaker. If you ever get caught in Russia in such a situation the words:

"Moto visa pra-lah-dee-nee." (Visa extension) will come very handy. I spent the night again drinking *piva* and eating strange kebabs. Wondering which way to go, since now that the import document had been sorted I could go east or I could go west. I thought about it in the terrace outside the hotel sipping my *piva* stealing their WIFI after guessing the password. I saw Maria the hotel receptionist a thin pale slight Russian woman come out of a side door and asked her out. And immediately noticed a ring on her finger which put to bed the thought of anything else going on. Maria had the very slight smile that would brighten up your day and her cuteness was irresistible. She was happy to go with me to the nearby Carlsberg bar and she spent a couple of hours teaching me some useful Russian while I taught her some useful phrases in English. She was Russian though and drank me under the table not even looking slightly drunk. We parted company about 8pm with a table completely covered in beer bottles and I fell in with a small group of Germans who were staying in the hotel to do a big project they all couldn't talk about. The decision of east or west would have to wait and effectively I slept on it after numerous beers and some babe watching. I noticed that Russian women were odd in that I was burning badly and I have dark skin naturally while Russians would spend even more time in the sun than myself and yet still stay a ghostly pale white.

I returned to the hotel and found I was letting off an enormous amount of gas and had runny poos, which stank, to high hell. On top of that I would bring up the pancakes I had eaten earlier a very bad sign as I didn't seem to be able to eat anything.

Let me get this out now. Russians are an odd bunch in that they eat things cold that you are supposed to eat hot and things for desert at the start of the meal and starters at the end. Most confusing quite often sausages were on offer, which were completely raw, as you would find in a supermarket stuck on your plate. The usual experience in a Russian café was you pointed to something you recognised out of all the Cyrillic text and you were greeted with 'nyet', and kept on doing this until something was on the menu. Usually *kartoshka* (watery instant mash potato) and Goulash beef as well as *khlep* bread, which was obvious it came out of a bread maker though quite good.

I suffered giardiasis and campylobactera poisoning throughout my Russian trip. However since I guess you don't want to hear about my stories of runny poos and lifting my helmet up 45 minutes after eating anything to throw up what I had just eaten I'll just get it out of the way here. Although I had a few mishaps where I got the timing wrong or I was stuck at a particularly tricky bit of road and couldn't stop having to hold the vomit in my cheeks until I could stop. It might sound disgusting but it was either hold it in or have your helmet fill up with vomit and the associated smell that came with it. This was particularly problematic when you set up your tent for the evening. You would have giardiasis-enhanced gas, and it was a stark choice gas yourself in the Dutch oven or run outside and be eaten alive by the mosquitoes.

Hamburger and *kartoshka* were common with the hamburger served cooked but cold sometimes frozen. That said I did have some ridiculous being ill moments which will of course be mentioned in due course. But overall Russian food was cheap but generally the hygiene standards were appalling to non-existent. Russians of course had developed a tolerance to it and were probably much better for this. I suppose they would suffer much less from the western problem of being too clean as in the western nations. If chemicals are used to kill germs constantly your immune system has no chance to build up any tolerance and thus you become weaker. I remember seeing some sort of wife swap where a woman was disgusted that a family had made her children eat things raw to build up their tolerances to germs. I have a feeling that the person who ate the raw food would be much stronger than the person who only ever ate clean food.

A friend of mine once exemplified this. He said, "I don't care about germs, germs inside me are stronger than any germs in the food here," I think he was right as he would eat at filthy (but cheap) restaurants and suffer no ill effects. Even drunken stumble into restaurants proved to be little difficulty to him. I wondered how he would have fared out here. Russians and Siberians in particular seem to love their microwave ovens though and in each café I stopped at you would hear the loud ping of the bell as the microwave finished its processing.

In the morning I felt fairly good...other than running to the toilet more than once in an hour and being sick at the same time. The good feeling was more to do with the fact I had gone to the front desk and swiped an enormous number of their painkillers. A good fist full and was quite literally buzzing. I stopped at the Internet café I discovered and plotted two routes one home and one towards Siberia. I sat and thought about it, if I didn't do this now I would never do this and promptly decided to ride Siberia with the thoughts of "now or never". I wasn't going to fail or give up. Leaving Rostov was easy, just through a police checkpoint and away.

18 : STALINGRAD

The edge of one of my print outs said I needed to go north via the M4 to get to Volgograd (Волгоград). The name sounded familiar some how but I wasn't thinking about that now. This involved a trek on a Russian motorway. Russian motorways are good at least in the western part of Russian they were good. They were identical to the 3 lanes with shoulder and Armco on the inside type motorways. Except that Russian motorways are how can I say it different. There are fewer restrictions on stopping on the shoulder so that the shoulder and the grassy section to one side is generally full of people selling fruit and vegetables. Even picnic tables were set up on the verge with families sat there having lunch, it seemed bizarre as motorway rules in the UK are so much stricter than this. Evidently the motorway was still not complete yet as about 100km down it turned into a gravel track fairly shallow gravel where I suspected they were about to lay down the tarmac to finally seal the road up. Though nobody actually slowed down for the gravel even launching off the sealed sections and catching the air momentarily until they hit the gravel skidded a bit and continued on as if nothing had changed.

The road turned to a fairly good sealed road that was fairly straight interrupted by many cross roads and long trains. I counted upwards of 54 cars being pulled by two locomotives and a surprisingly large number of people sat on the roof. I should have been clued in to the fact it would take a while when one of the lorry drivers from nearby got out a gas stove and started making *chai* kindly offering me a shot glass and taking a photo on his phone.

I went towards Volgograd and didn't quite make it having to camp in the middle of nowhere but somewhat close to the road as the grass seemed kind of smooth but would cut you on touch. The problem was that although the ground looked good to camp it was an illusion. The grassy parts the ground was lumpy and baked hard meaning I had to set the tent up on the track itself. Very little happened here other than being buzzed by a MIG of some kind. I'd seen him circling and flying around in the distance as no more than a fly sized object in the distance. I think the MIG pilot wanted to have some fun and snuck up on me, well as far as a jet aircraft can sneak up on somebody. But I was wearing a motorbike helmet with earplugs. I felt something rumbling behind me, any bikers who read this will know that you can always hear or feel a big engine behind you usually a Subaru or something, but a glance in the mirror nothing, that's really odd. As the rumble grew louder I looked in the mirror again still nothing. I stopped for a sip of water and something was approaching low and fast very low and VERY fast. I ducked and got buzzed by a MIG who climbed near vertical the second he passed me standing by the side of the road. I wonder if he understood the finger I gave him while I was on my arse in the gravel.

I'd set off early as per usual and the road turned bad corrugations constantly jarring my spine and passing through some of Russia's industrial heartlands I thought this could well give Baku a run for its money as I passed huge decaying rusted factories, mines completely and abandoned villages. Along with dying animals and people by the side of the road. It looked like a mad max dystopian future everything was derelict whole towns would be just a gigantic pile of broken wood where you might imagine houses to have been.

A small highlight to this was a roadside snack stall in the middle of nowhere; an old Russian babushka sat sleeping. She woke up as I stopped the engine of the XT and scarpered into her armoured bunker type general store. I bought myself a bottle of chemically tasting orange and attempted to talk to her. Now and again people would come out of a bunch of bushes and order something from her at which she would pop out of her armoured cabin to the table next to the store. They were almost always after this thing that was kept under the counter. After much difficulty in getting her to sell them to me she pulled out a sort of camping cooler and opened it up, at first glance it was stuffed full of jeans. Dirty no filthy jeans. She then peeled them back to reveal her goods that turned out to fist sized pasties hidden underneath the jeans evidently to keep them warm. They were nice warm and creamy potato pasties. Almost identical to one that you would buy on a high street for a pound without the meat. Instead they had finely chopped herbs and some sort of gluten to make the simple potato melt into your mouth. She smiled back at me and offered me some more which I gladly took up for later on and smiled at me a Richard Kiel smile but said nothing. She was evidently quite happy to see me or to be selling some of her produce. For 5 of these pasties I paid her 23 roubles, which is less than 50p.

With the sun beaming and gleaming with a shimmering heat effect like you might see in a movie in the distance. The sun beating down on my black leathers so that the seat and my jacket were unpleasantly hot to touch I thought I best make tracks. I told her my best goodbye in Russian and she waved me goodbye in response.

A strange thing happened about half way to Volgograd during the day the daytime sky turned to night. There was a huge tree clearance going on and huge pyres of wood were being burnt there was so much acrid smoke that it seemed to get cooler and darker while I rode through that area. Even the XT choked a bit on the smoke. At least it got rid of the black flies, which would swarm around you the moment you stopped, or maybe the smoke was stinging my eyes so badly I couldn't feel the small black flies bite me.

A few miles short of Volgograd I passed a gigantic steel statue of Russian tanks heading to the sky it dwarfed everything around and glittered into the sky. I stopped to take a photo on my camera phone and noticed the 1945 in big letters at its base. A police officer trundled up and spoke remarkably good English, though I don't know how he knew I spoke English.

"Good day."

"Hello."

"You wonder why this monument is here?"

"A little."

"It is to commemorate the victory in great patriotic war, many men cross river Volga at Stalingrad. But now we say not Stalin grad as Russians do not remember Stalin so nicely and we say Volgograd."

"Ah that's it! The battle of the Volga ~ Stalingrad." The turning point of WWII. Which tied up the German armies. For you Neanderthals out there the Battle of Stalingrad was Hitler's biggest failing is if Hitler had simply passed Stalingrad south to the Caucuses and North to Moscow Hitler would have won the Second World War. Several more miles in I saw a statue, no ordinary statue a gigantic statue that would put the statue of Liberty to shame. A gigantic statue of mother Russia holding a sword called the "The Mamayev Monument". Which at its base has engraved all the Russian soldiers who died at the battle of Stalingrad. I didn't manage to find the eternally burning flame though I had read about though. The structure was so gigantic and the names almost endless. It is actually bigger than the Statue of Liberty at 67 metres tall. With 200 steps symbolising the 200 day siege testament to the number of people who died in the battle of Stalingrad the plinth was about twice as tall as I am and I'm 5ft 7 inches. The sheer number of names gave an eerie feeling. The Allies may have won the war but Russia had paid the price in blood. I've heard riders say the same thing about the Northern France battlefield cemeteries I have only passed through that area and never explored in depth.

I rode around in circles for a bit, and stopped for a mouth full of water and a man approached me and asked me what I was doing this far South in Russia. I told him that I was to go to Vladivostok. I had again lost my tools while the XT was parked up in the customs yard and my battery charger, not that I had anything battery powered to charge up anymore. He started showing me photos of his GSXR750 through his phone beaming them to my phone each and every time. I asked him where I could find a tyre and bike shop and he announced follow me as he got into his Lada Samara. We drove through a few industrial estates and some looping dusty roads he led me to a motorbike shop Bikercity34.

I had a look inside and noticed that the prices for used motorbikes were astronomical. A typical £2000 motorbike you would buy in the UK in Russia would cost £6000 and they warned me to be very careful. Bikes are incredibly precious in Russia the XT would easily get stolen if I was not cautious. Vasily the chief mechanic shook my hand and had just what I wanted a 90/90/21 Metzelier Karoo, well it had to do as beggars can't be choosers and my TKC80 was looking decidedly un-knobbly and worn enough to be mistaken for a slick tyre.

Vasily changed the front tyre for me on a big machine while two of the mechanics ran around looking for tyre levers and patches. The patches were found quickly but no tyre levers. Instead they bought two huge screwdrivers. Vasily and his assistant then angle ground the edges down significantly and heated them both up with blowtorches bending them into tyre levers. They engraved into them "From Russia with love". While this was happening I was offered the obligatory green *chai* and Jammy dodgers. Alexei one of the mechanics was about to sling my tyre into a skip type thing but I asked to keep it as riders before my trip in the UK had told me never to sling a tyre as it might be very useful. This Russian Lark was starting to grow on me. We took photos shook hands and hastily an escort was arranged. The bike shop closed early and 8 bikes mostly cruisers and some scooters gave me an escort to the edge of town all honking their horns waving at me, "Dos vit danya!" They all shouted as they I rode past the police checkpoint that marks the edge of all Russian towns.

The road out followed the Volga River North East around Kazakhstan I wanted to get to Samara and spent the next two days camping rough having significant difficulty finding a rough campsite. There were good ones here and there but had cars parked nearby or were guarded jealously by dogs that waited until my tent had been pitched. A few times in fields but men on bicycles told me to leave. The difficulty was compounded by the fact that good-looking campsites often turned out to be bad. Flat grasslands turned out to be swamps when I turned off the road. The sight of my front wheel sinking down to the forks was enough to stop me in my tracks before I went in too deep. This was a huge pain as I would stop carefully climb off, tip the bike over gently and drag it back up the embankment which is more difficult than it sounds. Besides this nothing much interesting happened though the mosquitoes and horse flies were getting incredibly thick.

However the road narrowed from a multiple lane road down to two not very wide lanes missing barriers at the side and the road became part of the scenery. This rather than a motorway where you simply cruise at high speed and you are physically separated by crash barriers lampposts and a central concrete barrier here you were up close. With trees, rubbish tips cafés whizzing by it was so much closer than you would get on a motorway. Made even closer riding a motorbike as there was no cage to separate you and the scenery. No windows no glass to look out of as if it were artificial in a glass case somewhere.

I stopped at roadside café strip whereby I rolled along into town and noticed lots and lots of skimpily dressed women beckoning me on. I turned into the sort of truck stop behind a ton of cafés all with women with short skirts and low cut tops to entice weary passing travellers towards their particular café. It has not happened often but I was sat on the bike and 20 young tall skimpily dressed women all approached me dragging me this way and that. I settled on the non-skimpy dress wearing babushka's shop for supper. I figured that if they need to do that then their food couldn't be much cop. A surely Babushka served me a satisfying snack. A few of the younger Russian women decided to sit down with me anyway as foreigners that is non ex-Soviet foreigners were rare here. The odd few bikers passed but many generally entered Kazakhstan earlier or had taken the northern route. Most of them seemed interested in chatting to me and they were so very young yet with lots of baggage. They all seemed to be under 24 years old and married with at least one child. I discovered in Russia in part due to the Orthodox Church there was an incredible pressure to get married. In the UK we might call somebody a spinster if they are in their forties and not married but this happened in Russia for people who were not married by the time they were 23. My dad often feels the same way about me in that I'm a freak of the family I'm not married and I'm 'old'.

I rode on for a few miles down the road finding a nice little campsite through a scraggly bush onto an old long disused track, though the ground was unsuitable anywhere else but the track.

I woke up in the middle of the night to footsteps and rustling thinking oh shit I've been rumbled mind jumping to the video of the Hammer gang in Russia. The footsteps got closer with a clicking and somebody tapped on the side of my tent. "Hallo hallo?" Said the man outside.

The person turned out to be a typical German cyclist crossing Russia. Rather optimistically on a tourist visa i.e. 30 days and had chosen to camp where I had camped. I loaned him my stove and spoke a few sleepy words before turning over to sleep again.

"Danke." He said and I heard the hiss of the stove tick over as he cooked something up making various noises in the night trying to put his tent up as quietly as possible but failing dismally. I heard various *schisse* every now and again as he was having difficulty. I got up out of self-interest to try get some sleep and helped him pitch his tent to another "Danke." And before I knew it he sat blocking the doorway to my tent and decided to inform me against my will of his wanderlust in a typical German manner. This involved telling me about his life in great painful detail. In Germany I've experienced this many times. In that small comments in Germany are dangerous. In Hamburg to one side of the Reeper-bahn I was with my friend Emily. I made a disposable comment, which would normally in the UK be responded to back with a one liner such as thanks. I wasn't in the UK though and such a comment to a German fellow this was open season and my downfall of that particular evening.

"Nice pub you have here herr," I said in an off the cuff manner not expecting anything untoward to occur how naïve I was then.

"Ah I am very glat that you like my bar..." He started. I thought it would be the end of that but he kept going on and on and on. Going back I am sure to the unification of Germany by Otto von Bismarck. With me glazing over unable to escape as Germans by enlarge are quite big people. He had manoeuvred to corner me so that I could not escape.

Daniel or at least I think it was Daniel provided similar deep and painful detail, which I half-heartedly nodded to pretending to listen. I'd heard Krupp engineering and all sorts but I wasn't paying too much attention, as I wanted to sleep. This progressed to asking about me a million questions about my trip were passed back and forth. However he was nice enough to provide vodka, which was a welcome surprise. I told him he wouldn't make it on his visa and he might try to get the train. Eventually however he let me go back into my tent where I fell asleep like a log. The problem is he had inadvertently pitched his tent on a column of ants. In the low half tone darkness of the night Daniel didn't notice them nor did I. It was a fairly decent tent the expensive ultra light kind I can't afford internal flysheet super single skin. The ants with cruise missile accuracy dodged my tent but managed to go round to HIS tent and into the only hole near the front vent where the column squeezed through the tiny hole and one by one entered a couple of platoons and a panzer division silently.

A loud shouting of Nein! And *schisse* disturbed me, as I was dreaming of something. Much muddling of torchlight and crashing slapping sounds and angry wave of unpleasant sounding German was sprayed machine gun fashion. Now I don't know about you but German to me sounds like an incredibly harsh language. I never studied German in high school but imagine if you are a German child being castigated in German you'd be in tears from the harshness of it even if it were a mild telling off. However perhaps that is just my Neanderthal uncultured mind. I heard some packing noises and zips being done up and rolled over back to sleep.

I did not see him in the morning so perhaps he was going the other way. The road followed the Volga River for several hundred miles, before curving away before I got to a city called Samara, which passed a huge industrial plant outside. Just looking at it Samara seemed incredibly run down. Although trees had been planted everywhere to minimise what people could see. I could still see that it looked very run down in a rustic sort of way.

Samara (Сама́ра) was tricky I had totally run out of Roubles and managed to get into the old town first with short single story houses falling apart and turning to dust and roads with potholes all over. It looked like a gravel track that the road had worn away so much. I had followed the trolley buses in this far. To get to the centre most major Russian cities have trolley buses so it's a good idea to follow them and you'll get where you want. I couldn't find a working cash machine or an Internet café and rode around the old part of town for a while. I finally asked some teenagers on BMX bikes and tried my terrible Russian on them. So terrible in fact that they asked for me to speak to them in English. There were no Internet cafés, WIFI any bookshops or ATMs nearby other than McDonald's that was under refurbishment so that too was worthless. Asking around other people seemed to ignore me and I sat on the XT for a few minutes wondering what it is I should do since I had no idea which direction to head to and no ability to find out or get money from anywhere.

Along came my solution, a big white Africa Twin and a biker called Serge who spoke no English. Some passing of my phrase book back and forth and he found out I needed a bankomat (an ATM) and led me to one and also a map. Which he again took me to a bookshop to buy one as the old technique of google maps was far too crude to be of much use here. En-route a reason why the Africa Twin was rejected was revealed to me his fuel pump failed in the middle of a busy street and through some tubing I had I fixed the fuelling problem for now. The problem is with Russian bikers is that they know their home roads much like I know the home roads on all the city streets in Manchester and the surrounding countryside and he started to engage in bike to bike combat with me. Riding at impossibly high speed through cars filtering down side streets through car parks across petrol station forecourts. Such that I crossed the tramline for the nth time and put the power on too soon and soon found myself in a massive tank slapping in progress. With cars in front and nowhere to turn to at the sides I had to filter into the narrowest space I have ever seen between a bus and a Kamaz lorry.

He phoned up a friend who spoke English who asked me if I needed more help and or a place to stay. I said no, but would like to meet his biking club anyway for photos and to give out a few souvenirs my Hong Kong flag patches and some of my postcards I had bought from France and Italy. We arrived outside a tower block and found a shipping container in the grounds outside this was the Samara bikers club. There was much shaking of hands *spasibas* for helping me out. The bike club also graciously accepted my small gift of postcards and patches. Then came a revelation from Serge and Mikhail, that they had been on their Africa Twins to Aktau in Kazakhstan from Samara and at least 300 miles of this road was perfect sealed asphalt road. Part of it was *pimat* (stone) meaning a gravel road that was regularly graded. And there was a road from Aktau, which went north and around the Aral Sea.

I was momentarily taken aback, the fears I had had in Georgia discussing with Tiffany was that I would not have made it and in reality I could have ridden through Kazakhstan via those roads. Instead I had gone a different way for a non-existent reason. Though alas I had also had some excellent experiences in Russia so far but only a few days in Russia seemed to be terribly uniform in its culture and customs I saw. Even in the UK you move a few hundred miles in each direction (well not sideways anyway as you would end up in the sea) the culture and even the language changes in a subtle manner. Though Russ in Istanbul had said that Kazakhstan was a bit empty and full of nothingness so I thought of that instead to alleviate my disappointment of not going there. I am however very happy to report that Russia seemed to be completely uncorrupted I had of course heard horror stories of police corruption either it didn't exist I'd gotten lucky or the job of ratting up the XT was working. So far police had never given me any trouble the worst they did was what they did to other car drivers i.e. stop for the odd paperwork check and a hearty. "Good luck English boy!" Or sometimes they stopped me and told me to put my lights on.

This was completely different in Kazakhstan in that the police in Kazakhstan I was told were incredibly corrupt. I told them about my Azeri story and they confirmed that sort of thing happened to them in Kazakhstan such that they would ride over the sand and Steppe around places police checkpoints would have been. It seemed that I dodged a bullet there. I was offered a bunk at Serge's flat but declined and said I had to be going. Many photos were taken and a mini escort of two Africa Twins led me to the police checkpoint. As a matter of thanks I stopped at a petrol station and over estimated the petrol I needed and ended up giving them 9 litres as a token of my appreciation for helping me out.

The plan from here on in was as I got to each Russian city was to look for Russian bikers and ask for their help. Obviously I felt a bit of a bum doing this though. I was also kind of worried about using up all of their hospitality. But generally to be a biker who does not ride a scooter or a 125 you have to be fairly wealthy anyway in Russia. However I did not want it to be the case that future bikers who come through tomorrow might not be treated so well by the local bikers due to me exhausting their goodwill.

The road out was long and straight to Chelyabinsk and it was getting dark, time to find somewhere to camp. Here out on the steppe there was ample opportunity to camp. Parking up for some supper at a local café I found a Russian ZZR1400 pilot who had his seat off and fiddling with something. This was Andre his bike had broken down and he needed to be 100km in a town nearby the next day he had been waiting for a Kamaz driver to pick him up. But it was late and the truck drivers had gone to bed. He had a look at my map and pointed towards a nearby town and got some rope. I didn't understand what he wanted but I soon realised he wanted me to tow him, and so it began. In the dark with no streetlights under a dark grey sky I towed him 100km over rough gravel patches over a broken bridge through a police checkpoint. We even stopped three times for him to run into a roadside café and buy himself a beer. Eventually we arrived and I followed him into a café cum pub where we consumed beers a Russian beer called 9. This was the percentage of alcohol content as if we were on some sort of beer production line with beer bottles whizzing by at terrifying speed. I imagine that I did a helluva lot of damage to myself such that in a few years time I will wonder into a room and forget why I went there. I found a nice spot just behind the roadside café where we had been drinking and set-up my tent half heartedly until the buzzing of mosquitoes made me put it up right and up inside.

The next day I got to Ufa (Уфа) en-route to Chelyabinsk (Челя́бинск) and didn't stop for long other than to go through a no entry sign. A Russian police officer warned me not to do it again. This police officer spoke perfect English and I confused the hell out of him speaking to him in Chinese. He wasn't really too hard about it really just citing that I should be more careful in the future about this and just wanted to take some photos. I had heard there was the Ak47 museum in Ufa but asking the police officer with lots of pointing and Kalashnikov being said back and forth I was told it was in a completely different city and I would have to back track north west to find it, oh well.

The road out of Ufa was nice. It had turned into wide sweeping grasslands lined with trees with 100 metres of clear grass beside the road on each side. Russians would be sat lying in these patches sunning themselves. Now and again there would be a roadside seller under a cheap umbrella or leafy tree branch selling all kinds of vegetables. Potatoes mostly but there were some unidentifiable purple things flowers and even moonshine vodka. In the grassy sections there were even families with horses and carts. More often though were butchered Ladas with the back end cut off. Men and women alike would work in these grassy sections using sickle and scythes to cut away clumps of grass and pile it high into the back of their vehicles. I presume to feed their animals back at the ranch. The horses and carts, the battered Ladas at least a quarter of a century old along with the worn road and soft golden sunshine made it seem as if I had stepped back in time. And that somehow I was standing out massively with the XT being 'new' technology. 1970s tech was new here, although there were of course other cars on the road. This section of Russia has two roads going towards the east and the majority of the traffic takes the northern route.

I was riding along as normal and had waited at a railway crossing for a very long time watching people make tea as the barriers came down. I accelerated as normal after the barriers went up and the ramps recessed back into the road I set off as normal but something felt wrong very wrong after the first turn a few metres away from the level crossing. The bike was possessed and was playing buckaroo fighting me and I was struggling to control the thing as it bucked left and right left and right lock to lock with flying from one side of the road to the other side of the road, into the path of an oncoming Kamaz lorry.

19: IMPACT!

I locked the bars back right into the correct lane and back to the other side and into a gravelly outcrop and into a ditch at the side of the road. I got up unhurt as I had been thrown clear and had a look. My less than 1000km new front tyre was toast.

I immediately put through an emergency satellite phone call through to my support team in a convoy of Land Rovers who were shadowing me a few miles back carrying all my food, tyres and fuel supplies and for a mechanic to come fix my tyre. A cook to make something hot and delicious for me to eat and also a doctor to check me out. I then stopped daydreaming and came to my senses.

My front tyre had been torn open with the now ruined tube hanging through the gash. It had been an incredibly fortunate escape I wondered what had caused it. It was ok though as I had kept my old worn front tyre from Volgograd. I cut off the tyre on the rim, which was in such a bad condition it would be pointless to keep and put my old tyre back in which was nice and easy, as the sun had warmed up the carcass. Except when I went to look for my pump it was missing somebody had filched it. I suspect it was the cyclist from a night before as I had loaned it to him in the evening sleepily to pump up his tyre and don't remember being given it back. So I started waving down cars and the first car to my surprise actually did stop and he did have a pump to loan me and although slightly shaken by what had just happened put the wheel back on while the old man who I learnt was called Viktor watched and waited to see if I was ok.

The boys from Volgograd who had made me these tyre levers had done just the trick these tyre levers were truly excellent. I bid fair well to Viktor and went back to investigate for what had just happened. A small strip of tyre was attached to a sawn off metal pole part way through the middle of the crossing. I suppose in hindsight this never bothered cars, lorries or motorbikes (as motorbikes in Russia almost always had side cars). As the wheels on cars and lorries would pass harmlessly to the side of the burr in the road, another bullet dodged there nicely.

Chelyabinsk was a significant milestone in my journey. In that Chelyabinsk is past the Ural Mountains. Right at the bottom and thus although subject to some debate as some people state that Omsk is the start of Siberia. And Siberia was effectively supposed to be a tough place. I had noticed in Rostov-en-Danu and Krasnodar that mentioning Sibir to Russians would make them tell you stories of their own experience of Sibir typically, "I've been there. Many Kamar," meaning mosquitoes. What was worrying was how they held their hands a metre apart when describing the mosquitoes. It was quite common that such people would offer me a drink for good luck. Very few people had actually been there though with myths and legends pervading about the place from locals and foreigners alike.

109

The road to Chelyabinsk was long and tedious for a while. Harsh mountain climbs with little or no scenery with struggling lorries bringing the pace down to next to nothing. At least the sky was nice and clear and it was a warm day. Though a regular feature at the side of the road were wrecked vehicles, lorries, cars and an enormous number of tyre carcasses. Even on the regular road works the men working there would let me through as priority. Russians it seemed loved bikes. Though I was surprised often to see people taking a pee against the own vehicles en-route. About 400km from Chelyabinsk the scenery changed dramatically. To frosted chocolate coloured snow capped mountains enclosing the valley. Almost like Grenoble weeks earlier but mountains much higher than in France enveloping the entire landscape with a serene valley road winding its way slowly through the plains towards Chelyabinsk.

Towards the middle of the ride I noticed cyclists in trouble and would give them a tow. At one stage I had 3 cyclists from Spain attached to my bike in a sort of train fashion. Although the scenery was wonderful and unspoilt it wasn't brilliant entertainment and the worn bumpy road meant speeds were limited to say the least.

Chelyabinsk formerly Tank-o-grad where USSR tank production moved to in WWII was isolated and very grey rectangular blocks of flats which looked slum like. With graffiti on the lower portions and big sturdy steel gates on the stairwells. As per usual I followed the trolley buses in and found possibly the biggest square ever, this was even bigger than Tiananmen square and on a hazy day in Beijing you can't see the other end of Tiananmen square. Suitably impressed I acted on my usual plan find Russian bikers and ask them for help. I got lucky and found some two Harley riders. Mikhail and Mikhail bikes converted to ridiculous gorilla bar choppers outside the world trade centre. They led me to a hotel nearby the river a fairly expensive and spartan place but a hotel non the less. I kept thanking them and took them to a nearby pub and bought them a beer each before returning to my hotel tired as I had gotten into Chelyabinsk quite late.

11pm I was woken up by the disco / nightclub next door. I got up to get my earplugs and suddenly have a thought, when is the next time I'm going to be here? I hesitated for a moment on seeing some seriously sexily dressed women queuing outside thinking oh shit this might be a fetish club. I have been told stories of fetish clubs that require mind bleach if you get queasy do not read the next paragraphs you have been warned.

One of my mates in deepest darkest London had gone to a fetish club under the arches somewhere in central London. As a favour as his mate who was gay had been his pulling wingman for a great number of occasions and he only thought it right to repay this favour to his mate. He didn't like it a bit with the mostly male clientele dressed in something not a million miles from Police Academy Blue

Oyster club as well as more overly pumped body builders. Incidentally if you do not understand that meme then you have never lived. This was most definitely NOT his scene. To pass the time quickly he drank lots and lots of beer with the inevitable consequences of needing to go to the bathroom, which was nothing out of the ordinary, except the urinal. Which firstly was one of those huge trough steel types rather than the individual type bowls. The second was that a man appeared to have fallen into it after maybe drinking too much. Going to help the poor man, he was informed that this guy didn't want any help and was what was termed a 'piss boy' a real live person who had a fetish of lying in the urinal being pissed on. Quite literally taking the piss. Everybody else seemed to be pissing on the bloke with free abandon but my mate thought this was wrong, very wrong and went out to drown his sorrows. Which lead the inevitable consequences of needing even worse to pee. Attempting to get a cubical but finding them all locked he had one choice.... piss himself or piss on the piss boy. As he did his business the boy in the urinal blubbered and gurgled appreciatively, his eyes locked onto my mate's eyes mine as he peed. It took me a hell of a lot of beers to get this story out of him.

I had a quick think about it and promptly went downstairs and was sucked in. For one night only I became Kawashima Sato. This was the only name I could think of as everybody kept thinking I was Japanese and for being Japanese I was absolutely sub zero cool, which meant everybody would buy me drinks. Corrosive modern pop sprayed out from the speakers alternating between techno and old 90s songs. At least 3 of my favourite songs came up 'Base creator by Bass hunter' and David Morales's Needin' you. Dressed in my biker jacket jeans and even biker gloves I felt self-conscious and kind of embarrassed to be looking funny these were the only clothes I had bought along so I had no real choice. But I imagined Janine my best friend saying this to me that changed my life several years ago:

"I too used to be hyper sensitive about appearing a fool, until one day I realized that nobody gives a shit about anybody but themselves. For 100% of the rest of humanity you might as well be invisible, because 5 seconds after you've exited their immediate field of vision, you're going to be forgotten forever. Assume that other people attach the same importance to you, that you attach to them - none. Hence if you embarrass yourself who cares you'll never see these people again after tonight."

I spent a little time babe watching, tall beautiful yet strange looking Russian women made strange by the disco lighting as their pale skin would take on what ever colour the light show sprayed across the dance floor would approach me and drag me up for a dance. They often said something like:

"You want to dance, come on just dance, no dance in Japan?". "You can dance with me, but no fuck da?" I thought about it for the briefest of moments and was out there in all probability causing quite a stir but I no longer cared.

111

"Da da!" I replied each time I was asked and sometimes there wasn't even a need to be asked often a hand would snake in grab me and pull me close. Incredibly beautiful skimpily dressed women would rub against me and rock me back and forth. I have never experienced it. It was as if everybody was on ecstasy but big blokes with machine guns at the door had a huge sign NO drugs! I think the Russians were happy to just be there. Hoots of whoooooooooo cheering happy smiling people everywhere surrounded me and enveloped me spreading a warm fuzzy feeling inside. If this was typical Russia (and it was) I absolutely love this place. I had time travelled back at least 13 years to nights out in my youth I had never expected Siberia to be like this.

I awoke on a pink sofa in a low rise flat complex thing covered in my own vomit in an apparently empty flat and wondered where I was. I took the stairs out and down and found nobody. Everything i.e. wallet phone was still on me but I was lost in Russia somewhere. I found out I was in a place called DolGoderevenskoye (Долгопрудненское) 30km north of Chelyabinsk and got a taxi back into Chelyabinsk back to the hotel luckily I had swiped a card from this hotel. I have no idea who took me home and if my dignity had remained intact. It may well have been the savage bear-wrestling woman from Tomsk far in the north who knows I didn't stick around to find out. Anyway if it didn't the woman would hopefully be looking out for a Japanese guy called Kawashima Sato who did not exist.

On the subject of Russian women if I may go off on a tangent for a moment, Russian women are bizarre to western eyes they are all tall thin pale and dress to kill and exceptionally friendly. In the UK this isn't often the case in the UK a woman who is tall thin and dresses to kill knows she is all that and acts all aloof. Though tall thin dressed to kill women are somewhat rarities in the UK, with the tracksuit being most common amongst the fashions of the UK. In the UK when people like me see tall women who are dressed to kill in an extremely sexy / feminine manner 9/10 times it is a cross dressing man. It is given away by the shoulders they are always wider than the hips. Ungraceful unnatural exaggerated walk and big hands. Or perhaps worse a whole bunch of men on a Rocky Horror show evening. This was highlighted in a story upon my return where in Manchester two drunken thugs attacked a couple of 'women' who turned out to be male championship cage fighters and promptly got more than they were expecting. Yet in Russia there were tall beautiful women who were dressed to kill who were actually women. Double even triple and quadruple takes had to be made to remind me I was no longer in the UK. The biggest of big differences was that when you looked at a woman and smiled she would look back at you and smile back instead of act all frosty, and it was perfectly reasonable to ask her for a *piva*. As beer/*piva* in

Russia is drank like cola is to us. Though that said they still were incredibly strong and aggressive when annoyed as I found out later anyway I digress.

I awoke to more kindness. As I now wanted to find an Internet café to say to followers that I was ok, and couldn't find one. I did my usual trick of circles until I was back at the hotel and a shop selling car parts invited me in, as I didn't look like a local and looked lost. He told me Internet cafés were born and died quickly in Chelyabinsk and took me to his head office in his car to let me say hi to my watchers get an update on my bearings and transfer some cash over. As again I wonder if British people would do this for a Russian lost in the UK?

At some point during the boring bit just before Omsk I noted that the main road went across into Kazakhstan. Presumably when this was built during the Soviet days this didn't really matter. It was all one super state, much like crossing from France into Spain or Italy is done with little fanfare. One moment you are in one country the next you are in another. But the USSR had been confined to the history books for 20 years so I had to go round. Or I was supposed to. In that there was just empty steppe and grassland as far as the eye could see. I had a think about it and went onto the grass. I went onto the grass and kept going south. I was eventually in Kazakhstan without a visa illegally. It looked remarkably similar to Russia 30 miles north.

I wondered as to how they said this bit was Kazakhstan and this bit was Russia in that both are large countries and the land is utterly worthless. I'd imagined a heated argument in the Kremlin during the formation of the USSR where ministers were arguing over the land:

"No premier you have it as part of Russia."

"No you have it."

"No you have it."

"No you have it."

"No you have it." Normally land is fought over like Demansky Island a mere 0.6sq km that nearly started a war between China and the USSR in 1963. But the steppe is essentially worthless, though of course the story of Kazakhstan and the USSR Bolshevik revolution and what the USSR did to Kazakhstan is no small beer millions died entire eco systems were destroyed and then some.

20: KAZAKHSTAN

I was in Kazakhstan illegally there was no way they could guard the entire border. Apparently the Kazakhs don't actually bother to guard the border from their side in many places. Instead relying upon the Russians to do this instead. I had a ride around and it looked identical to the grassy fields of which the sun made look like a field of gold with its slanted beams.

Cross-country riding on the steppe was easy. This was the same latitude as that of Mongolia that gave me a bit of a confidence boost. Though most of the steppe of Kazakhstan was destroyed by Khrushchev's 5-year plan that turned most of the Kazakh steppe into arable farmland and cotton growing land. Russ had informed me that I wasn't exactly missing much as Kazakhstan was just huge flat and open with nothing to see and expensive to boot.

I had however heard that it might be the Promised Land in terms of petrol. Kazakh petrol I had heard was cheap so cheap they imposed a tax on foreigners by charging them a slightly higher amount. I'd heard that it was 20-30% onto of the fuel, which sounded bad. But when petrol was supposed to be 15p a litre 30% on top of that isn't a huge amount. It's one of those taxes you wouldn't mind paying. I cannot confirm this though as I did not stick around to ask. I can imagine the scene though two Kazakhs complaining about the high cost of fuel as we do in the UK. They would probably die from a heart attack if they heard of how expensive it was here.

However I could see that riding here would be awful if it rained, but it didn't rain while I was there. Obviously being there illegally meant I didn't interact with anybody or see anybody from closer than a few miles away. I did not want to be caught without a visa in a country not exactly famed in the world for its human rights record. Nathan was somewhere to the South by now I guessed somewhere near the Cosmodrome near the Aral Sea. I wondered how he was getting on as Tiffany had told me he was going to do the deadly bit solo Aktau to Aralsk.

Effectively I had my chalk mark and made my way to Omsk. It was kind of immaterial anyway. From the Russian side I got a very good impression of Kazakh steppe. The agricultural fields of farmland end and all you only see the grass of the steppe. A golden straw coloured carpet that rolls on seemingly forever not till the vanishing point of the horizon. There isn't the slightest elevation at all. I crossed back into Russia also illegal again but if nobody sees you do it, then it's not illegal.

21: SIBIR THE BORING MIDDLE BIT

Omsk is most definitely Siberia people will argue that Chelyabinsk is not Siberia. They have a point, as it is not in the Siberian administrative area. Chelyabinsk Oblast is its area. A quick history lesson Siberia is a gigantic place at 5.1 million square miles. It is bigger than the US and Europe put together with a population of 30 million. Several trillion mosquitoes to keep you company and that's only in the bit outside Omsk (the mosquitoes not Omsk). The origins of Siberia are unknown some people say it means the sleeping land from an Altai or Turkic word, others state it was from an ancient city called Sibir the biggest in ancient history that was ransacked.

I like to think of it as the sleeping land myself. 8 months of freezing cold weather where it goes down to -45C on average everywhere. In Oymyakon where Maciek Swinarski managed to get in 2007 it got down to -71.3C. Even in the short summers the ground is still permafrost a metre or two down, and anything north of Yakutsk the permafrost is um permanent. Therefore there the land slumbers through time. Siberia was used as a dumping ground for the unwanted parts of society. Criminals' and political prisoners mostly. First by the Tsars then the Bolsheviks. People were sent there generally to die and die they did in their millions in effect being exiled to Siberia was a sentence of death but worse. As people survived for a few months only to succumb to starvation or the cold. A precious few survived and decided to scratch out a living in the harsh landscape rather than return. It is interesting to note though that Josef Stalin himself was exiled to Siberia twice. He managed to get back home before he rose to power and plugged the holes in the *gulag* system.

It was similar to the British transportation as punishment though it proved to have a less happy and prosperous ending. In its current state the American Colonies and Australia where the British sent their own unwanted.

Most of the 33 million people live in the cities littered along the Tran Siberian railway in cities or isolated villages. With curious states within states, such as the Altai republic which is a zone which covers Mongolia / Kazakhstan / Siberia which is home to Turkic Asiatic peoples. The Buryat people also formed their own republic around the Baikal region and the Jewish Autonomous region near Khabarovsk. Siberia however has been enjoying a minor revival lately oil, gas and gold have been found in many areas in the most isolated areas. Siberia is also home to the high tech military factories of the Russian war machine today.

With plentiful resources and the world hungry for forever increasing amounts of what Siberia has, Siberians may have a brighter future. Although such resources are not unlimited in a few places I passed the *taiga* was absent from deforestation. I am not surprised when Russians in Western Russia looked at me in a puzzled manner as to why I wanted to visit Siberia.

Arriving at Omsk (Омск) I pulled the same trick. Find a biker a Harley rider this time at a car wash called Sasha on a re-badged VX1800 pretending to be a Harley and got him to show me around. We had an unsuccessful time looking for a front tyre the only one being found was a tyre worn nearly as bad as my TKC80 on the front. Which was badly damaged now holes appeared between the knobbly bits of rubber. You could almost see the tube inside and it was becoming dangerous to ride on this tyre. He was unsuccessful and I thanked him anyway with him offering to take me to his bike club later on but having to go to work shortly. I declined and attempted to find a hotel en-route. I managed to find an Ikea, a Tesco super store even a porn cinema but no hotel. Until I remembered a sign I saw earlier on. Though this was no normal hotel and looked like a really big house with numerous guests leaving. A disproportionate number of women it seemed, I pulled in and asked:

"How much?" (Skol-ka Roubles?) I asked.

"How long do you want?" Replied one of the men.

"Erm I want to stay the whole night." I felt puzzled by this.

"When will you leave? How much time do you need?" I was asked again.

"Erm 8am," I said. I was led upstairs and there was a huge double bed 4 camera's in the corners of the room and it finally clicked when I saw mirrors positioned in various places. Mirrors on the ceiling. Mirrors to the side of the bed and one above the Jacuzzi. The place was to be rented out by the hour. I had thought nothing of the 3 incredibly sexy women getting into a Mitsubishi Shogun outside dressed in incredibly revealing clothing. This was a place people took their mistresses and prostitutes. I slowly backed out.

"Two thousand." They offered.

"What! 2000 no way."

"Two thousand dollar one night open bar, you take?"

"No way it's too much." But if it was less I wouldn't stay there anyway. I imagined what stains people had left on those sheets. I'm mildly surprised Russians seem to think that dollars to non-Russians are nothing. As with the extortionists in Krasnodar who wanted a huge amount of money the same thing occurred here. Perhaps they should visit and realise that the world outside Russia isn't the land of milk and honey. Luckily I found a place for 700 roubles for 12 hours, which was right up my street.

A large group of Russians were crowded around a table outside and motioned for me to join them. Sveltlana could speak excellent English and we chatted about mundane things. Things like why I was so far from home and all that type of thing. They went to buy me many beers all night upon hearing I wanted to get to Vladivostok. A strange moment occurred when they asked if I wanted to go and pool.

"No I don't swim," I said. Which isn't quite true I can swim a little but don't like to swim at all.

"Nyet, nyet we mean billiard."

"Ah, oh ok," I replied. Russian pool / billiards is weird in that you have one red ball and 15 white balls without any markings on them. The Russians I had befriended temporarily were just knocking them about into pockets ceaselessly there was no cue ball just knocking of balls around which confused me in my drunken state. The games seemed to take absolutely forever as well. Another quirk of Russian billiards is that the balls are almost the same size as the pockets meaning any less than perfect shots did not go in. I suppose this would prevent the jammy gets who play pool back at home. You know the kind where you intend to sink a ball in one pocket ricochet off four cushions and sink another ball and manage to call it a trick shot I was storing up. I did quite well at least I think I did well since I did not know the rules at all. The rest of the evening was drinking the bar dry of everything, with them picking up the tab, I REALLY liked Russia now.

The next place to go to was Novosibirsk (Новосибирск), which Sasha said I had a very good chance of finding a new tyre. Novosibirsk happened to the biggest city in Siberia and is effectively the capital. Riding out of Omsk I felt fairly good at this, as I was half way across Russia already. There were only 4 more pages to the end of Russia on my map. In that it was a double edged sword in that Russia is great for some things but the food poisoning and expensive lodgings meant roughing it more often than not.

Outside Omsk the scenery changed wide grass lands copses of trees and for the first time in a while I started to feel cold. With overcast skies and a very quiet road I stopped off at a small café with a balding Boris Yeltsin look alike. He beckoned me in. This place was the only café in miles, and stood outside looking at the road you could see the vanishing point on the horizon both ways. The road seemed to be endless in both directions with barely any traffic in sight. By now I had learnt to stop and eat at cafés it was cheap and sometimes good, aside from perhaps the giardiasis I regularly got from the food. Though I didn't know which café was the culprit as I had been to so many. They had given me a gift that kept on giving and giving and giving.

There is nothing sensational, outstanding or worth mentioning to see, but this region cast a spell on you by its huge distances. The vastness is incredible and it's monotonous touch, which allows you to ride and at the same time engage yourself in deep thought without danger.

Riding here wasn't a difficult task. It was essentially a case of keeping your hand in a certain position to keep the throttle engaged in top gear. Otherwise sitting on the bike doing nothing. The odd few miles were spent standing up to relieve the pressure on your rear end. Which was copiously producing gas from the general food poisoning and hoping a wet one would not come out and spoil your day even more. That was until you need fuel for either yourself or the bike. The monotony wasn't even resolved by my phone acting as an MP3 player. The hours of songs I had managed to cram into it had started to repeat themselves. And it was hard to dance to techno or get all pumped up while sat on a bike on a mercilessly straight road. Though the Tchaikovsky 1812 overture seemed quite apt in that it seemed to be an incredibly long build up to the high point. A sort of a mirror of my trip exactly. I even thought that it was almost like prison. You would be sat there riding nothing to do bored with an aching bum that had gone to sleep. Even though the XT had a wide generous padded seat, which I had made more generous by replacing the foam. Your bum would still ache. This was however markedly better than the DR and DRZ400 seats I had tried before deciding on the XT. Those seats were horrible. Like sitting on a cheese wire as it worked its way into your crotch. This experience may have been one like in prison. Although I must make the point clear I have had no first hand experience of prison, it's from what I've read.

The oddity was that the most mundane things were things to be celebrated. Plain wooden house, a tyre at the side of the road and so on. Another peculiar oddity was that poor road conditions were to be celebrated. You would go over a bump and have something to think about for a while and come over another one sometime later and think ooh. And compare it to the other bump. Of course there was the constant danger of falling asleep. Something I've nearly managed on a fast moving motorbike. But since have taken precautions such as resting and tons of coffee and Red bull. Often tyre marks would cover the road in tracks that would sweep over both sides of the road. It seemed that the drivers on this road had the same problems of falling asleep. This too was soon punctuated by the odd wreck. One wreck, two wrecks, three wrecks, CASTLEMAINE! Yes it got so boring I had to resort to bad puns to keep myself entertained.

Falling asleep was something, which I suppose was all too easy when in a sealed warm environment almost laying back like the seat in a car.

I stopped at an old café was more of a truck stop. By now my Russian had improved quite a bit. Well.. I now only made a little bit of a prat of myself. I could order eggs and bread. "*Yetso pyat klehp pyat*," (six eggs and six pieces of bread) You may think I'm greedy for eating six eggs and six pieces of bread but the cold was getting to me. Also when Russians give you bread although you might think of a slice of bread as being a big square they cut them into soldiers so 5 pieces makes up one slice we are used to in the UK.

"*Plim in eee.*" (Dumplings)

"*Plov.*" Which is a sort of rice dish with rabbit or lamb in small chunks. Looking at the un-cleared tables it was evident that they had already had their morning rush. They immediately asked the normal questions you get:

"Vih Atkuda?" (Though the vih is almost always silent) He asked me.

"London," I replied.

"London? A dien?" he replied wide-eyed. This means you did it by yourself?

"Da." Immediately he called to what sounded like Natasha and more food was bought out to me. He refused to accept any money for the food though I did try he sternly refused.

"Welcome Leon, Sibir."

"Spasiba." I replied at which he went on at great length as to what could eat me bite me and kill me. He said kamar an awful lot and held his hands as wide as they could go which was discouraging. Then said:

"Mead-vi-zhonok."

"Ni me pana mi." (I don't understand)

"Druk druk druk, ah." He stood up and held his arms aloft and growled. He meant bears that will eat you and warned me not to camp in Siberia. If the Kamar didn't get me the bears would. We couldn't communicate very well but he was a quite funny and would enact jokes I couldn't understand. I only understood once I got home. One I did understand was a little performance he put on for me. He got out a tiny shot glass filled it with vodka and said, "London," and skolled it. He got out a tumbler and said, "Moscow," filling it with vodka and again skolled it. He then picked up a vase and pretended to pour vodka into it and said, "Sibir," and gave out a crackly laugh.

Novosibirsk was fairly close in Russian and Siberian terms only 400 miles it seemed to be a constant climb towards Novosibirsk and surprisingly cold even during the daytime. I noticed something odd here. The road signs went backwards. One moment you would pass a sign saying 600km, and then the next sign 30km down the road would say 650km and the sign after that 655km. I often wondered if my mind was playing tricks on me. It was always too far to go back and check if I had actually seen what I had seen.

I gave an Asian looking woman a lift for about 50 miles and she thanked me graciously. After she got off she opened her coat and there was a baby inside. I'd have never taken her if I knew she had a baby. In fact I do not like to take passengers at all. In biking it is ok well it's not ok. It is more acceptable to kill yourself but it is much less acceptable to kill others. This is perhaps why motorbike insurance is of a magnitude cheaper than car insurance. Though seeing as this road wasn't exactly busy not seeing a single vehicle almost all the way other than going the other way I'd have felt worse about leaving her be. Russian public transport is supposed to be quite good actually though. In the middle of empty sections in the middle of nowhere it seems there are bus shelters and bus stops. Now and again you see a white transit van, which is a mini bus picking people up.

I arrived at Novosibirsk at 7pm and saw two bikers parked outside a motel and decided to stay the night. I wanted to ask them in the morning where to find a bike shop for tyres (*Shinya*). For the privilege of 1500 roubles I had a bed. I also had the pleasure of warm beer. But painfully hot water than more than made up for it. Though the bikers were noisy and had called girls in lots of girls. I heard at least 4 different women's moans and they kept it up for a very long time. With me finally admitting defeat and turning the TV on since there would be no sleep that night.

Russian TV is generally dubbed American TV that is amusing to watch just for the ridiculousness of it. It appeared as if they only had one person to do ALL the voices in Russian. So here I am watching this film with Stallone and boy in a lorry. Sly asks the child a question, and is replied back to in an identical voice from the child. If you listened very carefully you could hear the original soundtrack underneath. After 4 hours of noisy sex I got up and slept under the bike in my sleeping bag that the babushka running the place didn't like at all.

These guys Andre and Mikhail had actually overtaken me outside Omsk it was an Africa Twin boosted to 800cc and a Goldwing. They were both en-route to Barnaul to cross Mongolia. I thought for a moment if you can cross Mongolia on a Goldwing you could cross it on anything. The Goldwing was odd though the front end had longer forks and there were bits of steel bolted on to protect some of the bits from off roading. I got an address and rolled on into Novosibirsk, which seemed really small. Power station as per usual in the middle, everything built around it until I crossed the bridge and went into the real centre.

I landed in a big square that could have been Times Square in New York or a big square in any city. With the only noticeable differences being everything in Russian Ladas everywhere and trolley buses. But a good mix of white Russians and Buryat people going about their daily business. Banks ATMs the whole shebang and I went nuts for a few hours enjoying a Russian knock off of McDonalds, Internet cafés, supermarkets even.

I came to my senses and realised I still needed a tyre, and completely conveniently a Russian on a Honda XR250 came out of a side road. He decided to help me. This was another Sasha who was a Chechnya veteran and had been shot in the head. He had a severe stammer and loved to show me his scars. He spent the entire afternoon helping me out for no reason other than I asked him.

Although at first when he lead me into the suburbs I thought uh oh is he taking me to be hammer ganged? But no this guy was great but we didn't find any tyres in the city centre shops. He sat for a moment and said:

"You moto-cross? Da? Nyet?" he asked.

"Da," I replied. At which we went down a few small back roads and went to possibly THE worst road I have ever seen. I guessed that this was once a road that had worn away so badly there was nothing left but the tiny edges. Potholes inside other potholes you could have lost a Kamaz truck down some of those potholes. Steep first gear hills, deep ruts and puddles with snapped steel poles with nasty looking burs on them. That would rip a huge chunk of meat off you if you hit it. Hard and scary yet strangely fun. We ended up near another power station and there I found a yet another Metzelier Karoo just what I needed.

Tanya the shopkeeper inside was shocked at the state of my TKC80. There was pretty much just canvas with the odd bit of black rubber carcass left on it. It was way past its lifetime but I had no choice. I bought the tyre for 4000 roubles and set about to fit it myself. I reached for my tool bag and noticed it again had gone missing stolen yet again. I went in to get them to change the tyre for me for 150 roubles.

I didn't know what to do to thank Sasha I tried to offer him a few roubles but he refused. I tried to say I'll buy him a *piva* but he refused took some photos waved and rode off. I felt kind of bad as he had helped me out for the last 4 hours purely out of kindness and I had nothing to give back to him. As before I feared that I would use up Russian hospitality for those who came after me. A big choice now had to be made. Tssanganur via Barnaul or Irkusk and enter Mongolia via Altanbulag...

I could enter through Tssanganur in the Altai on my Hong Kong passport, for 14 days no problem or go to Irkusk get a 30-day visa. The lack of tools meant there was only one choice as Maciek Swinarski years before had said he suffered an enormous number of punctures in Mongolia. If I had nothing to fix them with and no way to get tools even in the biggest city Novosibirsk I couldn't risk it. And chose to go to Irkusk via the seldom-used high route.

I started to ride out and passed a railway car café and popped in for lunch. Surprise a Georgian man was working here. Usually it was a babushka working a roadside cafés. This man was great though he made the best *plov* I had ever tasted so far and possibly the best *plim-in-ee* I'd had on the entire trip. Meat dumplings seem to be common the world over. He actually cooked his food quite hot unlike at other Russian places he spoke fair English:

"You do not have iron belly of Russian. I cook hot for you," he said. I appreciated this greatly but the damage had been done much earlier and some hot food would not get rid of it that easily. His two helpers outside sat on my bike to take photos and I rode onwards towards Irkusk. Just in time for the weather to close in and change from the nice warm sunshine to torrential rain. My water proofs had generally fallen apart by now. They were still water proof but in another way that they were proof of water.

22: SIBIR BAPTISM BY FIRE

I managed to get into Kemorovo (Ке́мерово) and found that the town completely lacked hotels or guesthouses. Kemorovo seemed to be a heavily militarised town as soldiers were everywhere. Patriotic signs of various military things lined the road. The rain pounding down as it had been doing since Novosibirsk. I cruised along I felt exhausted and finally found what seemed to be the perfect camping spot near a big wall behind the tree line of the main road. Slightly muddy but that was ok, as it would make it easier to put in my tent poles. Except the moment I had finished putting up my tent I heard the unmistakable roar of a jet engine and realised I had camped at the end of the runway. I tried to block out the sounds with my earplugs but the vibration and roar made them ineffective. I struck camp and rode slightly out of Kemorovo and found again the start of a *taiga* forest and a small clearing down a short mud track with a tiny pond visible in the distance. It was isolated enough from the road that the whoosh of cars was barely a whisper. I fell asleep without eating generally exhausted from the rain, but for some reason woke up and felt something wasn't right and needing to pee. Not wanting to pee on my tent I put my boots and jeans on and leather jacket on to prevent mosquito damage and crawled out of my tent.

The next thing that happened was scary. I'd bought the torch out with me but it was a fairly weak LED type thing and as I stumbled to the tree line and began to pee. As I looked around the pond I got the shock of my life. I saw a set of yellowy eyes as high as my chest. Which seemed not to have an outline when I shone my torch towards it. I don't know why obscured by bushes or something but it seemed to just watch me.

I didn't know what to do since I wasn't finished should I run back covering myself in pee? Is it a bear or a wolf or something else? I thought back to the guy outside Omsk who told me about all the things that could kill me, his grin after he told me got me kind of angry. Why was my bladder so big today, in that the pee just wouldn't stop coming when normally I have a sip of water and have to pee almost immediately. Even my guts were betraying me. At least the warm steam rising up from it obscured my view of it. But that was worse in that if you can see something coming for you, you have a chance to fight it off whatever it is or get a blow in first. Finally I was finished I didn't even shake properly. But I backed off slowly and the eyes ducked down presumably to drink I backed slowly to my tent and jumped in reaching for my hammer. A tent wasn't exactly going to be much protection for whatever was out there, with thoughts of a wolf no worse a bear might be out there. The couple of microns of ultra nylon may have been highly useful against the rain but against claws or teeth it didn't seem too protective. I lay there all night scared with a hand on my hammer until the sun rose. Little sleep was had and my morale dropped like a rock.

This wasn't a very good morning as my stove had packed up and needed disassembly to clean out its guts as I'd run it on the filthy Russian petrol. Not that I had any water to heat up. I had a sick curiosity to go to the pond and see what might have been there. Although I am no tracker and wildlife means very little to me I might have been able to get some clues. But I was greeted with a thin blanket of snow that got heavier during the day. The man made junk at the roadside standing out more than ever in the thin blanket of snow. I discovered that this junk served a purpose as when I stopped for a break in a sort of a lay by people would be fixing their cars. They would root around in the junk looking for usable parts bits of wire or whatever. Most impressively were the Siberians fixing their cars. Evidently the snow didn't bother them and they would be fixing their cars in little more than jeans and a T-shirt. They would lie directly onto the ground without any sort of ground mat or covering and shrug off the cold. Siberians were tough no doubt. They were however grateful for my cups of coffee after I had cleaned out my stove it seemed as if the toughness had never been lost. I'm pretty sure that the US continent was just as wild and rough but decades of affluence had made the descendents of first pioneers soft. No such thing had happened in Siberia. Nothing much happened for the rest of the day other than the snow falling softly onto the road and sticking. Though as a small side effect I did see some rainbows and the oddest thing, a backwards rainbow where the violet is at the top and the red at the bottom. Siberia was proving to be very strange. In that only a few days ago I was roasting in the Russian heat.

The snow stopped briefly and got heavier as I got to Krasnoyarsk and again found nowhere to stay having to camp out. I was a tad annoyed now how can it be snowing in June! I was rewarded for my anger at the sky by huge blobs of hail. Little marbles bounding off my visor and threw in the towel just outside Krasnoyarsk. Camping in a sand quarry infested with a million mosquitoes although all I had to eat was noodles and soup I had quite a large portion of mosquitoes in my soup so it was almost meaty. It was insane as I stood up outside my tent it was like those people who wear beards of bees, but instead this was mosquitoes. Looking down at my jeans they were coated in a layer of mosquitoes such that there were more mosquitoes visible than jeans. How Siberians dealt with this I never know. You could hear the high pitch wheeeeeeeee of their wings as they desperately tried to enter your tent and suck you dry I swear they were bigger than mosquitoes I'd seen anywhere else. The problem made places like Europe seem like an under 5s bug show.

Much to my chagrin I discovered quite quickly that I was camping in the worst place as behind the sand quarry was the Tran Siberian railway. All through the night I heard tuk tuk tuk tuk tuk tuk tuk tuk as the wheels crossed the gaps in the rails. The Russians sure know how to build one hell of a long train.

Riding over the Novosibirsk hills, which are enveloped by a forest of pines and birch trees. After thousands of miles of straight roads, I could now ride again through curves almost sports bike country. If only you could get a sports bike in here that is as the straightness of the roads and immense distance and low service intervals would have made the trek out here even more difficult. Sports bike country or not I took the road fairly cautiously being on a trail bike. And the fact that the roads in Russia are somewhat slippery due to never being washed of oil spills like it is done in Europe. Quite a number of bikers die each year after having non-lethal crashes. Where they simply slide off the road through the bushes and are metres from the road but remain undetected and die from exposure. This is something I did not want to happen. Deeper and deeper I went in to the east. Where I was once hemmed in by farmland and swamps the sides of the road transformed into powerful forests the vastness of the *taiga*. Siberia's *taiga* forest covered an area the size of Australia a deep impenetrable wall and maze of deep green vista that went on endlessly up to the horizons. This caused problems in that there was only a small grass verge in which to camp if I wanted to camp. Though as per usual the grass verges on the Siberian roads were immaculately kept. Torrential rain came and went through storm cells that lasted a frustratingly short time. I would stop put on my waterproofs and it would stop. Eventually my rain gear became my standard riding gear due to the cold and regularity of storm cells that would get you wet in the 30-40 seconds it took to ride through them. The cold was also noticeable enough as I had to wrap a T-shirt around my neck and chin to keep the cold air from entering my jacket. My old instructor had always said that cold air will always find a way in and it did.

At Kansk the road deteriorated badly. An old man who came out his house and decided to say hello had warned me about this. Waving his hand up and down. "Pi-mat," (stone) he said and moved his hand up and down in a manner as if it was to be badly corrugated. As if to further illustrate the point pushed his hand around as if to motion dropping off or dying. He then went through the usual questions of where are you from, where are you going. The usual answers of London and Vladivostok were given at which he gave out a whistle to indicate it was a massive distance. He smiled at me with a steely grin, literally another Jaws impression and said something in Russian that I did not understand. What I did understand was a bit of it emphasised by the throat flick and a coy wink of an eye.

"Davai! Malenka vodka!" he exclaimed. Which means come have a little bit of vodka with me. We will end up drinking for the next two days and depart as the best of friends. I thought about it and said "Da," as I wheeled my bike in I noticed a seriously strong smell of petrol. Stronger than the normal smell of petrol when you have an Acerbis endurance tank. I looked down and had a check and the Y piece out the bottom of my tank had become disconnected on one side leading a petrol leak.

This was incredibly lucky as in previous occasions I've had similar petrol leaks experimenting with making secondary and even tertiary fuel tanks. These made the bike catch fire while I was on it. Using branches leaves and mud to put out the flames.

I wheeled the bike in and removed the tank and went inside. The old man and I exchanged names and he was called Lev. We had a shot or two and his son stepped in while we were on our second shot and joined us he was called Yuri. Yuri spoke reasonable English meaning we barely had to pass the phrase book back and forth. He also asked the same questions that his dad asked with some extra ones he asked the prices of things, food, water, petrol (which shocked him) tax (which shocked him again). He then started to ask some deeper questions. "Robota?" (What is your line of work). And some memorable ones.

"Do you believe in God?"

"No I do not."

"Why do you not believe in God? In Siberia myself and my father believe in God"

"I don't see any evidence."

"Ah but I believe that you believe in God, many people say they do not but inside in reality God helps you though us you lose benzene we are here to help."

"How much is, how you say work girl in England?" He asked.

"Excuse me?"

"Sex, roubles girl!" Lev exclaimed having not generally patronised such women of the night I made a guess at £100.

"5000 roubles probably," I guessed. At which both Lev and Yuri saucer eyed whistled in amazement how much it was.

"In Russia, no need Roubles," stated Yuri.

"All you need is vodka and a free hour!" at which he cackled a raspy laugh. I stopped drinking there as I needed to get some more fuel. I had passed a petrol station kind of thing a few miles back. Yuri demanded to drive me there in his Kamaz, thinking well when is the next time I'm going to get to ride shotgun in a Kamaz lorry? I took the tank off the bike and jumped, more climbed into his cab as he fired it up. The noise inside was incredible. I was starting to worry for my safety here as Yuri himself had had a few and had started to slur his words a bit from barely understandable Russian to completely unintelligible Russian.

The vibration and the noise each time he floored the gas pedal was amazing. The fact that he seemed more interested in a magazine while he drove me there seemed even more amazing he was generally asking me questions or flicking idly through the magazine. You could feel the raw power of these hardy lorries. The vibration, the smoke that seemed to pour into the cabin whenever we stopped. Kamaz lorries and Ladas are the only machines capable of surviving Siberian winters, when Siberians effectively never turned them off. I filled up and I was driven back and reattached the tank taking my time to sober up a bit while Yuri found me some fuel hose and I used a cable tie to attach it to the nozzle. He then invited me in to his home again where we drank hot sweet black tea. It was so incredibly sweet that the bottom third of each tiny shot glass was filled with sugar. This along with a saucer filled to the brim with purple runny jam, where I was instructed to scoop up a small spoonful between each cup of tea. It was delicious and incredibly sugary with an earthy taste. Soon enough it was late afternoon and Yuri came back and a flurry of Russian was spoken between them and I felt I had outstayed my welcome and stood up to leave but to no avail. In Siberia they force feed their visitors. Hard boiled eggs, tough salami, boiled ham, fried pork fat, bread, a rock hard cheese that needed to be literally sawn to little bits and 3 chicken legs were bought out with thick mayonnaise smothered all over. Yuri and Lev would not take no for an answer and had to bend my arm to get me to eat an enormous portion of goodies. Siberia had flowed into my heart, as I utterly loved this place now. The desolate wilderness where people had little granted incredibly hospitality I felt terribly guilty about eating their food and any attempts to recompense them for what I ate was ignored.

We exchanged firm handshakes. I gave him a postcard and a flag patch, which he gracefully accepted. Yuri took some photos on his camera phone and gave a heartfelt Dos Vit Danya! I waved as I pulled away from them. I wondered if such things would happen in the UK if a Russian on a road trip came about.

I stopped for petrol at what you would not consider a petrol station. It was 4 lorries tanker lorries with a hose attached to them and they opened the tap let you have a few litres and closed the tap. It also had possibly the longest money tray I had ever seen. 3 metres long I pulled it out a little saw no draw then kept on pulling and pulling until it fell out. I suppose out in the back and beyond they were paranoid around these parts. In that in the UK we complain if we do not see the police if something bad happens to us within a reasonable amount of time. But in Russia off the beaten track there may not be a police officer for days if not weeks.

The road was a nice road for a while, but again decorated with damaged machinery and tyres. It swept through thick forests of trees on either side nice and

127

a smooth good surface and was mostly sports bike country for a while. It then got bad. First a few square potholes here and there where the road had been cut away for some reason. Then more and more and more until the potholes became the road. And it was time to stand up or have your spine shaken to bits. Red dust filling the air from lorries taking it slowly it was hard to see anywhere. I was completely surprised by a police checkpoint in the middle of this, in that even if he put up his stop sign to me I would have no way to see it.

The road stayed like this passing through villages into a gravel road and twisted round a few hills. I had gotten maybe 120 miles and needed more petrol, standing up high revs in low gear was sucking the petrol through faster than I imagined and I'd had to swerve around most of the holes making my path even longer. I stopped for petrol and was greeted with, "Nyet!" For almost every pump until I found one unlabeled pump which I was told by the petrol station babushka it was 50 that's fifty five 0 octane petrol, take it or leave it.... I ended up taking it.... and thankfully the XT didn't knock or pre-detonate and ran on it as normal just a tad rough though but I had to take it. Part way through the road improved again and I passed a bloke on a motorbike coming the other way. We both stopped I turned the bike around and took my helmet off and said hello.

This turned out to be Tomoro. Who was riding a massively over laden SR500 with at least 4 of those huge backpacks you sometimes see backpackers carrying on the back of his bike. No sump guard, badly worn crash bars, and scratches all over.

We said hello and asked where we were heading. He was going to Los Angeles the long way; I was going to go to Japan if I could make it. As it was late and we seemed to be in a good spot, we turned off the road down a small meadow. With purple and pink flowers under the shade of trees with a convenient stream nearby and pitched our tents camp.

We collected wood from the forest and quickly started a 'smoky fire', to keep the giant man-eating mosquitoes away. Before putting our tents up then turning our talents to food and beer. I'd bought a big plastic bottle of beer and a big bottle of vodka as a sort of gift or bribe to villagers in case I needed to camp nearby. I was kind of surprised when he pulled out a double burner stove and started to prepare a huge meal even managing to cook rice with a steamer of some kind. While I only had instant noodles and a few packets of soup. Some how Tomoro had managed to keep things that needed refrigeration on the bike fresh. I don't know how he did it as he kept a tarp over most of his luggage slipping his hand underneath to grab things.

We chatted as to why we were out travelling and we seemed to be a mirror image of each other. Tomoro had rejected the Japanese way of life, which is indoctrinated into people to be corporate machines. In Japanese society if you do not conform you are made to feel to have betrayed your colleagues and countrymen. The brainwashing went so incredibly deep. He had stood up one day working at some corporation I never heard of and decided to go travelling. It sounded kind of familiar to why I had left on this big trip as well. Much beer was consumed chilled nicely by the cool stream and we slept well in preparation for the next day. As Tomoro was heading west and I was heading east we briefed each other about what we would find. I told him about the Omsk cheap hotel which he would have to pass and showed him a photo. Since there hadn't been any decent accommodation since Omsk. He told me about the state of the roads east.

The Amur highway he mentioned was very bad. But I thought if he could make it on a cruiser type bike then I could too since the XT is designed for that sort of thing. I did worry that he might not make it as towards Kansk my bash plate really had been used as the bike bottomed out on some huge potholes, which were like bomb craters. It was often a choice of big pothole to the left or to the right. We said out goodbyes and swapped details offering each a place to stay if we needed it and waved him off while he took numerous photos of me. He suddenly realised how little equipment I had just jeans, and two bags and stopped and asked really if I was going to be ok. I said I'd be fine. We said a final farewell and set off our separate ways. I never heard from him ever again and never discovered if he ever made it to Los Angeles.

This was to prove one of the longest rides I have ever ridden time wise. Tomoro I thought was wrong as the road went on for quite sometime and was smooth as silk new sealed road. It soon changed to side roads where quite literally a bulldozer had driven through the *taiga*. People had torn up the trees to make a barely navigable track through the forest. It had rained the night before and this was hard-core mud riding with deep up to my forks mud and enveloping my chain. I had imagined that this was the slightly easier route but it was proving to be anything but as the mud got deeper and stickier. Both my wheels turned into balls of mud with thick globs of mud being sprayed onto the engine baking the instant it touched the cooling finds. The road was a tease it would go through a muddy section then turn back onto the pristine sealed road surface for a mile or two just enough to make you let down your guard and clean off the mud from your engine. Then back to the mud. I often faced stark choices where there was a slippery foot wide ledge beside a large muddy pool go through the pool or over the ledge. I often chose the ledge sometimes walking the bike over with me walking through the edge of the water. If this was just mud it would be fine but it was interspersed with big rocks with sharper ones here and there. Along with the worn *taiga* to each side with broken twigs and sticks sharply sticking out at angles, which I was worried about taking my eye out on, there, being no medical facilities here for 1000km.

I kept getting stuck having to tip the bike over several times just to get out of the mire. This was just insane as the mud road kept on going and going and going and seemed endless. I had a look at my watch and I was doing barely 15mph at some points. Now and again there was some relief in that sometimes the earth was packed so hard that it did not disintegrate into mud. Though in riding in the tyre tracks of lorries they forced you to ride faster than I wanted. More relief was had when the road sometimes about a mile or two before the sealed sections turned into deep gravel. Not perfect but it was better than the mad bad mud bath I was having at this time. It seemed endless and just kept going on and on and it was extremely disorientating as you would suddenly come to a sealed section with no road signs, no sign of the sun to decide on which direction to head out to.

Until I passed a hotel area in the middle where two hotels and service areas on the sides of the road I had had a lucky escape here. As my rear tyre valve was leaning over quite a bit. I scored some tools from a lorry driver and a Lada driver who happened to be stopping for a rest and put my rim locks back in which proceeded to give me a puncture twice. For a biker in Siberia surrounded by mosquitoes pinching my tube was perhaps the most disheartening thing in the world. In effect you had to start all over again the process of removing the tyre and fixing the tube and there would still be that chance that you pinched your tube again.

It was still light by 3.30pm and I thought just a bit farther and the road will be good again. Unfortunately it didn't get good for a long time. I was averaging 35mph generally stuck behind lorries unable to keep the momentum up and getting bogged down to a stage where I was down to 20kph. But with nowhere to stop the tree line going right up to the side of the road I had no choice but to keep going.

The road did finally improve for a few miles where small huts lined the road and people selling their vegetables sat by the side of the road. The road turned into what I call the dead zone. In that the road turned to sealed tarmac but to the left and right were deep fetid swamps with legions of mosquitoes. This alone would not describe what I saw but every single tree in the area seemed to be dead. Not a single leaf for miles and miles and miles and miles. No explanation of this other than a Tunguska event perhaps it could have just been giardiasis enhanced farts everybody had. I found out when I got home that it was generally caused by the intrusion of man the road that had been built had disturbed the permafrost that lie beneath all of Siberia. The permafrost would simply never recover and refreeze leading to the wet mud coalescing into swamps, which drowned the trees. Siberia's version of Mother Nature had acted vengefully the swamps that appeared were a perfect breeding ground for mosquitoes. This makes me wonder if there ever were as many mosquitoes in the earliest days of Siberia as there would be considerably fewer swamps due to man. But on the other hand the intrusion of man had been comparatively tiny in that Siberia is gigantic and the wounds and conquering of man over Siberia was barely in its infancy. Though the swamps also served the people to a small degree in that I saw the odd person standing in such swamps chest deep apparently fishing in these swamps. How they do not get eaten alive by the mosquitoes is unknown.

Also a stark reminder of the fact I had no tyre tools was a tyre skid mark. This went on for 100s of km swerving left and right left and right all over the road. The road turned into dusty deep gravel track. This wound its way through a few small villages that were no more than one horse towns. Where I had to ask for directions, as it was not immediately obvious where to go when the road forked. The roads had been rebuilt or re-cut in so many places it was difficult to see where the roads went. A few of the towns seemed to be dying in that they were occupied only by old people who sat by the side of the road trying to sell their dust covered fruit and vegetables cultivated from the land. There was still nowhere to stop and camp with the Siberian rail line close by and the gravel road following it as a partner sending choking dust into the air as each vehicle drove past. There seemed to be a constant haze of dust and particles in the air, which hung in the air long after the vehicle that had kicked them up had departed.

Once the road became sealed I passed two Icelanders Lars and Lars, who had just come from Mongolia. They had good news the road got better from here on into Irkutsk with just a few unsealed sections that were mercifully short. I had to disappoint them however in that they were in for some very bad roads ahead of them and nowhere to camp. But they didn't want to camp as they only had a few days left on their visas and would just about make it to the Ukraine if they rode quickly.

When I finally looked at my watch it was 11pm (it was actually midnight as I had crossed a time zone). Siberia does that sometimes in that the sun stays just above the horizon until 1030pm and it doesn't get dark until 2am in the mornings. I had effectively ridden for nearly 20 hours. I found a large potato field to the right and rode off towards it over the hard pack earth setting up in an ideal campsite. It appeared as if somebody had been there before as there was a flattened clear area and lots of rubbish from prior campers. This little campsite was good, at least 2 miles from the road so the wussh of cars was completely absent for once. There was a similar effect with the railway so that there was a serene silence. I set up my tent putting the tent pegs into the dark soil easily for once along with the ends of the tent poles. As I did this an Italian on a bicycle approached from the distance he had also seen me turn off the road into this field but had not reckoned I had gone so far in. He wasn't particularly talkative and I did not catch his name. I was glad for his company psychologically though. I think the bottom of my morale had fallen out. During a few of the previous occasions I lay in my tent thinking what am I doing here? I'm in the middle of Siberia with a million mosquitoes for company and felt lonely. The presence of another rider albeit without an engine was very welcome. Tomoro had given me a much-needed boost when I camped with him. I suppose this is just a hazard of travelling solo and it is a force that forces you to interact with the locals. Though in Siberia people are somewhat far and few between.

The mosquitoes were pretty bad and there was no loose wood on the ground to make a fire to repulse them. Living tree wood does not burn particularly well either but I had developed a tactic against them now. I wrapped my spare T-shirt around my neck and face. Then stuffed whatever into the bottom of my helmet and kept all my riding gear on. The mosquitoes were completely ineffective against me. Granted my helmet would steam up and I would lose a pint of water through sweat. Once you set your tent up you could jump in quickly pull the zips closed kill any you found inside and only then take off your clothes. This though had its weaknesses. If you leaned over too far a gap of vulnerable flesh would be revealed between my jeans and leather jacket that was a sport cut and thus very short. Though it must have been fairly effective against ticks too as I managed to avoid this particular horror of Siberia.

Worst still was taking care of business using the countryside as a toilet. Although this wasn't the first time as I had been like a bear doing it in the woods for quite some time by now. However this is where giardiasis came in handy as you would pull your pants down and it would leave your lower bowel in seconds you had a quick wipe and scarpered. Though you had to be very careful on what you used to wipe. In that wet wipes make up removing wipes were fine although they felt horrible to handle. What was most definitely not ok was using things that LOOKED like wet wipes. Things such as leather conditioning wipes or scouring strips. Using one of those creates an intense burning sensation, which rivals eating a too hot curry and it getting revenge on you when it comes out of the other end. Some prior mistakes made were horrendous. Something to rival when preparing chillies and forgetting to wash your hands BEFORE you went to pee in the toilet. Such things made funny practical jokes but blood curdling screams when you did it accidentally to yourself.

Peeing was less easy you would have a single piece of vulnerable flesh exposed. And it didn't come out instantly in one quick go allowing you to scarper meaning you had to pee while dodging the mosquitoes making it go everywhere which wasn't much of a concern except that some would invariably get me. Even with matrix style dodging there would always be a mosquito that got you alas I got my penis sucked several times in Siberia just not the way I expected it. I was just glad I wasn't a woman having to take care of such business out in the wilderness.

Toilet issues aside though there is no way around the mosquitoes when cooking though, you just couldn't do it inside your tent. So cooking was done in a very basic (read fast) manner.

As we cooked which was more heating water for yet more noodles the other guy laid out his bivvy bag we saw in the distance a pair of head lights. A grey van approached us from deeper in the field with a man handing out the side door holding a handgun.

23: SIBIR THE SECOND BORING BIT, WELL NEARLY

The van stopped right next to my tent and lots of men piled out holding various nasty looking things axes, saws, and even a few pitchforks. We were stunned for a moment until the man holding the gun that turned out to be a strange radio thing, which he was trying to get better reception with.

He seemed to say the word kamar an awful lot and he was right we were covered in the things almost like a beard of bees, well not quite I heard him say something in Russian and caught the end of it.

"Davai, malinka vodka!" Thinking uh oh. My liver giving out a sigh of exasperation. But having a quick look around at the desolate fields around us and the basic food we were eating we decided to take him up on his generous offer. I was about to get onto my bike but he motioned for us to get into the van a UAZ type thing. We the Italian and myself looked at each other and climbed on board. But not before grabbing a bottle of my own vodka from my bike a short drive we were in a farmhouse.

The men in the van were a work gang to harvest the potatoes it turned out and had been working all day and were about ready to relax. It was pretty basic with the walls lined with bunks but there were piles of empty bottles of presumably vodka. Like I would stack up in my student days and pronounce "didn't we do well!" We were virtually force fed dried fish, cucumber and tons of mashed potato and toasted many times. Jokes were told; solemn sounding and cheerful songs were sung and much joviality was had. Although I did not understand them they sounded like happy songs which most people sang and slurred the lyrics to after a few drinks. I was asked again about prostitutes and their cost and was given the same answer everybody roaring with laughter. They also asked me about London if it still had its pollution problem. Through some passing of my phrase book back and forth it transpired that they thought London (which I don't have a great deal of experience with by the way) was constantly shrouded in smog. They insisted that this was real and I said it wasn't. Their teachers had told them it was like that one of them disappeared for a moment and pulled a book out of a satchel. Out came a copy complete collection of Sherlock Holmes.

It transpired that Sherlock Holmes in parts of Siberia was still used as English teaching materials. The schools could not afford to replace them with more modern texts. Which was the reason they kept wondering why it wasn't true. Sherlock Holmes is at least 200 years in the past, and it had given them an archaic view of London, with its opium dens. Holmes apparently a respected person even being a heroin and cocaine user.

At 5am we were dropped back at the campsite just in time to be greeted by a torrential down pour which would rasp against the side of my tent the rain as was so heavy the Italian asked if he could come in. Both of us were kept up by the torrent of rain hammering the side of the tent. I was utterly wasted and this didn't stop me falling asleep quite quickly. When I awoke it was dark and I the storm still raged outside quite heavily leading to me yet again turning over and going back to sleep after a gulp of water.

I awoke early and the Italian had gone leaving a gash down through the mud and deep footprints. I saw this as bad. If he had to walk his comparatively light bike out what would I have to do? Slowly, slowly I rode out collecting an immense amount of mud with wisps of steam as muddy clumps were flung from the wheels hitting my down pipes completely coating everything below my knees in mud a big ball of mud. Yet still amazingly keeping it upright I do not know how as I cannot wade the XT both feet down. I managed somehow to get near the road where the perfectly fine mud ramp yesterday had turned into a mire. There was nothing for it but absolutely gun the throttle and hope the momentum powered me up the slope. So I rolled, more slid the bike backwards and found a slightly firmer section and put it into 2nd and gave it some gas. The bike surged forward gained some grip lost some grip and jumped onto the road sliding this way and that. I tried to put the brakes on but these were covered in mud too. Unable to stop I promptly slid into the mud on the other side of the embankment where the road was on. Luckily this was covered in thick grass and the XT gripped onto this nicely so I powered up the side of the embankment yet again just managing to stop before going down the other side. The weather this morning was atrocious so bad that things, big hairy caterpillar things had crawled into my helmet causing a yellowy squelch when I put the helmet on and a nasty itch on my scalp. My clothes had not dried from the night before, my waterproofs only offering proof of water. It got to a pretty low point when my crotch was completely soaked and entering a café I would squelch my way in, in my wet boots.

As I didn't pass the cyclist I guessed that he must have gone the other way westwards. I wondered how he would make it through the gravel and mire I had experienced a few days prior.

24: IRKUTSK, SIBIRSKY EXTREME AND THE BAIKAL.

The ride in through most of the day was heavy rain and storm cells punctuated by heavy hail. Typical Siberian unpredictable weather which varied between sunny one moment and rainy the next. With threatening looming gigantic clouds up above. Small satellite cities of Irkutsk with mazes of pipe work and worn way and incomplete roads where complete sections were missing meaning cars snaked left and right to stay on the better sections making it a bumpy dangerous ride. Things cleared up as I approached Irkutsk the sun came out and burned away the wetness necessitating various stops to rotate my riding gear so that everything had a chance to dry out. The roads and terrain flattened out so that I could have been in the Dutch countryside. A brilliant blue sky I could have drowned in dominated the landscape. Even making the usual rubbish dumps in the *taiga* just outside small towns only a mild nuisance. The entrance into Irkutsk was a wide sweeping area full of car and lorry mechanics and dealers, in remarkable similarity to the outer parts of Dijon over 10000km away.

I got near Irkutsk (Ирку́тск) whose coat of arms is a panther or tiger or something holding its kill. I rolled into town past the big Hotel Angara. A big concrete rectangle laid on its side with small slits for windows. Which was predictably a relic from the old Soviet days that faced the square. I imagined it would be almost exactly like the hotel I had seen in Azerbaijan and also in Rostov-en-Danu. Which was pretty obvious as no amount of refurbishment could hide the harsh apathetic functional concrete construction. I did a few laps not sure which way to go and went to look for the Mongolian embassy asking people for directions. It is on Karl Marx Street behind the DHL if you are interested. I evidently discovered that it was a Friday as the Mongolian embassy closed early on Fridays. I also had an encounter with a Russian military convoy of buses either that or prisoners, where a police car led several buses through an incredibly narrow street. I didn't realise it was a convoy and filtered in between them, the bus driver gave me an incredibly dirty look as if I wasn't worthy of existing, much like the guard at the Sochi ferry port. I often wondered why people got angry or stressed like that, in that it never helped anyway.

Curiously Irkutsk in the parts that I saw anyway completely lacked the mazes of combined heat and waste pipes in the town centre where I lingered for a while I saw none. Perhaps they were buried as cities like that cannot survive a Siberian winter without such heating.

I had a choice go to Ulan Ude that might take me two days and go to the consul on Monday or settle down in Irkutsk. After several nights camping I didn't feel massively up to camping again and decided to settle in Irkutsk. I went to the big Hotel Angara and asked how much for the cheapest room. Already at this early hour on the sofas in plain view of the surly looked like he could snap your neck in a cinch security guard were two women. They were enthralled in a puzzle book. They were dressed in micro skirts the tallest high heels with thick makeup and stripy tights. Though some places had women of the night here it seemed that they were women of the day and night. Though I may well have been mistaken as the women in Siberia and Irkutsk that was the regional capital seemed to dress incredibly sexy anyway.

The Hotel Angara unfortunately wanted 3250 Roubles something out of my reach. But conveniently had an Internet café in the lobby. Which was at the time packed with Australians who generally mistook me for a Buryat local.

"Oh you're a bloody POM, how you doing? I'm Peter what's a POM doing out here so far from home?" said Peter.

"I could ask you the same thing, what's an Australian doing so far from home?" I replied.

"Well me and the wife just retired and decided to go see the world somewhere free of tourists but this place is bloody full of them."

"Yeah well there are tourists and there are TOURISTS."

"I see what you mean mate in that I'm just here to use the Internet café. But bloody hell mate some of the people I've met travel but don't want to lose any of the comforts of home so I don't know why they bother in the first place," he said.

"I understand the feeling," I responded.

"Well you probably do but then you probably make us look like tourists how long'd it take to get here?"

"About a month," I guessed. As I hadn't been really keeping much track of the time, as it seemed completely pointless. I didn't really have too many appointments to keep. I managed to gather quite a large crowd of tourists some of whom thought that I was a liar. There was still a popular misconception that Irkutsk could only be gotten to via the Tran Siberia railway. Or by taking a flight into Irkutsk. Google maps didn't exactly help either as still in 2009 there were large sections missing from the map from Kansk onwards to a few hundred kilometres north of Irkutsk.

One of the tourists turned out to be a tour guide called James. James had been here for a while from Canada and warned me that Irkutsk is a fairly dangerous city. There was apparently a serious drug problem in Irkutsk. He took me round the corner just behind the hotel and there were needles everywhere with a few people knelt down shivering in the blistering heat of the afternoon. I managed to find a hostel the Baikalier located behind the DHL offices in one of the concrete tenements just off the square of the Angara Hotel. A small cosy 400-rouble (£8) hostel that was basic but comfortable. Unfortunately it was stunningly hot inside even in early afternoon. The girl who ran the place asked that I go get some flip flops generally as I had been on the road for quite some time and removing my socks was an unpleasant event in sight and smell they were able to standing up by themselves. I had a feeling that if I left them alone for long enough they would breed and a new life form would emerge from my scummy socks they were that rancid.

Irkutsk seemed strange there wasn't a single pub in the place I could find only restaurants which charged exceptional prices even for Russia. I did see the 'English club' complete with a fake Queen's guard soldier wearing a giant bear skin on his head and oddly a kilt which wasn't quite accurate. I used to think my job was bad but seeing this thought otherwise as he marched up and down in front of the club while tourists both Russian and non-Russian appeared to mock him. I managed to find the big market place where small shops with bored looking Russians attended to them. I investigated the basement shops that sold a ton of power tools but none that were useful to me so I resumed my flip-flop search.

It seemed that everybody everywhere was sat around drinking his or her *piva*. Men, women even fairly young children who could not have been older than twelve perhaps thirteen. I had read somewhat later that *piva* / beer was actually starting to gain serious ground on vodka as the drink of Siberians. It's the other way round in western Russia where beer is cheap vodka expensive. However the marketing men managed this in Siberia by advertising beer almost as a soft drink. Something virtually for children and thus people consumed it thinking it was completely harmless. I'm not sure what to make of this if you drink beer to get drunk you will do less damage to yourself than some of the rocket fuel I had seen posing as vodka. Home brew moonshine called *samogon* was also popular, though I think beer was the lesser of the two evils. When I drink lots of beer I get a stomach ache long before I can do any serious damage. While with vodka with the 80%+ strength I saw in some places you would drink lots quickly and do more damage than beer. I heard of a sobering (no pun intended) remark before I had left that 95 million people in Russia had alcohol problems men and women alike this was an enormous number out of a population of 142 million. Though the government was at a loss on how to tackle it. The Tsars, Catherine the great, Lenin, Stalin, Khrushchev, Gorbachev and Yeltsin had tried. But made it worse via high taxes, which lead to home brewing. Though the government previously was so dependent on taxes from vodka it often went through the motions.

138

There were also lots of *kbac* sellers with big tanks of *kbac*. I had seen this in Georgia as well and many of these tanker type things by the side of the road. It was supposed to be a bread ale type thing home fermented barely alcoholic but refreshing almost like we envisage shandy back home or root beer. Russian marketing men were played the patriotism card with *kbac*. They too advertised it as a soft drink but as an antithesis to the almighty colas of the world, these marketing men were actually winning. Though based on cost if I made less than $100 a month I would probably drink *kbac* too. 2 litres was barely 12 roubles. Cola comparatively of any of the two major brands cost 30-35 roubles per 500ml bottle, which was almost TWICE the cost of petrol. It would have to be something pretty damned special to cost more than petrol considering vodka cost less than petrol too. Cola is nothing special though it's just all the marketing hype surrounding it. An extremely wealthy investor was once asked if he was given 200bn US$ if he could overturn the cola monopolies he said there was no chance of it. Interestingly though all of the western branded soft drinks were placed in remotely locked fridges. Beer and vodka did not seem to need to be locked up in such a manner. You would pay first and somebody inside would press a remote control to unlock the fridge for just a moment. If you slacked in speed a tirade of Russian would be spat at you from the babushka behind the counter.

I found my flip-flops in the outside market a nice pair of deep blue made in Russia for once flip-flops for a reasonable 300 Roubles and made my way back to the hostel. I walked back to the hostel and thought I'd check up on my post at an Internet café down an alley way and spotted two bikes. A BMW bike a model I had never seen before and one of those 650 BMWs I had rejected out of hand earlier due to cost weight and lingering issues BMW never got round to fixing.

Inside were Walter and Tony the core of the Sibirsky Extreme project. I had never heard of them. I had heard vaguely about an adventure with Maciek Swinarski, Chris Scott and some others but had heard little else even that it had been canned when Chris Scott couldn't make it. Maciek wanted to finish the 666 MotoSiberia project and go where no bike had even gone before. They were staying at the local bike club the Baikanor that was cheaper and better than my place so I decided to have a look. When we arrived with Walter and Tony leading me there it transpired that the XT was possibly the oldest rattiest bike there with the least amount of equipment clothing and tools.

Completely conveniently Tony needed a 17-inch tyre. I wanted to change over my worn tyre. Though to say worn is wrong as the Trellebourg tyres are made from plastic as I had ridden nigh 10000 miles from Turkey and they looked remarkably new. We decided on a trade he'd change my tyre over and could keep the old one if he did all the legwork. Which was good as I was going to change it just over the border and find a skip to sling the old one. At the Bike club were also various other riders who had made it this far.

Hannes a Fin he had limped here on an Africa Twin with a broken shock absorber. He had attempted to get to Vladivostok and back in 30 days. Who everybody called the buzz saw. As he would keep everybody awake through his incessant snoring. He had even kept Walter and Tony awake and it was a great relief when he finally vanished off one evening for a shag. Must have been something to do with his habit as he had a pannier full of tins of snuff. Though he had the most sexually active fingers possible as everything mechanical at least got totally fucked.

Andreas and Claudia on a F650, which no longer looked like an F650 as it had been tourateched so heavily that it looked different. Claudia was on a new F800 BMW, which again was tricked up and wide as a bus quite literally. I figured Andreas's bike was worth at least £35,000 in touratech parts if bought new. Claudia's was bike probably worth £40,000 as they had the most trick of trick parts. Gigantic 60 litre fuel tanks, hard cases, secondary tanks on the back, you name it the original thing on the bike had been replaced by touratech gear even engine bolts had a touratech logo on them.

Rough tourers like Nathan, Tiffany and co as well as the original Mondo Enduro and subsequent terra circa group scoffed at such things. I think namely as they cost a packet and tended to reinforce the idea that to do such a trip you needed a hell of a lot of money. While Walter not quite a rough tourer (yet anyway) decided on less is more in that it was important for him to save weight. Either Andreas and Claudia were exceptional off roaders or they took an easier route, as I couldn't lift the bike off the side stand with luggage on it. The important consideration with the XT was that I could lift it up fully loaded with minimal effort.

We spent the evening bitching about Long Way Round and Walter happened again to know Austin Vince the Mondo Enduro team leader as well as Tiffany. Tiffany whom I had met in Borjomi and briefly in no mans land between Georgia and Azerbaijan.

Walter affectionately called Tiffany his wife as he showed me his PDA with screen after screen after screen of emails and texts asking for advice. Walter also personally knew Maciek too it seemed that the world of adventure riders was a very small group. There seemed not to be more than 3 degrees of separation between each and every adventure rider known in the UK and Poland. Walter had managed to cross Siberia in 1994 the first man to do so on a motorbike on an XL400 Transalp. Beating the Mondo Enduro team by a whole year and yet absolutely nobody had heard of him. Granted in 1994 I was more interested other things I wasn't interested in riding a motorbike then I was more interested in riding other things like the girl next door.

I had to go back to my hostel and spent the night with Mila a Nordic woman who was pleased at the low cost of drinking in Russia. She claimed to need a mortgage to get drunk in Norway. She wasn't too happy as she had heard the stereotype that Asians can't handle their drink and I did my utmost best to prove her stereotype correct as she was downing pints at a rate of at least 3 to 1. Russians and the Scandinavian peoples' love their pints and like to have a pint or two. This is a common thing shared with Northern Europe, as their winters are harsh and cold too, pints of **vodka** though. Although I slept better than I had slept in the wild back and beyond I was still somewhat weary the endless travel and uncertainty and the need to generally constantly pay attention was tiring. Bikers sometimes think this is great. When you ride fast or for a long time due to the heavy amount of concentration that is needed this has a nice side effect that from the concentration used up you fall asleep easily at nights. Some bikers call this road meditation as it really does clear your mind. Though there was some sort of deeper tiredness I couldn't explain.

The next day I moved into the bike club. 300 roubles a night, washing machine, restaurant / bar attached what more could I ask for? If you ever pass here the *plov* and *solyanka* is absolutely delicious. It is a simple broth of meat, cucumbers herbs and spices but I think back to it today and I can almost taste it. Forget borscht I never found anything better other than at a hotel, which charged me ten times the amount I paid at the bike club. It is all Natasha knows how to heat up, if the chef is there anything on the menu is edible if Natasha is there only things that can be heated up are good. Natasha in 2009 effectively ran the bike club and lived there. I do not know if she still does. Walter and Tony prepared to leave doing the tyre switch somewhere. Walter took me to replace my tools yet again with limited success, as there were no tyre levers anywhere. As I moved in and settled in a Russian girl was heading out to Mongolia shortly and wanted an escort. She was to arrive later that day to discuss if she may follow me or I follow her.

Alas this came to nothing when she turned up on a YRB125 which didn't seem up to the job of crossing Mongolia. She looked an awful lot like Claire R who I had fancied years ago at an old work place which went absolutely nowhere and who left the company to avoid me. Well not really as I left that company first. Though a lot of women looked like her as she was a plain Jane type, but the reason I didn't take her was that she quite clearly had an awful lot of luggage. The Russian men at that bike club who were going the same way lied and said they were going elsewhere too. The first clue to this was that she kept talking about her ex boyfriend constantly and compared me constantly to him. When she talked to her friends she started to call me her man when we had only just met. She was an established rider at the Baikanor though with her picture adorning the wall. The core members being in framed photographs next to the bar. A black tape stripe on the corner marked a fallen rider. The Baikanor had rather a large number of black tape photos about a third of the photos out of 40 maybe 50 photos.

Although travelling with another rider would have been nice especially one that could speak Russian fluently it seemed more like a baby sitting mission to be frank and from what I saw of Mongolia later on she would be fine. Tony got back and photos were taken of Walter and Tony leaving. Leaving only Hannes, Andreas, Claudia and myself to sit in the downstairs club come bar to bitch about Long Way Round. And boy did we bitch!

To avoid being sued I shall say no more than this. The Book Long Way Round and DVD/TV series is not as exciting as it looked to be. There were some moments staged and purposely exaggerated in terms of danger, remoteness, funding, distance and most importantly of all acknowledgement. If you ever meet me in person I will give you my opinion of what these things were as that gives me a veneer of plausible deniability. Putting it in print most definitely does not!

The next day Andreas and Claudia left for Mongolia and didn't expect me to make it. Giving a doubtful tone as to the, "See you in Mongolia." This was the start of the terminal decline in Anglo German relationships as Germans in their Teutonic manner and efficiency sounded like they were talking down at me. Germans some how always seem to need to do it in their Teutonic style everything needs to be planned equipment everything. I imagined a ridiculous situation where a German couple planning a night out carefully calculating this and that. Ah let us see, let us go to a reasonable restaurant and come home for some efficient German sex ja? Though of course this was not representative of all Germans just Germans who had money. I suppose it takes a certain personality to become wealthy and sponsored bikers like Andreas and Claudia were sponsored which was good in one way as you can run up huge bills to give to BMW. But when you are spending your own money you want value out of it as you remember how hard it was to save all that money.

I spent that particular day drinking with Hannes and managed to wander into a big mall and bought a new camera an 8-megapix jobbie by Samsung, which was pretty steep close to 4000 roubles. I could get a cheaper one at home but of course I wasn't at home. We even had a short-guided tour of the open-air military vehicle museum. Hannes and myself spent much time drinking and babe watching as there were some incredible good looking and well dressed women in Irkutsk. A typical day would be to get up late walk into town check the post at the Internet café and go drinking with Hannes. Having stunningly attractive women walk down the street showing off, sometimes coming up to us and talking to us. Although they did walk back and forth to show off it wasn't in an aloof sort of manner. In the UK and China when you see attractive women nicely dressed they will often act aloof. They know they are hot and thus consider themselves way above you. I loved the way you can look at them smile and they will smile back. The fact that can I buy you a beer messaged across by *"pri-vet malenka piva?"* was most excellent as in Russia this is completely innocent as drinking is social and has no sexual connotations. You ask a woman in a bar or a club in the UK and it has all sorts of sexual connotations. I was surprised that this happened, as in the UK I would generally be greeted with a "piss off". I even considered the theory with them that women dress as they do because of the 9 months of winter where they spend all their time wrapped up. I was told that this was not true. Russian women would always dress well; in USSR times women's fashion magazines were considered to be contraband and would cost a huge amount of money 3-400 Roubles (a considerable sum in Russia today). Women all over the world are women, they like to look nice and feel special. The USSR being unable to control this allowed fashion to be an outlet of creativity in an otherwise drab world. I had seen this oddity in the original hostel where the girl looking after the hostel would change into a completely different set of clothes and do her make up (which she didn't need at all) just to go to a shop nearby for a loaf of bread. On her return moments later she would change back, turning a 5-minute exercise into at least 30 minutes of dressing and undressing. It was nice to see some people who took pride in their appearance, considering I myself had not bothered for quite sometime.

That was our lot for a couple of days, most frustratingly were that none of the pubs in Russia seemed to have toilets. The odd café did but pubs no, after a few pints you would feel the need to break the seal. Though you would not find anywhere to break the seal, which meant running to the big shopping centre I had discovered on the first day here. I think they could have made much more money by having toilets. In that you've drunk loads and loads do you stop and find a toilet moving elsewhere or do you piss yourself? One pub we went to an open-air type pub which had a combined kebab shop in the back everybody had to use the wall behind which was a little gross as it had been VERY well used prior to my own use even for the brown. Quite curiously also that younger people would come and beg overtly at us in pubs and bars. Anywhere else I doubt they would be let in. Old babushkas however would be more discreet they would rummage around bins or walk up to your table and collect cans and waste off your table and recycle them for money. I suppose they must have had their pensions destroyed when Russia's currency collapsed not once but three times.

I was suffering from cabin fever in a bad way. Although the bike club had a pool table and plenty of beer (though it being a bikers bar they would frequently run out) as well as live music almost every night which Natasha always attempted to get 200 roubles out of us for attending. Although Irkutsk is a well-known place to Russians and non-Russians alike, it is a very empty and hollow town that had been tuned purely for tourist money extraction. Themed Irish bars which had no real claim on calling themselves Irish bars, serving stout and some pictures of shamrocks does not an Irish bar make! I think people consider it to be a nice place as many people travel into Irkutsk via the train. After being cooped up in a train for 8-10 days it took to get here I'm not all that surprised people thought it was a welcome relief. Irkutsk was simply soulless and boring from the tourism exploitation. Though the economy had little choice it was do this or die like many other Russian cities.

I decided to visit Lisvyanka after checking out my post. Lisvyanka was 68km from Irkutsk south. On that note it is often thought that Irkutsk is on the Baikal it is not it's a fair distance away the water you see while you ride in is a river into the Baikal, the Angara.

My post did not give good news Alex T who was originally going to ride quickly across Russia to meet me had decided to turn back. After a nasty encounter with corrupt cops, which ended up with a gun being pointed to his head and bike issues as well. There was nothing left to wait for here.

I packed up and made the trek to Lisvyanka, which everywhere turned out to be completely full hostel and guesthouse wise. As I was preparing to leave an old Babushka asked in the local shop said, "*gastiniza?*" to me.

I replied, "Skol ka?"

"500 roubles," she replied. Immediately she said something after which sounded like is that too much? Almost apologetically 500 Roubles was fine (about £10) and I was led into a house at the edge of the village this middle aged woman was Svetlana (which seemed to be the typical standard Russian woman's name). It was immaculately clean and tidy even though the outside looked somewhat rotten. I hadn't figured it but 500 Roubles included dinner as well as she stopped me when I tried to go out for dinner at the local café. I was smothered by dish after dish of Russian food. Sausages and potatoes, 2 kinds of soup with monster size dollops of mayonnaise called drinking yoghurt smothering everything. There was also offered in small quantities some home made whiskey worse than it sounds. Moonshine was made in a filthy bucket at which you got impure alcohol. This had added to it various seeds which gave it a watery almost urine like colour when you are severely dehydrated. It had a nasty oily kind of taste and I was lucky that they did not want to go on a bender that evening.

In Russia circa 2009 most people still live below the poverty line of $42 US a month and thus generally diversified and had turned back to their land and catching fish. A little while later her sons' Mikhail and Yani joined us. Who worked as a mechanic and fisherman. They had both been to the university of Novosibirsk and thus spoke perfect English but were somewhat underemployed. It seemed in Russia people spoke perfect English or barely any however due to general poverty could not afford to move out nor afford to get married as their girlfriends had to support their families too. The collapse of the USSR had meant that promised pensions never materialised and those who did save in roubles were destroyed multiple times. In the days of Mondo Enduro in 1995 Russia was suffering a hyperinflation problem. They did once more before I arrived. The shops had things of decadence but freedom wasn't good for most people as it was only free if you could afford it. I think this is why maybe people always asked if I had dollars or Euros when I went shopping before finally letting out an audible sigh and accepting Roubles. It might also go someway to explain why so many people had metal teeth. If you invested your Roubles in gold and silver teeth you were protected against hyperinflation and could keep them safe lest somebody steals your teeth. There was much debate at the table that I could not hope to follow but with Mikhail translating roughly for his mother I got the gist of it.

"The old days of the USSR were missed by older people who had things to lose i.e. their investment in the system. When the system collapsed they were too old to start again and rebuild and would prefer the old soviet system to come back."

Mikhail and Yani had different view of all of this in that Yani said to me, "I do not miss the old system. I am too young to have experienced much of it, but today although most Russians are poor we at least have a choice. When before there was none and we were all captives of the system. It was inevitable to not fall over and collapse. Although the collapse has made us into an African nation we are slowly rebuilding for a better tomorrow, and we have the choice to do this for ourselves this time." This seemed rather patriotic, as the evening wore on many things were asked generally about UK life. But then a generalist taboo subject about religion.

"Leon, do you believe in God?"

"Not particularly, I'm a bit of an atheist." I replied Yani wasn't surprised at this however.

"I believe that you believe in God as people who say they do not believe are just denying in God but believe inside if you crash, you call out to God to save you." He responded.

"I don't call out to anybody," I answered back.

"I am certain that you do," Yani replied.

"Well...."

"The way you say a little bit shows that you have doubt in your heart." He left as a parting comment going out for a walk. I followed briefly to see the cool darkness of the Baikal and the few lights around the promenade and the whitewashed concrete building, which seemed to serve as the main social venue. Though all that could be heard was the soft lapping of the waves onto the pebbly beach of the Baikal. Svetlana attempted to get me to stay another evening. But Walter was correct Lisvyanka although pleasant had nothing much to do but sit at the dock of the bay wasting time.

145

The next day I decided to go to Oklon Island 50 miles north. Most of the road en-route was sandy gravel, which was easy enough to handle as I left the majority of my luggage at the bike club. I got onto the free ferry and camped out there for a day. It was wonderfully scenic and quiet the kind of silence everywhere bar the odd gurgle of water here and there that I could hear my own tinnitus out in the open. I can never hear my tinnitus in built up areas, as there is something called 'The Hum'. The Hum is some sort of low frequency hum (the clue is in the name), which the source of can never be identified.

A fire was made to disperse the mosquitoes and a eerily peaceful night, nothing went bump or made a noise in the whole area the odd muted splash of water on the shore but that was it. The morning beauty was wondrous, undisturbed nature green upon green with mirror flat water on a tiny peninsula I had seen the night before.

Back to Irkutsk to pick up my passport and visa and I was nearly ready to go bar one last big night out with Hannes. In the central drag of Irkutsk we went out drinking and our loud English speaking attracted an American called Louis from Los Angeles who everybody thought was Buryat. In fact everybody thought I was a Buryat too. Which in turn attracted two French cyclists who spent over 2 hours deciding what to eat when there was only Mongolian pie on the menu. This cosmopolitan meeting is an excellent argument for why people do not learn many languages in England. If everybody else on the planet is taught in school in the national curriculum to speak English, people like myself had it easy as everything was communicated in English. We got immeasurably drunk on black beer until one of the gang totally drunk said, "I don't like Russia you have to pay for sex!"

"What?" somebody asked.

"You pay for sex, you buy beer, buy condoms and rent hotel rooms for the night! So you have to pay for it."

"You have to pay for those things anywhere you go."

"No, no, no, back home I drive truck, you stop near woman on side of road punch her out fuck her and leave means free sex."

I sobered up significantly after that and we left the Frenchman who said this. While the rest of us went to the Stratosphere nightclub which was suggested when I got friendly with a café waitress who seemed like she wanted to come with us but had to work in the 24 hour café.

We went in to the complex and it was quite a big complex. It was sort of like a supermarket of entertainment, bowling alley, restaurants and 3 nightclubs in one place. The Los Anglesite and the other Frenchman went to get something to eat, Me and Hannes went to the Akula club and paid the appalling hefty 800 Rouble entry fee. However this was worth it as we were greeted with 100s of sexy suggestively dressed Russian women who filled up my notebook with email addresses and flirty and filthy suggestions. Very little was drank that night following the rule of men i.e. that in the presence of hot suggestively dressed women a man had to remain sober enough to fight. To their knowledge we were wealthy European guys and an excellent catch. Hannes earlier had told me of his exploits where Russian people although poor by our own standards lived contented lives and therefore although some were not really interested in you and more in your passport. Today it was less likely as Russians had considerably comfortable lives.

When leaving I got dragged into a taxi by a Russian woman and her friend and went home with them my imagination ran absolutely wild at this point. A 3 some with two hot suggestively dressed Russian women. Conversely a terrible thought occurred to me. I might be hammer ganged and end up on some video site being battered by hammers and slowly tortured to death.

I had a choice death or a date? I thought for a moment and thought it was worth the risk. After Ulana whom I just learnt her name, got out the taxi and we were in Suburbia. I went in to talk for a while, or tried to but got my clothes torn off me. I got absolutely battered seriously battered. Russian women are shall we say different and enormously strong so that you are being used as if you are a dick on a stick. It was hard and aggressive and I was lying there like a dead body with rigamortis in certain areas. Afterwards I was completely embarrassed almost felt violated and wondered oh shit what is her name? I thought of hundreds of Russian women's names: Tanya? Olga? Svetlana? Anna? Tatiana? Sophie? Natasha what was it oh God what was it? Considering I had taken a serious beating from a passionate act I wondered what she would be like angry. I decided to play it cool and call her babe, which seemed to go down well. We got out of her bed and she suddenly said something in Russian, ending in Segie going to the door.

Oh shit Sergie? Who the hell was Sergie!? Her boyfriend? Her brother? Perhaps a hammer gang psychopath waiting for me? Who had waited all night exploiting my vulnerable situation? Oh even worse her dad, oh God... she opened the door and a piebald cat strolled in and jumped into her arms. I took her to a café and we had breakfast and I said goodbye swapping email addresses. She never responded to me to anybody who is interested and her name was Galina.

I returned to the bike club and packed everything up, one last attempt at tools at the car place Walter had taken me. The first shop I walked into supplied tyre levers, which were cheap but burred and rough needing me to buy a file to clean the edges of burrs. A new pump and a valve corer tool were welcome additions to my tool kit all easily found by myself where Walter had failed.

The Russian girl still didn't have her visa yet as Russians perhaps due to extreme animosity from Mongolians when Mongolia was occupied made sure that they were both expensive and took a very long time. She had been waiting for 2 weeks and there was no news. I suppose it was understandable in that Russians only 30 or 40 years before had taken many Mongols out to the Steppe and put bullets into the backs of their heads it was still in living memory. I generally wasn't prepared to wait much longer as I was seriously getting cabin fever in the bike club. Not to mention Hannes snoring was appalling and would keep everybody in the building awake.

It was a shame as she was a direct clone of a certain Claire R I once asked out and blew me off. Though my memory of course could be playing tricks as I have not seen Claire R in over 3 years when I used to work in Manchester city centre. In the office she was a quiet generally didn't talk much other than work, which was perhaps because we worked on different floors. We had exchanged oh all of 50 words with each other during my 15 month tenure at this company. She was engaged at the time but suddenly split up and saw my chance, but was unsuccessful. I always considered plain Jane types who were quiet at work to be exciting outside work to make up for the lack of interesting things happening at work. I know I used to be. At work I would be completely blank get on with my work type. The staff knew I was a biker and that was about it. But each weekend I would go about tearing up the tarmac of the Northwest with various friends and beyond making up for our dreary day lives. Though this (Claire) is a dead end, as I never go back ever it's just a quirk of mine although this is a moot point, as I no longer have any contact with her.

Though he was storing up his sleep probably. Hannes had ordered a new shock via DHL and it had taken a very long time to arrive. 2 weeks by the time I left it still had not gotten out of Russian customs. Which meant that he had only 5 days left on his Visa to get to Finland. 5 days to cover 8000km maybe more. Though Hannes was upbeat about going west even though he had failed to get to Vladivostok. Going west he crossed time zones the other way and would gain an extra 7 hours on his trip west. Being stuck in Irkutsk for the best part of 2 weeks he was looking forward to things we take for granted in Europe. Petrol stations that let you fill first. Petrol stations selling things other than petrol and cigarettes and such like. And he had been daydreaming about a big fat steak, as steak wasn't something to be found in Siberia.

Although Russian meals always have some meat in them, Russians consider you haven't eaten if you haven't had any meat. Particularly Siberians it always came in very small pieces in everything from *solyanka* to *plov*. A steak in Rostov had cost me 900 roubles and out in Siberia not many people had that kind of money.

25: ROCKET FUEL AND THE RUSSIAN SAS

The ride to Ulan Ude (Ула́н-Удэ́) was a pleasant twisty road that cut through the thick *taiga* forest of the Baikal area. I didn't see a place called the Bolshoi Calais I had been emailed about. This road had plenty of off turnings all over. The road although not very challenging was nice to ride quickly like a sports bike for once even if the back wheel didn't like it much. Passing a few small villages filled with Asian Buryat looking people. I'd left fairly late in the day and reckoned that I had to camp out. En-route 100s of roadside stalls were selling fresh and dried fish the pungent aroma was overpowering at times. I didn't make it that far today considering Ulan Ude is 240km from Irkutsk. I stopped in a good looking field far from the road which turned out to be a busy fishing area. The odd Russian would come and tap on my tent. Asking to sit and pose on the bike and for a postcard of home, which I duly gave them as they were getting really dog-eared in my rucksack.

Before sunset a middle-aged man came by my tent and offered me a better place to camp. The back garden of one of the houses as this campsite proved to be especially busy with people going to a nearby pond carrying the odd fish back and forth. This was Vladimir who turned out to be ex Spetsnaz, i.e. Russian Green Beret / SAS type. He took great pleasure in showing me a large collection of photos and his Spetsnaz campaign badges, which included Afghanistan.

I undid my tent and followed him back to his house that was on the edge of the village and quickly put my tent up on a bare part of his vegetable patch. We then went inside his little house, which looked to be fairly rotten from outside with the wood deeply eaten into from mould. Inside was as the other Siberian houses I had seen was immaculately clean and tidy. Out of a side room came his wife whose name began with a Vylia maybe. She didn't look pleased and was tying her hair into sort of a beehive style as I went in. An argument ensued between them which sounded bad and I tried to hide away in the corner while this happened. She left the house shortly afterwards giving me cold hard stare and Vladimir started to show me things pinned to the wall above the sofa.

It transpired that he had been to Afghanistan in the 1980s. The patch was like a batman insignia, and he was remarkably strong and fit for his age. Afghanistan was nearly 30 years ago and this guy was in his mid 50s. I wasn't sure until he showed me his prized possession his knife gun or gun knife. Subsequent searches on wikipedia this is called a Ballistic knife. This only ever issued to Spetsnaz forces ballistic knives are even illegal in the US of all places and the photos had the same tattoo.

Spetsnaz GRU are tough they are reputed to be even tougher than the SAS. Their training regime means that many are killed during training so the group is an absolute survival of the toughest and hardest men who survive the training. I was convinced. Seeing he had little reason to lie to me. One of the questions he also asked me which stood out was I think why I was going to Mongolia as he said Mongolians were all thieves and very bad people to which I had no answer.

After he showed me his photos he prepared dinner quite quickly. It was something he called *Sala* or *Salak* or something. It looked like raw chicken strips dipped in egg and herbs. He skewered a piece with a knife and poked it in my direction. I was cautious but not wanting to offend my host I ate it and it tasted like smoked salmon with a creamy sort of texture and mellow almost mayonnaise after taste. This was supposed to be a Siberian speciality though I never found it anywhere else. I ate this along with some bread salami and some old cucumber, which seemed a bit past it.

I had prepared for such an event by bringing along a huge bottle of super vodka. Super vodka in that it was brewed triple strength to save on transport costs. Much like various New Zealand or Australian beers I heard of where it comes double or triple strength and you dilute it to make it into normal vodka. Though vodka is actually declining in popularity to beer in that what can only be called camaraderie of drinking lasts much longer drinking beer than drinking vodka. I gave him a flick of the throat and he grinned a metallic smile that would make Jaws jealous. This was a huge mistake as Vladimir was partial to the odd drop of vodka. He found a loaf of bread and a wilted cucumber as a sort of accompaniment to the vodka and started the drinking. He was drinking it much faster than me as I was mixing the stuff with orange powder and water. This orange powder I had bought in Irkutsk. As plain old water was a bit uninteresting and this was a re-hydration pack of some kind or at least I thought it was. A few hours later Vladimir blinked slowly and leant backwards in his chair falling asleep. I finished a final slug of vodka from a fairly big tumbler and barely made it to my tent.

A small tip though is this if you should ever find yourself travelling through Russia and come to a small village is this. It is to wait and watch villagers about their daily business. They will visit a certain unmarked building, which is the village shop. Sure there are actual shops that look like shops in Russia but these are placed to get people travelling on the road who don't have the time to search out a village shop. These shops sell everything you can imagine food wise. In the middle of Siberia you would often see Snickers, Mars bars, dairy milk amongst the Russian chocolate and crisps. Even Walkers and Nestle had made big inroads into Russia. Russians and Siberians in particular have an incredibly sweet tooth.

I woke up considerably later just before dawn as I emerged from my tent he came out and started shouting in Russian acting furious I think demanded to know who I was and what I was doing camping on his land. Giving me a suspicious look without a hint of recognition and gave me what I think was a tirade of verbal abuse in Russian. This was bad as Russian Spetsnaz in Afghanistan had some horrendous tactics to use against the Afghan people during the Soviet occupation. When one of their officers was taken hostage they would drive into a town capture the town leader and slowly cut him to pieces over the course of a week. After a few shows of force the hostages were returned unharmed. Or Spetsnaz would kidnap insurgent leaders and torture them not for information but to make examples of their enemies.

Surprisingly he just shrugged his shoulders then strangely went inside and motioned for me to come in and have breakfast I was given a plate of eggs with him eying me suspiciously all the while. As we finished his wife came back and they had another argument at which Vladimir sort of remembered me from before and offered me some *chai* in way of apology. I didn't mind though, and went outside to get the other bottle of vodka for them and left it as a parting gift as they refused to take any money off me when I tried to stuff a wad of 100 rouble notes into their pockets.

Hannes had warned me and told me an old Siberian saying which was apt at this moment in time:

"Ten roubles is not money. One thousand Kilometres is not distance and 40% is not vodka!" It was spectacularly true that night. The refusal of money happened an awful lot when you tried to thank people by giving them money, as their pride would not allow them to accept it in that it was just above begging. I think in their eyes and they rarely had visitors from out of town and a bloke on a motorbike seemed to be exotic. I gave them a few postcards instead, which they accepted gracefully and pinned on the wall immediately. Vladimir then went into a small cubbyhole and tried to give me a souvenir back. It looked like a large dark egg but on closer inspection turned out to be a hand grenade of some kind. I was sorely tempted to take it as it would have made an incredible souvenir but it would be hard to explain to customs officers as to why I was carrying an explosive device. They may also have taken the shoot first ask questions later kind of thinking if I took his gift.

The next day Ulan Ude the capital of the Autonomous Buryat Republic that was by passed by quickly as I would see Ulan Ude on the way out. Though I did see a big statue holding a sword similar to what I had seen in Volgograd. Also I saw the giant head of Lenin when I took a wrong turn through the town, across the enormous bridge spanning the river that ran through the town.

I rode round a few complicated junctions down to the Mongolian border via a sealed road that turned to sand and gravel in a few places but nothing too tough. Through spectacular scenery and the landscape becoming drier and more barren as I passed through. Thankfully the large mosquitoes vanished completely but were replaced by its smaller white brother that was harmless compared to its brother in Siberia.

Though here the bike had problems it started to rumble badly and displayed the same symptoms as the second day in France. It would cut out or rev in an unstable way I checked the wiring and found nothing wrong and continued on my way maybe I could get it fixed in Ulan Baataar. But was not hopeful as Walter had told me there was absolutely nothing there I would have to risk the 400km to Ulaan Baatar to see if I could continue my trek.

26: HELLO CHINGIS

En-route to Mongolia the people all seemed to look more and more Asian. Black hair triangular faces, and the café stops confirmed this in that everybody seemed to be Buryat or Mongolian immigrant. Although this had been happening since Omsk whereby the Russians were intermingled with pale looking Asian types not quite Chinese, not quite Russian. Though in Omsk they were in rather small numbers compared to the white Russians, though as I progressed farther east it was getting to an even proportion.

The road was fairly desolate with the odd patch of gravel or uncompleted road works here and there. The problem was with the sealed road it had been done poorly where thin layers of tarmac had been laid across uneven ground. The uneven bits came through the tarmac exaggerated and magnified making it a slow and slippery trek to the Mongolian border. This was made all the more difficult by the bike randomly cutting out for reasons unknown at the time. Though the landscape became much more barren, greenery seemed to vanish if it wasn't beside a river and it was getting noticeably warmer than the previous days. With sand gravel and grass seeming to completely envelope the road at various points in defiance of the sun and lack of water. Curiously the Russian government allowed this overgrowth on this part of the road. All through Siberia and the western parts of Russia the road edges were immaculately kept. An extremely common sight was of a work gang with petrol strimmers cutting back the grass and plants at each side of the road. For 1000s of miles the roadside was immaculate even on the unsealed sections I had experienced previously. The road might have been a death trap pot holed to hell boneshaker but always the grass verge was perfect.

Passing through the border town I saw many strange signs. Although Russia is filled with strange signs the border crossing was particularly strange, in that there were triangular signs similar to that of no motor vehicles without the motorbike above the car... What was strange about it was that the car appeared to be on fire, sign after sign of this, which I thought, was strange...

No cars allowed on fire? I did have doubts to if a car was on fire the driver would calmly follow the signs and evacuate the vehicle at the proper designated location. In Irkutsk Hannes and me has seen a strange road sign of a pair of sunglasses and wondered what this might signify as well you wont find those two in the Highway Code. Upon my return home I found that this sign meant vehicles carrying explosives were limited to 30 tons.

As per usual with Russian border towns there was very large military presence packed full of tanks APCs and generally men walking around in military fatigues. It was in the norm though with a total absence of the drunken people Russian towns usually have. The town seemed to be nothing more than infrastructure for the military base, i.e. brothels, bars and a sort of grocery store. This town seemed oddly deserted and the people that were there didn't want to speak much even if you went up to them and said hello.

An oddity was that in the middle of nowhere not stuck in a shop or anything was an ATM booth, which looked decidedly out of place. Almost Japanese like vending machines that are in the most out of the way places. Twisting through windswept roads I felt like I was going in the wrong direction stopped for a map check and waited for a moment for somebody to pass by to ask. People did pass but didn't stop; the first people to stop were a pack of 4 cyclists two from France and two from Germany.

"Ah so you must be the mad English man ja?" They asked.

"Erm yes how do you know me?" I replied.

"Ah Andreas and Claudia on BMW pass us two days ago, they say you are very crazy. Why are you so crazy?" At which he went into great length at why my trip would fail well recanted what Andreas had said behind my back.

"I do my trip my way he does his trip his own way, anyway I travel light the lighter the bike the better it is off road," I replied. Andreas of course I'd met in Irkutsk, and although he never said it to my face he had been incredibly critical of my trip. He seemed to say one thing to my face and another behind my back. He had stated that the bike doesn't matter just go, but had bemoaned to his fellow countryman behind my back that my trip was utter craziness. Though to be honest I think Andreas has a vested interest in touring 'properly' i.e. hard cases expensive modifications, backup crews, forwarding of tyres and immense amounts of equipment. Namely as his tour was sponsored by Touratech and BMW. If people like myself, Nathan and Tiffany could do this trip with minimal equipment on old bikes without a single item branded touratech then they would be out of business. As people would go out there and use minimal equipment instead no sponsorship from that!

I did think at certain points he might have a point since I totally lacked maps unless you counted taking photos of them and stopping truckers to look at their maps. No GPS, an adequate water supply, clothing and had absolutely basic camping equipment. I suppose all of the extra kit would have added to my comfort GPS for example would have gotten me straight to places to sleep and eat without having to go round in circles around big unfamiliar cities. But I suppose with such things you lose a certain something *quid pro quo*.

HUBB riders' state that it is impossible to get lost all you are doing is exploring unexplored territory. Without GPS you get a much rawer experience you have to stop and ask for directions and in turn meet more people and see things off the beaten track. I've gotten severely lost many times in Europe touring and discovered hidden beauty spots, hidden camping locations, unspoilt vistas, this trip was no different. Some of the comforts would also have been useful purely from a morale point of view. As I had the bottom of my morale fall out once I reached Irkutsk though this might have been more to do with the numerous beers I had alone which is a recipe for disaster to be honest.

We (myself and the bicyclists) went onto the border crossing point known as Altanbulag and there was a massive queue the kind that goes around the block twice. As forewarned this consisted of the guard opening the gate for a minute pointing at people you, you and you as the lucky ones then slamming the gate and letting people bake in the heat for a few more hours.

Bikes, motorised and non-motorised however rule, as we could get right to the front and passed through with minimal waiting. Getting out was a paperwork struggle, health declaration forms, customs declaration forms in triplicate, migration card completion, visa registration work, and the whole shebang. That was just getting out of Russia...

Mongolia proved to be much of the same walking back and forth from one office to another to another. Where they filled in large ledgers of who went in and who had left the country. Then passing it onto somebody who entered it onto their computerised systems. In my jacket it was utterly cooking and for a strange reason the border point was bracingly hot. The customs procedures were slowed down markedly, mainly due to officials standing by to guess my nationality all very tedious.

"Buryat?"

"No."

"Mongol?"

"No."

"Kazakh?"

"No."

"Uzbek?"

"No."

"Taiwan?"

"No." Which would be repeated over and over and over at least the border guards didn't go through all 242 countries that exist according to the UN. And as an added benefit some of the armed border guards were quite good looking and would stop to chat at you for the most mundane things. As the border point was somewhat remote, 300km from Ulan Ude which wasn't exactly a massive metropolis, and 400km from UB which again wasn't a huge city. I plucked telephone numbers off the women guards well two of them and told them I'd meet them for a night out in UB.

I was in the inaptly named clearance zone when I was called over by some moneychangers and a first dip into the black market ever on my trip. I changed 5000 roubles in the form of 5x1000 notes and was handed back a brick of money. I counted 266 notes of 1000 Tugrog notes. This currency was weak really weak. Worse than the Russian rouble, in some villages and towns en-route quite a lot of Russian places always asked me for US dollars or Euros first. When I said I had none they would sigh and accept my Roubles. Of course this isn't as bad as the Uzbekistan money Tiffany had told me about via email. Where she changed 100 Euros and came back with a suitcase full of money. Curiously Mongolia does not have coins in their currency and their smallest of the small notes is one Tugrog which considering 2500 Tugrog was equal to one pound while I was there it was worth 1/2500th of a pound. I had read reports about Mongolia in Irkutsk during some downtime when there was nothing else to do. And Mongolia it seemed was the poorest country in all of Asia even worse off than Bangladesh, Laos, Vietnam and Cambodia. Missing coins I supposed they missed out on exciting pub games such as table top rugby and there wouldn't be anything cheap and convenient to throw at people except maybe rocks.

27: MONGOLIA

Here I was in Outer Mongolia. Inner Mongolia is actually part of modern day China, but the outer bit made it sound all the more remote and extreme. Even though I had encountered pretty remote and basic life in Siberia, which by definition should have been outer, Outer Mongolia. As a teenager we had joked about Outer Mongolia being the most remote place on earth. I would see. I got out to the open road for about 30 seconds and into a petrol station. In Mongolia at the petrol stations the attendants pump the petrol for you and then take your money. A stark difference to Russia. Where you pay first and risk over flowing petrol tanks. Petrol was an equally pleasant 1100 Togrog per litre of 98-octane petrol such that I didn't even feel the need to use the 900 Togrog stuff at 85-octane.

The problem with big denomination money is that even though you are spending bog all with the excellent exchange rate, because of the big numbers involved, it feels like you are spending a huge amount. In that it's not often in the UK I hear somebody ask for twenty thousand of something or even ten thousand of something or even one thousand. The most I've spent is probably on my student fees, and even that was a thousand and it would take a fair bit of getting used to. This is sort of like the psychological experiment where people always seem to think that highball pint glasses are bigger than short and stout pint glasses. It is identical but psychologically something tells you the tall one is bigger.

Minutes later I was back onto the open road ... the ONLY open road in Mongolia well paved road anyway... My immediate impression of Mongolia was that it was one massive golf course a massive, massive one. Ironically Andre Tolme in 2006 did just that over 11,880 strokes playing golf all the way across Mongolia. The grassy plains punctuated with sandy bunkers here and there, although you couldn't really see that much from the road. As the road was enclosed in trees allowing only the smallest of glances through the trees either side of the road. It seemed less as if Mongolia was suffering from desertification more as if some how the grass had managed to grow out of sand and it was slowly being turned back to sand. I would pass obvious tourist traps like the Chingis Khan secret history camp on a hillside, or the Authentic Korean Mongolia experience, how can that possibly make sense? I don't know how they figured that one out at least they were honest that it was designed to be touristy and no need to be cynical about such things as you do in other places.

Go anywhere touristy elsewhere and the words authentic, traditional and hand made is applied to all sorts of stuff even tat. What they mean by traditional is that it is lifted out of encyclopaedias and remade in some factory in China. Hand made applies to the fact that somebody had to plug in the machine that produced it etc.

157

Worst is possibly local prices for you! Now I wonder what use a countryside nomad would have for a gigantic carved wooden horse, how many Mongolians buy that sort of stuff? Only mad or seriously wealthy ones so local prices means nothing! A few checkpoints which took 500 Togrog as a toll and I was at Darkhan before dark and continued on my merry way to Ulaan Baataar, but didn't quite make it as it became dark earlier than I expected. A schoolboy error here had caused this, as time in Mongolia is one hour in front of Russia.

The cities in Mongolia appeared to follow the Russian model. A big combined heat and power station in the middle or to one side and the city sprawling around it. Big steel pipes sprawling along the side of the road I guess for carrying hot water in the winter as combined heat and power seemed to be popular here as in Russia. This was not surprising as Mongolia was an ex USSR state since 1921 and had only relatively recently shaken the shackles off and been allowed to ferment its own destiny. I stopped off at a café for water and cup noodles. Strangely the owners of this roadside café were not Mongolians they were Koreans with a bizarre American accent from the Deep South. It was incredibly bizarre for a Mongolian looking Korean man to be speaking to me in a deep southern droll. I swear it was Jodie Foster's brother in a disguise. It transpired that these Koreans got sick of Korea and moved to Mongolia.

"How ya'll duiing thare fella?" asked Kim.

"Erm I'm fine thanks," I replied.

"Wut would you like to be eating this fine evenin' sir?" Kim inquired.

I pitched the tent up on some farmland on top of a hill generally in preparation in case the bike wouldn't start on the button I could bump start by rolling down the hill. Careful to not pitch near a cairn which held some sort of religious significance as I had witnessed car drivers sometimes stop near them and perform a quick ritual. As I pitched my tent I marvelled at the complete lack of vicious black mosquitoes. A pesky tiny white one did bite me but it left no real impact, as they are bigger and harder in mother Russia. The wind however had other plans and decided to keep me up all night making the thin walls of the tent flap furiously. For once the soft sandy soil the tent pegs went in easily by hand. So did the tent poles, with some big clouds on the horizon the guy lines went in as well just in case. It was an uncomfortable night as it was at an awkward angle where I kept sliding down the hillside out of the tent. But and now and again the wind would catch the lip of the tent flapping it up before the guy lines bought it back down again. Now and again I would hear horse gallop near my tent I would pop my head out the tent get looked over and eyed suspiciously and without so much as a hello or before I could utter hello they would ride off again. The people would pop out of nowhere and come and have a look no matter where you stopped. It seemed almost as if the nomads hid behind rocks and popped out ready to greet you whenever I stopped to check something on the bike or to re-tie a strap. This is probably why on the road I would see tiny no horse villages which had nightclubs in them. I wondered how lively they could be. Stopping for just a few minutes' generated minor crowds so that must have been how they made their turn over I suppose.

Ulaan Baataar or UB as everybody calls it. I suppose when your capital city is called Red Hero it sounds odd to be saying take me to the city of Red hero. I sometimes feel the same way about Hong Kong. The fragrant harbour in Hong Kong people just call it central or crossing the sea. So instead of ah you are going to Hong Kong is never said it's more like oh so you are crossing the sea then? While Bolton / Manchester / even London to me are meaningless names. I digress UB was still a fair distance away and it couldn't have proven to be of greater contrast to the mostly empty countryside. A city of lights neon signs, hotels casinos well after the ugly industrial bit anyway.

Riding in I was greeted with the power station and a sort of grey drab industrial sector, which made me think of Baku. Though of course I have never been to Baku but have been there vicariously due to the many grisly accounts of other riders. Appalling amounts of traffic lots and lots of traffic mostly Japanese 4x4s lots of them. I was surprised that a country of nomadic horsemen had so many cars. Considering there was less than 500km of road in the whole of Mongolia it was even more of a surprise it was nose to tail all the way into the centre. Fortunately or unfortunately depending on your point of view, Mongolians it seemed treated cars like the Iron horse and would go off onto the grass at the side and pop back onto the road again. The odd one or two this would be ok I suppose but it was 100s of cars doing it.

I had always imagined UB to look as I had read it, i.e. picket fences around *gers / yurts* leading a sea of white into the city. Instead I got tenements blocks and blocks of vaguely square concrete tenements. These looked worn and rundown covered in barred windows and the odd piece of washing. A wide 3-lane road led in and out to the heart of the city. This wasn't the Mongolia I had imagined, nor the Mongolia Walter had mentioned either. Though granted Walter hadn't been to Mongolia since 1995 and there had been 14 years of progress.

Progress seemed to have spoilt it a bit. The Mongolians were stuck between two competing worlds. The countryside and the big city style living even the population of Ulaan Baataar had increased markedly in the past 10 years doubling. It was a stark contrast to the rest of the region petrol stations malls, advertising by big international corporations. Though I was happy to report that there wasn't a McDonald's in Mongolia at all. It is one of the last countries in the world not to have a McDonald's instead they had clones like Big Burger and Berlin Burger. Long may it remain so free of such intrusions. I wondered if they would have the same disappointed people like in western countries where the TV tells them to chase

159

unattainable dreams. Dreams of being movie stars or rock stars. I was beginning to think advertising wasn't a good thing because of this as it skewed people's values and made people think that happiness was material and owning things. Though there was a good smattering of independent shops here and there, with marques and shop names most definitely not western or eastern. Fashion shops called Wanko, or Destroy hair styling or Long Cok. I wondered if English literate people had played a nasty trick on some of the shopkeepers. The trick often being that when somebody doesn't understand a language they are vulnerable to pranks. As such when they think they tattoo in Korean or Chinese or whatever says love or hero or hard as nails or something like that. In reality it could just say chicken fried rice. Or that they had just left it like that unable to afford to change them or refused to admit they were wrong. After all Mongolians are Asian people where face is important. In that it was reminiscent of what Alex had told me of his first impressions of Japan. Where old ladies would be seen walking in pink t-shirts labelled 'happy joy gay wanko walking club,'

While in the countryside the nomads were happy to survive winters and have enough to eat for the last 2000 years. I wondered how long this could all last. Pondering which would eventually win. Although if the more modern way won it would have been a pyrrhic victory and it is unsustainable anyway. I rode past a massive compound that turned out to the Russian compound where many of the Russian bureaucrats and their families lived those that chose to stay after the collapse of the USSR. It had been the seat of power in Mongolia when the USSR was in charge.

Unfortunately Ted Simon wasn't there to greet me either not that I would have anything to give him. After getting lost in the small city centre I found UB guesthouse that was in a small alleyway behind the main street and was turned away. Then I found the Golden Gobi and was let in and took my jacket off. Having not taken this jacket off since Irkutsk even for sleeping she shrieked as the inevitable stink rolled out. I was told not too politely to go somewhere else at least the owners drafted in their employees to carry my things.

It is pretty bad when you get thrown out of a $8 guesthouse I suppose, however I was taken over to the Chumbee hostel instead. A tiny quaint little place it was cheaper at $5 and with the most helpful owner possible. This place served as the overflow for the Golden Gobi and it seemed to be closer and friendlier than the Golden Gobi that was run like a tight ship and very corporate manner. Apparently if you stayed at the Golden Gobi you were expected to book a trip with them and would be asked to leave if you did not. Although next door to the Chumbee was the friends' touring company who would come round and ask if anybody was interested and link up travellers. Though with the XT here this was unnecessary for my circumstances. I went for a short walk to get my bearings and noticed the oddest things that the sedgeway had caught on at least in the police force quite significantly here. Police would roll around Sukebaator Square on their segways in big laps.

The bin lorries were strange. I always wondered what this catchy tune was playing in the back streets where all the hostels happened to be and it was the bin lorry playing a soft almost ice cream van type musical tune which made everybody run down stairs with their rubbish. I reckon a child born in the UK would be mighty disappointed with this. That's if they had not been told the old trick some parents use on their children, that the ice cream van only plays that tune if they have run out of ice cream.

A good wash was desired though. Having not had a wash since Irkutsk that meant days and days ago well three days. I decided to go for a wash or rather get somebody else to wash me as the Chumbee showers were constantly occupied and the grime on the shower head just dropped onto you meaning you never got clean. Additionally the fact that showering at the Chumbee had no privacy so anybody could wander in use the toilets, maybe take a photo and walk out so it wasn't my cup of tea. Showering at the Chumbee the door could have had a door alarm that played the song the performer. So I popped out and into UB massage, which is reputed to be 100% vanilla and clean. Not too far away across from the state department store that everything was congregated around.

The state department store is private now and according to people I spoken to as little as 10 years ago was the only high rise building in the entire country, now there were plenty.

I needed first to go to an ATM, which isn't easy although there are plenty of ATMs in UB and in quite a few countryside towns these days there are few, which are in English. There are plenty of Russian and Mongol ones but unfortunately only 3 English text ATMs in UB that I found. I found one opposite the Beatles monument and went inside to get some Togrog. Going in there was a door and 4 security cameras for a single ATM room no bigger than a toilet cubicle. I went inside and fumbled for my still at crotch location card. The guard immediately came out and started to shout something in Mongolian at me. Presumably with the big beard thinking I was some sort of vagrant about to take a whiz on the ATM. I retrieved my card and said 'just a minute!' to him in English and he backed off almost bowing in apology. This beard malarkey although nice in that it kept the mosquitoes off (as I had not shaved since the UK) and made you look manly rough explorer made everybody here think I was a bum. Still I got my money out the ATM again a virtual brick on money for just £50 of Mongolian currency and left with the guard keeping a beady eye on me. This ATM experience was ok I suppose and guards are a good thing too. In that it would prevent the thing that sometimes happens in the UK where muggers take you to an ATM to draw cash. Though there seems to be something wrong with all the ATMs where I live in that they are all badly placed. The ATMs near where I live in Manchester seem to always be on some little dark side street where there is a sort of alcove effect nearby. Where you are always convinced there is an assailant waiting to cut your throat.

A mate of mine once told me of his experience as follows. "I'm still shaking from an incident that just happened, coming away from the cash point tonight, I was just putting my wallet away when two guys jumped me. After the initial shock, I managed to knock one out before I hit the ground. On reflection though, it probably wasn't the best time to have a wank,"

After I had gotten my cash I weaved my way across the street past a huge monument to the Beatles, which was odd. In that any link between Mongolia and the Beatles was extremely tenuous. I looked on the menu and super comfort massage body wash massage for 30,000 Tugrog not bad about 12 quid so I go for a punt. The woman at the desk thought I was a bum because of my beard and nearly called security as I entered but as I spoke in English to her and her mood changed immediately.

I'm led into the back room put all my valuables into a locker and strip down to a towel and go into a wet room with nobody inside. In comes a cute as pie Mongolian girl who wearing a cute blue frilly bikini top and non-existent skirt. She barely went up to my shoulder. Though she did have rather ominous beefy pop-eye like forearms that was a little bit disconcerting, as they didn't seem to fit her body shape. Looks can be deceiving however as she motioned for me to lie on the bed type thing that was covered in a disposable plastic sheet. She threw alternating hot and cold water all over me that was nice and invigorating, and then started to soap me up nicely nothing sexual about that which was terribly disarming after I had tensed up on from my Turkish bath experience.

Now was the horrible bit, the exfoliation. Girls I don't know how you can do this on a regular basis but she had these gloves which were like mini cheese graters. Sort of like steel scourers used to get rid of those deep baked stains off pots and pans when you have made a pasta bake. Which if you use on soft Teflon will remove it clean from the steel base of the pan. She scrubbed and scrubbed, causing me to almost scream, and scrubbed and scrubbed. As if my tender flesh were a particularly troublesome stain. I somehow wondered if I had gotten into a BDSM session and she was the Sadist and she had only done a small patch on my arm. I wondered if I would turn out to be like one of those hanging corpses in the film Predator stripped of all their skin. She was pretty thorough rubbing my skin raw and showing me a pile of skin she just scraped off me the size of a grape fruit Woo! Thank goodness that was over. I was pretty glad when she stopped scrubbing as I worried I might vanish and disappear down the plughole. If this was the super comfort body massage I wondered what the rest of the things on the menu would

162

be like. The super clean bones massage, super heat-exfoliate facial massage though maybe I was being a wuss as there were no audible screams from the other rooms. The next bit was good. She started twisting my joints feeling for tension and massaging them out bit by bit this was good very good. But it was just to let me put my guard down for additional torture as she cracked each knuckle of my feet and hands this girl loved seeing a pained expression on my face. She washed me down once more and washed my hair and washed my fine beard before showing me out of the washroom. With total irony as I made my way back to the hostel I got splashed by a lorry, in possibly the only dirty muddy puddle on a UB street. So much for being clean. Well admittedly only my jeans got dirty, or rather dirtier than they were previously.

The next day it rained hard Mongolian style, which meant that UB flooded with foot deep murky muddy water in the streets. This was exceedingly dangerous, as the streets were not always sealed. Manhole covers completely missing hidden under the murk were also a hazard. Twice I saw some backpackers bravely go out into the rain and cross the road vanishing completely submerged into a manhole and swimming back up in horror of what had just happened. Some of them took it with good grace and thought it was comical others did not and took it far too seriously crying and whining about it endlessly. This was compounded by no electricity meaning there was little to do, shops could not heat up food. Internet cafés could not open and beer from bars was impressively warm so that I did nothing for quite some time until invited out to play basketball in the yard outside the Chumbee when the rain let up a little.

The Mongolian men being tall and well built could almost but not quite dunk the basketball. It was a fairly uneven game between the tourists who came out of the Golden Gobi and the Chumbee to participate we (the tourists) lost.

Later on I met with a couple of young women backpackers from Paris who were asking for trouble as they watched me play. In that they were strange French people in that they were vegetarians. A vegetarian in France is considered to be freaky by the French themselves. Out here in Mongolia where the people don't understand what vegetables are or even have a word for vegetables they would be in trouble. Though they were not that extreme though in that they would eat some meat things on account that they had no choice in the countryside. On their treks even though they had a large card written in the curly Mongolian script saying they did not eat meat. An extreme vegetarian would be an anecdotal I heard at a party once where a mate of mine started seeing a girl who was a strict vegetarian, her vegetarianism was so extreme than it included non ingestion of man meat, their relationship did not last long.

A similar vein of eating meat when you are not supposed to exists in Tibet. In that the Buddhist people there eat meat that is somewhat against the Buddhist doctrine. Though to say Buddhist is also wrong as there are so many variations of them. Anyway in Tibet Buddhists eat meat as they have no other choice nothing else grows there and there is no other source of food. Granted meat is also good for harsh environments like the Mongol steppe same thing in Tibet I suppose. A story I heard was even though Tibetans do not like being occupied by the Han Chinese they have found uses for them. The Tibetans will eat the meat but don't like the killing. Thus they will hire a Han bloke to do the slaughtering. If there isn't a Han person around they will approach a yak and suffocate it with mud and straw stuffed down its throat and walk away for an hour or so. When they return oh dear there appears to be a dead yak it's a terrible shame to waste it.

The French girls had come on the Tran Siberian train they had switched at Irkutsk for the Trans Mongolian train fairly recently too. Incredibly they had seen my bright orange non-conspicuous tent and distinctive bike from the train thinking I was some kind of nutter in Siberia as they recognised the British number plate. They were quite fun for an evening where we whiled away the evening with warm vodka and salty bitter slammers. A Canadian who also spoke French joined us and they would say silly things thinking I didn't understand until I spoke to them mid way through the evening in fairly good French and pink faces emerged through the room. Not that it was anything severely nasty said about me though. They did share their maps with me and showed me some decent routes to go through that they had taken in a Russian jeep into the countryside that were not too difficult to cross.

The day after I went to find the Oasis café and managed to find Andreas and Claudia who were surprised to see me as well. I stayed the night in an over priced *ger* with no roof which meant shivering all night long. I didn't find the place particularly hospitable as the place was packed full of Germans who would politely invite you to sit with them but speak in German across you jamming you in the middle. Understandably I was one of the few non-German speakers there but it felt incredibly isolating to be there. Though this seemed to be happening to the French couple that were staying there also. Though all of the German travellers there were incredibly well equipped Kamaz lorries with the kitchen sink. 6X6 lorries that would not look out of place in the Dakar rally. I imagined they were turning their noses up at me as Germans had always done at not being properly equipped for such an adventure. Curiously none of them dared to attempt the Amur highway when I asked them about it, fearing it was too dangerous even if they were fully equipped with the best touratech gear money could buy. Even the German Kamaz equipped lorry drivers were a bit shaky about taking this route.

The next morning I spent time riding around the foothills of UB city, which were impressive and quite easy. What was less impressive was the enormous amount of rubbish strewn on the foothills meaning punctures were frequent and annoying. It had taken me about a day to go nearly a full lap with 4 punctures and I decided to call it a day after running out of patches and getting tired of repairing my inner tubes.

Mongolia is definitely a place for a mousse, not a moose it would be hard to stuff a big wild animal into your tyres. But a mousse is essentially a much thicker (up to an inch) thick inner tube which is much harder to puncture but on the flip side gives a much harder ride as there is less air in it and it wears along with the tyre, normal tubes if fitted correctly do not.

The evening was spent in one the ubiquitous Irish pubs. UB had well more than its fair share of Irish pubs, which had absolutely no claim to being Irish pubs, nothing, even vaguely Irish. No people waiting around waiting to kick your head in. Many of them didn't even have black bread, stout of course. I'm not sure how they claimed that they could be Irish pubs by enlarge they were fairly deserted. I spent the evening with an actual Dubliner who was passing through who made the same complaints about the Irish pub claims. There was a similar pub on the main road, which claimed to be a traditional English pub. This made a slightly better effort 2 warm ales on tap. A proper steak and kidney pie and the odd few black and white football photos and scarves of Liverpool FC strangely enough. The Mongolians who stood outside on the stairway throwing up after drinking too much added an air of authenticity too. Though in UB this seemed to be everywhere people drinking too much. Now if they just had a bunch of blokes standing around menacingly ready to kick your head in and overpriced beer it would be truly authentic. Though each pub and restaurant other than the most expensive ones also seemed to follow the Russian model being they were built without any sort of toilet facilities. Typically this meant drinking near the hostel where there were guaranteed to be toilets. With giardiasis this was a double whammy and so the Milstar pub became a favourite hang out. Cheap enough to drink plenty, close enough to the hostel and comfortable enough with its wide leather seats so you could sink in for a long night.

Here I said goodbye to the French girls who were leaving on a trek to the Gobi before taking a train to China for a flight back to Paris from Beijing, as it was markedly cheaper. I quite liked them they were non-guide book carrying LETS GO types, which I admire greatly. I also have some more contacts should I decide to go to France on a future tour.

Alone the next morning I was getting bored of UB. The city is comparatively tiny, although it is a massive place for Mongolians with 800,000 people to a city boy like myself it was tiny. Hong Kong alone is 10 million people in a tiny place. UB I discovered after a few lazy walks during empty afternoons waiting until it was late enough to start drinking was in effect a Cornish town. Towns in Cornwall are single road towns with the odd side street and back street. UB was effectively the same it had a big central road with a few back streets and nothing else. Once you got away from the state department store colloquially called the centre of town where all directions lead from you get into decaying tenement areas. Places where pool tables are standing in the street, poor people in ragged clothes sit around drinking beer. Playing pool, surrounded by tall uninspired architecturally square concrete cubes which were essentially slums. The ground levels covered in graffiti and bars covering every possible entrance (and exit) thick steel doors covering each entry to these buildings and just open dust and gravel at the foot of each building. The odd burnt out building here and there are a reminder of the riots at the end of 2008 with no money to repair them. Tarpaulin sheets were put up in a feeble attempt to hide the damage, it seemed like a mini version of any other generic city you may find anywhere on earth. I even managed to get to the edge of the city that was bizarre in that cities anywhere else sprawl out into terraced houses or flats then turn into suburbia. But the edge of UB was abrupt. You could stand with your back to the city and it would seem as if you were in the middle of nowhere (essentially this was true though as Mongolia is the middle of nowhere) and turn round and be faced with a quasi-modern city.

I decided after the second day of being alone, as other backpackers seemed to keep to themselves and Mongolians in UB seemed indifferent to my approaches to them to talk to them. I decided to go out on a little trek out there to the real wild of the open steppe to the real Mongolia that had been in my dreams.

28: THE OPEN STEPPE, THE TAHKI HORSE! FALCONS AT YOUR WRIST & THE WIND IN YOUR HAIR

A simple trek was my first outing to the countryside a trek to Terej national park 70km from Ulaan Baataar northeast. I'd gotten sick of the Chumbee Hostel granted it was cheap and friendly but with no common room and very little to do in UB bar sitting in Internet cafés to make calls and update my status for those who cared. UB had little to do in the day time since I'd seen it all. Seeing it all is rather easy in Ulaan Baataar it's the biggest city in Mongolia. City is a bit of a misnomer as it had a population of 800,000 people a mere town in the UK. The hostel owner had told me to not stop near large encampment of *gers*. As this would be expensive and to pull up to a small encampment or even better a single *ger*, everybody has a horse in the countryside she said.

Away I went the sealed road actually continued for a fair few miles out of Ulan Baataar and remained sealed for a while until the Terej turn off to a small track. The track was punctuated with checkpoints that had excellent tarmac for about 5-10 metres before fizzling out. The road was utterly deserted of vehicles and I was the only vehicle for miles around. The constant breeze, which had kept me up days, before was still blowing through the valley. The steppe as far as the eye could see stretched out endlessly and seemed to go on forever. A lot of people say that Mongolia has a big sky, and they are right the scale of everything around you. Areas where you can stand and see nothing but grasslands punctuated only by small white dots the *gers* of the nomads. This sight was impressive and incredibly humbling. It felt however like a place you don't want to break down, as there is nobody to help you. A few ratty bikes buzzing around in the distance leaving columns of Martian coloured dust were all there was for company and large birds of prey. Which circled ominously lazily in the purest bluest of blue skies. The road became just a gravel track that was easy enough bar a few big rocks displaced from the side of the road and twisting down a narrow valley towards a checkpoint.

5000 Tugrog tourist tax for a permit and away I went over the rickety old wooden bridge. It then got a bit touristy very touristy in fact in that huge tourist camps consisting of huge numbers of *gers* next to large hotel complexes. Keep on going the hostel owner had said to me in my memory. That is until I got to a place called UBII. UBII was a gigantic complex. It looked completely out of place in such an open environment.

While I was sort of regretting my choice to have come here a little bit a small heavily tanned man jumped out and Hello, hello? Hello, hello *ger* rent? Cheap! I said no initially and wanted to see what was up ahead in the village where the road turned to mush yet again. I bumped into some Swedish people who thought I was a local, and 3 guys from UB. All 3 of them spoke in heavily accented English with an American accent. They found it funny that I was riding cautiously in their village over the deep gravel tracks all over and I stopped to say hello. In Mongolia I quickly learnt that your bike if it is not Russian or Chinese is up for a test ride no ifs no buts they are going to have a go. The three guys there were J, K and B they'd told me their Mongolian names, which were tongue twistingly impossible for me to pronounce. It's ok they said when we were studying in New York everybody called us J, K and B. Usual line of questioning with a Mongolian twist.

"Ah you came all the way from England? You are English?"

"How come you look Asian?"

"I joked with him that I was like Michael Jackson but backwards."

Though they had a sort of pained expression on their faces when I said this I didn't realise why until much later that Michael Jackson had died.

I felt what is the harm in it in that there is nowhere to go and not enough fuel in the bike to get more than 10km surely they won't steal the bike and these guys had BMW cars out in the village why would they want my bike?

A lot of people had said that the XT600E was most definitely not an off road bike it was just styled to look like one having not done too much extreme work on the XT I was semi inclined to agree. Some rough sections some unsealed bits hardly counted as off road I thought the muddy bit north of Irkutsk may have counted. Considering many of the country bikes in Mongolia were 350cc 2-stroke air-cooled bikes of Russian origin that had slick tyres the XT was something of a high tech bike at least to people in the countryside. Though it probably only looked that way as the XT is 1970s technology with semi modern styling.

Cue the oldest guy there taking the XT for a bit of a spin. When I say spin I mean literally spin as he spun it round and round on the spot kicking up choking dust and sand into our faces before gunning the throttle and speeding off up the valley. I got concerned when he didn't come back after 20 minutes and went inside a nearby bar to wait. Coming out after 20 minutes more I finally heard the XT coming from an impossible direction from behind. There are no roads behind though.... puzzled I waited.... and waited with the unmistakable single getting closer and closer. Sat at the outdoor snooker table the XT got really close, but nobody could see it...I'm getting worried now but the other guys just say don't worry he is the master. I'm greeted by the sight of the XT flying through the air from underneath as the kid who borrowed my bike decided to jump over the pub I had been in moments before and land spinning in the gravel a few metres in front of us.

"Nice bike," he said.

"I told you he was master!" He had confirmed it was an off road bike and it was ME that was the problem not the bike. A bit like Chuck Yeager in 1950s Korea where after a duel he stated to the man who berated the F86 sabre vs. the MIG 15 claiming that the Russians had an advantage their aircraft being better. This resulted in a two way duel where Chuck and his friend had a air to air mock battle with Chuck in the F86 sabre and his friend in the MIG they switched planes and Chuck won both times, he is famously recalled as stating.

"It's MAN not machine."

We spent the evening playing pool with these guys and I rode back cross-country more than a little drunk. For all you safety nazis, I was off the road and in Mongolia it is not illegal to ride drunk either and could only have hurt myself, which I didn't hurt myself or anybody else.

Dinner was served and two Americans in a 4x4 convoy arrived and occupied the gers around me a ger each. We chatted about general things that tourists who cross paths talk about. I also picked up their telephone number as they said I was welcome to go to their ranch in New Mexico if I happened to go across to the US.

The gers were almost sauna like but it was good this time as the outside really was cold and the owner of the ger came in now and again to put some more dung or twigs on the fire. Though this was a low valley and not too cold and it was the middle of the Mongolian summer too. Apparently these gers here were fake, namely as they had steel poles which were concreted into the ground and never moved. I would have to wait another day to see a real one.

The whole area had horses and more horses tied up to non-gers in that the locals of actual Terej village had seemed to abandon the ger and had wooden huts instead. The poverty here bordered on the verge of unbelievable as people who had bare houses with just a stove outside and a pile of wood to call their worldly belongings. Strangely most of them seem contented in that their lives were simple and poor but worry free. I guess they didn't have to worry about mortgage payments or bills in the post either. Although one unpleasant sight was a house where the husband and

169

wife both had advanced stage cancer. They could never afford the surgery to attempt to cure it at an earlier stage and sat there their faces obviously full of pain. Watching the world go by with their neighbours taking the horses for a stroll now and again.

I was joined by a wealthy ex USN couple that were essentially travelling the world with a big land rover defender. They had done what many people are afraid of sold everything they had and decided to spend the rest of their lives travelling. They were quite interesting characters regaling with me with the when I was a boy type stories of their own mis-spent youth. Though this attracted plenty of people who wanted to sell us all sorts of services. Genuine Mongolian dinner cooked for you! Or being allowed to hold and have my photo taken for 10,000 Togrog the huge *burkut* (golden) eagles some of the people kept. I had my photo taken but the bird was huge imagine picking up your Christmas turkey and putting it into the oven, it was like that but even heavier. I was however more concerned with its razor like talons that I was sure it was going to tear my eyes out.

Morning came and it was overcast and raining. I packed up the bike and rode out through where I came in. Except that it had turned into a mire of deep slippery mud. My front and rear wheels both turned into big balls of mud and I had to get off and walk the bike out at some stages just to get to the gravel track road.

I had a look at my options and decided to go back to UB, but I stopped about 3 miles down the road and saw a track leading into valley leading down to a flat plain with a sort of track going into the distance. With nothing really in UB waiting for me I went down it passing a large group of *gers* until I came to a one *ger* stood alone with three horses outside and quite a big pile of rubbish to one side. The horse being the family car if in case somebody wanted to pop down to the shops or something. Through the universality of sign language I told them I wanted to ride a horse and stay with them for a day or two. To my complete surprise the daughter spoke English, as she had been to study in New York. I had made an identical error in Encamp in Andorra almost a year before.

Paul and myself had entered Andorra and went into a bar. Paul had asked for two beers in Spanish then French, and the barman piped up in a thick Australian accent, "So you want two beers do ya?"

I arranged for 2 days and one night for a quite reasonable 65,000 Togrog which was about £30 all in. Which were horses, meals, a guide and a place to sleep for one night. I must confess that don't like horses. Call me weird for choosing to ride a horse for two days but it was one of those things that you just have to do. It's like going all the way across the world to say China and not eating any Chinese food. A bit like Ewan and Charlie then who bought dehydrated rations for the entire trip. But seeing as all of the other people in the hostel were suffering from my giardiasis enhanced gas expulsions I saw their point. Or going to Belgium and not drinking anything. Mongolia is **the** country of the horse, or the *Mori*. Mongolians are proud of their horses the *takhi* horse the only wild horses in existence and the Mongolians 900 years ago had ridden them to Europe and back.

If you go to Mongolia and not ride a horse it's an experience missed out well that was my excuse anyway. The reasons I don't like horses is that horses have a mind of their own they are sentient intelligent animals. If some random bloke came up to me and jumped on my back I would be mighty annoyed to have to carry him for miles and miles. The key difference was compared to a machine like a motorbike is a horse makes its own decisions. A motorbike there is direct control you do something and the motorbike will respond in a particular predictable way each and every time as it is a machine and as long as it is maintained well it will obey your commands each and every time. Maybe that makes me a bit of a control freak or something. Paranoid I kept all my biking gear on and it still didn't feel safe.

A horse was bridled up and I was asked if I wanted a traditional Mongolian saddle or I could choose the 'wussy' leather Russian saddle. Considering the Mongolian saddle was made from wood and one false slip would mean I would be childless forever I chose the Russian saddle. My guide was Salar, which was explained to me to mean hero of fire. I got on my small grey horse and went for a ride around the valley floor. Chu I already knew was the command for giddy up and my guide was saying it so often that it sounded like a train.

We trotted along painfully, as Mongolians keep their stirrups really high. It was obscene and on the back of a horse I was assuming a sort of porn star position with my knees at 45-degree angles to my side up to my chest. I also sat on the horse wrong as it kept hammering my balls. Trot argh, trot argh, I felt that my testicles would end up like boysenberry jam until Salar noticed my severe discomfort and showed me to almost slouch in the saddle that worked nicely. I was shown how to turn left and how to turn right. It's like riding a motorbike and even the need to stand up a little bit and press your weight through the foot pegs / stirrups over rough ground. I even made the horse turn all the way round in a circle and back again several times much to Salar's confusion and thought hey these horses are different. All other horses I've ridden (and admittedly not many) generally follow the lead horse or a well-trodden path. It felt like you had as much control as you do when you've crashed your bike and you are sailing through the air.

It felt ok for a while as if the horse had been incredibly well trained that is until the horse for some reason went nuts and bolted with me grabbing its neck and holding on for dear life. Salar quickly caught up and grabbed the reins and said something to the horse, which snorted at him wickedly in a defiant manner.

We crossed over a small valley with steep hills and into a small cove full of Germans in their Kamaz lorries complete with kitchen sink. We waved took photos well the Germans took photos of me no doubt clinging on for dear life and said

171

goodbye. I was seriously put to shame when a child of no more than 6 or 7 years old rode past me at full gallop without a saddle just reins not even holding onto the reins eating something and carrying a bag in his hand... pesky little brat!

As we passed into yet another valley we crossed a deep river when I mean deep I mean deep. All I could see was the head and neck of the horse sticking out of the water moving diagonally across the fast flowing river. This was an un-crossable by bike or Jeep it was so deep. Wet boots and wet jeans no matter. I was just glad to be out of the fast flowing water.

Through another shallow valley and we saw a giant statue complex thing of Chingis posed for photos and continued on. As the sun set giving me one of those Kodak moments. Maybe even a Marlboro advert look if viewed from afar. We trotted towards a *ger* which stood out in contrast to the green and golden grass like big button mushrooms in the distance. Salar approaching made a traditional Mongol greeting of please tie up your dog. It's supposed to be sacred and important to make this greeting and apparently talked about his animals getting fat or something.

This was not a moment too soon either as from biking accidents, standing up on the foot pegs for 100s of miles through Siberia my knees were absolutely shot. And pulsed in pain shooting up and down the calves this in addition to the dull ache in my spine and shoulders. Mongolians do this everyday they are tough as old boots and then some but seeing the harsh barren landscape they had to be tough to survive.

The *ger* was a small neat round felt tent with a wooden frame with the design unchanged since probably the days when Chingis was hacking Chinese peasants to death when he rode the steppe. The *ger* was in effect a comfy tent that could be packed up in an hour allowing people to wander off to follow the pastures for their animals. Although I suppose this would also be highly useful for avoiding the in laws.

Being invited in I carefully stepped over the threshold, which appears to be important in ALL Asian cultures for some reason. Google provided no answers when I returned to Ulaan Baator, but this is just the way things are. Similarly along with not stepping on the threshold you are never supposed to whistle or decline anything that is offered to you, as it is the height of rudeness. Though I suppose as a visitor this was generally accepted that you would not know all of the customs, though some of the customs such as acceptance and offering of tea, passing items to each other in a certain manner are universal through Asia, a bit like.

"Please pass the salt dear."

They chatted briefly, which to me sounded like them hacking up spit. I had assumed since Mongolia was occupied by Russia they would speak Russian but everybody seemed to spit when you said anything in Russian. I think they were trying to say to me that they hated the Russians and that they were all thieves. Which was curious as Russians said the same things about Mongolians. The Mongolian language curiously enough called Mongolian seemed to me to be tongue twistingly impossible. I got as far as the word *Mori* (which means horse and can be interchanged with *takhi* and the word *kushiru* that was a Cornish pasty shaped non Cornish pasty thing.

The *ger* was compact and small again tiny stools, which made people sit in a sort of porn star position again. Small narrow beds with thick blankets on them surrounding a big iron stove cosy very cosy indeed. Strangely enough and completely out of place was quite a large TV. Which on deeper investigation led to a satellite dish and a set of solar panels and some huge boxes of marine batteries hidden in a box behind the *ger*. Technology of this sort even infiltrated to the depths of the steppe. I suppose in the wintertime it would give them something to do. The winters were harsh when I mean harsh I mean harsh. –10C was a warm winters day –35C was quite typical and the Nomads would hide in their *gers* around the fire. Unlike Siberia that had combined heat and power stations to keep the people warm, these people relied on fire, vodka and food to survive winters. Although I suppose it would piss you off immeasurably if a programme about somewhere hot came on. I heard another horse trot outside and another hold your dogs greeting which I had learnt from the hostel lady. And a Swiss bloke stepped in and to an look of horror of his guide stepped onto the threshold of the door way and sat himself next to me with a cheery hallo.

The family in the *ger* next door came to greet us the husband called Oyunbileg and the wife called G. She wasn't actually called G but her name was so complicated and required unusual tongue twisting tone I couldn't for the life of me pronounce it. Since I can't read the Arabic looking Mongolian script, which to me looks like wiggly wobbly lines, G would have to do. They beamed smiles at us with their weathered leathery faces and were quite happy to see us. We were offered us some Mongolian tea which looked like white water and tasted like white water. We were offered various treats, first a bowl of what looked like butter twists you might find at a Christmas party rolls but smaller which tasted of nothing.

G then went outside and bought in a worn plastic orange bucket in with something sloshing inside in.

"Yoghurt, eat, eat," she said. Looking inside it looked like jelly white jelly, which quivered as she put it down. I was unsure about this but in Mongolia it is considered incredibly rude not to at least try something that is offered to you. At least I wasn't offered testicles like the LWR boys. A small bowl was scooped out for both of us and we both ate it at the same time. This was different it was incredibly sweet and delicious unlike the bitter slightly sour taste of yoghurt back home.

Then *aruul* a sort of a tangy musty bread type thing that was unique though the Swiss guy whom I now knew as Simon didn't like it. *Biroban* a sort of pastry thing made with wheat. And possibly the thickest cream I have ever seen thick enough so that your arm would get tired scooping it out of the little clay pot they had presented it in. It was supposed to be fried in animal fat as well; you could feel your arteries clog up and get chest pains just eating it. Oddly enough I never actually saw any fat people in Mongolia other than foreigners. The few times where I did see Mongolian women in UB in their short skirts and hot pants and tight tops they had the most amazing bodies. I was actually told about a bar where it is sort of a nightclub and Mongolian women come out every half hour and get their kit off but never managed to find it.

We were left alone to wonder and I chatted with Simon for a while who turned out to be suffering from advanced wanderlust. As dinner was still a couple of hours off and noticed aside from the toilet outhouse there was absolutely nothing no signs of civilisation at all in this valley. Just these two *gers* out in the wilderness. With nothing for miles but steppe essentially just grassy plains.

Dinner was *buuz*, meat I was told. Simon was curious and asked what kind of meat? To Salar as his guide had gone off elsewhere, 'yes meat,' I ran through my head what Mongolian meats there might be sheep, goats, cattle, horses, yak, marmots, rats, pigeons, chicken, camels, and that isn't even a comprehensive list. Though we cannot judge them by our standards I suppose since this is more an issue motivated by survival than anything else.

"But what meat is it?" Simon protested.

"MEAT!" Insisted Salar curtly. It is perhaps best not to think about it much, but surely it couldn't be as bad as mechanically reclaimed meat or hot dogs. Having seen mechanically recovered meat be manufactured and processed you never want to eat that stuff again. The cheapest hams and meat slices in the supermarket are cheap for a reason if you don't want to know skip the next paragraph:

In the 1950s the last traces of meat were taken off the bones by blokes with knives, today they use a high pressure water jet type thing to get absolutely everything off the bones this was supposed to be the 'notch above the bottom rung stuff', the bones are then apparently heated to extract even more 'meat' out of them and sprayed again with the water jet. Which got the last traces of 'meat' out of the carcass which was usually discoloured from the process of heating and spraying so that it became a grey sponge like substance that had colours added to it and it was rolled out into sheets of ham.

Or sausages, you can read any packet and they will say belly pork, but when they 'belly pork' stand up and put your hand on your belly, where exactly does your belly end does it go farther down so that when they say belly they mean perhaps cock?

174

Something that you shouldn't think too deeply about I suppose.

Mongolians don't eat vegetables in UB they have potatoes and a strange salty pea salad type thing and ramen. Which is imported from Chinese factories. Apparently there isn't a word in Mongolia for vegetables either. The *buuz* was sort of a Ravioli type thing full of chewy fat and served along with thin slices of fat. Oyunbileg was curious why I didn't eat the slices of fat provided and I told him in England we throw that stuff away. Oyunbileg translated to the other people in the *ger* who had trotted in on their horses and there were audible gasps about the room. I was told by Salar meat without fat is bad food. And the more fat a piece of meat has the better it is and it is considered more delicious than one with lesser fat.

I sort of felt bad now in that I had frequented a small restaurant where they thought I was Mongolian but born overseas and thus unable to speak Mongol. The first time I went there I was provided a sumptuous number of mutton slices all very lean and tasty...as time progressed and I became something of a regular there the mutton became fatter and fatter making me think this was getting worse and worse. Finally when the whole plate was just fat I took a nibble ate the potatoes paid and left never to return. From their point of view they had given me a lousy meal to start with which turned into an excellent meal to a Mongolian's eyes at the end. It was a small cultural difference. At least this misunderstanding didn't end up in me being shot at though.

Dinner was over and we were ushered out to stretch our legs. It was beginning to get dark and kind of cold enough for them to light the fire. Fire apparently again is considered sacred. We were invited back in and some other men had come from *somewhere*, as I couldn't see another *ger* anywhere in the distance or had earlier. They started to talk about horses. Mongolians do love their horses and they ran out of fingers counting the number of horses they could name. To me a horse is just a horse you get brown ones white ones and black ones. Sort of a cleaner variation of the game we played in Capadocia about different names for sex. I wondered if Mongolians had a variation of the children's game top trumps in the UK top trumps was all about cars, tanks, sports cars motorbikes or guns all mechanical type things. I ran with this thought for a minute of Mongolian children playing top trumps comparing the statistics of horses, but couldn't think of any meaningful statistics you could compare.

One of the men got up and poured me a glass of water. Which tasted like water and smelt like water i.e. nothing this turned out to *shimiin arkhi*. Mongolian style vodka, not as strong as the vodka in Russia mind but still nicely pleasant. I had half expected *airag* but that was to come later. Simon seemed to be drinking a ton of the

175

shimiin arkhi stuff not realising it was alcoholic. After a few large glasses he generally sat very quietly rocking back and forth with a coy smile on his face.

Airag was next thing to be offered to me. A large glass bigger than a pint glass was offered to me and it was fresh very fresh. It was sort of like a glass of Advocat the horrible yellow stuff that each and every household has. Usually a bottle of gifted to them that looks like custard, which everybody hates yet, it strangely stays in business (the people who brew advocat that is). It was so fresh it had horse hair in it, a fair bit, well made a nice change from the human hair found in most Mongolian food even in UB. It was part and parcel of life in Mongolia for hair and food interaction except maybe at the seriously westernised places like Berlin Burger and their copied Big Mac.

I was motioned to bottoms up in one go, which I did. It was sort of like yoghurt you've kept out of the fridge for a while with a lingering rotten feet aftertaste. Not that I eat rotten feet particularly often more smelt them. But riding in Russia I never had much of a chance of washing things. Probably why the bears never came for me yet. Salar came up to me and patted me on the back after I'd had another pint of the stuff, and told me.

"People in Mongolia have iron belly, you are not Mongolian you do not have belly like us, many people with no Iron belly shit many times from *airag.*" At which he gave out a raspy laugh. Oh how I hated this man at this very moment.

At which he chuckled and patted my stomach great! My genes being already lactose intolerant along with being cursed with giardiasis I thought why didn't he tell me before I'd had almost a litre of the stuff! Giardiasis was an even bigger bugger to have while riding on a horse. On the bike it was a case of stop kick side stand down and run into the bushes.

On a horse this isn't half as easy you have to get the horse to stop which invariably doesn't want to stop get off the horse and run somewhere discreet which is easier said than done since the steppe of Mongolia was desolate. Salar was very much confused about this whenever I suddenly vanished off the horse. But the *airag* consumed meant it was going to be a very, very long night.

A bloke on an old Russian motorbike turned up with a couple bottles of Chingis brand vodka.... As a side everything in Mongolia is Chingis Branded you name it vodka, insurance, restaurants, rock bands and even chocolate bars. In UB I had seen adverts, which advertised everything and ended with a resounding Chingis at the end of it. Mongolian TV had a terrible habit that is repeated throughout Asia in that they repeat exactly the same advert as the last one just so you don't forget. Sometimes the same commercial would appear four times in a row that was most irritating but I wasn't in Mongolia to catch up on TV though so it was tolerable.

Chingis as he was locally known not Ghengis was completely outlawed under the iron rule of the USSR. As well as taking people to a pit in the desert and putting bullets in their heads the Russians had outlawed any media or mentioning of Chingis. A media blackout since effectively since 1921 when the Bolsheviks marched on Mongolia. Mongolia upon the collapse of the USSR suddenly freed to become whatever it wanted to become had turned to an ancient national hero. Chingis Khan to conjure up the spirit of unity amongst the people in the turbulent period that followed. Though Chingis gets an awful lot of bad press, sacking villages and general pillaging but then having made the biggest empire in the world you had to get your hands dirty. The British Empire did the same along with most other empires. Omelettes cannot be made without breaking a few eggs.

I'd prepared for this with a bottle of Siberian vodka that was graciously received. We were not as hard-core as the Russians as we had a bottle of mixer and a couple bottles of cherry cola. But before any serious drinking ensued we had to perform a small ritual dipping your finger and splashing a tiny amount of vodka to each of the four winds and dabbing it on our foreheads. The evening was jovial and merry with throat singing some incomprehensible form of dance and chatting about horses presumably.

Everybody got up to leave at 8.30 and men clambered onto their horses incredibly drunk. While still merry their horses carried them home without much of their input. A few of them fell off getting back on and falling off again as the Russian stuff was way more powerful than they were used to. Mine was close to 80% Chingis is 37% strength. I felt kind of embarrassed about this I suppose it was kind of difficult to take their keys off them if they got too drunk...

At least horses have one benefit over motor vehicles in that the horses will bring you home no matter how drunk you are. The same can't be said about cars and bikes. Though I thought I saw the look from one of the horses as it snorted and blew out a cloud of warm breath... "Here we go again." *sigh* as if it happened all the time, before it trotted off at quite high speed into the darkness. I wondered how they could navigate actually. In the dark the XT headlamp was ok at best but the adventure motor biking hand book told people never to ride at night and I had broken that rule more than a few times off roading.

I took this as a chance to ask about sleeping in Mongolia without blankets, something, which I had read about 5 years ago. But had never actually seen this trick. This was where Mongolians can sleep in the depths of winter wearing just their clothing to sleep in. In the summer no problem sleeping out in the open but winter too cold. Standing outside on a summer evening felt cool at times in winter seemed insane. Salar for a few Togrog showed me. He went out and peeled off a bit of the steppe sort of almost like turf pulling it off in slabs and dug out a shallow grave about 3 maybe 5 inches deep. He then walked around looking for pebbles and the odd Brussels spout sized stones and put them into a pile. He then went off on his horse and came back with a big bundle of twigs, where he got them I don't know as I hadn't seen that many trees.

Oyunbileg seemed a bit unhappy at this and seemed to argue with Salar but not in an unfriendly manner. As he did this he then made a small pile of twigs lit a fire that crackled satisfyingly and eventually threw in the rocks while we sat around watching what happened. Once the flames died Salar went and kicked the contents of the fire ash and stones into the grave he had dug up earlier. He then went inside the *ger* to get something. He emerged a minute or two later holding a large felt blanket. Which he lay over the hot rocks and motioned for me to lie down on it. It was nothing at first then it got hotter then unpleasantly hot sort of like when you first make a cup of tea and hold onto the sides of the mug but it's too hot for a while. In the 10 minutes I lay there I felt like a sausage. I had to turn over constantly, as the bit in contact with the ground was too hot. So I turned over, but this meant that another part of my body was comparatively cold meaning it was like a slow spit roast. I had to get off and go back inside, as it was intolerable.

Come 9pm we were pretty much asked to go to bed. G piled a ton of felt blankets on top of me and pretty much pinned me to the bed which itself had plenty of blankets on it already. Oyunbileg would be staying with us. He put his head down and fell asleep the second his head hit the pillow block thing. I hate that...in that I always have trouble sleeping no matter where I am. Insomnia is terrible, what is more terrible is that people you tell about your insomnia love to say something insensitive.

"Oh really you have insomnia? Well me I'm out like a light the second my head hits the pillow." What a nasty thing to say! You don't go up to people with AIDS or cancer and say I'm perfectly healthy thank you very much. Or go to a man without legs and say my legs work perfectly you wouldn't do that so why do people say they can sleep like that?

The night was cold as Gorkhi-Terej is apparently on a high elevation plateau in that with my head sticking out of the covers my body was nice and toasty but my face was exceptionally cold. Though through the tiredness and ache in my thighs from riding all day I fell asleep after maybe an hour.

I awoke to the sound of wolves. They sounded really close the *airag* earlier or the giardiasis was getting its revenge on me and I had a choice shat my pants or go out and let it out. I thought shatting the bed would be nasty and this not really a valid choice. Thoughtfully there was a torch by the door and I stepped out only to be met with a chilly wind like stepping into a meat locker. I fumbled back in and put my riding gear on and gingerly stepped out. I had a look around and saw Salar still sleeping on the hot rocks, seemly perfectly content with the faintest wisp of steam rising from below him. His breath making an even bigger column of condensation rising into the night sky. I wondered why Salar had not really wanted to show me, he thought I was being a little shitty bastard of a tourist and wanted him to sleep outside away from us. When in reality I just wanted a demonstration of it and the hazards of mis-communication strike again.

The outhouse was a fair distance away and I made my way over this tiny rope fence they had up which was more like 4 posts with a rope tied around it like a boxing ring. I heard yet more wolf howls. Bugger this I thought and pulled my pants down about a third of the way to the outhouse and suddenly relief. I suddenly thought oh shit it will still be here in the morning a watery frozen pool of cack. Putting that thought aside from more wolves howling and not wanting to be dragged off by the wolves I went back in.

I'd been to the outhouse earlier and it wasn't exactly very good. It was a hole with a wooden box around it so I didn't exactly miss much. In fact on that subject a mate of mine had been to a similar outhouse in South East Asia when he went in, the toilet was just a deep hole with a bit of a board and a rail to hold on to. To one side was a fairly hefty stick that looked kind of worn. As he crouched down to deposit his stool he felt something try get up his rear end. Something wet and warm. In shock he jumped up and saw a pig eating his shit, people had been using the stick to beat off the pig and poo in peace.

I awoke with a chilly face; though Salar looked completely unconcerned and unaffected by the chilly night he had spent outside. Though he did give me a few exaggerated cracks of his back to emphasise his discomfort. I asked Salar about this in the morning and he said, "Ha the problem is you do not have a Mongol nose." Feeling about 10 inches tall I explained to him that I only wanted to see not for him to sleep on the hot rocks outside. Oyunbileg and G laughed at this when it was translated back over to them. This was apparently a technique for sleeping only used by Mongolian bandits who travelled ultra-light and only bandits where supposed to know how to do this. And Salar had to be convinced with some Togrog before showing me, it wasn't much to me but it was enough to feed his family for 2 months.

For breakfast we had deep-fried in butter doughnuts more cream and some semi rancid butter of some kind. With the amount of meat we had eaten I was surprised we were not served something meatier for breakfast. I don't know perhaps something along the lines of say, Meatabix? Served in milk for breakfast. I had a moment where I imagined all the Weetabix commercials I had seen in the UK like have you had your Weetabix today? I had a feeling of an advert in Mongolia. Have you had your Meatabix today? Or the terribly annoying advert I recall where a lorry driver does the old snafu.

"It's Weetabix but made with oats." The advert would be instead slightly different to this and my own rendering.

"It's Weetabix but made with meat."

"Should have called it Meatabix."

As Mongolians scoff at people who eat vegetables and I suppose Weetabix would be considered similar to the fodder that their animals eat in my opinion.

Simon and I didn't want to leave the *ger* it was so toasty warm from Salar lighting the fire again. But nothing lasts forever as we stumbled out and got onto our horses to be led back to where we started. It wasn't that far a ride thankfully free of rivers and I was deposited back again to waving people with their big lorries nearby the camp to my XT. My XT looked a bit sorry for itself as this was the first time in weeks I hadn't ridden the XT and it felt unfamiliar in a strange way as I had had a break from it.

I was glad of the experience though as the Mongolian way of life is vanishing potentially forever overgrazing is destroying the steppe. The goats raised for cashmere eat the grass out by its roots and thus the topsoil is blown away in the wind. Rabbits did the same thing to Australia the soil blew away and the land is irreparable. It's a shame as the Mongolian nomadic way of life is possibly the last vestige of true freedom away from state control. Away from oppression and still a decent if hard life amongst the wilderness. This sort of living isn't even possible in Siberia anymore.

29: SAND, SAND AND MORE SAND

I rode back cross-country to go back to UB to rest and get back into civilisation for a while before deciding to go out on another trek. I managed to stay at a different guesthouse with the Chumbee being full for a night, which was not pleasant. For an expensive guesthouse they yet again had horrendous toilets that were filled to the brim with turds and I was assigned to a *ger* with no roof and froze all night.

I'd always wanted to see the Gobi and hear the singing sands. Andreas and Claudia had other things to do and were preparing to go for a cross-country ride. Lucky for me another guy on an Africa Twin called Andreas but from Italy turned up.

Andreas and Claudia were gone heading south to get some nice photos and we rode out of UB southwards towards the Chinese border on easy sealed tarmac roads slightly worn but nothing too serious. We stopped a few times to take photos passing a gigantic hill completely covered in head stones. I'd wondered where Mongolians buried their dead legend has it Chingis was buried in a hidden spot where 20,000 horsemen rode over the grave to hide the location.

We thought about climbing the hill but thought this might be a serious mark of disrespect, and just took photos instead, and paying our homage to the *Ovoo* a cairn like rock pile at the side of the road. By walking round it 3 times in a clockwise direction bowing and leaving a trinket of some kind. Mongolians do not believe in God. Although Mormon missionaries were common in UB, it was easy to spot them miles off, as they were the only people with clipboards, short sleeve shirts and ties. Mongolians instead believe in Shamanism that seems quite apt for the environment. They believe that there should be harmony between the earth and the sky and that they should look after nature. If they did this nature and the spirits would look after them a simple deal. If in need they would ask the spirits for help advice and solutions to problems by a Shaman going into a trance although this was risky as there might be evil sprits amongst those that approached the Shaman in his trance.

Andreas had told me about similar trances in South America. Where on a Friday night people would sit around in a mud hut and blow *Yopo* up each other's noses and sit contentedly for hours watching the colours, as there was precious little entertainment in the South American jungles. I didn't see a Shaman go into a trance though, but it did seem to us outsiders that it was an excuse to get totally stoned and get paid for it. As the Chumbee hostel owner's father was a Shaman and had become wealthy before being shot by the Russians for being a Shaman. If it didn't work then he wouldn't have gotten wealthy. Onwards and outwards we went with nothing much to see bar steppe and an odd mirror ball thing put at a junction.

I stopped to watch a single man on a horse holding a very long pole drive his cattle down a valley way with a lone dog. I felt privileged to have seen that it seemed completely effortless on his behalf. I'm sure that it is in reality quite hard work but the Mongolians and their horse expertise made it look as if it were nothing.

A few little roadblocks popped up now and again almost always occupied by leathery-faced Mongolian men in the middle of nowhere. A cobalt blue sky was above us and we generally made excellent time to Choyr where we stopped for lunch. Children and older men alike asking all sorts of questions we didn't understand swarmed us. I left Andreas to deal with them borrowing his camera to take a few choice snaps of Choyr as I had yet again lost my camera, with only my phone camera which wasn't very good. I decided to push on and take more photos and turned back to take my memory card out of his camera and give it back to him. His Africa Twin sounded dodgy and he wanted to turn back to UB while I thought I would take a small circular trek in the desert.

Though the Gobi wasn't much desert like as I had expected. Expecting a Lawrence of Arabia type entry it was mostly grasslands for quite some distance until I saw the shimmering rocky demarcation zone. Behind this dunes in the distance. The ground started going bald with bigger and bigger sand bunkers in the grass which became rocky and rough with patchy almost gravel like surface until the bunkers became the landscape.

I decided that my trek was so small that I had barely any supplies on me bar a couple bottles of water, no food or anything else. I had of course zero sand experience but had been told by Tiffany to accelerate and keep your speed up else you will bog down and be stuck forever.

I had put in my rim locks in place earlier that day in preparation for this. In that you run super low pressures and the tyre goes flat but acts as a fat footprint spreading the weight kind of like a caterpillar track. Well that is supposed to be the theory anyway but I had worn down one of the burs on a convenient rock to prevent any more punctures, which were the bane of off roaders. Outside Choyr I had let my tyres down even more. The rim locks were in theory to grip the tyre and prevent it spinning asynchronously to the wheel, which it had a high likely hood of doing so if under inflated. This if caught early is no problem, but if caught too late will drag along the tube inside the rim .The tube is held in place by the valve and it would tear the valve rendering the inner tube utterly useless and irreparable.

The Gobi isn't what you think of a desert. Gobi meaning place of little water in Mongolian, in that it starts out as grassland, which thins out into a rocky lunar type surface similar to what you would see from the photos of Mars, but with smaller rocks. This marked a sort of demarcation zone that turned into dry riverbeds and eventually the dunes right at the Chinese border.

At the first small dunes I sat quietly for a few minutes attempting to hear the singing sand the Gobi is famous for but heard nothing other than the slight sounds of the wind. Perhaps I was in the wrong place. The first few sections were remarkably easy as there were tyre tracks and the sand had been compressed a fair bit. The next bit over a small dune easy as well. I was growing in confidence and on the flatter sands was doing exactly as Tiffany had described put on the gas and you skim over the top of it sort of like a speedboat as long as you accelerate hard you won't sink. I was having a cracking time bouncing along the small sand dunes. When the bike just as I was powering out of a tricky bit of sand it had one of its turns and choked as it if were coughing on something. Power came back but I had slowed and dug the bike in deep really deep that I was in trouble.

I tried brute force to yank the bike out which only made me tired and sweaty as hell. I tried to tip the bike over but it was buried too deep and the wheels might bend if I did this, which would put me into even more trouble, so I began to dig around the bike. Unfortunately this proved to be not so good either as I dug handfuls of sand away more would spill down and fill the hole I had excavated, seeing as the dune was the size of a dump truck I estimated I would have to shift several tons of sand to even get the bike out. For a moment I panicked not knowing what to do. I had feared this in Kazakhstan around the Aral Sea and without support had decided to avoid it completely. I had a think and thought only way out of this is to get help.

I climbed a nearby high hillock and looked at the landscape the horizon was covered in heat haze and blurred so that nothing much could be seen. In the distance was a small *ger* to the north where it was slightly greener. I am scared of being lost in the desert so got my small collection of clothes and buried them while I walked towards the *ger* making a sort of a trail to the bike.

The dunes did not last long and soon I was onto the grassland still tired as this trek the bike had essentially taken me absolutely everywhere such that I didn't have to walk far at all. I stumbled towards the *ger*, knocked and there was nobody there, no horse tied to the post and thought I was in trouble again.

I decided to wait and finished off the last of my water before a boy trotted up on a horse. Through sign language and showing him my crash helmet he figured I was a motorbike rider and he went off without a word to find help. He returned with a leathery-faced darkly tanned Mongolian man on another horse that was a fair bit bigger than myself who thankfully could speak Russian and through some back and forth phrase book exchanges realised my motorbike was stuck in the sands. The words *pisok* (sand) and *moto* were said a lot. A half bottle of vodka was produced to help us consider the situation more carefully with the customary blessing to the winds.

Chuluun (I think) came with me to the bike thanks to my trail, which was easy to locate. Both of us by sheer brute force dragged the bike out and pushed it to his *ger*, which wasn't that far away. It just felt far away as I was terribly unfit. We then set about the incredibly important task of finishing the quarter bottle of vodka and the task of seeing what the problem was. A bit of jiggling on the sand covered wires and the engine oil light came on, success. Chuluun was just about to ask for a go as Mongolians will before it spluttered and died yet again. More jiggling and it started and I pumped up my tyres and left it to stand for a moment idling. I gave my small collection of sweets mostly mentos to the boy and a packet of cigarettes to Chuluun making a small cultural error of not giving him a light. Even though I do not smoke cigarettes are useful. They always make nice little icebreaker and seeing as a packet was 25p it was hardly any problem. They were way of a thank you gift. Nomads this far south don't get out much and a few mentos and chubba chups seemed to mean the world to the boy.

I said goodbye to Chuluun and his what I assume was his son with them with them saying something I couldn't understand in Mongolian that I presumed meant good luck! I limped back to Choyr but there were no mechanics there and I kept the bike running for fear of not being able to start it again. Putting petrol in just in case and splashing water over the fuel filter in case it was vapour lock, which hissed as it instantly vaporised on the hot engine casing. As I went to fill up with petrol I was motioned to stop the engine. But couldn't, they were ok with this once I paid them first to put fuel into the tank.

I met a pair of Italians on what looked like XT200s as they had thin tyres and a much thinner profile. They had just returned from the Chinese border and had attempted to smuggle their bikes into China. Apparently it is fine to ride your bike in China. It's just getting it across the border that is the difficulty as soldiers at the border will check the cargo of lorries quite carefully. In that the Chinese police are a little bit like the Russians. If they see you at some point where you are not supposed to be they will assume that because you are there you must have gotten past the prior checkpoints. And thus your paperwork must be in order so they just let you pass.

A pair Germans in 2006 had managed to cross Siberia entering Russia via Ukraine riding down to the Chinese border via Mongolia. They had enlisted some help and smuggled their bikes into China on the back of a lorry carrying bricks for $150 each. The construction around the border around 2006 had given them many places to hide and unload the bikes. With bricks looking as if it were a solid cube.

They managed to ride to the Laotian border; they were not stopped by police and were not stopped for riding on the motorways, which is illegal in China. They now have become tougher as a result and there are fewer lorries with building materials suitable to hide motorbikes within.

A similar thing exists on the Laotian border in that you park your bike half a mile from the border. Get your stamps walk back to get your bike and the customs officers are compelled to help you as they will get into trouble if they do not. This revelation seemed to kill the prospect of riding all the way to Hong Kong where I could leave the bike permanently. Alas this turned out to be unviable and for starters I did not want to have a temperamental bike in China serving only to attract the wrong sort of attention the kind I did not want.

So I limped back to UB my desert adventure cut shorter than I would have liked. Pulling into the Chumbee, the XT completely grey now from the dust and sand. I had the hostel owner make a few calls on my behalf to look for a mechanic to have a look.

This involved following a mechanic on XT500 around town while he fixed other people's bikes. We would be riding along and be flagged down by people at the side of the road. He would have a look at the bike fix it with something off his tool bag and then ride off. I followed him out to a shantytown on the edge of UB I could just about make out the lemon slice building at the base of Sukebaator square. We pulled into a yard completely full of bikes piled high and stacked in shipping containers in various states of repair. With quite large numbers of XT225s piled up in a corner and some exotic bikes 2008 R1s and 1000RR FireBlades I wondered where they used them since the road in from Altanbulag / Sukebaator was quite rough.

A mechanic in one corner was testing engines in a corner by starting them with a welder and to the other end another mechanic was changing tyres somehow not using tyre levers. He just put his hand into the side of the tyre and pulled against his foot and the tyre came off in his hand along with half the spokes. For the XT it was nothing serious it turned out to be a wire which had snapped inside the plastic sheath which only revealed itself when one end of the wire was pulled and it slipped out of the plastic covering frayed bit from the inside. Also that the multimeter was giving erratic readings on the battery when running, a quick rummage around found a reg rec which didn't have the same number of pins which was made to fit and the bike ran fine from there on in. 10,000 Togrog and 5000 as a gesture of good will for their help and I was riding back to UB. Though when I say that it sounds easy in that it wasn't in that the difficulty was that the reg rec on the XT was hidden under the tail bit just above the taillight. Which meant removing my side racks, the plastics on the sides then the pillion grabs which I had not removed as they made really handy bits to attach straps to and tie things down to.

185

After this the removal of the rack then you got to the reg rec. Though after a moment of deliberation I realised I could have simply undone 2 screws to get to it. Many riders nowadays are completely cynical about the hiding of parts here and there. In that you *have* to remove so many parts to get at parts that need to be repaired. Although Honda, Kawasaki, Yamaha, Suzuki et al may claim mass centralisation and or performance boosts and a more compact frame. Some things are impossible to remove (nearly) and make you think it has been designed that way purposely to annoy you or to get you to bring it to a main dealer. The VFR750 is a typical example of this. The single sided swing arm for the rear wheel is designed for endurance racing. It is single sided so that rear wheel changes can be quick. Except that somebody in Japan thought it would be a good idea to put the exhaust pipe and link pipe in the way of the wheel hub meaning the exhaust pipe had to be removed to replace the rear wheel each time you got a puncture. If I had to do that each time on my XT I'd have had to carry hundreds of gaskets. This design completely defeats the point of having the extra weight and complexity of the single sided swinging arm.

This is true for engine work too. There are bits that are just too small for people of normal sized hands to manage. Although the XT was not too bad for this since it was old school technology. Modern bikes are tiny in their proportions often requiring tiny hands to get things our like spark plugs or air filters. The kinds of people who were generally employed as models for hamburgers and porn films to make the 'meat' look bigger than it actually is. Though some Japanese things are insane in their design anyway like cam chain tension springs. Some Japanese bloke one day thought ah I know this tiny weak spring will hold the cam chain in place. Perhaps I am far too cynical.

30: CHINGIS RIDES AGAIN

I got back to UB just in time for Nadeem festival starting and it became impossible to find a place to stay. Although of course there is always the backup of putting up the tent I generally wanted to avoid that. I only had one night in the Chumbee. Here I met the Bavarian bikers Andi and Simon also two other guests of the hostel who came from Holland Ingrid, Matilda, and Euan who was a kiwi. The Germans had just made it to UB where they would turn back as they didn't want to do the Amur highway. Also as quirk the Germans could not exit via Korea, as Germany never signed an international agreement in 1931 accepting IDPs. They had effectively reached the bit where they would turn round and do the mind numbing roads out of Russia and back home.

It was the weirdest of weird things. Ingrid looked identical to one of my ex work colleagues one called Jackie. She let me ramble of for a good few minutes probably not realising I was speaking to her. I asked her what she was doing here only to be spoken back to in a European accented English making me go purple with embarrassment. She quickly hatched a plan involving me finding helmets at the Oasis and the German bikers and I taking the girls and Euan up to a remote village to watch the Nadeem festival countryside style.

This involved a mission to Oasis guesthouse to get helmets combat filtering the 6km out of the city through heavy traffic without any protective gear for myself bar my gloves. This experience felt oddly liberating in that a motorbike career of being good and keeping my helmet on always restricted your view to a slit, which you peered out of. The visibility was excellent and without a jacket my forearms got strange tan marks but the wind from riding like this was glorious. Combat filtering or attack filtering is something pretty silly, which we do in the UK, in heavy traffic it is prudent to slow down. Combat filtering is filtering at high speed through dense traffic, it was dangerous but it felt good to be alive even though this kind of riding may have stopped this being the case.

The Oasis café where I bumped again into Andreas about to leave Mongolia for good via the Altai, whom I mentioned Andi and Simon were his big fans. 5-10 years ago Andreas had written an adventure biking book that was the best seller in Germany. This book was virtually the German version of Mondo Enduro, except flush with cash. Oasis café could only rustle up two helmets so Ingrid and Matilda had one each but Euan my passenger didn't which was a little disconcerting, kill myself ok, kill my pillion no.

187

We went out of UB towards a town in the North through a road between the power station and the airport. This was fun chasing two big BMWs with 200% more cc than me with more experienced riders than me with a pillion sans helmet on the back. Needless to say this got quite exciting as the road deteriorated into rubble. We arrived in the small town that I can't tell you the name of as I forgot, where there was the ending of the festivities. The archery had finished and the wrestling was in its final match. The prior year champion a massive mountain of a man who looked like a sumo wrestler judiciously guarding an enormous plate of Mongolian doughnuts. While after we were invited into the judges' tent for no reason other than we were the only westerners at the event. I even managed to meet another Hong Kong person who was Ingrid's friend from Rotterdam who was constantly mistaken for a Mongolian exactly the same experiences as I'd had myself.

But this was the start of a love affair between bikers; Ingrid back home in Holland had a CB750. Andi and Ingrid were getting really close. Although from behind it was impossible to see if anything was going on while riding. They wandered off by themselves and started to leave the 4 of us behind. Simon turned out to be an out of work helicopter pilot while Andi turned out to be doing a 4 month trip combining both of his vacation periods for 2 years together and thus was being paid to do this trip. I had thought of doing that myself but circumstances made this impossible.

Euan vanished and we ended up riding back without him. After traipsing up a hill where we suspected the horseracing was and I was booted out of the Chumbee hostel when we got back to UB. Though strangely I managed to get back first out riding them on the rocky roads. The XT can still give BMW a run for its money even though it is a bike that cost 1/10th the cost of the BMWs add in the accessories and luggage it was 1/25th of the cost. While Ingrid found me another extremely new hostel called the Nomadic way run by Bujinlham Daramjaw who forever after was called Bridget. Since we attempted to call her Bujilam and got it wrong plenty of times much to her chagrin.

This was the second time I'd been booted out of a hostel. However the Nomadic way was a short walk away where there was room for me and my pile of junk. Although the XT would have to be parked in a secure car park some distance away it was nice. It was an apartment except that the bedrooms were filled with bunk beds making it into a sort of hostel. I'd made dinner plans with the Germans, Ingrid and Matilde and had some time to kill and decided to stick my things in the wash. This was actually a cheaper and better condition hostel with free things that cost money in the Chumbee though of course we are talking Mongolian money that in any case was pennies difference. It was however nice to be getting a bit more luxury than I had been experiencing for a while.

I had also decided to shave and say goodbye to the beard that I had been growing for the sheer hell of it. Generally my personal grooming being generally completely alone on the road had gone to hell. After I did it I realised why every Mongolian in Mongolia was treating me like a bum, as only bums had such beards. I visited the same shops and restaurants and they treated me completely differently it was now ok to pay after I ate; certain things on the menu suddenly became available to order. I would suddenly become transparent to cops. It was mildly odd that Mongolian men (other than beggars) were cleanly shaved. Even in the countryside with no obvious source of water the men were almost always perfectly cleanly shaved I do not know how. In the Nomadic way as I cleaned up and got dressed in the second dorm I met Doug, perhaps the most entertaining person I had met so far on the trip.

31 : DOUG

Here I met the self-styled theosophical professional backpacker Doug. At first glance was unconventional. For starters he was a lot older than anybody else and reminded me of myself, but older. A virtual expatriate Canadian Doug had effectively left Canada to travel the world and had only returned 7 years prior to this moment to renew his Canadian passport. 17 years straight travelling meant he had some stories to tell, some highlights were the sky burials of Western Sichuan and funeral pyres in India.

Most remarkably one evening in the hostel with the other backpackers named Rob, Leanne, Crystal and Christian we sat around drinking beers asking what we each did. Teacher, doctor, gap year types, me the adventurer and the only person left to answer was Doug.

"So what do you do?" I asked.

"I don't work anymore." He replied

"So what did you do?"

"Oh I worked as a double for things."

"Like what, oh I was the back of various actors in various TV shows."

"Oh like who?" Doug had worked on several remade versions of classic Sci-Fi as the hands back of the head and feet of a certain actor. So when you saw a hand fondle the boob or buttock of another actor or actress say Tricia Helfer it wasn't the actual actors hand it was his. His favourite story was that he had even sat inside a tank of KY jelly for 12 hours while they filmed certain sequences. Doug and I got along as unconventional people who don't fit anywhere. Doug never fit into Canada and was unconventional I felt I didn't really fit as a white collar and we got along stunningly.

We met with the Germans and Ingrid and Matilda and had dinner whereby Ingrid ordered the safest thing on the menu spaghetti. Which looked pretty awful and much Chingis vodka was consumed far too much but when the stuff is 10,000 Togrog a litre you can't complain. Although your liver and stomach lining might.

Ingrid and Matilda would end up going on a big bike trip down to the Altai with the Germans as the helmets I found them could be rented for a whole week. As they vanished off this left me Doug, Crystal, Christian, Rob and Leanne to go see the Nadeem festival and keep the beer factories in business. Crystal was terribly naïve having never seen the viral video known as 2 girls one cup, or the worse one guy one cup. For those who haven't seen it don't, you cannot bleach your memory and mind. We even managed to find some Muppets 2 girls one-cup parody that spoilt her childhood memories of Jim Henderson's Muppets forever. While Rob a medical student who had recently finished his final exam showed us some disturbing pictures of the parasite Billy Connelly joked about the one that swims up a stream of urine. Mr Goatse has nothing on these photos.

I spent most of the 3 day Nadeem festival with Doug we connected in a certain way as misfits leading different lives. And not seeming to fit into normal society whatever that was. Though around this time Mongolia was loaded with tourists, tourist tourists. Ok for sure Doug and me were effectively tourists too but these proper tourists were something else. He always had a travel story to tell nothing to belittle you or make your own travelling experiences belittled but some really good stories, such as sky burials where he had witnessed it a month before arriving in Ulaan Baatar. In western Sichuan in China as with Tibet the ground is frozen solid permafrost all year round so the dead cannot be buried. There is also no wood so the only option is to mash the bodies and bones up by hand and feed it to birds of prey.

Normally somewhere touristy people will stop in front of others in the process of taking photos. Or walk behind people taking photos and be ushered a thanks for being considerate. In Mongolia it seemed those manners were left behind in their home countries. When we went to watch the unveiling of the 9 white-tailed banners that Doug commented that the 9 tails war banner of the Mongols looked identical to the warcraft banner of the Orcs. There were tons of pushy tourists with their cameras literally pushing in to get a good photo while we stood there just happy to see what was going on. People change their behaviour when they know they are being filmed or are having their photo taken, and thus it's not always a good thing to be doing this.

Confident that we would wait for the horses to pass us, the tourists chased it like an accident solicitor after an ambulance. Such that a wave of tourists hit us knocking us over. A pushy fat French woman even stepped on my hand and shot me an incredibly dirty look and said something probably abusive in French to us if it were my fault. I got up and dusted myself off and the wave continued onwards. We got the last laugh though as the French woman continued to lumber on and pushed over a police officer onto his backside while starring into her camera. She suddenly turned into the sweetest and most apologetic of people, but the policeman thinking I was Mongolian had seen what had happened to me and Doug nodded his head solemnly as the policeman reached for his cuffs.

Watching the games here and there with me buying local tickets that were 10% the cost of official foreign tickets. This included the opening festival, anklebone shooting archery but no horse riding as that happened outside the city and it's not really possible to watch this, as the course was 32 km long.

We were slightly under whelmed at the Nadeem festival in that when we first went to the stadium we walked past it without realising it was the stadium. The stadium was no bigger than a conference division football ground and was less than 3 stories high the train yard nearby looked bigger. We went inside and sat on a partially flooded spectator area on solid concrete blocks splayed around as seating. The under whelming continued as the opening ceremony began which was little more than a few people stood around dancing waving pink and yellow banners around and included an angel from the heavens who gave Chingis his divine rights. Young children making tall human pyramids and also young children and old men alike doing horse stunts that would not look out place at a cowboy rodeo. Though granted the atmosphere was somewhat subdued by the heavy rain and strong dusty winds and a sea of umbrellas covered part of my view. The Mongolians didn't care though as they just sat in the rain getting wet, they are obviously made of tougher stuff.

All I could say was that TVB (a Hong Kong TV channel) had done its research very well. The costumes that the Mongols wore bore incredibly similarity to those of the bad guys in TVB period dramas.

We did see the Mongolian wrestling final though over three days, which ended up going well into the night at the finals. The men would wear chest less shirts which legend had it was to prevent women from entering the games, which covered their arms, pointy boots and trunks. The wrestling was almost like sumo in that they would spend a long time dancing giving ritual thanks to the spirits of the hawk holding their arms aloft like school boys playing aeroplane. If anything besides the soles of their feet touched the ground a wrestler would lose, there were no second chances. It seemed kind of harsh that a wrestler could have trained all year for this and be out of the knockout tournament in a matter of seconds. It wasn't about size or strength but a huge element of skill as the finalists were a skinny bloke and a man with a massive belly. However wrestling for the most part seemed to be rather relaxed, almost as if it were cricket at the end of the knockout stage. The wrestlers would do their sumoesq ritual thanks to the sprits for a while. Then they would grapple leaning on each other until they got bored then breaking up then leaning on each other again until they got bored or cold again. It felt like cricket you could go off have a 5-course meal and return and not have missed any of the action. Perhaps they were tired as none of the moves such as leg grabs or pushes seemed to happen at the final, which was a bit uninspiring. I half wondered if they were just doing this wondering how long they could keep it up, talking to each other.

"Look do you think we should finish up and go home now?"

"Nah lets just lean again for a few more minutes I'm avoiding the wife."

The larger fatter bloke won to an ecstatic cheer from the crowd probably after the skinny bloke got bored and there was much dancing and presenting of awards. Oddly enough as we sat and waited for a chance to exit people around us seemed to be discussing the final match at great depth, when to our westernised eyes all it seemed to be was just leaning.

The whole festival also seemed incredibly commercialised. There wasn't a moment at the stadium where you did not have the opportunity to buy food or some tourist tat coca cola or a western branded snack of some kind. The sellers seemed unhappy at their jobs in that his ancestors had once been part of the golden horde. They had carved out the biggest empire on earth and yet here he was just a cola salesman.

The anklebone shooting was a tad more amusing a small box would be placed about 3 or 4 metres from a man sitting on a stool. He would flick his wrist to flick a sheep anklebone to try and knock the anklebone off. This in itself wasn't amusing as they again took a very long time to take their shot. The highlight of this was the throat singing when a target was hit. A virtual choir of high-pitched throaty voices and caterwauling would be sung or chanted that you wouldn't hear anywhere else (except maybe a Mongolian TV advert). Which bellowed through the room reverberating off the walls and almost sounding like a Buddhist monastery chanting session but without the tapping on the hollow blocks.

We also managed to find a microbrewery where the band Altan-Ulrag played. Although they only played a few songs this was an impressive experience a mix traditional Mongolian folk music combined with rock. They didn't miss a beat. Although I nearly did as this venue called IK Mongol served German food and I had ordered metre long sausages off the menu. It was expensive for Mongolia but we thought what the hell. I had expected them to be curled up sausages and thin to make up the length. But these sausages were something else as thick as my wrist and lay out in one long piece and to be eaten WITHOUT a knife and fork. It took me over an hour to consume that much meat though the 4 litre tankers of unfiltered beer helped. That was most definitely not like Oktoberfest beer. Oktoberfest beer is heavily watered down this stuff was extra strong 7.5% stuff yet nicely smooth at the same time.

Doug left a couple of days later on a bus to the Chinese border after sharing information how to obtain a visa for China circumventing the hoops that the Chinese government make you jump though. I was sad to see him go as I lost my drinking and hang out partner for now as he agreed to meet up with me in China later, as he had to do visa runs back and forth. I wonder what he would see on his next trip to Laos and Cambodia. He'd seen all sorts of things you were not supposed to see. Low caste Indian people cracking open the skulls of people being cremated to prevent skulls from bursting. Indian beggars who would share out their proceeds communally. Bodies floating down the Ganges River. Human bodies being cut up to be fed to vultures at sky burials things few people would ever see. I wondered if it was worth it, in that your normal person working in his or her own

193

country leading a normal life would never see this sort of thing, in effect it was experience or comfort. He had chosen experience I do not hold him in contempt for his own personal choice.

Rob, Leanne, Crystal and Christian left the same day leaving me alone Christian and Crystal went to the Gobi while Rob and Leanne went to Irkutsk.

Although we went through the usual formalities of swapping email addresses and names so that we could find each other on facebook I doubted that I would ever see them again and even if I did it would feel different. That was the other side of the double edged sword of meeting people in that if you meet people it is inevitable that you one day have to say goodbye to them. It is the same with bikers, in that the group I left in the South were a big diverse group whom I did manage to see again but many had died in accidents and thus I never really did get to see them again.

Though the hostel had new guests two Frenchmen who were making a film about the nomads and Euan from before along with his German buddy whom he met on the train. Tobias who had been suffering from extreme wanderlust as the Germans put it. They each had their little projects. Euan was attempting to circumnavigate the planet comparing each method of transport with aircraft and Tobias who was running away from German military service and thus little happened between.

Though Tobias had had a rough time in UB getting his cameras stolen by a thief with a razor blade who cut it out of his bag and replaced his camera with a brick. Although I don't condone what happened, it must have taken quite a bit of skill to do that. To add to the woe Tobias had been mugged by a huge Mongolian man who demanded $100 or be beaten up and managed to run away. He just wanted to leave UB as soon as possible and enlisted my help along with his friend Michael a French guy who was staying at the German hostel. At which I made a little discovery that Ulaan Baator had a Nazi bar and this set the scene for another little mission to find the said bar and have a look. A few days so later a guy called Rick (This is not his real name and I changed this to protect his identity) joined the hostel but insisted on being called Richard (again not his real name). Again with fresh victims we did the old drinking while asking questions until it came to Richard.

"So what do you do?"

"I don't work anymore."

"So what did you do?"

"Oh I worked as a double for various things." This began to sound familiar almost déjà vu in fact.

"Like what?" I probed.

"Oh I worked as a stunt ass." At which everybody in the hostel spat out their beers stunned into a silence the kind that would occur if Turkey could talk and Bernard Mathews walked into the room. Or a certain Mr Glitter walked into a room of parents offering to baby-sit. In that moment of silence everybody was stunned, civilisations rose and fell, suns were born and died, ice ages thawed.

"A what!?"

"A stunt ass." Now to those who don't know what a stunt ass is, it's quite simple in porn films the male actors are always paid less. This is completely different in gay porn films quite often heterosexual porn actors will be asked to perform gay for pay. I.e. heterosexual actors would be asked to film a porn film for a gay audience. Several famous porn stars famous in the heterosexual world started off as gay for pay porn stars a quick search on the Internet will find you who as I don't want to mention it here. However sometimes you get a really famous male porn actor who wants the money from gay for pay. But doesn't actually want to 'bottom' and can't bring himself to go through with it so enter or is that received Rick. So with some extremely clever camera trickery the camera is stopped and the stunt ass is bought in to 'receive' as the bottom for the scene and again be switched out for the money shot. This I suppose makes sense as I assume it would hurt like buggery. He did however listen attentively to my Turkish border story and remarked comically.

"Well when a bloke shoots at me arse I normally just wipe it off." Rick had done this in the 90s at the height of the demand for a couple of years. He had made enough money doing this in a few years to retire and live in Asia for the rest of his life. He put it this way:

"In that you guys working in offices you are getting metaphorically done in the rear end by your bosses. You sell your bodies and minds to your bosses for a pittance. I sold my ass for an awful lot more who is the smarter one?" He did have a point as he was 36 and had been retired for a long time having travelled for the last *fourteen* years. What struck me as most surprising is when Crystal (who had come back) didn't believe him. He would search online for a few minutes and find a film he played the double for and pull down his pants exposing his bum. It really was true it was his bum on screen 'receiving' it was identical perhaps a little out of shape but it was his rear end though I didn't particularly want to press the point and investigate in great depth. I was in Mongolia and it would be incredibly strange to be asked so what did you do in Mongolia then? People would expect something horse like something to do with the countryside but it would be very bad if I said well I watched hours and hours of gay porn to check out this Rick fellow I met for a short period, what sort of traveller would that make me?

Rick did have some bitterness though in that in the industry meaning the San Fernando Valley in California. There would often be held porn star awards Oscars if you like. Though perhaps that should be stiffies? (I checked online on my return and they really do exist). Categories exist for best anal scene or best bukkake scene though how on earth you can get an award for such a thing is beyond me. An anathema Rick had had was that the person he *portrayed* in various films had received awards for their on screen performances, even though it was him who was doing the actually down and dirty work. Rick was a bit bitter about that, in that it seems in many big production studios' and firms' for some reason there is a complete lack of acknowledgement. Just how ruthless is that?

Richard wasn't half as fun as Doug though he did help me to find the Nazi bar in UB, which turned out to be nearby the Chinese embassy. Though he refused to go in and left after a day at the hostel to go on some kind of jeep tour to the Gobi. With cabin fever reaching terminal levels I went in and it wasn't that impressive. While the one I had been into nearly a decade ago in Austria had hot suggestively dressed women in Nazi uniforms with a booth near the door where you could buy replica Reich marks. Which was well worth the hiked up price of the beer to be served by tall blonde women in tight leather cat suits as you quaffed your bier. This bar had a few pictures of the leaders of the third Reich, some steel tankers with Swastikas engraved into Nazi beer mats and beer that cost triple what it cost anywhere else.

Though once some of the crowd discovered I was not Mongolian one of them approached me and lifted his sleeve to reveal a swastika and tried to intimidate me. After not rising up to the bait several times I they left.

In Mongolia there is severe anti China sentiment. Everywhere I looked there was graffiti around which said 'Fuck China'. Chinese construction workers were regularly harassed from what I saw. There was similar sentiment towards the Russians and Koreans. People would have prejudice against their neighbouring countries just because they were different.

In Russia I'd been told that Mongolians were all thieves and scum, while in Mongolia I had heard that Mongolians thought Russians were all drunks and thieves too. While both the Mongolians and Russians hated the Chinese. In that everybody had an uninformed opinion of each country when as an outsider travelling through those countries I could see that most of it was patently false, though I didn't get to see the view from China yet. I imagined that everybody hated China as the Chinese were making money and it was partly in jealously in that in Siberia and Mongolia everything seemed to be made in China. The economic prosperity did not seem to be happening in Siberia or Mongolia and this was their reasoning for the dislike of their neighbours amongst other things. Though the roots of this probably went deeper than you'd think. Mongolia has almost always been occupied in some shape or form since the Empire of Chingis collapsed. At around 1600 the Manchu armies occupied Mongolia, they gained a brief period of independence from 1911 when the Qing dynasty collapsed for a period of nine years. Then came the white army refugees, who pillaged UB proclaiming to be the 9th reincarnation of Chingis then in 1921 the Bolsheviks, came and made Mongolia a satellite state of the USSR.

Though I put a caveat in this for the black market, it really is called the black market where the people in there REALLY are thieves. Bags cut open with razor blades in an extremely stealthy fashion were normal. Gangs would stand by the gates waiting for obvious tourists to stroll in and rob them blind sliding in slowly behind them cutting their bags opening and passing it to their compatriots and playing completely innocent. Go on search me I don't have it when they were caught afterwards or even in the act.

People upon seeing white tourists approach would turn signs over for a higher price so that tourists would often be charged double or triple the normal price. Though again this was a case of pennies as the Mongolian currency was so incredibly weak. So weak I found that nobody in the world wanted to change it bar the money changes at the border points and even then at a terrible exchange rate.

Even though the black market was dangerous and full of shysters I liked the place, you could literally buy anything. Well as long as China exported it. I nearly bought myself a Mongol horse riders rain suit since they seemed to keep the rider perfectly dry. Alas it was non breathable which is bad, in that you don't get wet by the rain instead you get wet from your own sweat not evaporating and pooling into your clothing. Police bike boots used to be like that. I remember in Plymouth being friends with a bike cop who described at the end of a long hard shift on a scorching summers day he would remove his boots and be able to pour out his sweat, YUCK. I didn't want that happening to me all over.

But the sight of Mongolians buying and selling haggling. The smells. The sounds the bartering, the un-refrigerated desiccated samples of mystery meat. Even a small animal trading area where large groups of men would pick out an unfortunate sheep or a goat. Picking wasn't pointing and saying I'll take that one, men in their *dels* possibly their Sunday best would leap into the small enclosures and have a good feel of the animals to feel if they were fat enough to buy. In almost an identical fashion people in the UK would do to a melon or a loaf of bread. Sometimes they would take it away, a Mongolian take on a take away? Other times there would be a slaughter there and then, but not how we would think of slaughter. The way we do it in the west and Muslim countries is that we cut the throats of animals with or without stunning via electricity or by gassing the animals. I do not want to get into the politics and or ethics of food production and slaughter. Effectively if you want meat, animals have to die. So until scientists have made a cost effective version of laboratory grown meat there is no other choices animals have to die, simple as that.

A couple of boys or teenagers would hold the goat down while it struggled to be free sensing its fate attempting to stand up and break free from its current position. The boys held a pair of legs in each hand and put a knee to the neck while one produced a greasy dark knife from a small holster secreted in his clothing. One of them would then make a thin cut into the chest much to the protest of the goat who was in a do or die moment in struggling to free itself. A boy with small hands would reach in and squeeze the heart to stop it beating. He would remove his hand, which was covered in a sort of reddish mucus. The goat or sheep would then suddenly stop struggling kick a few final spasms and then be still and dead after a few moments.

Slaughter was done in such a manner to preserve the blood and to keep the blood in the body and thus make the meat more succulent. Even though Mongolia and Ulaan Baator was a place of plenty the Nomadic heritage of the people meant that they rarely wasted anything. There was virtually no blood spilt and the people performing the slaughter seemed confident enough to be wearing their best silk *dels*. The goat was taken to a patch of ground to the side where an old woman perhaps in her seventies would prepare it though preparation wasn't quite as you would expect. It involved holding a gap in the carcass open and throwing in hot rocks from a fire and covering it in something I couldn't identify. I came back a few hours later and watched them use a blowtorch to remove the hair. The gut was then cleaned out of the rocks previously stuffed in and the carcass was put above a coal pit to cook while the men went off shopping. It was totally impressive experience that I doubt you would see in many places in the western world. This is a real Mongolian barbecue the stuff you find in restaurants in UB and in other countries like so many foods is an invention. I remember when some people bought fortune cookies to Hong Kong and the people there were surprised it had bits of paper inside it.

These markets are actually quite dangerous places though if you blend in like I always manage to do they are quite safe. But the appearance of cameras means you pretty much put a flashing sign on your head-stating tourist! Touts would harass obvious tourists relentlessly even to the verge of threatening behaviour. Even the Mongolian tourist board which half heartedly push boxes of leaflets at each wild Mongolia trekking agency had stark warnings about the markets.

32: BIKERS LOVE STORY, GOODBYE MONGOLIA

The Germans had been away for a while taking Ingrid and Matilda out of UB and had been unseen for a while. The Germans, Ingrid and Matilda came back and Ingrid had gotten even closer and in the hostel. She put a sheet over the open doorway and were noisy all night. Pretty much forcing me to go outside and spend the evening drinking until the morning. In effectively 2 weeks they had again circumnavigated Mongolia with passengers. Such that Andi and Ingrid decided to ride back to Europe together a love story made in bikers heaven perhaps?

Though not before grudging letting me have a go on their BMWs that I immediately did not like. They were heavy wide and very tall which seemed to be the antithesis of bike design. The lack of feeling through the front via the Norman Hassock copied suspension where BMW apparently waited for the patent to expire rather than pay royalties, meant you could feel nothing. The fuel injection meant that you felt disconnected from the engine. I poured some power on expecting results, the engine span a bit faster, but I imagined the computer controlling the FI system thought NEIN and declined to let me have any extra power. Andi however very much liked my XT in that it seemed light and could be thrown around with little effort and it was missing the vulnerability of the airhead design of the BMWs. Though the airhead design is quite clever (Tiffany's GS850 has this too) in that with the twin airhead there was no need for waterproof boots as the air that came off the cooling fins was warm enough to dry your boots quickly.

I felt that the Germans had made a fairly big trek and if they can do it on heavy BMWs 1250s two up with a ton of equipment then so can the XT. Which led to me packing properly this time. Buying 2x5 litre bottles for water, a 5-litre can for petrol and another backpack stuffed with food and medical supplies as well as a print out of useful Mongolian phrases and several bottles of Chingis brand vodka to curry favour if I had to. Lucky for me the hostel had a good map that showed the paved roads and the track roads through Mongolia, which I made my plan.

A small diversion to Khustain Nuruu to see the *takhi* in one of the areas they have been successfully introduced back into. As the *takhi* actually became extinct except in a few German zoos at some point in the 1990s. Then over to Khovsgol Lake, Altai, Jarglan UB, a simple little round trek. All at cities which had airports, which meant if I got hurt I could buy my way, back to UB and buy myself a flight back to Berlin or Seoul. I went back out the city past the power station and onto the other paved road that adjoined on the entry to UB or so I thought. I managed to make good time to get to the edge of Khustain Nuruu, which was a small park just south of UB. The going was fairly easy nothing more than just a bit of loose soil but infinitely better than deep mud of the road to Irkutsk. As I was heading west brilliant beams of slanted sunshine greeted me as I made my way over the plains into the nearby park. A small easy river crossing that was surprisingly deep and fast flowing in the middle was powered through and I soon caught a glimpse of the *takhi* horses.

They generally stood still in small clusters mere dots on the landscape but easy to spot as the young horses were a pale white colour even though the adults are a dusty brown colour. To my eyes they looked odd, odd in that they did not look how you may think a horse may look say a horse in the Grand National race. But they looked much rougher and wilder. Slightly shorter stockier and with a maine that looked rough like an upturned broom almost as if it were a cow with its shorter head. You could never make a why the long face joke about them. It was almost as if somebody had painted a zebra into this dusty colour. As I approached they all stood and looked at me as some sort of intruder but the steppe was a bit rougher and standing up on the pegs to keep my balance at slow speed I got remarkably close. About 50 metres maybe less and could see the small almost toy like mini white *takhi* young horses though these seemed to be in the process of changing colour too from the pure white.

I rode north-westerly from here on again over easy steppe mingled with small loose stones where it proved easier to ride by the side of the established tracks. As the crisscrossing tracks meant that the tyre tracks were constantly disturbed and you would have that loose internal organ feeling. Apparently in the Mongol empire Mongol couriers who rode massive distances wrap their middle in super tight sashes to stop their organs moving around and thus death. I was soon out of the park as it is comparatively tiny and back onto the last of the sealed road.

Moron where the road abruptly ended and turned into gravel track for a short few metres which then turned to hard pack earth with trails leading this way and that. I stopped wondering which way it was to go waiting for a while until a minibus / converted van came across and asked them where they were going, eventually one of them was going to Moron and I followed them until the tracks petered down to just two which were going the same direction. I pulled into Moron pretty late and noticed it was actually a fairly modern city although many people lived in single story huts in the shadow of a nearby mountain. Internet cafés, hotels, restaurants were all common here. I was disappointed really in that I had wanted more of what I saw in Terej. But Terej was actually slightly artificial too.

First port of call was a local bar where again there was bike testing where my XT was comparatively high tech and many people sitting on the bike.

A small crowd developed and they wondered whom the bike belonged to as I blended in perfectly but I was happy for them to sit and look at the bike and for some of them to have a ride around. The XT was a hit to the guys I let ride, considering the bikers there had some seriously rotten bikes with steering so notchy you had to go over a bump to be able to steer I didn't even think this was possible. Wheels with a third (or more!) of the spokes missing, completely missing brakes, exhaust down pipes that just vanished though oddly the chrome on the bikes was kept immaculate.

Seeing as I had a ton of food and a ton of water I filled up at the petrol station near the market area where it was noticeably more expensive at 1300 a litre (woo hoo a couple of pennies more expensive) and rode out of town to camp to deplete some of my food reserves to lighten the bike you see.

The morning was slightly chilly even though it was overcast during the night so that no stars could be seen. I'm pretty sure a few horsemen visited me in the night. On that note I had always seen plenty of men riding horses but in Mongolia never saw a woman riding a horse or for that matter a motorbike. The women in Mongolia are hard as nails the land makes them that way, but it was an absence that I only just realised. Riding through the tracks was easy as it was dry. I could understand the difficulty riding here if it rained, and I was kicking up lots of dust it was worn grassland and uphill for quite a while with the odd camel punctuating my journey here and there and the odd herdsman in the distance who waved to me.

I had decided to go to Hatgal a fishing village on the shores of Khovsgol lake, the tracks thinned to one or two all going north, and it wasn't really something I could miss. A small wooden hut village that looked like it was Russian more than Mongolian and I could have mistaken it easily for Russia if it were not for the Mongolian flag and all the horses around. It was so like Siberia that they even thought of everything including the millions of mosquitoes and black flies as well as a little bonus. Black fly are utter buggers, they are unlike mosquitoes. Mosquitoes breed in swamps and still fetid water and DEET masks your presence. While Black fly DEET actually attracts the damned things and to boot the things lay eggs in running water. Though it wasn't as if I had any DEET though, but they made a huge mess of my visor and clothing requiring some scraping when I got back to UB. The Black fly is probably why the Mongolians around here all smoked as the flies were like cold air and would get into tiny spaces. The traditional usually purple silk or felt *dels* the Mongols wore in the countryside seemed incredibly vulnerable to black fly not to mention lacking in body armour or abrasive resistance, but that's going a bit safety nazi.

201

I managed to bump into the French girls here again whom I'd had a party with in the Chumbee hostel as they were setting off for a trek up one side of the lake. I remembered how much the other horse ride had hurt my knees and spine and declined. I followed them for a few miles on the XT but turned around when they crossed a river where only the top half of the horse was visible. Another night was spent here in a rotten guesthouse hostel type thing. I'd generally been spoilt in that accommodation was so cheap in Mongolia there was little need to camp such that for a very long time I had had a roof over my head and a bed to call my own. The previous night had seemed terribly spartan and uncomfortable in my tent cheap yes but compared to modern comforts it was rough and uninviting. Walter, Andreas and Hannes had all said that they bought tents and camping equipment but camping was for emergencies only I suppose I saw their point of view now.

I made it back to Moron and filled up again and stocked up with provisions as it was not possible to go south on a motorbike at least that it what I was told anyway. I headed west to go the 160 miles to where I could turn south to a town called Altai, except I never made it. I rode out crossed some dry rivers and some easy shallow streams which were no more than half a foot deep at the worst but still fast flowing I rode down a stony track preferring it to the soil as the edges of the ruts would crumble and make you slide uncomfortably to one side. I kept going and stopped to make some lunch and put my foot down which sunk not a little but an awful lot ridiculously the XT got stuck in a swampy bit. I looked around and it was patently ridiculous as there was no swamp anywhere around bar a car sized swampy bit to one side of the road where I was and had ridden into. Swamps are bad in that they are always easier to get into than out of, like a bad marriage or asymmetric wars like Vietnam. I was stuck and was so close to the edge that I thought the old trick of tipping the bike over then dragging it might bend the wheels that would put me in a world of trouble. I tried rocking it back and forth even attaching a ratchet strap to a nearby rock but the bugger wouldn't shift. I sat nonplussed at what to do and had a think about it, and thought I would have to find some Nomads again to help me out. I decided to make myself a cup of coffee before wandering off to a *ger* I could make out a few miles away about the size of my fingernail at arms length.

While waiting for the water to boil I looked up and in the brilliant blue sky saw a solitary airliner leaving brilliant white contrails across the otherwise empty sky. I wondered what everybody was thinking onboard looking at the nearly featureless open steppe. I didn't suppose they could see my situation. For just a moment I thought back to the last time I had taken a flight. A warm cabin, on demand entertainment, 3 square meals and as many snacks as you wanted. The entertainment of attempting to get the telephone number of one of the female cabin crew. The actual travelling via flying was incredibly lazy in that all responsibility for movement and control was delegated to the pilots. I snapped out of this pretty quickly though in that this trip was to try something different. Travelling like that in an airliner made the world that is huge seem small and insignificant. Whereas I'd sacrificed comforts for this and generally you do not travel overland if comfort is your priority. It seems odd in that people will travel all over yet not want to forsake their home comforts. I'd been on a guided tour of China before where we travelled everywhere in an air conditioned bus ate at restaurants that served exactly the same food each and every meal. To counter act this highly linear form of travel I often went out for walks by myself into the non-touristy areas.

The coffee was pretty awful like all my coffee while I was preparing it a couple of Mongolians, boys really turned up on a bike and watched. I asked them for some help and they came and tugged the bike a few inches through the muddy bit and sat back on their bike and sped off. I was a bit annoyed at that, until they came back with two bottles of vodka to think it over we polished off a bottle of vodka and another bloke arrived on a horse. All of us just yanked the bike and it was free but both tyres were flat annoyingly necessitating a slow repair and of course the important distraction of finishing off the second bottle of vodka. Which necessitated camping there for the evening. I was way too drunk to ride, as I would most likely hurt myself. The morning came and with it heavy rain and I thought about it for a moment and decided to turn back to UB, in that if it rained in Mongolia the tracks became very hard to ride and I did not want to overstay my visa. Namely as this had been tightened up with big fines due to people overstaying as it was so cheap. It wasn't so cheap anymore. Thankfully the earthy tracks were not too slippery and I tended to ride to the side of them instead where I would get less wheel spin. I made it back to UB with 3 days left on my visa.

I picked up my Chinese visa and decided to leave for Altanbulag but didn't quite make it. I got to the border and the insurance booth was closed, so had to turn back as the booth didn't open at weekends. En-route I passed a gigantic steel wicker man structure built by Hyundai industries and took some photos before getting back middle of the night back to the same hostel which was now empty. Though the recon trek as I called it to the border I met another rider.

This was Lilly from Switzerland. She had come the very long way having gone down through Africa up through South America, North America and over to Japan. She had been through central Asia several times. I did not get her second name. She was into her 3rd year of riding and had come from Japan most recently she was riding an XRV650 Transalp that predated even the Africa Twin that I had bought originally. She was carrying an enormous amount of kit. With four hard boxes (two at the back two on the side of the petrol tank) 3 roll bags and double tank bags. On top of this to boot her Transalp had a first gear problem, namely it didn't have a first gear and was seriously worn.

To add to this she was a purist vegan and upon meeting her thought that our very own British woman adventurer Tiffany had some serious competition.

Her plan was to cross Mongolia two up with her father who was flying in later that day and ride back across central Asia before it got cold. What impressed me was she had so much equipment it took seven trips up and down the stairs to the bike to get all her gear. Though her equipment was quite vast in that she had a hookah pipe a portable oven (which sounds remarkable but it was one of those steel boxes that is heated from underneath) a ton of spares tools water filters and food. When she first turned up at the hostel I had been unable to lift the bike off the side stand it was so incredibly overloaded. Considering Lilly was fairly muscled and Tiffany was incredibly small I was markedly impressed.

I introduced her to the Germans and the Oasis and she decided to move there until her father arrived as they did the German thing of talking to each other in German across me. But this was ok as in a day I was to leave to go ride the Amur highway.

Before I left I did manage to get invited to a motorbike race, as I was preparing the XT for departure. Oiling the chain, checking the tension, cleaning the carb and checking the wiring. Adjusting the valves in the secure car park porta cabin and borrowing their rather thinly pressed tools, like something you would find in self-assembly furniture. A couple of Mongolians walked in on me with a KLX200 that was poorly. They saw what I was doing and asked if I could fix it. It was merely a severely fouled spark plug and some dodgy wiring, again with the test ride of my bike. In Mongolia you have a bike you HAVE to give test rides out to people. For my sins I was invited to a bike race. 9am Chingis international airport I was told they would even come to the hostel and pick me up. I got there the next morning and was amazed. The most common bikes were Russian made 350s. Mostly Ural outfits one after the other with the odd sidecar combination thrown in and the odd Japanese bike there. Mine was one of 5 Japanese bikes the XT550 being one of them, the others being KLR650s and a DR650.

A crowd gathered to test my bike and I reluctantly let them while they gave me their keys, as they had a ride around I had a look at their bikes. Broken spokes, loose spokes, wobbly wheels on impossibly loose bearings, open carb, completely bald tyres with the canvas or steel hoops visible from afar. And suspension suffering severe stickiness, as you would push down on it and it would stay down for a minute before popping back up. I even saw a bike, which looked like it had a solid steel hub in addition to a front wooden wheel hub with no brakes madness! It reminded me of home, in that I myself and some of the bike forums northern group have been guilty of some of the above and we are all still alive and kicking.

I wondered how effective these bikes might be for the race. I actually wondered if I had been entered into the race myself worryingly as they all pointed at me with thumbs up and shook my hand. Alas I was not entered into the race, I don't think I would have won anyway. Looking at the skill and ability of people to ride such rotten bikes I was in awe at the way they just bounced over the landscape kicking up stones. Though this was mostly obscured by the massive amount of dust and sand kicked up by the bikes. The motorbike was just an Iron horse to them and my we have to get some of those Mongolians in competitive motor cross. They flew around the landscape making clouds of dust without helmets or any other protective gear.

The good news was Lilly had provided me a location of a hostel in Ulan Ude and that I had some first hand recon information about the Amur highway that was recent this was excellent news.

33: DAVAI MALENKA RUSSIA!

It always felt sad to be leaving a place. Although there is the usual swapping of email addresses and contact details there is always a thought in your mind we'll probably never meet again. When the chances of meeting people in the UK again are slim, 2/3 of the way round the planet, which is hard to get to, it is unlikely we will meet again. This applies both to travellers and to the people you meet who live in the places you visit. Again the border point was hot and humid unlike the rest of the country but the ride north from UB had taken considerably longer than I had predicted after 2 punctures from a nail, once from the nail itself once from the incredibly demoralising pinching of tube while putting the tyre back on the rim. Though the rim locks did come out to make tube repairs easier.

I changed my money at the black marketers just before the border zone and after I changed it another black-marketers offered me a 15% better rate, bah too late to cry about it. Could have should of would have. I crossed from the clearance zone and stopped to buy some insurance as mine had expired while in Mongolia itself.

"Hello, why you come so late?" Were the words of the Mongolian customs officer he closed the gate behind me and announced the border crossing has closed for today. He looked like he had packed his stuff up and was about to go home himself. Only the "gate closer" and his colleague are waiting for me to stamp the official exit stamp into my passport. Unfortunately the border is closed while I am still in no mans land. I asked if I could go back into Mongolia and use the hotel in Altanbulag town, but the guard said I could no longer go back in and the outer gate guard had stuck a hefty padlock on the gate already.

"*Gastiniza*?" I asked.

"Nyet *gastiniza* you have tent?" Checking the orange parcel on the back of my bike, yes. You can camp here as he motioned to a bit of scrubland where the grass was losing a battle against the bare topsoil. I prepared coffee and a meal attempting to put the tent up on ground as hard as concrete. I should have followed Tiffany's wisdom and gotten a self-standing tent or at least straps to tension the poles. The whole area was lit up with insects attracted to the light that I had trouble sleeping, as the light would seep through the fabric of the tent.

The night guards and soldiers changed shifts a few times in the night bringing me cups of white tea and sharing with me some of their snacks. Though it seemed that they were more checking up on me that anything else. I did wonder why as there wasn't exactly anything to steal and nowhere to go with high barbed wire fences on both sides of no mans land. I was having a positively Atkins moment in that I had consumed pure meat and fat the last couple days in Mongolia and this combined with the giardiasis had made it worse. The guards were treated to an oddity of a man getting out of his tent running a few metres away, a ship's fog horn sounding in a landlocked country. Then jumping back into his tent. I can't imagine living with anybody who advocates and practices that diet.

I got up early to be crossed out from the large leather bound ledger used to record entries and exits to Mongolia. Then slowly moved to the Russian side to be stamped back into Russia and the mammoth amount of paperwork this involved. Being stuck on the Russian side for the best part of 3 hours as the foot traffic for the border had opened before the vehicles. During the waiting I realised I had spent a good 14 hours not existing neither in one country or the other. Aircraft are so quick these days that you seldom spend more than 10 hours on a flight so you always land somewhere.

A good part of this was the customs document the customs lady gave me 2 months to get to Vladivostok. A darned sight better than the 8 days the beast of Sochi had given me. The soldiers did however go through my bags thoroughly opening each bag and unrolling each T-shirt and opening each box I had. They said it was Normaliya as drugs were smuggled from Mongolia. I guess it wasn't such a great job as he opened my bag of stinky socks and was visibly repulsed. I felt almost sorry for people in cars who were asked to remove seats and spare wheels and even more through checks of luggage.

The first destination was Ulan Ude to find a hostel, this hostel I had been recommended by the Nomadic way in UB city by Lilly who I had met a few days prior to this trip out to the border. Misha had worked here for a few years and had helped to set-up the Nomadic way hostel.

The ride out was uneventful bar a few rainstorm cells that no longer bothered me as I had my proper waterproof gear on and had wisely waxed my boots with some disgusting half wax grease I found in a Mongolian market place, though it did work. The rain had little effect unlike previously where a rainstorm would soak me to the skin and the wind chill would cause me to freeze onboard the bike. Though this was not perfect and cushy as you think in that there were two nasty little side effects. Firstly even though they were nice Goretex separate upper and lower rain proofs my crotch would invariably get wet. So when you took off the trousers it looked as if you pissed yourself, as a neat damp circle of wetness would surround your crotch accusingly. Additionally it was incredibly easy to overheat in them. This gave a similar problem to non-breathable fabrics in that you take them off and you are drenched but not by rain but by sweat. Goretex is supposed to minimise this but Ross had told me Goretex is only 25% breathable if that. Oh well it beat being totally cold and wet on the bike.

What was more worrisome were the multitude of road works that had sprung up while I had been in Mongolia a temporary metal bridge I had crossed on the way in was absent meaning I had to ford a shallow but wide river. Fuel was also problematic. The petrol stations I had passed on the way in to Mongolia were not deserted and empty today however they were. The usual surly Babushkas would be absent, no point in staying in the bunker when you have nothing to sell I suppose. Which meant I slowed down considerably to save on fuel just in case. Although I did manage to get within 70km of Ulan Ude before finding a petrol station with some 70 Octane petrol for sale which would have to do until I got to Ulan Ude take it or leave it, I took it.

I had however thought heavily on Bunjee the girl who ran the hostel's day-to-day administration. I'd developed a kind of attachment to her in that she was very sweet a little naïve and didn't have huge expectations of whom she would marry but I think this was general loneliness of being on the road. Where small things became amazing and taken out of context. A bit like Irkutsk it is an unremarkable town but after 10 days on the Tran Siberia railway it seems glorious.

I'd decided to stay in Ulan Ude for an evening before heading out to Chita for another night to tackle as much of the Amur highway as possible. I was apprehensive about the Amur namely this came about from stories from other travellers. My map was pathetic just a card of the hostel, which said take the number 7 bus. As I was heading into Ulan Ude I saw a couple of backpackers and decided to ask them for directions assuming they had stayed in this hostel. I had reached to take a photo of Hanija and Wojek, and noticed my camera was missing which made me furious again.

Hanija and Wojek were a couple from Poland. Somehow they had managed to hitchhike from Wroclaw all the way out here, without paying a penny to any of the drivers who picked them up. It had taken them two weeks to get to the bus stop they were currently sitting in. They were heading to Magadan to ride the road of bones in a Kamaz bus/truck thing as their summer vacation. Although they didn't know where this hostel was they gave me ominous warnings about the road finishing after Chita (Чити́нская). There is no road; it is impossible they said, were discouraging signs of what was to come. Everybody so far had different opinions about the Amur highway. Walter as far back as Irkusk stated it was a graded gravel road and hence easy. Every German I had met had doubts on **THEIR** ability to do this road, and said that I would fail on this road. While Poor circulation team did this road in 2008 and had great difficulty crashing 3 times. Though their team Alan and Geoff rode a pair of big fat triumph tigers a monster of a bike that weighed in at 300kilos before you put luggage or fuel in the bike even more with rider.

My XT was comparatively light as a feather I had reduced the XT's weight down to 142 kilos. I was barely pushing 45 kilos myself and had 10 kilos of luggage 200 kilos all in fuel water equipment everything I reckoned I had a good chance of finishing this road.

I was unable to find the hostel and was about to cross the bridge into town when I stopped next to a taxi about to ask where this place was when the number 7 bus stopped and I decided to follow. Disappointed the taxi driver gave me a, "Dos vit danya." I followed the van like mini bus to the hostel. The bus stopped at a dead end and I was approached by a group of Buryat people who all wondered where I was from and followed the getting old by now.

"Vih Atkuda?" Line and many people offering their homes for me to stay in for free, with yet another photo opportunity where 100s of camera phones were taken out and my image taken for prosperity or something. I was even offered a slug of vodka, which I accepted and quickly made off for the hostel down a muddy track that couldn't be considered a road. Now I don't condone drink driving but this was NOT a road and there was nobody about anyway to hurt bar myself.

I pulled into something that looked like the photo I recalled online a day ago and knocked. A tall thin woman stepped out and I said, "Lilly told me this was a nice place to stay."

"Ah Lilly from Switzerland! Oh welcome in!" The hostel was near deserted bar two Israelis en-route to China and the family themselves. Tanya her daughter (which I forget her name) and her husband who again I forget the name of. The hostel which was a giant converted house was quite nice outside the wood used to build it look recent with small narrow but comfortable beds and a kitchen to cook your own food. The Ethnic hostel is in the middle of nowhere though in a small satellite town of Ulan Ude which meant that all there was for dinner were noodles. In all honesty I'd had enough of noodles but the local cigarette shop stocked nothing but noodles so noodles it was.

This shop was the old style shop where everything was behind the counter with plate glass separating the customers from the counter. It was incredibly frustrating speaking little Russian. It was a pointless case of wait in line and tell the till operator babushka what you wanted who would prepare an invoice. This invoice would then be taken to the pay window, and then you got an invoice off a second person that was stamped. You then took this to another surly faced babushka who would think about gathering what you wanted who would then give you a receipt to queue at another window to pick up the goods. Before you could leave you would have to get a final stamp. I could have spent a very long time to the annoyance of everybody else. I'm not surprised this system was hated even in USSR times. In Krasnodar the Russians there had adopted the shops we are familiar with but with triple full body sized turnstiles and surly guards.

Tanya had much to say about Lily all of which seemed familiar. Tanya was actually from St Petersburg and had come out to Siberia to teach before meeting her husband here and deciding to settle down. We ran out of things to say really as she had only ever been in Ulan Ude and St Petersburg. The long ride here had made me thirsty cutting our chat short. Luckily the place had an attached mini bar, at 25 roubles each beer (that was 50p) it was expensive for Russia but not expensive for me. Strangely it wasn't Tanya who ran the mini bar it was the daughter who was at most 8 maybe 10 years old. It felt kind of wrong to be supping Russian beer being served by an 8 year old. For starters she wouldn't have the strength to drag my drunken carcass back inside. So I only had a few while chatting to the Israelis who were actually leaving in a few hours before turning into bed.

Ulan Ude is the capital of the Buryat Republic a virtual autonomous region of Russia. It seemed rather harmonious in that the Buryat were here first descended from Mongolians around the Altai region. In that the Buryat people seemed to fit in with the White Russians immigrants from European Russia. They seemed to get along. In that in the Tsarist days there were blatant attempts at subjugation of the Buryat. Forts the Cossacks built were burnt down and so on. There seemed to be a sort of overall sense of identity of Russianess. I never saw Buryat people discriminated against like I sometimes see in the UK even to this day. Although I admit my view of the area was the thinnest of slices of life and not long term. Though in prior imperial colonies there is always some not getting on with the conquerors. The most extreme examples perhaps being the Native American Indians and the Aborigines of Australia who were slaughtered wholesale and treated as below the settlers. I read later that it was because the Siberians and Buryat in the past had forged a sort of symbiosis. The Buryat would have trouble with food supplies, technology and medicine. While the Russians would suffer themselves. Siberian winters were too harsh for the settlers. Hence they taught each other certain things and had got along ever since. I wondered what life would be like for Tanya's daughter being mixed Russian and Buryat.

I left early to make the 900km to Chita a long ride which was sealed and completely uninteresting here there wasn't even *taiga* to look at. Just endless flat fields with the occasional outcrop of trees here and there. But still easy enough to ride without trouble. A few police checkpoints punctuated the day stopping me generally for a chat nothing more than any formalities. Not even asking to look at my documents, which was fine by me. I was ok with that the police manning the checkpoints here must get incredibly bored as the traffic was mostly going the other way and they generally stood around doing very little until a vehicle passed, days must have been very long.

One strange sight though about 50km before getting to Chita was a casino in the middle of nowhere. I stopped and had a look and it really was a casino just before a police checkpoint. I wondered how they made enough money, maybe all the cars from Vladivostok the drivers stopped to provide them with enough trade.

In Chita there was only one hotel, which was expensive at 6600 roubles for the cheapest room. I was sorely tempted though in that this would almost certainly be the last bed I would encounter for a while as the Amur highway is supposed to be desolate. No hotels until Khabarovsk or at least 300km from Khabarovsk as Lilly had told me that there was a truck stop there. Instead after declining their final offer at 6200 Roubles I set out to find a place to camp, which turned out to be a small village just outside Chita.

This was the first time ever I was told Nyet to if I can camp in their village. I went to the next one over who invited me with open arms. They were greatly pleased by the bottle of vodka I had bought for just such an occasion and it was my turn to say, "Davai, Malinka vodka!" With a flick of the throat and a sly wink I received a wide smile back and a flick of the throat back as a sign of recognition along with a brotherly hug, which was completely unexpected. Things that I did not understand were said in Russian but sounded friendly and welcoming. We had a merry time without understanding each other much, and some mellow songs were sung which I also didn't understand.

The night ended abruptly sometime just before dawn as many of the villagers sulked off and tended to their machines which they had left on all night after starting them earlier on. The room was spinning like crazy and I just jumped into my tent half-heartedly and fell comatose. Waking up now and again for a mouth full of water or turning over now and again lapsing in and out of consciousness occasionally poking my head out of the tent to throw up it was that bad.

I felt absolutely terrible the next day, or at least I thought it was the next day and didn't get out of my tent till 10am. The Russian fellow who let me camp the night before came up to me and said a few phrases in Russian. I only understood Sevodnia (today) and puchisa (yesterday). I told him roughly I'd be gone soon as I wanted to make a crack at the Amur highway and be finished by Friday in 4 days time. I was told.

"Nyet this is impossible," in fragmented Russian and English.

"Why Friday is 4 days away!"

"Nyet today is Tuesday."

"No it isn't."

"Da, today Tuesday." I had a glance at my phone and realised I had been so incredibly drunk I had spent nigh on 30 hours passed out blissfully unaware of the passing of time. The Russians who had welcomed me thought I was trying to stay here for good seeing as they all had gotten up and were tending to their vegetables or fixing their cars or whatever it was Siberians did during the day yet my tent was still there.

"You, Black sheep," he said and cackled with laughter, "Malenka vodka?" he teased me waving a small bottle he had to hand. With a grin, which wouldn't look out of place from a Cheshire cat or our last Prime Minister I could see my green face reflected in the curved glass and knew I had to be firm, as he probably wasn't joking. Oh how I loathed this man right now, for the noise making my hangover worse, and twisting my arm to drink so much as well.

"Nyet! Nyet!" I groaned weakly and slowly and painfully struck camp that seemed to be an incredibly complex task. Which I had no dexterity for this morning having to re-roll the tent sheets several times before they fit into the carry bag. The XT started with a grunt a little longer than normal on the starter as I suppose it hadn't been started for longer than usual and baby steps almost. I waved goodbye to the Russian folks who had so kindly let me into their village and rode along the dirt track and back onto the road into Chita.

I rode gingerly the few miles into town round a roundabout resisting my usual urge to go round it and get my knee down as it was a slippery worn road. I found a café amongst a few shops stocked up on engine oil, some general supplies of noodles, chocolate, petrol and finally visited an ATM for money. As the Amur is remote and I wasn't sure if there would be a Bankomat anywhere till at least Khabarovsk. With a deep breath I retracted my steps back to the original turn off and started down the Amur highway the second most dangerous road in the world.

34: AMUR HIGHWAY

Vladimir Putin opened the Amur highway in 2005 to much fanfare, what he didn't say that it wasn't quite finished. Pre 2005 the bridges were not in place, and the road foundations had not been completely laid yet. Post 2007 the foundations had been laid mostly and around 2008 the Russian government started to seal up the road. Which was not an insignificant task as it was 2100km to seal up. Though Russia is throwing money at this road with 30% of GDP spent on this road alone. This essentially meant that 2009 was the in all probability the last year that it would remain unsealed. For the past 4 years it had been relentlessly sealed up to become a main all weather highway. Riders who I spoke to said it was close to 2000Km of unsealed road and this year it was considerably less.

An awful lot of people like the Germans I met in UB had horror stories to tell about the M58 Amur. Lilly said it was ok, but since Lilly was a hard-core rider who made Tiffany look like a newbie and me like a neophyte what it really was like could be anybody's guess.

I pulled up at a café and asked people. The results were varied, very good, poor, terrible no answer was the same. But if Tomoro had done it on an SR500 a non off road bike then what the hell I would do it.... seeing as the alternative was close to 10,000 miles the other way this was in effect the only way out. I filled up my spare can of fuel and stuffed my face like a savage at a café at the roundabout just before the Amur highway started. Considering a good hearty meal in a Russian café costs 130 roubles I ate like I meant it. 600 Roubles worth of food, I wasn't sure what to expect better to be safe than sorry right?

The first 80km was perfect snooker table flat smooth tarmac. This couldn't last and it did not last. It all changed rather abruptly after crossing over a single bridge the road changed for the worse. The road became deep gravel for miles upon miles upon miles then would turn to tarmac for a short time. I was taking it about 20mph carefully as the gravelly sections were deep but gained confidence and started to hit the road at 30 then 35mph average. The road was in various states of completion some sections it was just graded gravel that was easy to ride on sections with large rocks that formed the substrate. Other sections the workers were laying down a steel grid type thing onto the substrate other times it was completely excellent tarmac. There was a sealed section every so often to tease you into thinking it had finished but in reality it (the highway) was being built out of quarries in the middle of Siberia outwards to speed up the construction process markedly. Though it

213

would deteriorate pretty badly in places where there were rough corrugations where the grader had not been for a while. Bumps that jarred up your spine meaning the only option was to stand on the foot pegs of the XT. This isn't much of a problem for small sections. But the standing on the bike the weight on your knees and wrists was painful and exhausting as mile after mile of seemly endless unsealed gravelly corrugated bits with the odd car sized crater here and there to keep you on your toes.

The first day was a big one I managed to get about 338km into the Amur highway in 6 hours of riding, but at a high price. Each petrol station I passed was empty nothing not even lowest octane stuff that is sat in a bucket in the shed round the back, which I had happily used near Novosibirsk. So left with little alternative I went to the next one which again was empty then the next one until on an unsealed section I conked out of fuel dead and had to pour both my petrol stove can and my spare 4 litre can into the tank. Deep gravel for miles and miles cars and lorries would stick to one good path through so it was either choke on the dust trails or overtake. I chose to overtake which would put me on the deep gravel where the end would lose it but then suddenly snake back into place. Same with the front as it would dig in momentarily where you were sure you were about to go flying but gunning the gas would make it stand up instantly again. I was getting good at this. It was also getting quite thrilling in a small way as there was an element of danger that contained excitement. It felt a bit like ride 'em cowboy sexual position, where in the throes of love making from behind you scream at the top of your lungs another woman's name, i.e. holding on while she tries to buck you off. Though to be honest I'm not sure I could have tolerated a boring middle section like the Chelyabinsk to Novosibirsk section.

I limped slowly due to lack of fuel over deep gravel to a village and asked where the petrol could be found. They said nyet and put two fingers indicating 20km down the road. 20km later an airhead bike rider also indicated 2 that I thought meant 20 km farther on. I rode on slowly to conserve fuel even switching the bike off down hills freewheeling as much as possible and managed to get to a clandestine petrol station that had no fuel from the pumps.

Despairing I asked if he had anything else, he did. He had a can of old petrol in his car, which had seen better days as it looked like rusted water, but the XT being the XT would run on anything. I guess if I had taken a bike which was more picky about the fuel I would have had to wait for a tanker to pass which may have been days. Earlier on I had asked drivers at the empty petrol stations and they seemed to shrug their shoulders and say 'this is Russia! Or zafta which meant tomorrow, at one of the stations one of the car drivers had been there two days so I guess I got lucky again.

With the Armco barrier to one side blocking any attempt to get out to a better campsite I camped out less than a metre from the edge of the road on what used to be an old track which had a large pile of gravel poured onto it to block it. With the hard ground and exhausted it felt utterly horrible to not be able to set my tent up at least 5 times. I had wished I had a freestanding tent and made a mental note to buy a freestanding tent for the future. It was a good thing I had gorged myself earlier that day, as there were no cafés that were open en-route to my location. The night was fairly restless as cars and large industrial vehicles no doubt used in building the road would rumble past. This wasn't a sudden rumble though as you could hear them miles away. At first the vibrations then the noise itself, which became progressively louder along with the vibrations getting stronger. Once it passed my camp spot the process was repeated backwards with the Doppler wane of the engine as it passed into the distance. Although this was not all bad as through the mesh vents of the tent door I would see a vast array of stars like diamonds spilt on a black sheet. As this part of Siberia had no light pollution. I had managed somehow to miss this completely in Mongolia land of the big blue sky, as it was always cloudy at night. Though a clear sky meant a cold night and each time I did manage to doze off a large vehicle would pass by waking me up.

I awoke fairly early after catching maybe a couple of hours sleep to thick white fog, which had descended during the night. It was surprising how decoloured the world had become. In each direction a sort of grey washed out colour even the nearby trees a pale nearly white green the road nearly grey and the sky grey. As I was making coffee which is all I had in the morning these days I would hear a fffff sort of sound and a car whoosh by at high speed visible for a moment and vanished back into the greyness of the fog shroud. A battleship could have moved by metres from my location and I would have missed it completely as the fog could have hidden anything. At least this stopped the biting insects for a while which was scant relief and allowed me to pack up my tent and strike camp faster than usual. This sudden appearance and disappearance of cars, bus and lorries happened a few times while I was packing up my tent and rolling it into its carrying bag which was looking worse for wear more black tape than material it seemed. As I prepared to go I listened for a minute or two to make sure that nothing was coming through the fog and struggled for a moment to get up the steep embankment on the side of the road only to be narrowly missed by a car coming the other way. No wonder this is the 2nd most dangerous road in the world the fog continued only for a little while. Once I got out of the valley floor I was camping in melting the fog in the powerful Siberian summer sun.

Thankfully after only 55km I came to a café and again gorged myself. The babushka who ran this place wasn't particularly talkative. The number of dishes this café had equalled the number of tables a rather disappointing two tables and two dishes. Though she did have plenty of chocolate and ramen noodles which I stocked up on nicely. The road became rougher now as if it hadn't been graded for a while with big clumps of gravel sat in piles the whole length of the road.

The process of grading is where they get a huge bulldozer or truck with a spade on it to flatten and neaten up the road to a surface where wheels can grip. The fog had cleared and I rode onwards. The highway feels different from other roads in Russia in that the highway is remarkably quite flat flatness does not preclude bends however and I wondered how fast I could take them. When it crossed a short to medium sized valley instead of going down following the relief of the valley the engineers had simply piled enough stone and rubble to bridge the entire valley an incredibly engineering feets considering at some places I was at least 30 metres above the valley floor. This was good in that it gave a decent riding surface. Though this was bad, as you didn't feel part of the landscape it was far away almost like a motorway.

As another side effect much of the highway had Armco barrier blocking the steep sides. Tantalising untouched potential campsites would pass you by. There were small riverside clearings no more than a few hundred metres from the bottom of the roadside. Although it was possible you could stop near a set of stairs and walk down to the bottom of each valley this seemed incredibly dangerous to leave a vehicle like this stopped on the road. This didn't really stop Russians from doing this though as whole vans and minibuses of people would pour out of their vehicles and down the steps causing minor snafus of traffic as everybody wanted to get to the places were the gravel was the thinnest. A third side effect was that due to the elevated manner there were few roadside services. In the rest of Russia every 100-200km there is at the very least a café and or a petrol station or some combination of a petrol café even if the café was just a window on the side of the pay window to the petrol station.

Today was a more confident day. I was managing 55mph on the gravel and 35-45mph on the deep bits and corners. Yesterday had been a good introduction and I had managed to fight my instinct to slow down. I was quite proud in a small way of making my own significant column of dust. Today also had more traffic coming from East to West, lots of Japanese cars all covered in tape and cardboard to be delivered to Moscow and the rest of western Russia. I had noticed that the Lada although extremely popular was not as numerous as the Japanese car which was generally off a ferry at Vladivostok to be taken to the wealthier western Russia.

Cars would overtake you at speed not that this was a problem. The problem was that they kicked up choking dust. Much worse were the Kamaz lorries which kicked up incredible thick clouds of dust which were mixed with sooty exhaust fumes which meant you were never quite sure where the lorry was or you had to ride on the opposite side of the road to stay clear of the dust. Nothing really happened today other than making it to the M60 junction. Though from the dust and the exhaust fumes I had to stop more than a few times to remove the dust from my visor it was that thick.

The M60 is the road to Yakutsk and ultimately Magadan. A gigantic plateau had been created for this spaghetti junction like road as it went south as well to China. I had a quick thought and decided to go to Yakutsk that was only 650 miles away. As I turned towards Yakutsk who did I see? Hanija and Wojek the two Poles had managed to hitch hike all the way out here. They had managed to clamber down the sides of the embankment down one of the service stairways and camp next to a small river and washed. They looked quite pleased and told me they would look after my bike while I went to get some water for some coffee. As I clambered down the stairway it was a different world in the valley floor. The rumble of lorries was hardly audible passing sound waves in the air above but not down here. Here with your back to the road it looked like something out of a Tolkein novel green semi *taiga* punctuated by endlessly rolling fields and a deep valley where fog banks persisted not burnt away by the kiss of the sunlight. The greenery was unspoilt to one side with an almost chemical green scientists would have to create in a lab with a long complicated name. The Polish folks were confident that they would get to the road of bones and admitted that there was a road here.

The Kolyma highway, as the locals know it went all the way to Magadan. I had been informed that it should never be attempted alone the remoteness and lack of traffic and appalling road conditions meant riding it alone was incredibly dangerous. The road of bones is a name given by westerners though as the locals all call it the Kolyma highway. Legend has it that it is called the road of bones as every foot of the road cost the life of a Gulag prisoner. This road is 2000km long to put that into perspective. Due to the permafrost just below the surface bodies of the gulag prisoners when they died were used as part of the substrate to build the road, so that literally it was the road of bones. But then it is remarked often that in Siberia unless really off the beaten track you are always near the site of an ex-*gulag*.

Russian road maps become obsolete so incredibly quickly out here. I bid them farewell after sharing some coffee with them, as they looked cold with only small rolled up sleeping bags. I rode towards Tynda and ultimately intended to get to Yakutsk gateway to Magadan. Except I didn't make it to Yakutsk. The road from the M58/M60 junction seemed to kill my tyres with incredible frequency. In less than 120km I had five punctures such that my inner tubes both front and back looked horrible there were probably more patches than there was inner tube. My inner tube on the rear tyre was looking bad from any angle you looked at it you would see a patch and quite frankly I was running out of patches. At least I could change a tube pretty damned quick these days I had a stark choice keep repairing it or find a city and get some new ones. Tynda (Ты́ндинский) was less than 90km north and Khabarovsk still a very long way away so I decided to go to Tynda to find a *shinyamontawk* a tyre fixer as it ought to be no problem for them to fix.

In Siberia the people can fix anything if they say it cannot be fixed then it cannot be fixed and should be junked. On the outskirts of Tynda I found my *shinyamontawk* who didn't speak any English. As generally there was little need, this being the back and beyond of the back and beyond few English speakers came here. He had a look and understood my hand signals but said something in Russian and pointed towards town for some reason. I rode down to the outskirts of Tynda and once the road became sealed a few miles out of town and got yet another puncture. Annoyed now I flagged down a passing Lada and asked him where a *shinyamonawk* might be. He kindly wrote on his hand 2km, which wasn't bad, except that pushing a heavily laden trail bike with a flat front tyre is harder than you might think. I got to a small ramshackle shed exhausted sweating cobs and harassed by mosquitoes at every step. I finally found a *shinyamonawk* in a small log cabin by the side of the road and collapsed in a heap on his yard. Smiling out came David who asked the usual questions.

"Vih Atkuda!"

"London."

"A Dien?"

"Da, erm moto *shinya* njet Dubris!" I tried to articulate to him in a small hope that he would understand. He went inside and got me some inner tubes. No good they were 18-inch tubes, which would work for a while but would wear holes in them after a few 100km down the road. He instead took my wheels off balancing the XT on a couple of worn tyres and vanished into his workshop. He carefully peeled each of the patches off and replaced them to a much higher standard that both my tubes although they still looked awful were good again. I handed him 200 roubles that he accepted gracefully and I considered my options. I was about to get on the bike and turned to David and asked him, "*gastiniza?*" to which he replied, "Da," and motioned me to follow him. With the setting sun Tynda looked a watery yellowy orange although of course in Siberia the sun never completely sets it hangs just above the horizon. I followed David to a seemingly grotty low rise house with garden on a bit of a hill in Tynda and realised he had actually invited me into his home. Again the hospitality of the Siberians was incredible, his daughter Anna and Irina his wife who was a BAM worker (Baikal Amur Mainline railway) was home and greeted me in almost perfect if slightly accented English. I was shown to a small room at the back with worn but freshly crisp laundered sheets. Which were even ironed that heightened my guilt at taking up one of their beds.

Anna was gorgeous she had long slightly curled blonde hair deep blue eyes you could drown in. A slight smile that could have gained her a job behind the perfume counter at Debinhams. Usual formal questions were asked, oh where are you from etc but the conversation again turned to the subject of God.

"Do you believe in God?" I was asked.

"No, I do not believe in God maybe as we call Agnostic."

"In Siberia many people believe in God I am not so sure myself, but many believe as it is something firm to hold onto. The communists destroyed religion but Stalin bought it back. To spur men to die for war to beat Hitler. But how you say it was something he could not take away again so the state sponsored the church again. Leon don't be so harsh to judge people who do believe in that Russia is changing. When the Soviet collapsed, the church is the only constant thing in their lives. Russia has lost its soviet empire only a short time ago and in that time there has been an identity crisis. When the Bolsheviks took over it was the same oppression corruption under Stalin this got worse but now the collapse has changed everything that Russia does not know where it is anymore." She had a point there in that Russia had changed massively. In a world of change people like to hold onto certain things. Though I personally do not agree with it in that my life is effectively light I own nothing of consequence and can move, as I want. I actually like the unknown, as the old saying has it 'familiarity breeds contempt' how many of us have said we hate the places we live?

Outside a small crowd had gathered to look at the XT, as foreigners were a rare sight in Tynda. I heard North Koreans had been based here for a logging Operation in 2007 but North Korea was comparatively nearby. The North Korean camp was also completely forbidden to outsiders including the local Russian population. Many of the small crowd took photos of myself with the bike attracting the primary interest. Tynda is a small town and news of new interesting things travels very quickly as very little happened there to warrant entertainment. I wonder if it was as fast as bad news. If I could only make a bike powered by bad news it would get places incredibly fast, though I supposed I would not really be welcomed anywhere.

We went inside and I was again virtually force fed with enough food to feed armies. Large piles of eggs, some sort of salami, some omul fish pie of some kind, cucumbers and thick black bread which was insanely filling. My hosts seemed to be virtually shovelling food into their faces at an astonishing rate. They took this as me not being accepting of their hospitality and kept piling more onto my little saucer thing, "Eat, eat!" They would virtually demand. As Tynda was a cold climate people would eat regularly to keep warm in the winter and use the summer period now to eat similar amounts but vegetables instead of meat as the meat was saved till the winter.

We got back to chatting again about UK life the problems of Russia and how David and Irina had actually come from just outside Moscow. They had come here as they felt a million miles from the Soviet government and thus felt freer. David apparently enjoyed walking out into the *taiga* where there was absolute solitude (except a billion mosquitoes for company and perhaps the odd bear) in the UK when you go for a walk you have to pass more urban sprawl to get to the countryside so it isn't quite the same I think. With Irina holding a BAM job it was totally secure and even though the money was less than in Moscow it went much farther in Siberia than Moscow.

We discussed all sorts of things and a photo album was bought out of various sights of Tynda including a huge hammer and sickle monument in the centre of town and the Iron man dedicated to the BAM workers. It seemed strange in that through western Russia pre Chelyabinsk I had seen few monuments and statues harking back to the Soviet days. No statues of Lenin, certainly no statues of Stalin, very few hammer and sickle pictures statues or sculptures. The odd town limit sign was nicely decorated or had a miniature version of what the town produced such as fish, helicopters, tanks and such like but nothing overtly Soviet. Yet here in Siberia there were many examples of Soviet statues and monuments statues of Lenin were in each town. Ulan Ude with its giant bust of Lenin for example. The main squares and streets named after famous people such as Lenin and Karl Marx. I asked them about this as to why Western Russia had demolished their sculptures or removed them.

"Just because some art work is not politically correct anymore does that mean we have to remove them? There are some who still think highly of the Soviet system there are many children who owe their lives to the system. The great patriotic war (WWII) killed 30 million Russian men. Stalin adopted all of their children and had the state raised all of them, without it Siberia, Russia would be nothing." David replied.

Late into the night we retired to bed and slept peacefully for once. I woke up to be greeted with a big pile of eggs and bread. Not wanting to abuse their hospitality I tried to decline but more was piled in front of me. It was a teary farewell in that Russians generally tended not to travel very much in that since the fall of the USSR train fares and airfares have gone up due to the lack of subsidy. Even Walter had found people who he had not seen for 15 years in Siberia. I offloaded more postcards and a few of my books in English I had picked up in Mongolia and bid them farewell. As I did this they stuffed my bags with tons of food, which could have fed armies. Before I left though I was warned that I should not camp in Siberia. Or at least get well out of sight, as it was dangerous. I was half expecting a lecture on bears. But David told me to be very careful, in that Siberia had a massive unemployment problem. Although there was welfare system it was quite trite and people in sheer frustration were powerless and turned to crime. Such people might see me as an opportunity to increase their income and would not think twice about murdering me. In an expanse as big as Siberia I would be forgotten and there would be little chance of rescue. This was perhaps the same reason petrol station babushkas sat in an armoured bunker. If there was trouble there would be no help for quite sometime perhaps never. I shook hands. I had photos taken waved and powered out of town feeling kind of guilty at abusing their hospitality though to decline was a bigger insult I suppose. I wonder if they will remember me if I pass through in 10 years time. Walter had some people north west of Irkutsk remember him after 14 years time will tell I suppose. However by 2019 the whole area would have changed as the new roads and the expansion of the BAM would accelerate that change, but nothing stays the same forever. There might be massive expanses of Siberia but only 100 years ago there was almost nothing here how times change.

Heading south towards the Amur highway again. I made quite good time to get the Amur highway as I was much more confident to go at a higher speed with proper repaired tubes. Quite remarkably just beyond the junction was a huge hotel complex petrol station with tyre repair facilities with many Russians sitting there on a huge veranda type thing. The hotel was closed however but the café was open and some eggs were enjoyed although I had plenty of food with me from Tynda. I quite frankly was lazy and didn't want to heat it up again. How I could heat up a chicken leg and rolls containing hamburger type meat with a camping stove was beyond my camping stove cooking skills and boiling seemed a bit primitive. Although I could have safely turned round to get to here initially the meeting with David, Irina and Anna had been absolutely priceless, you would never find that in a Lonely Planet guidebook.

It seemed that the road to Vladivostok was much easier than before and would become easier over time as civilisation encroached ceaselessly on Siberia's hinterlands of the Pacific. Hell my trip was decidedly easier as in 2004 there were no bridges and 100s of river crossings would be needed considering the sheer number of bridges I crossed. Though I was still effectively in the middle of nowhere. Though quite nicely the Russians put mile markers or rather kilometre markers every 2 km on the Amur highway.

A curiosity was that there were road signs that pointed towards towns. Towns which did not exist, in that hoping upon a café I would sometimes follow them only to reach a large flattened down area of wooden ruins or an area where a town might be. Tell tale signs of neatly crisscross piles of wood that form the foundations of Siberian homes. Homes are built in such a manner to prevent the heat melting the permafrost and the area turning to swamp

It seemed that in the not too distant future there would be many planned towns along this route so that the Amur highway would not be such a lonely experience. Though no two journeys' will ever be the same the Amur highway I experienced would perhaps be the last of the old desolate unsealed road.

35: PAX KOREANA

I continued riding east relentlessly where the road flattened out and passed a few large villages where the sky was a deep pink colour from the low sun and a distant factory-pumping out fumes so rode on. The factory chimney was the tallest thing around for miles and stood out against the backdrop of green trees and wooden homes in defiance of the forest and fields. The rivers here were strange in that there was a mist that floated above the river in a ghostly manner even though the humidity seemed rather low.

As I was looking for a campsite I came across 3 bikers a DR400S a TT600RE (which is a direct descendant of the XT600E) and a XT225. All of the luggage piled up on the TT600RE they were looking for a campsite as they had started quite early that morning. I was also looking for a campsite for the same reason. They were quite surprised at my appearance. My black riding jacket and bluish jeans and helmet completely grey colour from the dust kicked up. I'm slightly picky with my campsites and rejected two in hope of finding a better one later on. One had been next to a large lake but the gravel road in was too deep to ford as it was flooded and a sandy one.

So together after a brief introduction we turned back. Back to the sandy campsite I'd found earlier which was through a gap in the Armco barrier. Across a few semi dry mud flats and into a small clearing which was nice and sandy. Perfect for pitching up a tent but for me alone I thought much too far from the road and too deep into the forest as each side bar the little goat track we came down was forest not especially thick forest but impenetrable by bike.

A fire was started which was essential to keep the mosquitoes at bay. The Koreans introduced themselves as Kim, Kim and Choi. Doug had joked that everybody in Korea was called Kim and he was 2/3 right here. They were on their way to lake Baikal for 2 weeks I was pleased to hear that the escape from Russia the Dong Chun Ferry still ran. They were suitably impressed regarding the distance I had come. None of them could have gotten time off work to do such a big trip, neither could I. I said I left my job to do this. This seemed to impress them even more as what I did wasn't done in Korea at all. They then asked me when the Amur super highway started. Putin had announced that there would be a 6 lane super highway through where we were now. I told them quite simply it did not exist and wouldn't for quite some time. This seemed to make them unhappy and talk to each other quickly in Korean as if they had severely underestimated the amount of time it would take them.

They had with them about 80 packets of instant noodles and it was all they had eaten, and were glad to be sharing some of the food I had been given in Tynda and some of the dried Omul fish I bought outside Chita. I taught them a few Russian phrases for better meals and told them about the Irkutsk bike club drawing out a crude map. I warned them about the petrol shortage I had experienced before. They had the standard 8-14 litre tanks on their bikes if my 29 litres had very nearly run out they would be in trouble. At this I gave them my spare petrol can, as they might need it. As it was early the Koreans decided to go for a ride farther down the track that went on for quite some distance and I was left alone. In the space of a few minutes after the noise of their engines and exhausts became muted by the *taiga* there was absolute silence. Silence almost imposing and oppressive silence, although the odd mosquito came for an attack it seemed deathly quiet almost as if there were something wrong. If you recorded this on tape the hiss of the tape would dominate over any other sounds. If somebody else were there to ask they would say.

"Can you hear that?

"No?" cupping a hand to an ear. "No I still can't hear anything."

"Well it's because there are no sounds to hear." I set about doing the usual maintenance checking the chain tension and oiling the chain and was disappointed that I had 3 tight spots in the chain. Just where the oil seals had burst in the chain links and oiled them thoroughly while adjusting the rear wheel slightly to compensate for the chain stretching.

Surprisingly a sound did come but from the road and my solitude was broken, becoming two. A cyclist turned up he had seen us in the distance vanish from the road and had guessed where we were camping and shortly before it began to get darker the Koreans popped out of the *taiga* lined track. They had been for a short 4-mile route there and back ending in an industrial rubbish dump like many places did in Siberia now we were five. This was Jim from Birmingham, who was on a big trip, which he described only as, "I'm not going back." Jim had ridden here from Chita having taken the Trans Siberian railway from Moscow to Irkusk. He had 18 more days to get to Vladivostok, as his visa would run out (which was about 2600km away). It was voted pretty much that Jim would stay in my tent that night as the Kims' & Choi were sharing a 3 man tent and were quite literally packed in with me not being that much better since I slept diagonally in my tent as I could never get it perfect. The need to be quick and jump in meant I got little practice, if you were not quick you got eaten alive by the mosquitoes.

We asked him what he saw and he effectively said the road, much like the cyclists I had met in Mongolia had said. The problem with a bicycle is that it is comparatively slow. Add in some hills and a head wind and it's like walking with a cart. Hence cyclists on their short visas had to hurry everywhere spending 10-16 hours a day riding averaging 15-25kmh so in a day theoretically managing about 2-300km a day. Russia is gigantic meaning this had to be done day in day out. His bike looked pretty battered to hell but then my bike didn't look that much better, but looks were unimportant in Siberia. The fact that it works is the most important thing. Curiously he said something that was on my mind too that Siberia could easily be mistaken for Scotland. If you were kidnapped say and kept unconscious until you were dropped off in the middle of Siberia you could very well mistake it for Scotland. The only material differences being that people here spoke Russian but were quite cheery like many Scots I have met and that the midges which come for you in clouds in Scotland were replaced by horse flies and mosquitoes. Although mosquitoes were bad you could still smash them to bits and grab them to squish them satisfyingly if they had sucked you. There would even be visible bloodstains on your hands were you had crushed them. You can't kill midges in such a manner. Jim also smelt REALLY bad on a motorbike you smell but since you do not exert yourself at worst holding the same position for hours you smell bad but not sweaty bad smell. Jim did smell and could give skunks a run for their money. Although he did have some stories to tell about Siberia. In a town after Chita I had just passed in only a few minutes he stopped there. He alleged he was mistaken for a Russian by a couple of drunks who started talking to him in slurred Russian. Thinking that he was some how ignoring them but merely not understanding what was being said. One of them pulled out a revolver, which presumed, was used against bears or criminals and started screaming at him in incomprehensible Russian before his mate screamed "nyet!" and they ended up fighting over the gun rolling on the ground while Jim had made his hasty escape.

Though surprisingly that night I fell asleep quite quickly and didn't wake up which was just as well. That night we had our first, and hopefully last, encounter with a Russian Bear. It's something that Russians joked about to me since entering Siberia but I had never really expected to happen. They would sometimes show me their rifles and old hand guns used to defend against bears or would offer me some bear meat stew, which I didn't really think was genuine. Jim described it like this in my unconscious state I was blissfully unaware, which was a good thing I suppose.

"At first I heard and felt the movement of something outside walking around as if one of the Korean blokes had gotten up for a pee but the footsteps sounded really heavy too heavy to be a man and out of step with the footstep of a human. They were slightly muted not like a person at all. Followed by the sound of heavy breathing the kind you get off stalkers on the phone. It was taking its time, moving slowly around the camp. Sniffing and prowling probably intrigued by what it had found. For a good twenty minutes I lay still and silent, watching it's silhouette

224

against the wall of the tent and trying to remember what kind of bears you found in Siberia, black or brown. One would chase you down and kill you the other would climb up trees and kill you. I was shit scared as I had a Mars bar too which I saved half for breakfast and thought the bear might want that." I expected the Koreans to take the piss about it when we got up but each of them had been scared silly in their tent totally terrified and visibly shaken by what had happened that they hadn't gotten a wink of sleep. Due to this they told me they had decided to camp at petrol stations instead the hard concrete not exactly comfortable but the smell of petrol would keep bears away or so they said anyway. After breakfast of last night's leftovers I exchanged details with the Korean guys on the off chance that we would meet again in Seoul. They would be back in a couple weeks time.

They also gave me some information saying that I could enter Japan without a carnet. They had all been over to Japan from Busan with their motorbikes and instead of a carnet de passage had dropped a bond to a company off and bought insurance when they arrived. This was food for thought. I had never expected to be able to get to Japan without a Carnet-de-passage, which just couldn't be justified on the cost of nearly £1200 for one country.

Jim had to set off early as he was slow on his bicycle, and I passed him within 20 minutes after letting him leave. After a few more miles the road again turned to gravel track but better than previously and the speed was high over the gravel as I flew across it and that was it. The gravel ended completely or so it seemed. Stopping for a minor celebration I thought I had done the Amur highway in less than 3 days and had a small celebration of 4 eggs instead of the usual 2 for lunch, although I did not like to waste food I had to throw away the remainders of what David had given me in Tynda as it was oppressively hot and the food would start to rot visibly in the heat.

Punctures continued unabated though to Magdagashi where the road turned ok. It was sealed but badly worn with yellow streaks of the substrate poking through the tarmac. The punctures were the most frustrating bit to be honest. Although I only had two punctures I kept on pinching the tubes causing more punctures. I eventually ended up swapping the inner tube for my spare as the tube had so many patches on it that it was getting ridiculous. Not much progress was made as I had to stop so often and I ended up about 400km from Khabarovsk and ended up pitching my tent on a patch of gravel. The gravel in small powdery lumps the size of peas. It was remarkably comfortable actually again close to the road and in full sight of anybody driving down the road. Armco barriers and swamp prevented any camping elsewhere. Out of curiosity I took apart my rear wheel to have a look if there was something causing all those punctures, a quick feel and blood oozed out of my finger. A tiny sharp piece of glass had embedded itself that was barely visible on the inside of the tyre. I wondered how it got in there, as there were no signs of entry from outside the tyre. I put it down to carelessness. I had a last look around before feasting on chocolate bars I had bought earlier I didn't want to attract bears tonight. To be frank I was kind of shaken up near Novosibirsk by the eyes incident still and was paranoid about last night's bear encounter. Although I did not experience it myself, I thought that bears might be out for revenge as some people in China did nasty things to bears. They would capture them and hammer a tap into their gall bladders and tap their bile as some sort of medicine.

I had effectively left Siberia at some time during the day though there isn't really any marker to announce this. Russians do not consider this part of Russia to be *Sibir* they consider it to be the Russian Far East. Siberia is strange in that sort of way it is a different place. Geographically Siberia is part of Asia, politically it is Russian, and yet Siberia feels as if it is somewhere else neither Asia nor Russia. I felt this when many Russians in Siberia generally considered themselves to be Siberians first Russians second. They even have their own dialect of Russian, which wasn't completely different from western Russia. Yet slightly *piva* for beer in Siberia and *pivo* in western Russia for example slight and small differences like that. In a way it was a world of its own though invaded by man it felt neither here nor there. It stood out in Asia with non-Asiatic looking people bar the minority Buryat people. They ate different foods and had a completely different culture. It was as if there was a time portal just beyond Chelyabinsk. Which the exit was here. As it was in effect stepping back in time for lack of a better way to describe it.

The next day was uneventful other than riding towards Bizobizan the Jewish autonomous region. In the 1930s this was Stalin's answer to the Jewish question. Stalin simply had a town built and encouraged (read forced) the Russian Jewish population to live there. I don't know how Jews feel about this though as in Bizobizan I couldn't find anybody Jewish not even at the elaborate candle arbre fountain (called a Menora) supposedly outside the Synagogue. Not really having any place to stay and being met with blank expressions when I asked for the hotel tourist or *gastiniza* I plodded on. I plodded towards Khabarovsk on the M58 where the road again turned to dust and gravel but worse. There road was un-graded gravel with deep corrugations. Man sized potholes everywhere meaning standing up on the foot pegs. No campsites anywhere that looked even vaguely reasonable again with the trees not quite *taiga* not quite forest lined the side of the road. Even Kamaz lorries and buses had to weave left and right using the whole width of the road to avoid the potholes. There was the odd bit of terribly worn sealed road before whittling down again into gravel.

Here I picked up a hitchhiker out of boredom called Alexi (I found this out later). Alexi was unable to speak and had a paper sign for Vladivostok we cruised along for about 120km before he asked to be let off and he shook my hand heavily and entered a roadside café. Alexi was unable to speak he had a huge scar on the back of his head which looked rather fresh and thus was unable to communicate with me via speech.

I did notice quite a large number of military bases high walls armed guards in blue camouflage army fatigues holding AK47s or is it AK74 these days guarding military compounds. I passed them every few miles. This was still the Amur highway following the Amur quite closely just 13 miles to the west lay China. And the Amur had almost been the cause of a war between China and Russia. From 1969 there was a gigantic military build up on both sides fighting over a few of the islands near here. Nothing happened though and with the fall of the USSR in the 90s China and Russia had signed a truce and backed down reducing soldier numbers massively and shared out the islands amicably. Namely as it wasn't really worth defending as Siberia was most definitely not short any land.

Since I saw so many soldiers APCs and the odd lorry full of soldiers I wondered what this place would be like in the 1980s before the stand down as there were lots of soldiers now and previously many more.

Again the road alternated between good and bad. A section where a lorry driver advised me to take a short cut over a sand pile, which was blocking the road, which continued, unsealed for a good 50km before it abruptly ended in no bridge. This was a bit disappointing. Seeing as the road was elevated about 7-10 metres above the river there was absolutely no way to cross this broken section and I turned back managing to go far too fast over the sand barrier and make the XT fly I hadn't expected that and realised that I shouldn't have taken the wrapper off the handle bar brace as if I had an off road helmet I would have lost my front teeth as the XT landed hard bottoming out the front suspension then the back suspension before bounding back.

The detour was strange in that although I was nearing the end the weather was warmer. There was much more variety in the greenery than the *taiga* of the Amur highway and the road to Irkutsk. The *taiga* had essentially vanished and been replaced by a deciduous forest with wide green leaves and thick tree trunks. People sat by the side of the road selling their vegetables, and the narrow country lanes with a so-so surface reminded me of Georgia which was over 9000 miles away physically and in my memory felt like a life time ago.

After nearly a week of camping I felt I needed a wash. The Amur River was totally off limits to wash in. Even though I got within 2km of it and could often see it from elevated parts of the highway and didn't fancy much washing in various pools of water I found here and there after stories Doug had told me in UB. So checked into the first place near Khabarovsk, a sort of truck stop. With the usual things you find at truck stops, old haggard workingwomen sat by the benches near the truck parking area who looked like they were dead inside without even a spark of life chain smoking over and over.

I managed to secure a room that was a good deal for 800 roubles. It was basic and had a Russian woman quietly ironing upstairs as I went in to inquire about the price. The Russian woman looked like my history teacher in high school. Like for like or rather it was how my memory remembered her. I remember her because as a 13-year-old boy I was incredibly impressionable. She always wore an extremely low cut top that was far too small for her as well as an impossibly tight skirt that seemed on the verge of breaking. Each time she stretched to reach the blackboard there would be an audible sign of pleasure from the other boys in the class room and plenty of miniature tents all over the place. It even happened to the older male teachers that she was the sex. My ICT teacher at the time once had to share a classroom with her and as he stood up to get something on a shelf nearby some of the boys at the back of the class one of my mates Keith would exclaim.

"Look out Simon, he's going to clothes line you!"

Anyway I have a theory about this. All around the world people look very similar VERY similar, in that although DNA can have a ton of combinations that makes the odds of winning the lottery seem good that only a few combinations are actually used. Combined with only a few combinations of styles it means that there are people who look very much alike. On this trek I had seen 3 people look identical to people I knew or had known at one time. What was surprising was that I didn't explore all that much in the towns and cities I passed through so there could well be more. In Hong Kong I once found an identical looking woman to one I knew in London as well although the only way to find out if my theory is true is to have a worldwide DNA database that I don't think is worth the price in liberty to pay for the confirmation or rubbishing of my theory.

Later I thought I had scored a fantastic deal a case of beer for 230 Roubles. I had difficulty putting it on the back of my bike. Some black tape put paid to that. I really did think I got the bargain of the century less than 10 roubles a bottle and these bottles were huge 600ml beers. Feeling hot and thirsty I downed one quickly then another. The taste was there but I wondered why I wasn't getting the warm feeling inside so I had another and another and was still perfectly sober I had a careful look and noticed I had bought a case of alcohol free beer. Which I hate, it's like going down on your best mate's mum it might taste the same, but it's just not quite right. It hadn't been a hit with the Russians as nobody wanted it I even tried to give the rest of the bottles away but nobody wanted it.

Thinking of the last few meals in Siberia although Russians do not consider anything near Khabarovsk to be Siberia anymore I gorged myself on the last Siberian food I would encounter on this trip. It might well have made me sick more than once but when was the next time I was going to encounter it again. The UK according to yell has ONE Russian restaurant well two of the same owner one in Liverpool and one in Manchester, but somehow it doesn't feel the same and it costs more. *Solyanka* my favourite Russian soup ~ 30 Roubles for a huge deep bowl in Manchester it is £10. I sat around the mini water park outside the motel having my photo taken several times by Russians here and there who had come via bus from Moscow (who must be insane) almost lined up to shake my hand.

That night I got an unexpected visit from some men in uniform.

36: BAD COP BAD COP

As I quaffed my alcohol free beer the door started to be unlocked with a key. It didn't quite twig until there were 4 burly men all armed with guns drawn poking me my side with the barrel. They motioning me to get up oh crap I thought, and hiding my modesty as to save weight I didn't have pyjamas, does anybody still wear pyjamas?

Apparently they didn't have foreign visitors often and somebody had called the authorities the police. I was semi naked and half asleep I thought I was being rolled until the light came on and there were four burly officious looking men. A quick glance. Police MVD (Ministerstvo Vnutrennikh Del ~ (МВД or Министерство внутренних дел) the semi militarised police force akin to state troopers in the US or Gendarmes in France.

I was marched to the front desk, which was mercifully just next-door and they demanded to see my papers. The cop with the Stalinesq moustache who was idling toying with his holster I decided would be the bad cop. His partner who was cleanly shaven would be the other bad cop. With the MVD guys just hovering near the back chatting quickly to each other in Russian that I couldn't understand.

I was questioned in what I felt was a harsh tone about where I had come from that day. Where I was going where was my bike. They had a look over the V5C and my visa and were satisfied. They were stunned to see the Sochi stamp in my passport and asked why I had only managed to get my visa registered 3 times through the length of Russia. I struggled to say it but I said *gastiniza*, holding my hands wide roubles hoping to get across costs lots of Roubles hotels so I've been camping. They understood and warmed to me immediately Far Eastern Russia is supposed to be a fairly laid back place compared to western Russia. The MVD blokes turned round looking disappointed and left leaving me with the two police.

They had many more questions to ask and it seemed the initial hostility was fear, generally fear for me. Russia had lived under the paranoid communist system for such a long time that the locals were virtually instilled to report me to the police and had them come check me out. Which is exactly what happened. Even though communism had fallen nearly 20 years ago old habits it appeared in Russia especially died hard. They wouldn't take my alcohol free beer either. But they did receive a few postcards from Italy that were the only ones I had left.

They went outside took a few photos and gave me a hearty pat on the back for coming so far and visiting them, and a heart felt dosvi-dan-niye (till I see you again) before speeding off elsewhere...

I decided to have a wash (the reason I was staying) there was approximately 30 seconds of hot water before it became icy cold and spent the evening in the bar trying to find something stronger. I failed miserably and went to bed extremely early. I dreamt that I was still in Omsk that night and woke up a bit flustered actually wishing I was still in Omsk as all that had happened all that I had seen was hard work riding but all worth it.

I had a brainwave, once I got to Khabarovsk (Хаба́ровск). I could ride off road the 150 miles to Vanino. A big port city to cross via ferry to the island of Sakhalin and get to northern Japan, then ride down south through Japan and take a ferry to Busan. I got into Khabarovsk and hung around the riverside near the Harley Davidson bar that was absent of any bikers attempting my usual trick of get a Russian biker to help you. Though here this didn't work, as even in the glorious sunshine there were no bikers.

Through the park one street up next to the bronze statue of a flying infantryman there were an incredibly large number of Russian women changing into skimpy costumes for some event I was unsure of. They didn't seem to mind me lurking turning my bike around slow as possible for a long glimpse and even smiled back sweetly enough to melt butter.

I didn't know if my visa would do it though and had to wait passing the time babe watching at the waters edge of Khabarovsk until 8pm. When I made an expensive call to Real Russia who had provided my Russian visa. I asked them if it was possible to use my Visa to cross to Sakhalin as I recalled that there was a check box on the visa application form as to if I had wanted to go to Sakhalin. This didn't cost anything extra but would take an extra 3 days on original application.

The news wasn't good and I had to leave via Vladivostok as I wasn't allowed in Sakhalin a couple years ago maybe. But now the Russians had an electronic database apparently at each entry and exit point and I saw little point in travelling 150 miles to be disappointed.

I rode on the ever-changing surface sometimes-excellent sometimes-terrible road that had not been graded for a while and was covered in deep gravel. Down past Luchegorsk. A mere 15km from Damansky island now called Zen bao Island (literally treasure Island). It was this little bit of rock less than 300square metres in size that in 1969 and the USSR nearly had a war a big one. For a whole year there were border skirmishes that led to an enormous build up for the next 30 years. This was supposed to be why there was a population explosion in China in the 1970s. Mao needed cannon fodder and lacking the sophisticated weapons of the USSR at the time would have to resort to the infantry rush which had worked so well (though at enormous cost) in the Korean war of 1951. There is an old saying of Stalin that quantity has a quality all of its own. Apparently the population in India is for similar reasons a war with Pakistan that never happened. In 1991 though on the fall of communism the Russian government ceded this island to the PRC.

It seemed odd that a river barely as wide as a football pitch had produced such divergent peoples. In Europe each border region has generally similar people. There was significant overlap, as the languages were all common with the Greek alphabet, the same kind of food generally was eaten all sorts of similarities. But yet here it was markedly and noticeably different over the river people spoke a harsh low atonal Mandarin. They ate noodles, rice and millet (though Northern Chinese don't actually eat much rice I could hardly find the stuff in Beijing). While less than a mile into a different country the people here ate cabbage, potatoes and bread. It was somewhat different to borders in other countries which was generally an arbitrary line drawn in the sand (quite literally sometimes) to separate two people who were very similar purely to fight or moan about for centuries.

As it was getting dark I decided to camp near here from Luchegorsk the road west turned into unsealed mud as I approached through a small track. This was definitely used by a vehicle owing to the deep parallel tracks that went into the forest. I motored in a bit farther and noticed a few derelict watchtowers and some ruined chain link fences and the odd bit of barbed wire. But a hundred or so metres from the river I found an excellent campsite in a small clearing to one side of the forest. This campsite might have been where a house had stood once as the earth was unusually uniform and flat, but soft enough to put my tent poles into after poking it a few times. I rolled the tent off the back of my bike and decided find some firewood to get rid of the mosquitoes of which there were still plenty. Even though I wasn't in Siberia anymore as I walked a short distance away to pick up a few twigs.

I was shot at again.

37: OLD HABITS DIE-HARD

A bright purple flare streaked up above me with thin trailing smoke I thought it best to stand still and wait. Through the forest I heard heavy footsteps and some fast Russian being spoken though I could not make it out. I shouted out to them "Privet!" (Hello) a few times but was greeted with no more than a few grunts each time. Out of the forest came two Russian soldiers who looked a bit waylaid in ragged uniforms. Both of them with stubbly heads and smoky almost absent eyes. They both looked as if they had not had a wash for a very long time. They approached me saying something in Russian. They approached closer to me puffing out their chests quickly throwing out Russian words at me confusing me for a moment. This was an extremely awkward moment to them I appeared to be a Chinese person who had crossed the Amur River illegally for some reason. As I had heard off Russians here and there that many illegal migrants came over to this side of the river to either beg or steal. I looked like the people just across the border and one of the Russians even tried so say something in Mandarin to me. Lots of nyet, and misunderstood words were passed between us until seemingly they gave up. But I think I had the benefit of the doubt in that the Amur River is deep enough for gunboats there was no way I could have crossed the river expert rider or not. There would have been no way to get my bike across the river, and thus they seemed to be slightly deflated perhaps disappointed that they had not caught a Chinese spy after all. They had a look at my documents and one of the men tried to leave with them but I stopped him with a quick nyet, and he seemed to motion he wanted a copy of them.

My documents were very carefully checked and photos taken on an old camera phone of each document and them holding onto them and holding it up to the fading light to see the high tech holograms implanted on British passports. Much as I hate to admit the UK passport is quite secure with its holograms. Its embossed areas cover the photographs and signatures. The upgraded Russian visa with its hologram and my visa registration documents all seemed to prove that I was genuine.

They seemed to be confused that I was Asian looking yet held a UK passport. I suppose this is understandable. I'd barely seen any non-white Russians for quite some time after leaving the Buryat republic. In the USSR people of all different colours were accepted by force. After the USSR collapsed there were many stories of racism by both the police and skinheads especially in the Moscow region.

233

I did actually wonder why they had taken photos of my passport I wondered if there would be a copy made or something to sell on. Though the UK government would foil that too as the customs officers have a photograph on file comparing it to the one in the passport not the person.

Satisfied they gave me my passport back and searched through my bags by testing the zips opening and closing them just going through the motions. I had hoped they would perhaps show me a place to stay. Maybe stay the evening there for a bit of company as the past few days had been a little devoid of meeting people in any meaningful way. Petrol station attendants behind layers of armoured glass or steel plate don't really count as encounters I don't think. Nor did surely faced babushkas that tended to the cafés of the region. I was motioned by them to leave, and pointed towards the track I had come down saying *gastiniza,* motioning me to leave. I had an attempt to say *"Malenka vodka?"* but they didn't seem to want to rise up to this as Siberians did. Though I suppose they would not have been Siberians seeing as I had actually left Siberia a while ago. I'm generally not surprised that the Russians still keep an eye on the Amur River region as even though peace accords had been signed in 1991 the area was still sensitive and people were discouraged from straying too near. For starters just slightly north east of here is Komsolonsk. This is where all the high tech military factories are located. Where the Akula nuclear submarines, the diesel sub, which surfaced near the USS Kitty Hawk in 2007, and the Su35 were being produced. China would very much like more of those things. These things are currently a built under licence agreement but I had heard later on that Putin had announced unlimited defence spending to add to the border worries.

I suppose this is the old if you do not understand something then it is easier to hate than to understand. Although perhaps an element of jealously in that China and the Chinese had made money in swathes from almost identical land and resources while Russia seemed to be in dire poverty 19 years after the USSR collapse. China in a way collapsed too. Its socialist dogma changed by Deng Xiao Ping to keep the PRC government in power at all costs selling its socialist soul for a capitalist dream.

38: VLADIVOSTOK RULER OF THE SEA

A few hundred miles was all that lay between Vladivostok, and me and in a few hours in the dark I got there easily arriving early in the morning. I had hoped to go to the lake that straddled China and Russia there was alleged to be a hydrofoil in which you could cross into China for 5 hours without needing a visa. Although I had a visa it was hard earned and I didn't exactly want it to be stamped in and out ruining my plans. I pulled up to Spasskoye and was told that the area around the lake was closed for security purposes today and therefore by passed this part. While I was here I saw Stass from Irkutsk at a petrol station in his van named Guts. From what I figured he was here to pickup bike parts. As I said Russians don't even consider the 4000km from here to Irkutsk to be any great distance. Unfortunately as in Irkutsk Stass did not speak any English and my Russian was still patchy. So we said nothing more than hello in Russian and English before parting company.

Down the smooth as silk highway up and over a hill and I had arrived. A big stone sign stating Vladivostok in cyclic (Владивосток). I'd seen this sign so many times in my dreams and from other peoples photos that it almost felt familiar.

As I rode in I stood up on the bike punching the air and promptly fell off at low speed hurting my shoulder quite badly. The damage was not severe just very slightly bent handlebars and the mirror stalk becoming even more bent, but that could be resolved by turning my head. A few photo taking angles moving the bike and neatening myself up and it was time to find somewhere to stay. I had no idea where to stay actually and sought about finding an Internet café to look for a hostel. Unfortunately (though I did not know at the time) there was some sort of military festival going on and this meant I had to filter through about 20 miles of traffic before I got to Golden Horn bay. The traffic was appalling due to some sort of naval parade going on in the city. This led to some nifty filtering, which ended up in a large convoy of scooters following in my wake. This sort of thing used to happen at home an awful lot too when I used to work in the city centre. I cruised around asking people, "Parom Korea?" And was directed to various parts of the ferry terminal.

First to the wrong ticket office then a bunch of bikers on Hornet 600s. They were practicing wheelies back and forth up the promenade. The ferry ticket office was unfortunately closed and I was told to come back 'zafta' tomorrow making me realise that it was a Sunday today, as I had not kept good track of time.

235

I had heard of a cheap 500-rouble hostel called the Mix Mix hostel, having picked up a card with the address in Ulan Ude at the Ethnic hostel. Finding it would prove difficult. I had no map of Vladivostok. Google maps the good old backup solution to maps (which had gotten me half way across Russia), said it was on the Golden Horn Peninsula. Unfortunately though google maps doesn't have Vladivostok mapped out. Meaning I had to enlist the help of a taxi who also didn't know where it was. He stopped 5-6 times to ask for directions and finally lead me to a dangerous slum where there was no sign of the hostel just a few high rise flats and rats. A lot of rats in fact a helluva lot of rats. I'd bumped into a trashcan turning round and the whole thing was full of rats, and while I turned round I left many rat pizzas in the car park. Defeated I decided to return to the town centre and look for a hotel. Passing one called the Primorye and promptly checked in for 2000 roubles i.e. £40 I felt it was expensive but had little choice bar sleeping on the streets, which wasn't something I wanted to do. I also hate the fact of checking in late if you check in at 6pm you get effectively 18 hours to stay in the room for the same price as if you check in at 11pm (which is what I did) where you only get 13 hours. Seems kind of short changed if you ask me.... At least it was better than the experience I had at the hotel Hyundai. Where the doorman moved to CLOSE the door when I pulled up. The hotel Hyundai is incredibly exclusive in Vladivostok at over 15,000 roubles a night, too much for me.

Breakfast, pack the bike and ride off, had I known the ticket office was a mere 500 metre walk away I would not have packed up the bike alas all this packing and riding around led to a great coincidence. As I was parking up to go to the ticket office a taxi with an old man passed me by and a silver haired head popped out the window and shouted, "Hey, hey! Follow us!"

A short ride to a parking area ensued where I met Tony and Terry. Tony I had last met in Irkusk attempting to get to the artic circle, about 2 months earlier. Terry was to ride the BAM railway maintenance road to Tynda with Tony and Walter.

Over the next 4 hours I kept bumping into them in an attempt to find a cheaper hotel. But defeated I finally agreed to stay another night in the Primorye Hotel. I spent the day sightseeing trying *kbac* as it was my last chance to have a try it. I paid 20 roubles for a litre of *kbac* and Walter was right it was an acquired taste like stout is an acquired taste. It had earthy yeasty bread like taste with a hint of shandy and soil from the ground. I finished it and handed the bottle back to the seller. It was certainly drinkable but as said it was an acquired taste that wasn't to my taste buds as I generally like sweeter tasting things. This is perhaps why I am currently in the thrall of a mentos addiction a 40 a day habit.

On the sea front of Vladivostok was the S59 submarine. This submarine apparently scored an enormous number of kills in WWII and had been laid here as a museum much like the battle cruiser HMS Belfast in London on the Thames.

Clambering around the inside of the Submarine was quite fun and interesting and gave a *Das Boot* type feeling. It was cramped and it would be scary to be under the sea in that thing. Now and again there were Russians standing here and there to make sure you had a photography pass (250 roubles) and would pose in naval military uniforms for again a fee. I disappointed them though.

The rest of the afternoon was spent in the main square babe watching in my particular way. Also the local watching bikers' wheelie up and down the promenade opposite the submarine. Just before sunset where I went back to the hotel to look for Tony. Although this afternoon wasn't that pleasant in that I kept getting propositioned by prostitutes.

Tony had found the tyre I had given him in Irkusk to be a lifesaver, 1/3 through his artic circle adventure his rear was pretty much shot and he changed over to my trellebourg that I was going to throw away anyway. This he stated effectively saved his life, as there was no way on earth he would have made the sandy/clay mud tracks through northern Siberia. He was eternally grateful and kept buying me beer after beer. Steady on old chap it's just a tyre. I did get a mention in his blog about this, which pleased me a fair bit. We also met Arytom who was a fluent Russian speaker on a TTR250 who was leading a group of French riders through Siberia.

Tony told me about his trip and how they had gone to Magadan and not quite made it to the artic circle as it was un-ridable once they got within 10km so close but yet so far. Magadan turned out to be perfectly accessible as all the bridges had been built all the way to Magadan and the road was mostly graded gravel road. I could well have made it myself with the only drag being the need to ride back since I had no contacts in Magadan. It turned out that Chris Scott's book stated that the only bit that you should not ride alone was the abandoned section of the Road of Bones. In 1995 Mondo Enduro rode this section when it wasn't abandoned hence it was easier to ride than it is now. As each year passes the old section becomes worse and effectively impossible to ride unsupported or unless you have big balls.

The reason being that the bridges at both ends collapsed which meant the people in the villages were cut off from supply who eventually ended up abandoning the villages in between. Which meant there was nowhere to buy food or petrol. Along with this because nobody used those roads anymore they were no longer maintained. A grader coming along now and again not only makes the road easier to ride and drive on it also packs the ground in place preventing it from being washed away. It had been abandoned for at least 10 years and had fallen into such disuse that it was now deemed to be impossible unless your name is Maciek Swinarski who apparently managed it in 2007. Though Maciek isn't your normal rider of course and compared to his recent projects the abandoned section was a piece of cake for him. Of course people will cite Long Way Round as it being possible. But again the truth came out. In that Rayil who was known as, "Mr Road of bones" supported them time and again, such things were staged. Convenient Kamaz lorries that just happened to be passing were not convenient lorries that just happened to be passing at all. I suppose far out into the back and beyond it is difficult for people to assert what really happened. Compared to say going down to the local bike club and asking. The local bike clubs who know this are all the way in Irkutsk and Yakutsk not exactly accessible places even by air or train. I suppose the same musings could be said about my own travels, though I never claimed anything extreme and hard-core either.

Tony also told me about the madness of Maciek. Maciek's team had made it to Marenga first about 200km from Magadan. But it had taken them close to two weeks travelling through deep mud and unspeakable conditions. Walter had wanted to get to Marenga first but had been way laid in Irkutsk for days and days. He (Maciek) had been crossing rivers by swimming them and dragging his KTM over on jerry rigged pontoons. Madness but something utterly deserving of respect as there is nobody as tough as Maciek.

We had a nice night sampling the beers at a place where it was on tap, which was a pleasant surprise. With just me Tony and Terry being left propping up the bar by the night's end everybody said thanks swapped any relevant information and farewells were given to me as tomorrow I left for Zarubino. Tony was waiting on his bike being shipped in from Magadan to Vladivostok while Terry had come in via Korea and had given me an enormous amount of information regarding Korea and banished some of my misconceptions. I have often said it is important to take information from people who have recently been there as most important while armchair travellers cannot be relied upon.

Oddly enough Lars a traveller we met who just decided to up sticks and travel around for a bit managed to get a ferry ticket to nowhere that was listed. In that from Vladivostok, Zarubino and Vanino the only big ports nearby there were only 3 destinations, S Korea or Japan, he had gotten himself a ticket, which the destination was not listed, on any map. I wonder where he got to since he never did reply to any of my emails.

The road to Zarubino is actually north out of Vladivostok then curves back down towards North Korea again passing military bases that seemed to be manned completely by women soldiers is that womanned? I rode down a few sealed roads and into the countryside. I followed the river for a short spell. I noted that it was impossible to camp here as the river had steep banks and thick reeds so you couldn't tell where the bank ended and the river began. As I had been concerned about the vast amount of money I had spent in Vladivostok. Curving round some easy curves and asking for directions of a road works crew who were resurfacing the road I figured my way out and slowly rode towards Zarubino camping would save some money. It was a lonely long road for a while punctuated by the odd unsealed non-graded gravel section with huge pools of water. The Russians like everywhere else were building a new super highway to Zarubino that you could see from the diversion. The diversion scuttled along at the edge of the embankment that was a deep mud road. I'd thought that mud riding was over but a little reminder of some fun times previously. Sure it was hard work but you got to the end of it and felt some sense of satisfaction even though you were hot and sweaty. I had to ride on the verge to get past as Kamaz lorries went past without slowing down. As before on the Amur it wasn't the road conditions that were bad it was the crap kicked up by the lorries and the twisty nature of this road into Zarubino.

I stopped for lunch at what appeared to be a work in progress holiday camp off on a trail about 5km off the main road. Either that or it had become derelict as there was over grown grass all around and the tracks around looked as if they had not been maintained for quite some time. Inside I had one of my last meals in Russia cold beef burgers and *pilimee* dumplings and some *sashlik*, which is a sheesk kebab.

A man working onsite digging a huge hole came in and had a brief chat telling me about the history of this place. My Russian still wasn't great and I figured that it was derelict and was being rebuilt. The warm sunshine graced my back and I felt this wouldn't be too bad to go on vacation to for a short time. It was sad to see cabins stretching out to the woodland behind as Russians apparently no longer came here anymore with Russians being allowed to go to Korea or Japan for their holidays instead as it was cheaper much like we do in the UK. I left and went towards Zarubino again on this isolated and traffic less road and was stopped for the last time at a police checkpoint. It was a proper police checkpoint with the soldiers armed with AK47s. 9 soldiers and a commandant who sat at the desk upstairs in the hut. The document check was just a formality and he recorded me in his logbook. Asking where I was going 'Parom, Korea' seemed to satisfy him. The mood lightened significantly from here on and he asked me where I had come from in almost perfect English. My XT so far had made it all the way here without any indication where it came from. The XT never wore any stickers regarding where it came from and the number plate was indistinct from others.

"London, Chelsea Roman Abramovich."

"You like Manchester United?"

"Da," I said. Even though I really do not like them, and I mentioned Ryan Giggs, not wanting to repeat the mistake of Lois Pryce in Africa. We generally chatted about small things as I was in no particular hurry as the ferry was tomorrow. I gifted them the last of my postcards, which were getting a bit tatty now. One of the party ran inside to get a huge half bottle of vodka a small cucumber and a few pieces of dark bread and some salt. I was toasted as a bit of a hero, with a fat plastic cup of vodka and I was cheered for coming so far, and was gifted the rest of the bottle of vodka for good luck.

I stopped as the road became unsealed and seemed to have 6 forks and had a look at my map. I just knew I didn't want to go into North Korea. Although the thought did cross my mind to blag my way in, but I wondered how I would ever get back out. An hour or two later I turned off the fine tarmac road onto a smaller rougher road down towards Zarubino.

With the fine weather and clear blue sky Zarubino that Terry had said was an absolute dump looked marvellous. From the road leading into Zarubino and the island town was beautiful. While the town behind you as you rode in was kind of ugly which seemed to be neglected badly as it was tenements. They were worn concrete but this was hidden behind a convenient hill. Gravel roads with huge potholes and everybody there looking sullen and unhappy at their lot in life.

I went to find the local hotel and left when it was 4500 roubles per night and decided to rough camp in some burnt out buildings that were actually occupied by some squatters already. So I turned back to the village just before Zarubino where many people camped on the beach. I did too, well after some sand riding and some deep puddle riding which got scary when the puddles went over the top of the front wheel. I heated some noodles and for once due to the complete lack of mosquitoes blown away by the cool breeze off the Pacific Ocean I managed to put my tent up properly in the soft sand, which adjusted to my buttocks nicely. It suddenly seemed my tent was huge when put up properly. The irony of this was all too apparent as it was to be my last day in Russia. As I watched a magnificent sunset over the ocean where you could just make out North Korea over the waters.

Other Russians turned up and set their tents up beside me and spoke to me in Korean thinking I had actually come from Korea. When they discovered I was from England they seemed they were incredibly pleased. The old man said in broken English.

"Only England is Russia's friend!"

"In Great war, only England was druk (friend) of Russia." Well at least that's what I thought he said when he said England [something] druk, Russia. They had a look at what I was eating and asked me to join them with a sly wink and a flick at the throat (which I knew meant lets get totally mashed). This was Maria, Serge, Vasily, Vladimir and sons' who I only learnt the name of one being Sasha. They had come from a small town they pointed on my map, which I later discovered was Tynda. They wanted to come to the beach. Considering it was a good 1700km from Tynda to here I told you Russians don't consider 1000km to be any great distance. They had heard of my visit in Tynda that was unsurprising due to the size of Tynda.

The evening was a case of vodka, eating bread cucumber, raw sausages, and vodka, eating pancakes, mystery meat, vodka and vodka, oh and vodka. I had initially started with vodka and a chaser of beer. But was scoffed at by the Russians who insisted beer was just for children and it was how weak men drank. Vodka could be drank any way you liked as long as it was neat. About a 1/3 through the evening the world had tilted over slightly and they were playing a Siberian drinking game. Where we would eat sit on a picnic table, pour out a fairly hefty glass of vodka and drink it all in one go slamming the glass on the table. If you didn't skol it all in one go the vodka would be poured over your head. Sort of like an English drinking game where you drink a pint fast as you can and put the pint glass upside down on your head.

I tried heroically to keep up the British stiff upper lip and keep the pride but each round the glasses actually plastic tumblers with pretty cartoon cows painted on them started to get fuller and fuller. By the 4th one we appeared to be in the middle of an earthquake well I was anyway as the Russians all seemed sober. I kept getting vodka poured on my head. This might seem really wasteful and expensive but considering vodka in unmarked bottles (which was rocket fuel pretending to be vodka) cost £1 a litre and was even cheaper if you bought it from unmarked village shops it didn't cost much. Though I was sat there drenched barely making dents into my tumbler of vodka offered each time. Shots getting bigger and bigger each time. I was soaked I just hoped not to go up in flames as the men chain smoked and absently flicked their lit cigarette butts all over the place.

It was my fault really as in a small town before Zarubino I had stocked up on supplies uncertain what to find in Zarubino and had stocked up on some huge bottles of *piva* and vodka. Though some of my bottles were thrown or poured away as it turned out to be nasty moonshine posing as vodka that sometimes happened in some small villages called *samogan*. It was the cheapest of cheap alcohol and pretended to be vodka. I was fairly alarmed at when they poured it onto a plate and burnt it there was a fairly substantial residue. The party seemed to grow bigger as there were faces I didn't recognise and more people than had started but it was all happy and jovial. Culminating in a rousing rendition of hotel California Russian style, that song gets everywhere. Along with some Russian songs, which sounded decidedly Jewish with the common Jewish theme I hear everywhere and a bit like the theme tune to Tetris. I was half expecting a techno remix of Tetris to be played. I tried to escape numerous times only to be greeted with.

"Nyet! Stay your last day in Russia! Happy with us!" We even managed to rouse a tear jerking drunken slurring version of the Russian National Anthem. The Russian anthem (ex Soviet) is so good it has been written so well that even from the mouths of drunk off their ass Russians it still sounds excellent.

I finally did manage to escape about 5am and slunked off into my tent, thankfully the Dong Chun Ferry didn't arrive till 2pm that day. I didn't even get up until 11am. Well aside from poking my head out the tent and throwing up a chunky red vomit. And found that the Russians the previous night had already departed but had left me a small bottle of vodka with a 100 Rouble note attached with "до свидания Leon" written on it. (Dosvi-dan-niye) till we meet again Leon!

The morning was overcast which made Zarubino look ugly. The ferry hadn't arrived yet and I sat on a nearby dock going to a local café for breakfast the last Russian meal I would eat for a while, *blinchikee* with *malka*, (pancakes with condensed milk) had never tasted sweeter than now and the café seemed more like a home than a café. There being an open kitchen with a big square table where everybody sat. The waitress a pretty pale skinned blonde girl with blue eyes that I could happily drown in. She asked me where I came from and I handed her my last postcard of London. She called a few people from another room who all had questions and looked at the few photos I had taken on my camera phone. Bikers always seemed to pass through this spot they mentioned either in or out. Though the ones who arrived from Korea never stopped off here to say hello.

The ferry pulled into dock so I went into the ferry port and noticed the new ATM installed and the bank. These had not been here in 2008 from photos I had seen which was convenient except the cash machine ran out of money incredibly quickly and so did the bank leading to no Korean money to use on the ship. I met Jun here an uncertain Korean guy who was in the same bike club as the other Korean guys I met a few days earlier he was on his first big adventure hoping to get to London. He was riding a big heavily laden F650, but with slick road tyres spare road tyres and looked very unsteady riding on the 300-metre gravel section inside the port. Although I don't judge as harshly as Germans seemed to do his plastic cases and top-heavy loading seemed to be a bit suspect. I wonder if there is a Korean equivalent of Chris Scott to give adventure riders some hints as to what to do and how to ride off road. That said the adventure motorcycling handbook was a bit out of date with the newest edition being 2005 at the time and plenty of people had gone out before and had taken a baptism of fire. Myself before Capadocia had negligible off road experience though pain is an excellent teacher and it makes you learn quickly. I gave him the contact details of Tony and Terry hoping they wouldn't mind too much. Also a map and bade him farewell. He seemed to be somewhat unprepared as in South Korea they have immaculate roads almost everywhere you may want to go.

Though really I suppose it is better to start from the tough bit than it is to start on the easy bit like I had done. Europe is easy mostly sealed roads, plenty of infrastructure hence your bike gets worn out and by the end you are on the rough stuff being shaken to pieces. While if you started at Vladivostok you started on the rough stuff while the bike was in reasonable nick. Walter being the good guy he is did end up giving him an escort all the way to Khabarovsk and rebuilt his morale after some bad things happened to him (being mugged and crashing).

I went into the port facility filled out some paper work, got rinsed of most of my remaining Roubles going to various windows and handing over money. At least they were honest about it unlike politicians elsewhere who had to find some feeble excuse to justify tax increases.

"This is a tax to pay for the port improvements for 2009."

"This is a tax to pay for Federal tax of Oblast."

"This is a tax to pay for the facilities."

"This is a tax to pay for toilet improvements."

While I waited to board the ship in the departure area, where I was hero worshipped by various Koreans who had seen me ride through the port entrance and the actual departure area. I was finally allowed to ride the bike onboard. As I did I got me foot stuck on the pegs and dropped it incredulously in front of many crew. I was told to go back down the ramp and up the side stairway into the ferry. It seemed that the Dong Chun ferry had actually been repainted, as the last picture I had seen was it was a bucket of rust with an engine attached. The cleaner sides free of rust gave me some more confidence. Though the total lack of lifeboats and life jackets removed confidence this suddenly reminding me of a mate who had taken a flight in India.

He had taken a flight to New Delhi for a connection on another significantly older plane. This plane had 4-10 different airline names on the side fading away with peeling paint. Things such as the seats were not bolted down to the floor of the aircraft were common on this aircraft. The worst thing was the door. When everybody had boarded a flight attendant used a standard door bolt latch type thing shut across the door and a padlock used to secure the door saucer eyed he asked somewhat alarmed.

"How do we get out if we crash?"

"We don't crash," said the crewmember calmly. Sounded a bit reminiscent of my own travelling style when questioned by bikers you only wear jeans!

"Well I just make pretty damned sure I don't crash." Gaz formerly of Regents in Bury a bike mechanic said virtually the same things.

"R&G? Crash bungs? Engine armour? Biker armour? That sort of thing is tempting fate. Without it you will subconsciously ride more carefully."

39: SOUTH KOREA!

I had always expected South Korea to be a transit country. Get in, ship the bike and get out. The reality however proved different and half a day in I was thinking wow what a place! Terry a couple of days earlier had convinced me to stay a while and have a look around South Korea. Most if not all people got to Sokcho and headed immediately south for Busan to ship their bikes home in effect missing what Korea had to offer. South Korea had an awful lot to offer. I had an inkling of this from the 3 Korean men I'd met on the Amur highway that Korea was a place I should stay a bit longer. Korea however is often a driver/riders choice as there is no need for a Carnet to get to Korea. Japan demands that you have an expensive piece of paper called a Carnet that I didn't have. I suppose Korea has positioned itself nicely by doing this. I could never justify the £1200 for a carnet anyway or so I thought before the Kims' told me I didn't need one. Which meant I would try getting to Japan via Busan later on.

I was glad to be off the Dong Chun ferry to be frank. Even though the seas were fairly calm the ship is run very quickly. This is probably to minimise turn around times and to get as many passengers as possible from Russia to Korea and back. If there are 3 sailings a week and the trip takes 23 hours then they have to be fairly quick in turning the boat around. The fast running causes some small problems here and there. Not being flush with cash after Russia had proven very expensive I had taken the absolute cheapest ticket possible. This was economy B grade class. This doesn't sound too bad and it isn't THAT bad but a lifetime of sleeping on beds had made me think ouch. Korean style is identical to Japanese style where people sleep on the floor on a small square of foam with no covers and a leather pillow. This isn't so bad until you say turn on your side where your hip has nothing to dig into and pushes into the hard wooden deck. The solution to this is simple sleep on your back. But I'm rambling the problem with the ship running so fast is that it rocks quite badly in the water. This is not normally a problem as months ago the ship from Italy also rocked back and forth there were Pullman seats for this ferry though. The problem was because you are sleeping on a highly polished wooden floor on small foam mattresses. The mattresses slide in time with the pitch of the ship. Therefore in the middle of the night you can wake up in a corner of the room, piled high with sleeping people. This was much worse in the café come restaurant where the rocking of the boat would slide food all over the place. Hot cups of water would invariably slide off the table and make a beeline for your groin. Catching food wasn't good either, as you would catch food of somebody else (as I don't eat on ships), which they would thank you for and inadvertently get a hand covered with a thin layer of chilli oil. This was a problem if you rubbed your eyes or went to the toilet without washing your hands FIRST.

There were identical problems with the toilets which were of the squat variety sure you can hold on with both hands and wedged your feet under the stall dividers but when it comes to wipe you have to use one of your hands. Ample opportunities to fall into the squat hole/toilet thing was markedly unpleasant.

Although the engine noise really did not really bother me. I think I had learnt to tune this out completely and I had my earplugs. Earplugs meant the loud thrashing of the engine that sounded like it needed its carb synchronised and to be topped up with oil was reduced to a dull hum. Though the trip had gone quickly on account of the last Russians I would meet on this entire trip. A tall well built shaved headed Russian sat next to me and started to smoke and asked me the usual things, "Vih Atkuda?" Then asked if I would like to have a spot of vodka to give me strength for the rest of the journey. We went into the ship shop and bought a large litre bottle of vodka some Smirnoff orange flavoured. My newly acquired Russian buddies snarfed in contempt at this "vodka" being only 39.5% proof. And went to go get some mixer. To my mild surprise their mixer turned out to be yet another bottle of vodka which was stronger much stronger.

We first started with a Russian drinking game where 5 of us sat at a table with shot glasses the premise was this. You were poured a glass of vodka put 1 rouble on the table and knocked back the shot. Then something was called out and everybody ducked under the table another thing was called out and everybody sat back on the chairs again. This was easy until about 6 roubles were on the table at each seat when everybody could barely stand up from under the table. We ended up wandering onto the car deck completely drunken riding my bike around in the cargo hold around the containers and heavy equipment much to the dismay of the crew who came down perhaps due to the commotion and promptly threw us out.

Arriving somewhat drunken at Sokcho was pleasant the sun was shining, and there was a nice cooling breeze while we were ushered into the arrivals terminal. A simple stamp 90 days thank you very much. I love these civilised countries, which stamp you in on the border instant visa since visas had previously been a headache.

The headache came in the form of an Italian called Antonio. Antonio had come from Naples in a VW passat and spoke zero English and Russian relying instead on a point at picture book. He latched onto me immediately out of immigration and followed me to customs to clear the bike (and presumably his car) out of the ferry port and into South Korea.

Two hiccups occurred here in that we needed a large amount of Korean won to pay for the transport of our vehicles and lots of waiting around. Anybody who has been to Korea will know that your cards will only work in international ATMs that are a pain. Actually I only found 4 international ATMs in the whole of South Korea. Meaning I had to go and find a bank with an international ATM.

The shipping bill wasn't large by UK standards but the problem is the currency is so low value 10000 KRW is only worth £4 and I had to pay about $180US for the shipping, the bank decided to give me 1000KRW notes. I'm effectively carrying around a brick of money that isn't worth all that much. It's not so bad though I suppose as fellow traveller Tiffany whom you may recall I parted company in Azerbaijan managed to change 100 Euro in Uzbekistan. She came away with a huge number of bricks of money where the exchange rate is so bad they weigh the money.

The problem was communicating with the Italian guy who complained in Italian constantly. He expected me somehow to understand. 5 hours into the complaints I was getting agitated as he was complaining to me as if it was MY fault for some reason. We were unfortunately in this together. Waiting around for things to happen he said, "I think I am hungry I want macaroni." Whereby we set out on a mission impossible to look for macaroni. Suffice to say Koreans eat rice based pasta and ramen mostly and spaghetti rarely. After a very long walk around in the shops near the port the heat beating down on us. We found spaghetti but no macaroni. I'm sorry to any Italians or chefs who know different but Macaroni tastes exactly the same as spaghetti and when you are 8000 miles from home it's take it or leave it.... I shrugged my shoulders and suggested he eat the spaghetti instead. He stormed off angry with me and I waddled back via a back street to the ferry port.

On the way I passed numerous seafood restaurants the kind where the food was still alive and swimming around in tanks waiting to be cooked up. Tanks full of conventional looking fish, tube type worms, sea cucumbers. Even lamprey that is or rather was a British favourite at the time of Henry VIII it's actually not a fish but an eel like parasite, which bores into the sides of fish. The heat was impressive but more so the humidity especially for a coastal town drenched in my sweat and nicely enough the bike had cleared customs sort of. A hard faced man said we now go for inspection. Walking to where the bike was parked he started asking all sorts of intrusive questions, "Where were you born? What is your mother's name? Your fathers name?" Sort of reminding me of the Azerbaijan border. He was using a very harsh tone with me as if there was something wrong very wrong and I began to feel uneasy about this.

Finally just before we got to the XT he said, "Oh thank you very much I practice English with you." The customs officer. I discovered was called Kim had been taught by a rather stern man who would have done a very good impression of the drill sergeant in the film Full Metal Jacket. I'm like erm yes sure no problem a quick inspection no problems, I get on the XT fire her up and ride out through

Sokcho. Antonio had stormed off after not being able to find macaroni. He had missed the customs inspection allowing me quite frankly to escape from his smothering personality.

It was immediately apparent that South Korea was a world apart from Russia where shortages and shrugs of shoulders occur frequently. Shops had things on the shelves, brand names, 100 difference choices of noodles. Snacks everything! The whole she Bootle. I was very happy with this. Korea had clean food, clean tasty food (although heavily biased with seafood) I had started off my trip at a fairly respectable 12 stone (76 kilos) I arrived emaciated in Korea at less than 8 stone (50.8 kilos). It was a good excuse to gorge myself and put the weight back on. My clothes had felt loose each and every day. I didn't mind so much as it made it easier to get them off in case giardiasis had a go at me and it would let in cool breezes. I have to patent this one-day. The biker diet just go riding across Russia and you will lose a ton of weight. Even LWR who did not eat any of the food in Russia lost an awful lot of weight. Aside from food poisoning I have no idea as to why this was the case.

Unfortunately as I said earlier I had expected South Korea to be a transit country and therefore spoke not a single word of Korean nada nothing. I've always felt somewhat bad about going to a country and not speaking a word of their language. For Russia at least I had a phrase book. Although it's not really on the same level of badness as the typical English tourist. The kind who says the English over and over increasing in volume in a forlorn hope that the non-English speaking person would somehow mystically understand. In Russia at least I had a phrase book with which I had practiced with a Polish girl where I used to work.

Riding through downtown Sokcho was easier than expected bar the strange you can still turn right when the traffic lights are red thing that kept catching me out. Though the local riders seemed to be ignoring the traffic laws a bit. I would see a red light stop and other bikers would go up on the pavement around the traffic light and ahead as if the traffic light had never existed. I thought nothing of it until one car went up the kerb around the traffic light and continued on its merry way then another then another. As if the traffic light hadn't existed. A few laps around Sokcho and I was completely lost attempting to find a gigantic camping complex I had been tipped off about by Terry while we were in Vladivostok.

Sign language was the order of the day and lacking a map totally for even Sokcho I stopped at what looked like a hotel. I felt I deserved it even though I pretty much eschewed hotels through Russia. This was near the finish line I had done the hard parts and earned a night in a hotel. Hotel isn't the right word for it though in that they are called Motels. Although I'm pretty sure there are real motels like there are in the US Korean hotels are shall we say different...Motels in Korea are iffy the general clue was in the two pricing systems although at the time I couldn't read it there was a 'stay' price and a 'rest' price. In Korea motels are places where couples meet to shag. Korean homes are tiny and people don't leave home till their mid 20s. I had a thought of don't touch anything in the room. But this relented once I'd seen the room. It was actually quite clean or at least it seemed clean though Koreans are a very clean neat people who incidentally think other people are dirty but generally don't show this unlike their Japanese cousins.

On that note I discovered deodorant in Korea does not exist. Korean people do not smell at all. Having visited gyms in the UK the cheaper non branded ones you enter and you are hit by a wave of old sweat. Though I do like to use a particular machine at the gym when I can be bothered to join though. I used it too much once though and I was terribly sick but I LOVE it!! It's got Mars bars, Snickers, peanuts, chips and all kinds of good stuff!! I jest. In Korea there was a total absence of this body odour smell except in the hostels where westerners and non-Koreans tended to congregate. I have no idea why this is. Much later on I discovered that Korea has tons of gyms even though the general population is rather thin anyway. But then in Asia if you are female and size 8 you are considered a bloater. This doesn't really apply to the men though, though all of the men were thin wiry type. The only fat Korean man I encountered was Wendy's boss who was by no means gigantic. Oddly enough Korean people besides working lots for their corporations almost like *Zaibatsus* (Japanese corporations), often go to the gym. They are always very well hidden it seems in Korea in that they are unmarked and are discrete or the fact I can't read Korean script means I just didn't notice them. I managed to visit a couple of them to generally have a poke around. It seemed oft with line upon line of identical work out machines, to tone abs, calves, biceps, triceps and a million other muscles I've never heard of. All sorts of machines invariably marked Samsung or something. It seemed to me that if humanity were to collapse and fall into a new dark age in 1000 or so years time archaeologists in the future would dig up our cities and find all these exercise machines all designed to fit one person. They might think that our generation were sadists as we were obsessed with torture. As each town and city had rows and rows of machines thought to be for this purpose.

Though there was nothing on TV bar soft core Korean porn. Which was quite clever in that Korean law I assume prohibits pubic hair and insertions. The insertions law is taken to the extreme btw as I saw a Segal film where Segal stabs a man he is fighting repeatedly. Although I don't find inserting a knife into somebody's chest erotic in any way the insertion was blurred out or had a big black square put over it. This seemed to be taken to the extreme on some channels where a man being shot in slow motion would have small black squares overlaid on the bullet holes. The Korean soft-core porn was clever and pretty funny the faces the actors would make were hilarious as if it caused strange convulsions or a look of horror totally inappropriate. The clever part was the angles the actors were almost always naked, and it was filmed al la Austin Powers whereby the couple would have sex but there was always something obscuring their genitalia. A plant, a key ring, even a bowl of fruit, it became quite hilarious.

The morning quickly came and I was surprised at South Korea I had accidentally in my tired state left my keys in the ignition and virtually everything bar my wash bag onboard the bike. To my even bigger surprise absolutely nothing had been stolen. In the UK this would never have happened you leave keys in the ignition you turn round and the bike is gone.

Breakfast consisted of the ubiquitous cup noodles; except I had an inferior brand costing 300 Won it tasted like cardboard. How anybody can make something edible for 14p I don't know I do not recommend it! Their almond tea was nice though in a disposable paper cup which had a hideously complicated bit of plastic to lift the tea bag out of the cup. A piece of string would have sufficed all of this in a Buy the way. A shop that seems to dominate this part of South Korea. I returned to the bank and got yet another thick wad of Korean money (which was only worth £75) where I was virtually hero-worshipped. I was utterly stinking of sweat as I had not had a chance to wash my riding gear or clothing and yet here I was in a bank drawing out money being almost hero-worshipped by the staff of KB* bank who apparently had in what some people would say had only existed and not actually lived.

I almost feel sorry for Koreans born after the Korean War. They essentially copied Japan and indoctrinated the people into hard hard work, and absolute loyalty to the companies, much like in Japan. Although the initial generations of Koreans were happy to have survived the war the recent generations of Koreans had wanted more in life. I don't blame them, part of the motivation for this trip to escape if only for a while from this type of life. Although I had it easier than Koreans who would spend 18-20 hours a day 6 days a week at their companies at least I'd lived.

Having no map and all roads leading to the expressway, which bikes are not allowed on in Korea. I had to find a map and couldn't find a bookshop that sold a map. Korea other than for the convenience store that are open all day everyday has shops that open late mid day but then they do open till 11pm. Hence I was unable to find a map or a shop selling a map. I didn't know which way to go and tried my potluck asking 4 Russian looking people at an open-air café. They were visibly startled at me approaching them. In months and months I had not really taken care of my appearance, as usually it didn't matter and only added to the rugged traveller image people have in their minds.

"Hello," they said in a deep Mancunian accent, in unison.

"Where are you from then?" asked the tall one.

"Bolton," I replied.

"Hey that's just 5 miles from where we come from so what the bugger are yer doing out here then?" They asked.

"I rode the bike across Russia."

"Geez that's nuts! How did ya get through North Korea then?"

"I rode very quickly through it!"

"Geez!"

"So you did a ride like that Ewan fella, did yer come by yerself?"

"Erm yes but not like Ewan McGregor he did it supported." So the conversation went. It was nice to have a proper conversation with somebody and it made me miss home a little. I realised I hadn't actually spoken to anybody in English for quite sometime. Well with the exception of the other tourists in Mongolia which felt so long ago as if it were a prior life time. They gave me their spare tourist map and bid me good luck and off I went towards Seoul. But managing to pass Sokcho beach just before 11am. I had to stop and look. The water here is an impossible bright almost artificial looking shade of aquamarine blue. If you ever saw a photo of this you would swear that it had been touched up in photoshop.

Though it was a working day and the beach was deserted I spent a few hours reminiscing about a lake I had seen in Spain that had this same almost chemical blue. It was as if a huge number of chemical toilets had been emptied out. Though it wasn't all paradise. While the Spanish Lake, and another beach I have only seen in dreams were deserted with thick forest behind turning the beach into an enclosed space Sokcho beach was different. It was commercialised, heavily. A road ran parallel to the beach and the beach was lined with small huts that advertised cola and beach toys. Although at this early hour the shops were mostly closed it seriously spoilt the effect if viewed from some angles. Although if you sat on the beach facing out to the wonderfully blue water it seemed like a desert island you would only find in your dreams.

Although this didn't last as I turned the wrong way and ended up going down the coast a few miles to the south at Jeongdonglin. Another tourist resort it had the same blue within blue water and a nice cove. But as I approached something looked strange. Atop the cliffs it appeared there was a beached cruise ship, not a small one a massive ship that seemed to somehow have gotten to the top of the cliffs several hundred metres above sea level. This turned out to be the main tourist attraction around these parts but it was one hell of an eye sore. It was quite a clever technical trick they had done there, but it completely didn't fit into the landscape and spoilt the dream beach in my mind's eye.

The road to Seoul was a good one. I'd decided to go to via a mountain pass at Inchii where fabulous mountain views were everywhere almost like riding through the Alps between Italy and France, a marvellous sight. Where I stopped at a hot springs tourist spot and again was hero worshipped by passing Korean folks who would never dream of doing such a thing. Though I did have to stop at the peak to again diagnose the bike again as there were strange knocking sounds which coincided only when I accelerated. Unable to find this I tried adjusting the chain oiling it but to no avail. The knocking sound vanished after I started off down the road again only to return annoyingly on a twisty section with nowhere to stop. Not relishing the thought of the chain coming off and tearing my leg off I stopped in a lay by and readjusted my chain, looking over each link carefully. This attracted the attention of some passing Koreans who offered me a rather hairy peach and a bottle of water, excellent. Though with the stunning amount of grease covering my hands it was rather difficult to eat it, and wiping my hands on my clothing made my hands dirtier it seemed. The culprit turned out to be a fairly badly worn front sprocket which I could do absolutely nothing about I just hoped it would last till the end of my trek.

En-route to Seoul, I saw a sign saying "English village 8KM," this peaked my curiosity and I decided to go and have a look. The weather was certainly English it was drizzly rain for the past hour. Through twisting canyon roads I arrived at something odd. In a sort of a clearing surrounded by mountains, was what looked like an English village. Not so much in the style of thatched houses but it looked like a new build Barratt housing estate. It seemed truly authentic bar the classical music playing over the PA system yet lacked true authenticity of hooded chavs hanging around menacingly. I rode in to a big square in the middle and parked up to take a few photos as it would make a nice anecdote for anybody I might meet later on. Upon stopping a Korean man approached me and started to speak to me in Korean, as before I don't speak ANY Korean. I said in English, "I'm sorry I don't understand I'll be gone in a minute..."

The Korean's eyes grew visibly larger he said, "Hello, hello wait, wait!" And vanished off while I took some photos of the surrounding area. It felt almost creepy that somebody had built this in Korea. In Shanghai it is expected along with Hong Kong due to colonialism. But Korea is a pretty Alien place to the English. Just as I was about to start the bike another Korean man rushed out and grabbed my wrist.

"Come please, come," he said and led me inside.

"No, no I'll be going right now." Thinking I was in some sort of trouble. I was half expecting a cup of tea like in Turkey or Russia. But was taken through a winding corridor in the hidden complex past many empty rooms into a room to the side of the building, a classroom...

A classroom full of bright eyed Korean children. The Korean man who had led me in said a few sentences in Korean, and he then spoke some Korean to me. I suddenly had a bit of a sinking feeling in my gut. I realised he had put me in front of the class for an impromptu free English lesson from this apparently born in England Korean. Something they call a *gyopo*.

"Erm Hello children," I said nervously.

"Good morning sir!" They said back in unison and in an accent less English. There on followed an awkward on the spot language exchange class with myself telling them of my Russian adventure with many of the children a gasp at what I had done. Korean society is a very stiff society. One that I could almost consider a robot society where children are programmed to be corporate slaves. My adventures overseas would be considered a traitorous selfish act but something to be admired. As most of the population were unable to resist the corporate machines that controlled Korea.

Korea however is different from Japan while Japanese society indoctrinated their children into corporate slaves the Korean youth sort of rebelled. So although there is the Japanese corporate culture of doing things the younger Koreans are much less ready to accept that. Almost like unpaid overtime, well everybody else is doing it... So what's the problem? The mere fact that everybody else is doing it makes it seem almost acceptable to them. If I'm exploited and so are you it makes it all right then? A lengthy question and answer time where a Korean woman expected me to correct their English speaking grammar occurred and we crowded outside for photos of them sitting on my bike and photos of me on my bike. Here I learnt my first Korean word. Kam-sami-dah that meant thank you. I said thank you (for the experience) and started my bike to many camera flashes from camera phones and big cameras a like. I saw this as an opportunity to make my excuses and leave as I had been there for quite some time already and I pulled away from many smiling faces and waving of goodbye to me back onto the main road to Seoul.

I think this is a key turning point. I had been terribly undecided as to what to do with the rest of my life and this gave me an idea as to what it should be that I do for the rest of my life.

40: SEOUL

I began to develop a love for Korea for a very big reason. Korea is high tech and modern and yet is still not overrun by health and safety laws. People will ride around on their scooters without helmets minimal protective gear and take risks and not think any of it. As if it is normal though they do use steel scaffolding unlike the rest of Asia, which use bamboo instead. Children play freely in the streets, there isn't CCTV everywhere and the media doesn't appear to run constant scare campaigns like the British press does on a regular basis. Of paedophiles round every corner things like that which is probably why I liked it so much. A typical example was swine flu kills three people. In Korea people thought oh and so what?

   Britain achieved great things in the past, but imagine if the pioneers of past times had to obey the health and safety laws that we have to in the UK.

"Captain cook, you must perform the 'elf and safety risk assessment form in triplicate before you are allowed onto the island!" Though this is a bad example as it may have saved him from being eaten on his last expedition.

Or

"Sorry Isambard but you can't build that ship 'elf and safety won't allow it and nor will our insurers so you'll just have to forget about steam ships."

My map effectively said I needed to get on the expressway to enter the city, no other way in. Cruising round and round a man on a scooter kindly informed me I was to enter via Guri to get into Seoul. He asked the usual questions and was surprised that I had come all the way from London. Making my way through the heat I was tired and decided to call it a day at the first hotel I saw. As I could be there for a while looking for Kim's Hostel. Seoul is big very **very** big the entire Seoul metropolitan area contains 4 separate cities and 32 million people. It is the biggest mega-city in Asia in fact even bigger than Tokyo in the past few years. To put it to scale the Seoul metropolitan area inside the M100 motorway is bigger than the whole of Hong Kong. With an amazing 5 times the number of people living there. The first hotel I saw was the Hotel Boomlin that looked respectable with its large lobby free WIFI and bellhops. A place to park and a cushy air-conditioned room all for 45000KRW that translates into £25. Except the room had no windows and had a fire exit as part of my room which people would pile through if there was a fire. On my ride in I'd noticed an awful lot of shutters over windows, which made me think it was a fairly deserted area with shops closed everywhere.

A similar thing I've seen in the UK where town centres are all shuttered up a sign of the recession. Korea being an exporting country was in trouble from this recession too. And I thought much the same applied that these were just closed shops. I grabbed something to eat and went for a snooze.

4 hours later I went for a walk unable to sleep anymore and I realised why the hotel was so cheap and why there were so many shuttered windows. I had somehow inadvertently checked into a hotel in the Cheongnyangni 588 district. There was more hooking going on than in an Alaskan fishing village. It was like *De Wallen* in Amsterdam with 'barbershops' with stunningly beautiful Korean women standing inside them in skimpy underwear. Often under pink lights so it was sort of the pink light district, rather red light. My hotel was in effect an upscale love motel on the edge but did not advertise its 'rest' rate. Standing in the family mart eating my 50p foot long California roll, I was approached by a pimp who was speaking quickly in Korean. I said, "Sorry I'm not Korean I don't understand." Whereby he walked away from me and started telling the girls in his block I was not Korean. I later learnt that if you weren't Korean the girls would ignore you as if you do not exist. Which was fine for me as it was like walking through an expensive jewellery store as if you didn't exist but unable to touch. However I have nothing against them the individual workers themselves as they have to make a living somehow and put food on their tables. Again South Korea has no welfare, as we know it. Doug had said in Mongolia that such people as generally despised by other people frequently because they sell themselves for even less....

More comically I found other hotels in and around the area a themed one that from the pictures outside looked terrible. One of them themes was a wild western theme which rickety furniture and hard beds. Another was a space room that was all silver and glittery with plastic sheets I wondered who patronised these places.

I had to go here though as this was opposite there was a hospital come walk in clinic where I needed my shoulder and fingers looking at. Korea lacks a socialised health system and I'm not Korean anyway. I needed to pay first and claim back later though the bill was remarkably small $40 was enough for everything they did as the Korean won was so weak purposely to support exports.

Paying for it, medical care that is! Sewer mind! Was well worth it, but it didn't matter as again I could claim off my fairly comprehensive cover all travel and medical insurance. Koreans well Korean men at least get a feast for the eyes in the form of the nurses and even the women doctors. In that the uniforms they wear were something out of a fantasy well my fantasy anyway. The cutest of cute short white erotically starched dress uniforms which showed the curvature of their hips. Milky white tights and cute little paper hats and dainty little silver watches hung upside down on their chests like a broach. Cuteness overload yet still being sexy without even trying to be sexy it had to be a man who was the director of this place it was so obvious.

A doctor had a look over me twisted me this way and that which didn't bother me as I was attended by 3 nurses all curious to see this apparent new breed of adventurer who seldom existed in South Korea. Hence more virtual hero worship occurred there. I had my arm and shoulder scanned in something that looked like a bigger than normal laser printer with a Samsung sticker on it like everything else electronic in Korea. Then scanned again in a slightly bigger machine that scissored my shoulder in its vice like grip. There was nothing wrong; there were no broken bones of my shoulder and arm. They cut the tape and spanners off my fingers used as a temporary splint and scanned those too. It was nothing worse than a hairline fracture which they explained they could do nothing about other than let time heal it and to keep weight and pressure off it. I sighed my brutal regime of finger press-ups was over for at least a couple of weeks (yeah right).

Ironically I went to get some Korean barbecue half an hour later. At the big market place near the metro station and found a neat cosy little restaurant with a butcher attached to it. Taking a seat I was unable to read anything off the menu as is was in *Hanguul* (Korean text) something I can't read. But the waitress led me to the meat section to choose which cut I would like to have for dinner. I went through a bead curtain doorway and into the butchers shop and saw a large selection of pork and beef cuts. All of which were under a pink light to make the 'meat' look better.... the ultimate irony...

I went back to the hotel to watch the Forbidden Kingdom, as there was nothing else on bar yet more soft-core Korean porn, which the novelty had generally worn off from before. Jackie Chan was kicking ass on TV and I was soon asleep as this was nice quiet without insects in the bed or in the air and gained some restful sleep.

The next day after a long time spent ATM hunting and having to travel 2 metro stops just to find an ATM to accept my card. I went to Itaewon the supposed other party district of Seoul. It was shall I say not to my taste, in that Itaewon was full of MPs (military police) as the area due to the military base and seemed far too Americanised. American chains of various sports bars even the Korean shop sellers spoke in a corny American accent. It was a bit of a sick parody of China town or Korea town you sometimes find in cities in the UK or the US but of the US, which was odd. The prices for everything also came from the US and Europe too at 15000 Won for a beer too much for a pint of Guinness when Korean beer is 2000 a pint. Huge stinking arguments between tourists that is American and Canadian tourists would break out in a shameless manner. For the short time I was there I must have heard the most trivial arguments. One about the fries being the wrong shape the other where the girlfriend refused to get money from the ATM. The large crowds of drunken soldiers mincing around gave the area the sort of feeling that it might just spill over into a violent riot.

II

The heaviest rain I had ever seen drenched Seoul for a day before I decided to go out and find a cheaper place to stay. Though the rains only lasted a few hours it was enough to coat the streets in rain 3 inches deep. Forked lightening belched from the sky. Darkened clouds turning the day into night. And the sky into a chemical purple colour.

I had a recon ride outwards towards Guri from Cheongnyangni just to see if I could retrace my path as I may never have been able to escape Seoul other wise. During which the rain started again without much warning. I got wet and dried out again after a brief ride other bikers generally seemed to ignore the rain getting soaked. Though this was understandable as the powerful sunshine dried them out super fast. This cheaper place to stay came in the form of Kim's guesthouse. The trouble was Kim's was all the way across Seoul meaning having to ride all the way through Seoul. Which is where I saw that the motorbike in Korea is king and a law unto themselves.

Traffic jam? Filter through, big long queue that you can't filter through as it is too narrow? Go up onto the pavement and drive round it. The second bit i.e. go up onto the kerb was practiced by cars too. Part way through the day riding past the centre of Seoul I got near the statue of Yi-Sun-shin. The traffic got more and more crazy, motorbikes zigging this way and that. Scooters flying through traffic mounting the pavement going through red lights as if they were not there, with 3 sometimes 4 people on board straining the engines of the little 50cc bikes, which were popular. This didn't seem that unusual as I had seen some things similar in London and Manchester myself, it got iffy when I saw cars doing the same things and the pedestrians not looking at all surprised. All of this combined with the cheap petrol at 1005 Won per litre I had a minor epiphany. South Korea **IS** a biker's paradise. Road laws are non-existent, most bikes didn't even have number plates, and the roads just outside the cities were perfect sports bike country. South Korea for all its vices, which were actually good things in my book and the books of many bikers, South Korea was paradise. Bikers on bigger Japanese machines would pull wheelies, go across double white lines in full view of the police not wear helmets or gloves or any protective riding gear. The bikers in Seoul made me look like a safety nazi, scoffing at my leather gloves and helmet and tough army boots when I approached them to say *Annyeonghaseyo* (hello). The lack of riding gear the police would ignore totally people riding around in shorts flip flops and vests. It

256

took quite a while to get to Kim's having to cross the river illegally 5 or 6 times on the expressways that prohibit motorbikes but the police simply did not care.

Kim's was a place huge in suburbia of Seoul sort of. Which had so many beds crammed into the tiny space that you would see people walking in and out who were staying there yet you'd never seen them in a dorm. Unfortunately this was a Lonely Planet recommended hostel. The kind I generally tried to avoid and had even gotten onto the tourist map of Seoul. The problem with this is that it makes it popular and in being popular becomes expensive crowded and the service falls while the owner rakes in the cash.

Suburbia of Seoul looked remarkably similar to Suburbia of Japan. High fences sometimes concrete sometimes wood with gated fences. It felt almost insular, imagine a UK housing estate where high head height fences were surrounding each house. It would feel different, though I suppose people mixed more due to the smallness of the homes and the use of the metro system. Little Korean copies of Honda C90s buzzed about in these suburbs. Often ridden one handed delivering food. Food delivery was different in Seoul. A bloke would get on his scooter with a big top box sized box in his hand and ride to the delivery address. Inside the box contained steel plates and cutlery. The person who ordered it would eat and wash the dishes to be picked up with next day's meal delivery. Meals for Koreans are communal in that they would sit around a table and share several large plates and many smaller saucer sized dishes.

In the hostel I met several characters Christophe and Felix, who are travellers of the sort who confuse me a bit. They were from Germany and had decided to spend their two-week vacation out here in S Korea on account that it was cheap. What confused me was that they went out got drunk off their ass till 3-4am and then stayed in bed till 4pm finally rolling out of bed for breakfast before starting the drinking yet again. Ok so it was their choice it just seemed a bit wasteful to fly the 10000km to Korea to do something you could do at home and to boot German beer was vastly superior to the local brew Cass or Hite. My dad is particularly guilty of this in that he goes to far away destinations but always ensures that those places have cable TV, and he spends all his time watching TV there. I left them at a cute little Korean bar come restaurant trying to teach the welcoming computer thing the word 'schisse'.

Although Felix we found out sometime later was arrested at Incheon airport immigration due to having a Pyongyang stamp in his passport. In the DMZ (demilitarised zone) tourist centre there was a fake immigration booth, which had a fake stamp in it for Pyongyang. Felix had as a joke when we went there day tripping stamped it in his passport as a fake chalk mark. Look at me I've been to North Korea though N Korea you can actually get to from Beijing it just costs a ton of money about $10,000 US that's all. When he went to leave at the airport the

257

immigration official saw the stamp and he was promptly put under arrest and questioned for 14 hours missing his flight and having to pay to be put on the next flight out. There is a proper way to get into North Korea that is similar to what you'd find in Israel and Cuba where you have a piece of paper with the entry stamp printed on it which you would keep in your passport and remove if you needed to go somewhere that said you shouldn't go to those kinds of places.

The hostel was generally packed with teachers of English who had no other qualification other than being born in an English speaking country. It was funny and tragic sometimes in that some Americans with a deep southern accent drawl and dulcet tones were teachers in Korea. It felt similar to Mongolia but more wide spread. South Korea has so many private schools that there are hundreds of thousands of people teaching Korean children how to speak English these are called *hagwons*. I imagined in 10 years time when the children grew up that business conducted with English speaking companies would be less that successful as people would think you are taking the piss.

At Kim's I also met Gonzales an Ex USN Marine who had decided to stay in Korea for a year after serving at the Military base in Itaewon. Korea wasn't the land of milk and honey it seemed after all. We spent a few hours chatting about Korea in general.

"There are certain things you can't get here and had to get on the black market." He said. At first I thought he meant drugs.

"You mean drugs?" I asked.

"No drugs are easy to get," he said, "In Asia it is very easy to get drugs, as the medical services are all private. Much like in other countries in Asia if you want a prescription drug you just go to a pharmacy and ask for it. When you are asked for your prescription a 10000KRW or even 5000KRW note often does the trick." He explained. I knew that a similar system exists in China.

"Drug dealers had no business in South Korea, as there was no need for them when drugs are virtually legal."

"Oh it's like China then?"

"Yeah, well I always have to go to the black market to get smuggled protein shakes, biscuits and deodorants..." I laughed and asked him if he was serious, he said he was perfectly serious.

"You can't get this stuff in Korea and the government won't let people import them legally so the Marines bring it in their personal stuff which doesn't get checked." He explained to me. The South Koreans although had a massive army and all of the men under 40 could be called up to fight in case of war with North Korea meaning a military force of over 15 million infantry could be mobilised in hours. South Korea's government still wanted the US military backup and a blind eye was turned to the gentlemen's entertainment around military bases in Korea, notably a place right next to the military base in Itaewon called Hooker Hill. Though his protein whey porridge did smell absolutely delicious it was a mixture of ready brek (a British breakfast porridge) and this brown chocolate whey protein. I suddenly imagined being approached by a shadowy figure in the black market with shifty eyes giving a quick glance left and right to look for cops. Having to do shady deals over packets of digestives or a packet of Rich tea. Or say if I wanted the 'harder stuff' chocolate digestives. Or Spivs on the side streets, offering packs of oatmeal, selling it like it was cocaine. It's good stuff kid I'll sell you a half for 50,000 won, it's genuine stuff you can't get it anywhere else.

Or such smugglers fighting over territory fighting running gun battles, doing the odd drive by shooting to eliminate the competition and secure their rights to be the only ones to push chocolate digestives or oatmeal. This frankly seemed utterly absurd and I dispelled such thoughts out of my head. Korea is pretty crime free and nobody seemed to ever fall victim from it with the worse crimes being *Chikan* fingers (being molested on the train).

The other person I met was Simon. Simon approached me and looked like an Amish bloke on vacation. Simon would prove to be one of my best short-term friends during my stay in Korea and would revive my opinion of Germans. Simon wasn't your normal German. He had gotten bored while in North Carolina and thrown a dart into a map and hit Seoul. He was into his 3rd Bachelors degree, had done his MBA and was scouting universities for a PhD. His second PhD. Simon was the kind of guy whom you would approach and say get a job!

III

I managed to stay here for 2 days after failing to exit Seoul on account of getting seriously lost and riding in circles round and round for hours. I felt I didn't have the time to get anywhere interesting and decided to stay another day.

The key to Seoul is route 68 in that it traverses the entire length of Seoul and you peel off when you need to at the appropriate junction. The length of my stay was more determined by the availability of air conditioning as after Korea's wet months came a swelteringly hot month before it cooled down. Walking outside and standing in a pool of sweat was some thing I didn't like. I decided to explore Korea for the next week before giving my bike over to Wendy Choi my shipping agent whom everybody uses (say hi if you ever meet her) and so I left to go south. I had discovered off the Korean guys I met in Russia that river banks and beaches in Korea are fair game and are considered to be communal so fair game. So I pretty much went the long way round the coast of S Korea camping on beaches and under bridges over rivers, all perfectly above board quite often I would find other families already there.

This wasn't 'real' camping of course in that I would wash in various places including going to a motel for a 'rest' purely to use their washing facilities which was good value being £2 or £3 for the use of their shower and washing machines. But real camping does not exist in Korea. People there are far too attached to their machines. There is a campsite I visited near the world cup stadium, which is a 'campground', when they say campground they don't really mean it. I had a look it was cheap £6 a night. But it was just so wrong that it could barely be called camping.

The tents that were set-up on the pitches all had strange boxes connected to the back of them, which turned out to be air conditioning or heating ducts. En-suite bathroom facilities were nearby and there were huge restaurants and entertainment complexes as well as underground heating to seep into the tent. This along with free WIFI and low rent Samsung notebooks seemed to make camping so detached from camping as we know it in the UK that it wasn't camping at all.

"You want stay camping one night?" I was asked.

"Yes I want a pitch for my tent," I said.

"Why do, you ah have your own tent?"

"I've been camping in Siberia I have my own tent and sleeping bag." After a moment of awe having realised I had crossed from the UK.

"Ah this is forbidden for your own tent. You must use our tent only is forbidden to use your own tent."

"What? Why?" I replied.

"This is rule in Korea, I'm very sorry." Which just about summed up the official government designated camping in Korea. The cheapness of the accommodation everywhere though probably meant that camping was the last thing people thought about.

Though I suppose my camping in Korea was closer to proper camping than the Korean kind. Due to laziness however I would have breakfast and lunch at convenience stores and dinner in proper Korean restaurants. It was so cheap eating good food at low prices it made no sense to eat cooking for myself. Although this in itself detaches from camping too it was a nice compromise. Though it was not perfect as it often hard to sleep with the torrent of water passing nearby. Though the cicadas hissing in the trees gave the water a run for its money in keeping me awake at nights. Though cicadas big fat ones were everywhere in Seoul that there were trees. You would hear a hissing sound whenever you got near a tree and a huge palm sized cicada would hiss at you and crawl slightly up the tree to hiss at you again. I missed the absolute silence of Siberia.

I did however stop in a few cities on the way down managing even to go onto the expressways. I often stopped in small towns on the way just to have a look. These towns seemed to be almost positively Cornish they would have singlewide roads

260

down the middle of them with shops, petrol stations and houses to one side. This could have been anywhere. Though even out here away from Seoul there were considerable numbers of soldiers sitting around in jeeps or packed into the back of lorries. This gave me the overall impression that South Korea seemed a massively militarised society even far from the DMZ and the perceived threat of North Korea defences had been put everywhere. Technically North and South have been at war since the 1950s and there are on guard always. I generally wasn't exactly sure of what they were defending as these small towns were sprawling and finally petered out after a few miles. Though of course freedom isn't free.

This part of Korea also seemed to reflect China an awful lot too in that in the UK we keep grass verges as grass. In Korea many of the fields or roadside areas even rest areas were cultivated. I suppose this is because Korea is small and they need all the land they can grow food on. Farmers were also an incredible contrast to the affluence of Seoul, in that small huts made of board were on the edges of fields. Closer investigation showed that people had entire homes inside but miniaturised to fit inside. Many things looked very odd though that although farmers seemed to be poor and had little they would often have under a tarp a mini combined harvester or some other machinery. Though it was far from industrialised agriculture we have in Europe or the US in that now and again double-bent old women and men would tend to their fields by hand. It was bizarre in that there were no young people. The youngest person I found there was a 40-year-old man who spoke very little English so there was little interaction him thinking I was a *gyopo*. I suppose that many of them were tempted by a life of bright lights and the city working in fields or comfortable air-conditioned offices.

Strangely enough in China it is the ones who stayed in the fields who resisted the lure of going to the city who were the wealthiest. This is a strange reflection of the UK in that those who did the 'dirty' manual jobs are often wealthier than white-collar workers. It seemed a simple life possibly carefree and an interesting fusion of new and old living styles. In Korea only 60 years ago everybody lived like this as farmers tending to their fields.

The almost everywhere the roads were sealed bar the farms and the odd mystery track which I sometimes went down often leading to a ramshackle run down building where people slept. The roads were perfectly smooth bar some oddities, often on steep mountainous sections would have centimetre deep grooves cut into them for some bizarre reason. The scenery was of the Pacific Ocean or the mountains, which the roads were carved into. The view was usually ocean on one side fields mountain or rock on another side. I was actually getting bored of riding on sealed roads as sealed roads, which are perfectly smooth and grippy are incredibly predictable. It's like a politician on TV you just know what is going to happen next. On a small cc sports bike it would have been fun thundering around corners 80-140mph. A sealed road on a trail bike was just boring. South Korea was effectively super sports bike country when you got a clear bit. I had to ration myself to riding on the beaches and river banks to get to campsites but it was never the same as the off road bits done in Mongolia or Russia. Though it wasn't perfect a big problem was with the rural roads. In that on expressways motorbikes are not allowed onto (though there is little enforcement if you do decide to go on them). It was just start stop riding constantly in that there would be red lights every 500 metres outside the towns every 50 metres in the towns which would invariably be red so you stopped and started constantly which made for very tiring riding.

I noticed on the second day that drivers would ignore traffic lights totally outside the cities as nobody was ever crossing the road since 90% of the people in Korea lived in Seoul. In fact on the subject of driving in Korea...(you might want to skip the next Chapter if you aren't interested)

41: SEOUL
THE DARK SIDE

Seoul was pretty bad with big 4x4s everywhere a favourite being the Hyundai Santa fe which I personally hate. Not because of environmental reasons or space reasons (though it makes no sense to drive those things in Seoul it's too big). Kim who ran the guesthouse had two Santa fe parked up outside. But that's not the reason I hate them, the reason I hate them is because in the UK while I was riding I was knocked off by a Santa fe at a junction. The driver of the said Santa fe proceeded to gun the gas and leave the scene of the accident. The 4x4s were not the only bad thing though it was the riders. Although you would sometimes see the odd fireblade, R1 and such many Koreans would ride around on small air-cooled motorbikes.

The motorbikes were Dalems mostly a Korean brand that did not exist outside Korea. The only Korean brand I knew before this was Hyosung. The ubiquitous scooters were also a common sight. Dispatch or courier riders in London are considered a core elite of the biking fraternity to people in the UK and they sometimes milk this reputation. Those that don't get killed that is, one of the people I knew in Plymouth was an ex dispatch rider. He would have a schtick where he would show people his x-rays of all the metal in his body.

Dispatch riders in Korea are more like mules. Down town Seoul you would see 100s of bikers and bikes parked up outside shops. Shopkeepers would come out and demand something be taken to another shop client or whatever they delivered. A short session of bidding would occur. A rider was chosen to deliver that item and pile it onto the bike. In London this is usually no more than a letter sometimes a big parcel.

In Korea they think nothing of putting 6 or so gas canisters, carpet rolls, engines, compressors car parts even scooters on the back. Buzzing around the big cars stuck in traffic all jockeying for space and speed. They made my two panniers tent and sleeping bag look tiny in comparison. I had a few words with the Korean bikers and it transpired that the motorbike was generally considered to be a beast of burden something to carry cargo. While the car and van was considered to be transport for people. Bigger bikes and sports bikes were considered to be toys as well but were uncommon.

For driving and I think I figured out why in Korea, in that Korea much as they would hate me to say this is a mirror of Japan. In that in Korea being a Korean for the most part isn't great, although I am in fact describing the principle of habitation where people who live somewhere hate it. I.e. the English always bitch about the failings of England and Wendy would ask me why the bugger would you want to stay in Korea? Koreans have an ordered society such that much is demanded of people to conform to this society. Children who go to after school classes till 9pm daily. 2 years of conscription for the men it seemed to be a life that was lived to the obligations of others.

Hence I think at least that they feel they are only really free when they are driving and thus any thing that impinges on this they get mad at the wheel. This isn't to say there aren't any very good drivers in Korea however. To not acknowledge the mostly good driving would be terribly unfair to the Korean people. But it's the bad things that stick in your mind not the good ones I suppose as they make more of an impact. I also discovered what Korean brakes meant i.e. hammering on his HORN and not slowing down. I had quite a few close encounters with cars. Though I think overall I had a lot of slack cut to me as I was riding a UK number plate bike and the drivers would be thinking hey I wonder where he comes from.

Perhaps the best summary of Korean driving is a joke Doug had told me in Mongolia in a pub when warning me about Korean driving. As he himself had been there for a few months.

"The red light district, the only red light a Korean man will stop for." He joked.

Outsiders often see Korea as some kind of utopia. It is clean, things work and everything is nicely ordered almost as far as some people would consider it sterile and soulless or is that Seouless? I managed to stay there for quite a bit and started to notice things wrong with Korea. That is not to say that other countries do not have problems, but it's just the rather blasé manner in which it was generally ignored or accepted without question.

I'm not kidding in that Korean men seemed to regularly and constantly talk about prostitutes. Hongjin taking us out for an errand would invariably take a metro station that would mean we would have to walk through a Red Light district. Oddly enough he would approach them have a chat ogle them and smile walking away.

Through a few weeks in Seoul I must have seen at least 30 maybe 40 red light districts, some big some sprawling ones, some tiny just a strip of shops like a parade. Hongjin would spend hours in the hostel looking at prostitutes online it was completely open about it as if it was accepted and normal. In Korea going to a prostitute was almost expected drinking with random Korean men who struck up English conversations with me when was talking with somebody on the phone they would buy me coffee as thanks and suggest going to see a prostitute.

Bizarrely from the other side it wasn't disrespectful to be a working girl either, they just didn't talk about it. But it would be casually mentioned if people asked. South Korea as I said in my opening sentences is a very strange place. One hostel I managed to stay in just off Hongdae main road had a bunch of Americans staying there after having worked in Korea for 3 years and were about to go home. They had a similar experience that Korean men would talk endlessly about going to see prostitutes and recommend them to each other. One of them Elaine a Californian was particularly vocal about this. She stated that her bosses and co-workers would speak about it as much as the British talk about the weather. It was also strange walking out on the town with her on the way to a live music venue in that we would get wolf whistled and rude comments made to us by Korean men.

Another oddity were the enormous number of homeless people in Seoul. Korea is one of those countries, which is run like a corporation. Social security and welfare are low on the priorities of Korean people and it is virtually non-existent like just over the sea in Japan.

The oddity was that none of the homeless people I encountered ever begged for money. In a couple of the outlying parks and abandoned buildings in Seoul I saw people hanging up their laundry in neat rows indifferently to if they lived in those homes. They would keep their belongings neatly in an orderly fashion as they lay to rest for the night. It was I suppose a face issue in that they attempted to put a brave face on their situation to save face like many Asian people do it seemed a little extreme to be honest.

Of course it wasn't as extreme as China were people starved to death to save face. This was an incredible contrast to what I see at home in the UK. Where people aggressively beg or even threaten you for your belongings. That is not to say I haven't met some decent homeless people. It is perhaps the bad impressions, which stick in your mind more so than the good impressions.

I did however manage to get mistaken for a homeless person in Korea though in that my general look was somewhat scruffy for Korea. I had managed to use one pair of jeans for the entire trek riding, sleeping, partying, and going out on the pull only in these jeans. Though I must state that what appear to be dirt stains on my jeans are not dirt stains at all. They are crash stains that can't be washed out at all.

This mistaken identity meant I was actually invited to sit and chat with them once, and see some of the real Seoul. They were polite and immaculately clean, well dressed and shaven and it would be difficult to differentiate the normal citizens with the homeless other than perhaps their faces showed noticeable emaciation.

They seemed to state some of the worst fears of many people, in that many of them turned out to have once been high-ranking corporate officials. Or executives who had been become redundant over time and replaced with newer fresher faces that would work more for less and had hence become a liability. As an accountant I have witnessed this many times, unfortunately there is no accounting for the ruthlessness of humans.

I managed to stay with them for an evening; many of them seemed to be happy that they had survived the Korean War, which nearly tore the country apart. However they were completely reluctant to accept any charity or anything off me. I managed to share a few bottles of Soju with them on account that I wouldn't drink alone and it was only polite for me to offer them some as an honoured guest. However old people begging were a fairly frequent fixture though, in that it wasn't classed as begging in how we would see it. They would trail behind you write a poem in Korean for you. Fold an origami swan or bird (even though Origami is Japanese) and offer to sell it to you rather than outright begging.

42: BUSAN & THE LAND OF THE RISING SUN.

After a frustrating stop start ride down I arrived at Busan South Korea's second biggest city though it was a pale imitation of Seoul. Seoul has 32 million people Busan only 2.5 million. The ride down as said was unpleasant they seemed to absolutely love pedestrian crossings in the remotest of places with timed traffic lights meaning you had to stop lots and lots.

Though on the way south to Busan I did manage to go to a Jinjilbang I mistook for a motel. A Jinjilbang is a Korean bathhouse where people wash then jump into a whirlpool alternating between hot and cold. In that you would go in take all your clothes off shower and jump in a hot tub with 50 other naked Korean men. Now this sort of thing just isn't done so often in the UK. But I though meh nobody else cared so I went in as well. It was in stark contrast to what many people had talked to me about regarding bathhouses. In Japan if they discovered you were not Japanese other people would get out of the hot tub. While in Korea they knew I wasn't Korean and didn't care and would chat to me in very good English in the bath and in the sauna rooms.

Busan with a B not a P (as the government legislated to change it to a B) felt different it was no Seoul but it was still pleasant in its own sort of way most noticeably defensible space. Something Seoul lacked anywhere especially when people went to and from work. In Seoul you would be crowded from every direction just by ordinary people going about their day-to-day business. Busan also seemed to be markedly spread out in that as a port city it felt like Vladivostok. There seemed to be many long sweeping viaducts leading into the city. Old tricks such as follow the ferry port signs did not work unfortunately as there were three port facilities in Busan and I had absolutely no idea as to which one it was I was supposed to go to. Going from dead end to dead end-wrong area to wrong area. I decided to follow the KTX (Korean Train eXpress) tracks these are a raised platform above anything. This is more difficult than it sounds as the KTX tracks are suspended on a bridge high above the ground so that while the tracks can go over coves and bays you have to find some way around it. Finally after a few hours of trying I stopped by a taxi and did the oldest of tricks. Stop a taxi show him the address I wanted and follow the taxi to the ferry port, which I couldn't find the ticket office, as it was late I decided to stay the evening.

I had a few thoughts on getting to Japan now that I had gotten to in Busan. I spent an evening in an improbably strict rules hostel, which had no beds again Korean style sleeping on the floor. They obviously did not really do much business as I was the only guest that night but it was clean cheap and a bed (read floor) to lay down for a while before going out to explore a little. Busan had wide open spaces with relatively few people a nice sea front leading to the beach though it was overcast so nothing much was seen amongst the haze. I'd imagined if I had gotten there earlier there would be a fantastic shimmering sunset the kind you only see on postcards.

I left early in the morning as the place although clean had an owner who seemed not to really want guests. I think they were doing it to make a few extra Won in all honesty I didn't even catch the name of the owner manager of the place. Though she was good enough to write down the address of the ferry port and give me directions to get there on the metro. I went to enquire at the ferry port how much it would cost to get the XT to Japan and back. The hydrofoil wouldn't take the XT. The ferry to Hakata would though they wanted far too much money to get to Japan 492,500Won and that was just a single. I couldn't justify the cost for such a small leap and back as I knew of nobody in Japan who could ship my bike using LCL shipping (less than container load). Slightly defeated I travelled back to the hostel picked up my gear and dropped the bike off at a crating company who there and then built a box for the XT. An old man appeared with a small flat bed van, which he called a truck. The XT went into a big wooden box; or rather a box was built around it. Not to be seen again for quite sometime as I gave the shipping company instructions to hold onto it for a while.

I returned to the port and had a look at the ticket prices for the hydrofoil and they were quite reasonable and so took the hydrofoil to Japan for a reasonable £89 return I had reached Japan land of the rising sun as a million clichés would say all over the Internet in tourist brochures etc.

The time I spent in Japan was short and mostly consisted of visiting old friends here and there. Japan is a mirror reflection it seemed of Korea and Korea a mirror reflection of Japan. Japan though most definitely does have more vending machines though. With the oddest of odd things like vending machines outside convenience stores, which boggled the mind. It with the things that are sold in Japan from vending machines (used panties are a myth btw) you can spend quite some time never speaking to anybody. Upon my return I was sent a video of a robot performing demeaning repetitive tasks that in the UK and US would be reserved for minimum wage workers.

I supposed that this made up for the fact that Japan still had many JAPANESE ONLY signs posted up outside many shops. Conveniently written in Russian and

Chinese I'm not sure what they thought about Koreans though as the signs I spotted did not have any *Hanguul* script on them.

I travelled by bullet train to Osaka. To Osaka University where I had hoped to find Tina who always signed her emails it's not Lederhosen. She had gone to Osaka university for a few years a while back as a researcher. Last I had heard she had married a Japanese professor though this did not last and the staff seemed to say she had moved on. I did have a look at the year books though and saw her picture there and found out her middle name was Louise. We have never actually met having spent 2 years liasing with each other via email I like to do old turn up unannounced in a shocking manner. Half way around the planet unseen in the flesh ever with a 5-year gap was perhaps hoping too much and a severe test of my apparent power of coincidence. Though it's only coincidence if you bump into each other without expecting it or without fore planning.

I also went to see Alex who had moved away from London in 2004. He had gone on the JET programme (Japan Exchange and Teaching programme), which is run by the Yakuza who also run pachinko. A strange vertical game of pinball where the object of the game is to scoop the balls into a receptacle thing. You win a prize which you they take outside and exchange for cash with the local Yakuza. Alex had gone out and somehow did not manage to come back this is rather a common occupational hazard of Japan and Korea. Though I did make the precaution of phoning him first from Korea to make sure there was somebody to meet with in Japan.

Old friends never forget you and this was proof of that as we chatted and drank warm sake and chatted about old times. The decadence here was amazing even the toilet seats were heated. Though I can never get used to sleeping on the floor no matter how you dress it up with under floor heating. I sleep on my side and my hip digs into the floor. Meaning I toss and turn on the *tatami* mats all night long. Though he seemed to have gone a bit native in that he seemed to be pained when I walked into his house with my boots on though my cultural *faux pas* was overlooked. Though Alex did lead a stressful life in Japan, more stressful than his original life in Cornwall.

We spent an evening in a relatively empty bar with an old man in a suit dropping beer after beer. We sat at the bar drinking beer and small amounts of phenomenally expensive Sake called rice under the snow which was unique as it was drank neat and cold. A very old TV in the corner showing inane Japanese TV, programmes seemed to be lots of bright colours and people doing the silliest of things. The commercials though were something else. The song by James Brown about it being a man's world would be totally apt even innocent commercials for children's sweets. A typical commercial would go like this an obviously mature girl woman (probably late teens to twenty five tops) would be sat on a bench dressed in a typical Japanese school girl sailor suit costume. She would be holding a packet of some sort of candy. Another similarly dressed and improbably proportioned 'school girl' actor would approach the bench, kiss and or fondle the boobs of the first actress. Smile and give a coy wink and then walk off with the sweets that the first girl was holding before usually cutting to an eye catch scene holding the packet.

Nagoya was odd though that even bicycles had to pay to park at the Shinkansen (bullet train) railway station. The high speed trains were a novelty in that you got on and an hour or so later you would be in a completely different city when an hour in the UK on a train and you haven't gotten very far. It was strangely liberating, distance seemed to be no barrier. On the Korean KTX people would use it to commute from half way down the country granted Korea is small but 200 mile commutes were 45 minutes on the train. This was most impressive. I couldn't stay in Japan here long as the hotels were extortionate and I couldn't find a ryoken. The Dolphin hotel was £70 a night even though it wasn't that comfortable; to add insult to injury the bathing facilities were closed that day. Though the receptionist Amano was cute enough to justify the stay I suppose, though I had been spoiled by Korea so it was nothing special. I just wished I had bought the XT over, as the few petrol stations in Nagoya I saw seemed to be attended by women in hot pants and boob tubes. They sang happy sounding songs in Japanese when delivering petrol, and smiled nicely self-service is so overrated in the UK. I guess I would pay more if I could get this kind of service. Partly I also wanted the XT here as some of the skylines that are high country roads I could see from the train looked stunning and in perfect condition. Some of the passes overlooking the pacific were stunning which reminded me of the coastal routes in Spain and France over 10,000km away.

I also confirmed my dad's urban legend that in Japan vending machines and shops sell cans of drink in two sizes at exactly the same price. If you bought a small one it cost the same as the large can, and to my surprise the small cans always seemed to be sold out more often than the bigger cans from what I could tell at the vending machines flashing red LED lamps to indicate the sold out items.

I took the bullet train back to Hakkata a couple days later as it was just costing me far too much to stay any length of time in Japan. I was getting a Japanese experience in Korea anyway. Though that wasn't the issue. Japan just seemed over commercialised and sterile. Even though Seoul sometimes felt like that, Japan just didn't it feel right it left me cold as there was some sort of indescribable vibe of Seoul.

43: THE SEOUL OF SEOUL.

I took the beetle (hydrofoil) back to Busan as it was the cheapest option back to Korea and eventually got back to Seoul via the KTX which to boot only cost £20 for a first class ticket. 2 hours later 400km later I was back in Seoul. I never understand why public transport in the UK is so shockingly expensive when this was cheap fast and clean. Look at it this way a ticket into Manchester costs £4 (about 10000 won) while a similar trip on the metro in Seoul costs 400 won, even if you measure this in cans of coke it works out cheaper 8 cans of coke vs. ½ a can of coke cost in Korea the mind boggles.

Once I got back to Seoul, Simon and me moved out to a new hostel. Nobody touristy knew about well only Korean people knew about at the time as it was only listed on Korean websites via the Korean search engine Naver. The owner was Honjin Park who had lived in Seoul all his life and the place was more like a Ryokan in Japan where Japanese people passing through would stop off. I was plenty satisfied that nobody here owned a Lonely Planet guidebook. Most of the people there seemed to be visiting friends or family in Seoul from the Korean countryside and were thus Koreans you would meet everyday.

Oddly enough for such a high tech country VHS and cassette tapes were still all the rage. Park had a large selection of VHS tapes as well as cassettes he would put on now and again.

The mingling with Korean people was an eye opener. Korean icons in the UK such as Park Eun Kyung and Hwang Mi Hee whom many had made animated GIF files that drove men around the world crazy were virtually unknown. Park Eun Kyung? Hwang Mi Hee? Who are they? Even writing out the Korean *Hanguul* to them they would still give us back puzzled looks. However I suppose they are just another pretty face in the sea of pretty Korean girls who are everywhere in Seoul.

Most surprisingly was 'plays two guitars at once Zack Kim' who isn't just a pretty face and he has real talent who again absolutely nobody in Korea knew who he was either that or the people who I consider are iconic aren't really that iconic after all.

Park and his virtual wife Hwa Young (Korean women do not take on the name of their husbands) were a different sort of hostel owners. Completely unlike Kim's who would turn up in the morning pick up the rent and go out shopping for the rest of the day. Park would spend the morning cleaning everything perfectly. Then later on take us out drinking clubbing and generally do all sorts of things that you would expect parents only to do for you (Asian parents that is). In that on the hottest day of the year we were invited to a traditional Korean dinner of chicken and ginger hot pot made for us completely free of charge. Much to our protest he would take us out to dinner and pay for it. We would tell him it was no way to make any money as the money we had given to him in rent was spent almost instantly. He would run errands for us take us out to buy mobile phones, even postcards. I suppose it may have been some sort of cabin fever, as he seemed to play an awful lot of counter strike in un-busy periods. He was supposed to be a java programmer but the day Simon and me arrived he turned off his programming deck and never touched it again in our presence.

I most definitely needed to replace some clothes though and the Dongdaemun market proved excellent as Simon and myself went to gather new clothing. Difficult, as most men's clothing seemed to be corporate shirt and trousers. We did manage to find Dongdaemun market though and a place to get a cheap suit made. The market place was a buzz of activity. Tiny shops with benches and a cooler filled with tea where you would sit and noodles were made straight from the bag of flour sat on the shelf. Amazingly fresh though lacking in taste they were smothered in chilli, as Koreans absolutely love their spicy sauces. Numerous shops would shout for business the women working at them seemingly happy in their work. Anything and everything was made there on the spot. Soya bean pancakes from beans you just scooped up yourself out of a barrel of beans, huge jars of *kimchi* (pickled cabbage). Squid and octopus lurking around in fish tanks not wanting to be picked, although that's rather anthropomorphic of me. Though there were some aggressive beggars who tried to hide the fact they were begging who harassed us. They were begging by selling us warm chocolates nobody really wanted considering the imposing heat that even melted my supply of Mentos. Here Simon had a suit made it was so incredibly cheap to have suits made in Korea. Everything seemed to be cheap here as the Korean government deliberately suppressed its currency to export. He made possibly the worst suit I can imagine just because it was cheap. He picked a flowery fabric that would not look out of place on a Hawaiian shirt, perhaps even a chintzy sofa and had it made into a suit. It looked awful but grabbed an immense amount of attention of the female kind. The Dongdaemun area is strange in that it seems to be completely split into different areas, so that you walk a block in one direction and suddenly there are many shops selling compressors. Walk another direction and you go into the packaging district, the stationery or Korean dress district, nothing seemed to be mixed and we got lost more than once though this was no particular hindrance as the Seoul stream was always nearby which had the green Seoul Metro line underneath. The stream being one of the oddest features in the middle of the city. It was essentially a stream 200 years ago, which was used as a rubbish tip. But at phenomenal cost had been restored and turned into an attraction for tourists and Koreans alike.

For the next 2 weeks Simon and I lived the good life as people with hard foreign currency it was a paradise our money had 5-10 times the purchasing power of back home. With disgusting bouts of gluttony eating a meal for 10 between the two of us. We typically partied hard. Hard enough that it was all a hazy memory with copious consumption of Korean vodka and Korean girls who would approach **US** and ask **US** out from hearing our English banter in bars and cafés. They would also never say no to a slow dance to Spandau Ballet's song True either. It must have been our attitudes or the way we would ask them out without beating about the bush. Or that Korean conscription and military service meant that many of the Korean girls did not have their male peers hanging around to compete with us. Though it was somewhat apt this song that was so successful in getting Korean women to enjoy our company. The lyrics were completely apt to my general situation.

"I bought a ticket to the world, but now I've come back again, why do I find it hard to write the next line? Oh I want the truth to be told…."

I however digress; Korean vodka called soju we even had 15 litres in the fridge at the hostel. Though Soju was pretty weak 18% tops it was a more social drink than super vodka where by the 4th glass you were gone. Instead Soju was so weak that you could have many, many, many shots and still remain upright. Though Soju is sort of like Sake. Though Soju is consumed in groups it is a more social drink by Korean societal rules it is not to be consumed alone. Unlike say a beer which you might crack open at the end of a long day. Soju is supposed to be consumed only while seated in a group of 2 or more people. So as you drank it and felt ok but it would sneak up on you so when you got up to leave you would wonder where the floor went as you fell over repeatedly, which is a similar side effect of sake.

Though Simon and myself started to get jitters about Korea as a society it was TOO perfect, polite people, non corrupt police who were apologetic in dealing with you. Friendly people, no litter, crime did not even seem to exist in Korea at all. Though there were some good things too, in Seoul it generally didn't matter what your background was poor rich well dressed or like a bum, in Hongdae nobody cared. It was most definitely not like Lam Kwai Fong in Hong Kong where people don't go there to have fun and enjoy themselves they go there to belittle others to sneer and look down their noses at people maybe they find this fun I don't.

Surprisingly people (like me) would leave keys in ignitions and find the vehicle still there. Korea was strange it had a perfect transport infrastructure, good roads, and low taxes. Something just seemed wrong in that the whole country felt like the Stepford wives village that there was a big secret in Korean Society and we set out to find out the big secret. Our suspicions were aroused even more when we got

273

Park really drunk substituting his soju for some rocket fuel from Russia I had left and he very nearly blurted out the big secret. But suddenly realised he was about to spill the beans got up and went to bed without speaking to us. I did get a hint of what happened a few days later when in Hongdae near Sincheon. I passed a huge line of buses filled to the brim with riot cops. They generally ignored me as I passed, but I had something to eat in the ubiquitous family mart and came out into the middle of a demonstration that nearly turned into a riot. The kind of riot where police batons are swung relentlessly. A riot cop grabbed me from behind and cuffed me to a railing and started asking me questions in Korean one after the other. I think he thought I was being an arse as I didn't understand him and kept quiet. I finally said to him what's going on and saucer eyed he found somebody who spoke English and I explained that I had been dragged into this demonstration and that I wasn't even Korean (though I do an excellent impression as long as I don't speak). I was let go and thought hmm that's a bit of the underbelly the Korean tourism agencies don't want me to see.

The highlights of this two weeks of craziness were the subzero Seoul bar where we were stood around in T-shirt and shorts not feeling even slightly cold. We were thankful for the cool conditions as Seoul was in the midst of a heat wave. A few Karaoke joints where we stayed all night. A few Seoul metro games we used to play enjoying the Seoul metro air conditioning where we would go round and round on the green line of the metro, which let you stay on board as long as you liked. Our game playing was a guessing game of some of the Korean women. If she has had plastic surgery game. South Korea is THE plastic surgery capital of the world and on the metro it was weird we would see straight out of a comic book manga girls sat on the metro. Simon was harsher when drunk in that he would approach them and ask them how much their faces cost. Surprisingly the bastard usually managed to get their telephone numbers by doing this. I would get punched in the face. He had a killer line too; that South Korean women have a strange tendency to want to be virgins when they get married. Simon developed killer line to exploit this.

"Well you could get surgery to fix the damage I do later so it's no problem." Though Simon was a bit of a wolf anyway. In that he had managed to get three telephone numbers of airline hostesses just on the flight to Korea. He complained daily that their voice message and email inboxes were always full. I do not know what happened out of this.

Another memorable evening was a foam party we attended watching Korean girls in bikini suits running away screaming from a bank of foam was highly amusing. The foam did spoil our drinks though but was more than worth it.

I also managed to visit the south side of Seoul, which looked clean and clinical like Wall Street in New York almost a little bit soulless. Same thing with the COEX mall. The biggest underground mall in Asia there was some sort or electronics event, which again had the race queen promotional models lurking about acting about their silliness to grab the attention of the cameras, but again the men were generally not looking.

Other highlights included church; out of boredom on Sundays we would attend the Onnrui English Ministry or OEM for short where most of the English teachers in Seoul would congregate. It was incredibly full surprisingly enough. I found out later that South Korea is 50% Christian split between 50-50 Catholic and protestant and when I say Christian these people really would visit church. The service consisted of a typical 3 hymns karaoke style where a white ball on the screen would jump from word to word. Then watch the pastor with a quivering lip tell the sermon. Simon was absolutely sick he would mess psychologically with the pastor causing quivering moments where he was visibly resisting the urge to stab us in the face repeatedly. After this was a blessing session that made me feel uneasy. The blessing involved the pastor putting his hand on your head praying for you and 5-10 people giving you their power. Myself having nothing to pray for would dodge the pastors hands like a boxer as I feared if he touched me due to me being a total fraud, I would burst into flames. We even saw a Korean pop star called Brian attend that place though he remained inconspicuous and would slip out just before the end of the service. Quite curiously although Simon and Myself were total frauds we were the ONLY people there to put money on the donation plate and not an insignificant amount either 10,000KRW each namely as we never had any change, while everybody else just passed the plate on.

When Kim, Kim and Choi came back another Kim from Washington State and a native Korean who was also called Kim on an internship came back. We had some serious fun clubbing in Hongdae copious Soju consumption that caused us to be an even bigger magnet for Korean women. We didn't return to the hostel for 3 days and one of the Kim's managed to lose his cool and had a go at his boss afterwards after seeing how chilled and relaxed the European way of life was (Easy compared to theirs).

The Kims' and Choi who I had last saw on the Amur highway did actually all three of them run out of fuel where I had warned them and been stuck on a remote part of the Amur for days too embarrassed to ask for a passing car for help instead choosing to walk to a petrol station and back.

Though everybody left the hostel for various reasons, native Kim finished his internship and was about to go into the army for 2 years. Simon was there to check out universities to do his PhD. Simon's departure for a week was a funny event though; he had managed to pick up a few telephone numbers in the US and had managed to get a place to stay or so he thought, at the parents of a girl called Sang-Mi. With nothing better to do and the transport being so cheap I went to watch the unfolding disaster.

275

Sang-mi had met Simon at an international language conference in the US somewhere and they had swapped numbers on the assumption they would never meet again. He phoned her up and asked if she knew a place to stay, she immediately offered her place to stay. Her place turned out to be her father's house. So as we trundled into her dad's house with me carrying a ton of luggage that is Simon's luggage we sat down to dinner together. Sang-Mi's father Hong, made a mean Hamjungsuk. It is a meal where you have a cast iron bowl of soup with thin sliced beef and chilli oil with 50 or more side dishes that was delicious as was his private stash of kimchi.

"Can Simon stay here tonight father?" I assumed she asked in her sweetest Korean, with Simon a gasp thinking she would have already asked.

"No I am afraid he cannot stay here tonight." He replied back in toneless English.

"It is no problem. Sang-Mi can take me to a motel." Simon replied at which came one of those awkward silences. Motels are as I said before not places were people stay but a place where couples go to have sex. Hong looked visibly annoyed with a vein in his temple visibly pumping. I could imagine the thought in his mind he's going to take MY DAUGHTER to a MOTEL?! Korean men are all trained in the army due to conscription. They can all fight and practice Taekowondo and I imagined him standing up and killing us. But Simon stepped in with, "It is ok, I'm going to back to Seoul tonight anyway." Which killed the tension in the room and a bottle of soju was produced to calm everything down.

One day however Seoul seemed a bit subdued the news was that the president of S Korea was dead. But the more important news was that the boss of Hyundai (who was the real president of Korea) had gone to meet Kim of North Korea. Who had been reputed to be dead many times over. There were a few photos released to the general public that had some glaringly obvious photoshop errors contained within them. Park was convinced he was dead. The Koreans as a whole have used this trick many times Admiral Yi Sun-sin had died in 1592 and yet was still leader of the Korean Navy till 1892. I suppose it is bad to poke fun at the terrible conditions that the North Koreans endure but quite simply they have no choice, but this emphasises that the old tricks are still the best ones.

American Kim stayed for a few more days but was eager to leave to start his unconventional studies. He had sold up his lot in the US and come to Korea to learn how to cook authentic Korean dishes he had quite a passion for cooking.

We wasted a day out shooting in the middle of Seoul. It was odd that for £10 (about 20,000 Won) we could rent an assault rifle, which was tethered to a steel post, and fire off a full clip at a shooting range. Or for a lesser 5000 Won pretend to be Dirty Harry with a .44 magnum which oddly wasn't tethered to anything. This wasn't as good as in Laos or Cambodia of course where $50 US could buy you an

RPG (rocket propelled grenade). An extra $100 would buy you a cow, which you could use the RPG to blow the cow up which I'd been told about in Mongolia. People came and went and we just passed the time of day babe watching in Seoul, until one night Park suggested that we go to a nightclub.

A nightclub in South Korea can also be called a booking club. A booking club you will not find anywhere but Korea. The excuse is that men and women find it hard to ask each other out. Socially it is supposed to be a big no-no for a woman to ask men out. This along with the fact that a lot of Korean men were a bit nerdy you should have seen the Internet cafés in Seoul enormous complexes always full and people never seemed to leave ever. Generally both sexes lacked the confidence to ask each other out. Korean society came up with the solution called a booking club. Effectively it was simple you rented a table bought massively overpriced drinks about 10-30 times mark up and paid the waiter a fat 50,000Won ~ 100,000won tip. This would buy you a waiters services, the service of a waiter was to get girls to your table. You would sit there and point at a particular girl and the waiter between dances would drag a girl unwillingly sometimes genuinely, sometimes pretend, to your table where you had moments to offer her over priced beer / liquor purely to impress her enough for her to give you her telephone number. Or be impressed enough to stay. From what I saw it seemed like something similar to what we have in the UK. Non-gay men would go to gay bars to get drinks bought for them by gay men, the trick was not to drink too much or you would be taken home for non-consensual sex. The women were there to get free drinks and a small ulterior motive maybe meet somebody there but to not drink too much and be taken home for non-consensual sex. During my time there with American Kim we saw some seriously drunk girls virtually unconscious be taken home by men to the completely convenient motel next door.

What surprised me even more was that one of the women I saw there worked at the local family mart store on the corner nearby the hostel. Since I went there on an hourly basis to drain them of fruit juice, cookies, cup noodles and Korean California rolls. I had seen them drunk off their heads being taken to the motel next door.

The next day in the shop she seemed completely indifferent to what had happened the night before as an occupational hazard of bumming free drinks. Actually what happens in Seoul sounds kind of familiar to what happens in the UK, people get drunk and take other drunken people home. It's just that this was a tad more discreet with beating about the bush intermediaries and expensive booze. Though Simon, Kim and Kim managed to go to a completely different booking club much less sleazier than the place we had been to so I guess there were variations.

277

This was in contrast to some of the cute things that Koreans did. At Namsan Park in the middle of Seoul where the Seoul TV tower stands. Itself was a nice refuge away from the massive sometimes-overbearing city. It was a world apart in that it was built in such a way that it hid many views of the city and caught the refreshing breezes. At the top they had some, at least to my eyes at least. Some odd things. Young perhaps even some older Koreans would climb Namsan peak and attach a padlock onto the safety fence with a message of their love to each other and throw the key off the top of the tower even though signs clearly told them not to. This was supposed to 'lock in' their love for each other and ensure the relationship lasted forever. In addition to this the park benches would be a lazy V shape so that couples sitting on them would invariably slide closer to each other. This was kind of cute. If you were to climb the peak (or take the cable car if you were lazy) you would see many couples there watching the sunset over Seoul to the tune of a thousand cicadas. It was a romantic notion and seemed to be in stark contrast to that of the booking club.

I spent a few evenings with Wendy Choi and her co-worker friend Nora Lee buying each other dinner and convincing her that she should set up her own business. She was earning less than what many of the English teachers earned after 10 years of service. Like many Koreans I had met she was envious of my travels and had wanted to travel out there herself. But obligations i.e. work which she liked a lot and a fear of the unknown made her not go out there and do it like I and others who have encountered Wendy have done. I had a feeling she would never leave South Korea. Even though she was a worldwide shipping agent she had actually never left Seoul. This seemed to be something that I had wanted to avoid myself in that many people get caught up with the concept of stuff. As Tyler Durden once said.

"Things you own end up owning you."

In that people are so afraid to lose what they have now that they will not make the leap into other things that they might gain. Although I don't exactly know a massive amount about her life it seemed a shame to sell yourself to a corporation for the rest of your life. It seemed almost like prostitution especially if you did not like your job, though Wendy did like hers she often complained of the stress and pressure put on her by her bosses.

I should note that Koreans in many places are terribly poorly paid I discovered that the minimum wage there was 2500won about £1.20. Except that everything in Korea was much cheaper metro fares as low as 400 won (20p) and thus the purchasing power of the £ was simply phenomenal for a modern high tech country like Korea. Across the sea to Japan the purchasing power was non-existent.

Once all the dust settled and all the partying had been done through and through and I had visited almost everything in Seoul it was time to go. I wish I had been able to stay longer. I was almost tempted to stay when a Spanish bloke came to stay at the hostel. He was thin and wiry with long hair and a good-sized yet neat beard. I forget his real name, but Simon thought up an evil plan. As the Spanish guy spoke no English Simon sought to exploit this. Simon wanted to take Jesus to church and stand up in front of the crowd and announce, "Hello I would like to introduce my friend Jesus from Palestine." I am sure he would have gotten stabbed or something as Simon is sick.

I was kind of disappointed that I did not find out what the big secret in South Korea was. But then again is S Korea different from anywhere or anybody else? In that everybody on earth has some sort of dark secret the kind they won't tell anybody. Not their wives, family or even priests. They will never tell another soul as long as they live NEVER. Probably why I hate nothing to hide nothing to fear types. I have my secrets you have yours, I said before the human brain does not process negatives you are probably thinking of it right now. What is it? Are you a scat fan, did you diddle your boss for a promotion did you lose a game of soggy biscuit? Never trust those who say they have nothing to hide everybody has something to hide. South Korea itself and other countries and the other 6.4bn people on earth hide something too.

I realised what the dark secret was several months later or at least what I think the dark secret is. Simon to my knowledge shortly after I left managed to get a working visa and has been investigating ever since not making any progress into the dark secret.

South Korea had grown fast the UK took centuries to develop to the prime age of industrial might. South Korea had built up its ruined country from the 1951 war in less than 20 years. They had capitalism and western values pushed on them so hard that the traditional family model fell apart and material happiness was king. Spiritual and psychological happiness came a distant second if even considered at all. I suppose this is why younger Koreans rebelled against going all Japanese Salari man, which incidentally is a myth, Karaoshi (death by overwork) society. Such was the falling apart of society that many people did not fit and had no social safety net for their mental well being. Whereas in the past problems were discussed with family to resolve them. Values had changed and this did not happen anymore. Such that enormous numbers of Koreans ended up killing themselves as Korean society gave them a Hobson's choice conform and fit or conform and fit. A suicide rate of 36 per 100,000 people while the UK has 15 per 100,000 people. In a population of 48 million nearly 20,000 people chose to end their own lives. Although another theory I heard much later on but cannot confirm or verify if

279

there is any truth is that there are an enormous number of sex crimes that are simply swept under the carpet or ignored.

I was sad to leave South Korea as it felt like a nice place, granted if you were Korean and you lived and worked there it utterly sucked. People who work as expats always have better lives than the locals. This is of course true everywhere for example in Hong Kong expats also get sweet deals a 20,000HK$ monthly wage is considered excellent but for an Expatriate they want 60,000-120,000 monthly and even then consider it to be low.

An acquaintance I know from online had remarked that his experience in Japan was similar that his life was so much better than the average Japanese person. Japanese police would blink at his IDP (international driving permit) and let him go for road traffic offences. They did not want to bother with the paperwork or the trouble of booking him this may have changed though as his experience was in the late 1990s a lifetime ago in this day and age.

However a thought was that visiting a country is similar to the first cup of coffee you have each morning. The first time you visit it is always the best the second cup or visit potentially in the future will not be as good as some of the shine and things that impressed you will have worn off. As always familiarity breeds contempt the more you visit the more familiar you are.

However nothing lasts forever and will or want cannot change this. Considering I watched the life of one of the Kims for a while it seemed unpleasant and revolved constantly around work. Park had said to me that when he worked for somebody else his life was utterly unpleasant and filled with more and more work. Working well was rewarded by more work and he had never been home before 10pm from a 5.30am start. My experiences of Seoul albeit from a tourist viewpoint had seemed so nice that anything other than Seoul would prove to be a disappointment even if it was fantastic.

The ferry from Incheon to Tianjin was fairly empty it was laid out the same as the Dong Chun ferry. The only mild difference was the food and everybody appeared to smoke I mean really to smoke. REALLY smoke people all over the ship would be doing something and smoke at the same time. An awful lot of people had the ability to keep a cigarette in their mouths while drinking, or eating their cup noodles even biting into an apple all without moving the cigarette from their lips.

Family mart is Korea's 7-11 but worse. It's more like Starbucks but worse, although there are other marques of shops i.e. Buy the way, ministop, 7-11 GS25, IGR Mart C*Space etc. Family mart is utterly dominant. It's funny when you get directions in Seoul especially to hostels where they tell you to turn at the family mart then turn at the next family mart. It was especially funny to see on the Tianjin ferry three family marts' on one ship. The bosses clearly not content with being the monopoly onboard the ship they had to force it down your throat, as there was always a family mart on your deck no matter where you were.

Economy B class was much the same thing as the Dong Chun Ferry. That is sleeping on the floor in fact. The ferry in retrospect was a silly idea. The ferry took 27 hours from dock to dock, eating up an entire day and cost exactly the same as a flight cost. However nothing really happens on flights while the extended periods with little to do allows things to happen. As with the Dong Chun ferry from Zarubino I'd met interesting people and done some crazy things. This time however nothing really happened. Still for the super cheap flights you need to visit a Korean travel agent. These travel agents only speak Korean, their websites are in Korean and you need Korean identity papers to actually buy a ticket for these Korean companies to get the cheap tickets a ferry you just show up with cash. The majority of the voyage was spent sleeping and watching a few card games where large amounts of money were being won and lost per hand. It was unreal in that you would see thick wads of RMB played over one hand.

Chinese opera however was played loud over the ship PA system and it was impossible to escape this assault on my ears and by the reaction of everybody else on board everybody else hated it too. Good thing I still had my earplugs then! Though by that time they were pretty disgustingly covered in ear grease. My multi tools had been taken off me at Incheon so there was no way to cut the wires to the speakers that I so desperately wanted to do.

I really hate toilets on any vehicle, bar maybe the toilets on an airplane but since flights are generally short and fast visits to the toilets on aircraft can be kept to a minimum. The toilets were unkempt and smelt utterly disgusting and the smell pervaded the entire ship. Granted I had contributed to that smell earlier on after the ship wobbled and made me piss all over the wall, but these toilets were dangerous it was effectively a trough in the middle of a specific room on the ferry where people squatted over. This was fine first time I used it, second time I went in and the room was full of Chinese men squatting over the sewer kind of thing with their buttocks virtually touching each other. Chinese people have a remarkable ability to squat. I've got Chinese blood in me but I am unable to squat like they do, they squat with flat feet and can remain perfectly stable. It's kind of like feral children. If you don't learn how to squat in the first few years of your life you never will... With the ship swaying back and forth I passed and decided to hold it until I got off the ferry.

The ship pulled into Tianjin harbour masked in dirty smog towards a dirty yellow building which the ship docked nearby. Everybody got off the ferry and into immigration. I had been bricking myself since my visa had been acquired on a pack of lies. I cleared customs and immigration unscathed and came out of the ferry terminal and realised that I had absolutely no idea where I was. Fortunately I

282

managed to write the Chinese characters for train and was pushed onto a bus which was I assumed going to the train station. I assumed this was nearby due to the railway tracks that led into the port, it wasn't. The bus was a fairly new modern bus the kind that would not look out of place in the UK but packed a bit tighter that you would expect. What was most creepy was that the bus had a bizarre air suspension system that hissed in a creepy way. It sounded like a girl crying but nobody else seemed to notice. The bus stopped after a mile or so and a green fatigued soldier, who was some sort of PRC security guard got on board and said something in harsh tone less Mandarin and Korean. Since I didn't understand Korean or much Mandarin I just sat there and so did everybody else.

From being bored from the ferry my warped imagination had envisaged that he was asking for terrorists, brigands and thieves. Asking them to leave the bus to be arrested and it seemed faintly ridiculous that there was a sort of honour system in place in which terrorists and thieves would give themselves up willingly.

"Come on lads, no shame in admitting it," I imagined, "come on are you sure you wouldn't like to be a terrorist you'd make a good terrorist." At the very least he could have walked down the bus and eyeballed everybody to intimidate people but he just looked bored and disappointed as he left the bus after his announcement. Nobody admitted to being a terrorist or a thief and the bus rolled onwards. I felt it ridiculous since it was like a snooty customs official who would try to get you to admit something when coming back from somewhere exotic renowned for drugs an illicit substances.

"Come on, come on admit it you've got some drugs haven't you? I know you've got them you look just the sort." You are hardly going to look around for the coast to be clear and say "Yeah but don't tell anybody will you." …Actually I retract that as I remembered all those silly people who at check in who ended up on the news for joking that they had bombs in their suitcases. Though maybe one of the passengers did admit to it, since he said 'Jee Dan' which sounds suspiciously like the Cantonese for Jar Dan (explosives). Though I imagined the old Smith and Jones sketch at an airport where they are going through the metal detector and Griff Rhys Jones puts a machine gun on the tray to the side of the metal detector and is allowed through as it doesn't beep.

The train station or what looked like the train station, because it actually looked like a cyber man head from Doctor Who or a shopping mall and onto the pointy train to Beijing. I was the only person on the train it seemed and the snack trolley woman offered me each and every item off the trolley including some Lays chips, which were marked as cucumber flavour. Who comes up with the inspiration for these things? Unfortunately they tasted completely plain no cucumber taste but wait a sec that is what cucumber tastes like anyway! Also on offer were seaweed flavour mini pretzels, which tasted of MSG (monosodium glutamate) only MSG and nothing else. The weird thing is MSG only amplifies the taste that is inherent to the food it is put on how can you amplify the taste of nothing, maybe the crisps tasted like an amplified version of the inside of my mouth.

The train glided into Beijing quickly shadowed by a nice road passing small villages. Then grey houses and then grey flats then grey high-rise then through the murk looked like Beijing I couldn't exactly tell though the murk was incredible. On arrival I went upstairs at the train station and straight to window 16 which flashed English spoken here.

"Hong Kong ticket for one Sunday please."

"No ticket for Sunday, next one Monday." And came out clutching a ticket to Hong Kong in 2 weeks time. I hadn't expected to stay in Beijing that long actually. I came out of the railway station and realised I was completely out of my depth in that I didn't speak a much Mandarin. Also China had irritatingly standardised their writing system to simplified Chinese characters. I cannot read many normal characters much less simplified ones. Although I could semi get by, by de-toning Cantonese if that makes any sense.

Home for the next few days was supposed (I hoped as I did the usual thing of just turning up and hoping there to be space) Qianmen in a Hutong called the 365Inn, another hostel. Generally I hadn't done hotels for a while now as they were expensive and the fact that you don't get to meet others to interact with generally means a hotel can be a lonely experience. Also in hotels in China had problems as I had discovered in 2002 when I travelled around the Hangzhao area at Huang Shan. When you check into a hotel you will receive phone calls all night long asking nay demanding if you want a massage. I still had to find my way there yet. Some how I managed to find the metro and took a very long time to buy a ticket.

The government of Beijing seem to have a ticketing machine similar to what you would find in Seoul lots of destinations. Yet every ticket cost 2 RMB no matter where you went. Yet strangely everybody poked the machine a few times to get tickets leading to enormous queues. Each ticket machine also coming with an attendant whom I immediately felt sorry for as her job looked terrible.

Tourists (like me) would go and ask her how much the fare was regularly and she would say Lee Ang, Lee Ang, Lee Ang! I immediately thought back to a comedy sketch where a man is in a 99p store and regularly harasses the shopkeeper.

"How much is this mate?"

"99p."

"Oh ok thanks, how much is this?"

"99p! Look everything is 99p."

"Oh ok thanks, how much is this?" In an endless manner to windup the shopkeeper. The metro was unpleasant I mean REALLY unpleasant, imagine the Tokyo metro at peak time but with 3 times as many people crammed into smaller cars, sardines was not apt it was more like a black hole. People crammed at impossible angles and yet still able to push more people onboard. The worst part of it was I read the sign wrong and instead of 3 easy stops managed to go the other way on the loop. In a horrible twist of fate the stop JUST before my stop Qianmen the train stopped and told everybody to get off. Necessitating another squeeze into the train for 16 stops back the other way just to get to where I had started.

I was surprised at the number of tourists and by that I mean non-Chinese people who all seemed to be armed with the Lonely Planet guide to Beijing. It is actually illegal to sell in China curiously. Of course the 365Inn was never in the Lonely Planet guides. It was a case of check hostel world in Korea write down the address and a general map and go and find it.

Grumpy I got off at Qianmen and had absolutely no idea where I was and found that Kate Melua is a lying bat where apparently NO bicycles none at all (It happened to be a Sunday which explained their absence not that I knew this as I hadn't known what day it was for months). I stopped to get my bearings or try to and had a snack of melon on a stick. A cup of meat? And a sweet pancake. But hey with food poisoning I had to put back the weight or at least that was my excuse.

Unfortunately I managed to be caught short in general, public toilets should be avoided in China. The consensus is that you should hold it until you find a decent hotel or restaurant although this is no guarantee that the toilets will be nice or western style either. However going to a public toilet might be considered a mini adventure of sorts as you might come out with a story to tell, sort of like what I'm doing here.

I couldn't find the hostel and had eaten something iffy on the ferry and had to use a public toilet in a hutong. A nice little narrow pedestrian street in Beijing downtown. I've seen some disgusting toilets on my travels and thought it can't be that bad. But then again I had been spoilt by Korea where I had managed to find the best toilet in Seoul for 3 years running. In case anybody is interested it is at the world cup stadium. I went inside. Of course there were no doors in front of the 'pie pie boxes'. The first two boxes were occupied... in the third one, holy shit; no literally I mean holy shit. Shit was lying beside the hole in small steaming piles and in bright red paint in Chinese and English a warning stating.

"NO SHITTING IN THE TOILET"

Beside the hole! Who the hell is shitting beside the hole? I have never before heard about the 'no shitting in the toilet' rule. I found out much later why you aren't supposed to shit in the toilet for reasons I will explain later. I walked back and forward again and at the end, wow, surprise. I saw that little western style toilet with a wooden seat. I guess this is for old people who can't squat I was done in seconds. Next came a disturbing revelation, no sinks or taps to wash your hands. The revelation that all these people walking by with unclean hands and the thought of the food sellers who had most likely visited this place and not washed their hands YUCK.

This was supposed to be the improved Beijing though and in preparation for the Olympics they had been improved. I'd hate to think what they were like before the Olympics. Apparently I found out that Beijing's toilets near the Stadium are 5 star rated. Toilets, which flush. Toilets that have loo paper and sinks. It must have been the 5 star best toilets in Seoul that had spoilt me though if this was how it was after the Olympics what were they like before? It is sort of similar to when a fast food place advertises 'Now made with real chicken breast,' As a sort of advert which doesn't quite work it only made you think erm if they are made of real chicken breast now what on earth were they made out of before? With the sun beating down on me I and did the only sensible thing possible. I hailed a taxi, hao hao he said and beckoned me in to the incredible traffic of Beijing. It looked like the M6 on a Monday morning he drove 20 metres and into the huge throng of traffic. We waited while the meter jumped a few digits. After 10 minutes the taxi crept forward another 10 metres. A few more blips on the taximeter and we moved another 20 metres. After about half an hour realising I had moved the best part of 100 metres I got out paying him 20RMB (£2) the driver grinned at me saying xie xie (thanks) I must have been his best fare that day. As I had been dropped off at the side street opening to the 365 Inn I could have walked that 70 metres in 2 minutes. I asked another tourist where the 365inn was and was told it was somewhere down there mate. That was confidence inspiring 'somewhere'. Alas the hutong was completely dug up and people were shimmying along the pipes as if this was normal. Checking in it was a generally forgettable hostel like most hostels are like semi disgusting toilets and 4 beds in a dorm not bad not bad at all. I could have paid 10RMB less and gotten a 50 bed dorm but for £1 extra it was quite an upgrade...

The guy behind the counter did say ah you come from Mongolia? Erm no I came from Korea. So why did you get the visa in Mongolia, long story I told him. It was still fairly early so I changed into my shorts and went for a walk to see the local surroundings. It was all more hutong tourist traps and more tourist traps. A tourist hutong still isn't exactly great in that somebody seriously loves the colour grey, in that they are made from grey bricks. The pavements are also grey and so are the roads, which are all coated in a grey dust from the construction it felt a bit de-saturated in colours at first. As I walked there would be an assault on the senses big aggressive looking neon signs, flashing lights, 1000s of people wandering around and the constant changes in the smells, was this progress? There were also usual signs of progress, 24-hour barbershops that had the ubiquitous pink lights I had seen in Seoul. One minute it was choking exhaust fumes from cars and taxis, another few yards farther on and it was cooking meat, then rancid sewers, and then sweet smells. Luckily I look vaguely like the natives and therefore wasn't hassled much. But the tourist traps near Qianmen were like the markets down in Turkey except worse.

In Turkey NO I DONT WANT A FUCKING CARPET will suffice. In tourist trap shops in Beijing they have an incredibly wide selection of things. No I don't want a T-shirt, ah is ok I have fan, no I don't want a fan, ah but I have very good price sunglass! No I don't want sunglasses either. Ah so you want... and so on, unlike Turkey though people would grab onto your wrist and drag you in and refuse to let you go. My blending in was perfect and I escaped most of these encounters if I threw in a few spits here and there I'd have been perfect bar maybe the boots. Army boots are not seen too often in China and people would stare and think weirdo. In the blazingly hot heat of the season flip-flops and plimsolls were all the rage.

The frying hot sun baked down on me and I called it a day had a few beers had dinner in the hostel restaurant of burger and chips... it was the only thing on the menu with a picture on I could recognise. There were plenty of pictures of other things but since I didn't particularly fancy repeating what had happened in Spain a year earlier I went for the safe option. Alas not as safe as Ingrid in Mongolia who had the chicken and chips of the world spaghetti bolognaise but it was pretty safe anyhow. If you stay at the 365Inn never ever go down the alleyway to the left you will see into the kitchen and it is best to live in ignorance and bliss. Although I never did get food poisoned at this place much to its credit.

In Spain a year earlier I had rushed on a much faster bike to a campsite with concrete hard pitches.... by virtue that the camping pitches were solid concrete parking spaces with en-suite toilet facilities for each pitch. I'd gone in to the café and ordered a few Cerveza (beer) and in an effort not to embarrass myself pointed at a few things on the text only menu. I got deep fried brains and a horrendous dish where eyeballs looked back at me from my plate, though this was Spain and I was an awful long way from Spain.

Thankfully though beer in Chinese is still beer. But with a 'Jow' on the end. So those came thick and fast while I was accosted by one of the staff at the hostel. An incredibly pale skinned waitress working at the café attached to the hostel and a wispy moustached student also working there. During the evening it was decidedly un busy and they decided to chat to me. Or rather they took the opportunity to ask me questions about how much things cost in the UK (house / cars / motorbikes / food / beer / hookers and gin). Each time tapping into her little calculator how much all this stuff cost in RMB looking more and shocked at the cost of things. When I told them how much I had spent on this trip, (a fair amount lot of money) they both gave me an incredibly dirty look as if I had slept with their father or something.

I called it a night quite early that evening I slept or rather sweated all night in the dorm until somebody found the remote control for the air conditioner. It wasn't the heat it was the humidity that got us. My fellow inmates for that night were an Australian who was passing through an English teacher from the US and a Buryat girl who slept with a hand axe under her pillow.

The next morning the Australian guy gave me a prod.

"Hey mate do ya want to see the flag raising ceremony in Tiananmen?"

"Sure why not, just give me a sec." I slurred sleepily except it was 530am. The café out the front was closed and Beijing was still asleep mostly. We got to Tiananmen Square and marvelled at how big and impressive it was, with the smog you could barely make out the other end the Forbidden City. We parted company and I thought why not go to the Forbidden City? Loitering around until it opened up.

I paid the 70RMB tourist trap fee and paid another 200 RMB tourist trap fee for the audio guide and walked into the impressively large first courtyard of the Forbidden City that had an even bigger crowd of tourists being led around with blokes holding little flags up. A great many of them wore glazed kill me now expressions as they were in for a long tour a very long tour a 5-hour tour.

I was then greeted by no other than James Bond while pushing the first button on the audio guide at one of those marked spots where you press a numbered button. He told me in all about the Ming Dynasty who built a great deal of the Forbidden City. Roger Moore had been hired as the narrator of this piece; I was half expecting a double entendre at some point, as he would make suggestive comments the kind you would say to a girl.

"Why don't we go for a stroll around the court yard?" I found out sometime later on Roger Moore had recorded this in a studio in Chicago. He had never actually visited Beijing until late 2009 that was mildly ironic, as he sounded pretty knowledgeable. I spent time wandering around the large impressive grounds being largely impressed now and again for the next 3 hours until I felt tired, and decided to go elsewhere. Walking back from the end I passed the group with the kill me now expressions and the tour guide was talking about some sort of design here and there and the kill me now expression had changed to I want to stab the tour guide in the face. He might well have done seeing he was only at the 1/3 mark as the Forbidden City is a massive place. The evening was spent sampling impressively cheap and large bottles of beer at a few workers pubs.

The next morning I got up early again. To the hazy glow of the sun obscured by the pollution when I noticed a big shop hiring out bicycles. I hired a bicycle only to return it minutes later the pollution in Beijing is awful enough to make anybody feel out of breath in only a few minutes. Though this makes an excellent excuse for poor fitness I exchanged this for an funky 0.25 hp electric bike I rode well sat on the bike and pressed the button on the handle bar around the cycle lanes avoiding collisions. The problem is these electric bikes are fast and completely silent and people would cut you up and overtake on both sides. I finally made it to Tiananmen square where I got stuck REALLY stuck, cars, buses taxis buzzing past with no way across the 8 lane road I had been stuck there for quite a while until an old man on a bicycle casually slipped between two buses and made it. Seeing no other choice I went for it eyes closed and made it. In Asia in fact most of the world might is right and the bigger the vehicle the mightier they are. The electric bike is a lowly notch above bicycles. Riding in Beijing is not for the fearful or faint hearted, enormous numbers of people die on Beijing's roads each year. I had a feeling these were probably foreign tourists dying from heart attacks. As the locals didn't seem to even acknowledge the danger let alone fear it. Weird hybrid bicycles loaded to the gills like in Korea glided past me their motors straining with the effort.

I'd gotten off Qianmen main road and onto some quiet side streets and nothing could prepare me for this. I mean I've dodged birds, rocks and cars but nothing could prepare me for the torrent of spitting. It was almost like rain. I had heard in Beijing it was bad. What I experienced in Beijing was worse, in that since the Olympics spitting is said to be illegal and thus previously when somebody spat you'd hear them speak in Mongolian (or welsh) and then putoo. People would hack up for a good two three minutes look around then spit. Such that you had to guess when they would spit and slip through before people spat. It was amazing to see how people would hack to get rid of the tiniest amount of phlegm in their lungs hacking for what seemed like minutes perhaps hours. Though if I had to live in the day-to-day pollution I would probably be giving them a run for their money.

I made it to another tourist trap the temple of heaven. Although the temple of heaven is less of a tourist trap it is much more like an oasis of serenity and peace in the middle of bustling Beijing. Unfortunately there was no James Bond to talk me through the walk around. I decided to explore a little and go out of my way the 3rd and 4th ring was where I was to see real Beijing as the hutong preservation areas are just tourist traps that are pretend authentic. I'd made it to the third ring and started to feel hungry. With no restaurants about I followed some locals to a side street packed with food stalls where lots of things were being boiled, fried sizzled or roasted. I passed many people eating things off a stick, unidentifiable bits of meat. There was a huge selection of things to choose from.... as long as it came on a stick. Scorpions on a stick, grasshoppers on a stick, even a whole sparrow on a stick that puts a whole new meaning to a one-bamboo mah-jong tile. I managed to walk for quite sometime till I found a man selling what looked like meat on a stick; ok it may well have been snake I generally did not want to think about it better to live in ignorance. Which tasted nondescript and the sign worryingly said meat in Chinese this seemed a tad worse than Mongolia as I swallowed it down as in China the list of what is classed as meat is almost endless. Everything on a stick I suppose is more environmentally friendly though this is probably a minor concern. Everything in the UK is massively over packaged as if people are scared of contamination or something. In supermarkets single doughnuts would be encased in a plastic dome of plastic that itself was packed in a vacuum packed piece of plastic. At least the sticks everything was put onto were biodegradable and were made from trees that can be grown back.

Chinese folks tend to eat anything it seems, dragon fly nymphs, dragonflies, tiger bones, paws, anything that moves. Alas it's a cultural thing in that China has regularly has had famine for 2000 years. On my return I found a book called China land of famine and it stated that:

"China has had a famine every other year since 425BC till 1925, each famine varied in severity and sometimes were limited to one or two provinces." In Europe this seldom happens when was the last famine in living memory? The last one in China was in 1962; the last one in Europe was 1825. Though culturally we might find this strange I think a person in China would be confused about some British favourites like spotted dick or fried Mars bars, maybe even fried lard.

On the way back I stopped at a junction and glanced around as I waited to eye off to a gorgeous stylishly dressed, long straight silky-haired, oversize barely black sunglasses-wearing girl. I glanced over and looked over her body quickly and discreetly.... DAMN I said to myself! As she turned towards me I was fairly impressed with her face - nice skin, no perfect skin, a fine complexion, bright eyes, and glossy red lip-gloss. She was chatting away to her friend nonchalantly in putunghua then turned to face me and spat up the biggest gob of spit I have ever seen onto the pavement in front of me...

I managed somehow to find my way back to Qianmen hand in the bike and go for dinner, nearly getting run over by a bloke on an electric rickshaw. He asked me if I wanted a ride. I thought what the hell and wrote the Chinese for duck. He looked puzzled until I said quack, quack at him he said ah! With a glimmer of recognition in his eyes. He then spent the next 10 minutes taking me down some side roads to a gigantic place where I stepped in. It was a touristy place. Touristy place or not I was hungry and stepped in the whole place was occupied mostly with tourists. I was the only Asian person in there although overall the place wasn't that busy. I ordered Peking dack (sic) of course yes Peking dack (sic) just as it was written in the menu. I knew from earlier experiences Peking duck is just the skin, in that many tourists around me would order the suspiciously cheap (40RMB) Peking duck and be delighted to see a WHOLE duck wheeled towards them EACH. The waiter would then proceed to slice off the skin into sheets and take away the rest of the duck leaving just the skin and a stack of pancakes, leaving the diners disappointed. I'm not sure why though as they were left with enough meat and crisp skin to feed 5 people each. Though soup was made with the rest of the duck and soft meaty dumplings where offered as a side.

What struck me was that almost every culture that I had visited had a variation of steamed meat dumplings. In Greece it was '*oo-lahk-LEE mahn-DEE*' Turkey it was *manti*. In Georgia it was *kinkale*. In Russia it was *plim-in-ee*. In Mongolia it was small *kushuri*. In South Korea it was *mandu*. In Japan it was *gyoza*. In China *shuikow*. It was odd that through so diverse countries in the world they all had very similar common dishes. They often contained the same meats and vegetables inside and all where made in almost exactly the same way. It did make me think that peoples of the world had more commonality than we would like to admit as it probably had moved over continents over a very long period. Or that humans as a whole had some sort of neurosis, which means that they all have some instinctive urge to wrap meat in some sort of parcel of pastry no matter where they are on earth. I wonder what the British version of these dumplings are the closest I can think of is either a pasty or a pie. Though it was a shame that we tended to accentuate and fight over the differences between each other.

It did make me wonder if South America had such things in that for the most part Eurasia is connected and things move about. Maybe Columbus or Cortez bought some along to Central and South America.

I couldn't finish dinner it was great for just £5. I had a chuckle to myself watching some people have egg and chips. They travelled all the way out here and ate what they ate at home.

The next 3 days were taken up by going to Pingyao via Beijing west rail way station a huge cavernous place where the departures were similar to that of taking a flight having to exchange my ticket for a boarding card etc. Pingyao was where Rick from Mongolia was waiting for me, which was a (comparatively) short 14-hour train ride away watching the landscape turn drier and drier. On a hard seat in a car filled with people chain smoking and slurping cup noodle things noisily and digging their fingers into their nostrils up to the 3rd knuckle as if there were some sort of hidden gold in there. It was mildly hilarious that when the guard came round the cigarettes would be hidden windows would open and the cigarettes be held outside. The passengers sitting in the aisle just sucked the cigarette into their mouths. The train out of Beijing seemed to go through some terrible areas that were caked in black dust presumably from Daitong where 75% of China's coal passes through and is mined.

Though we didn't actually do much in Pingyao. We had a look at the Wong mansion. Which was a city thing where all the Wong named people are said to have originated from. We went to the set of the film *Raise the Red Lantern* Rick's favourite film and had a look at the city walls that are original Ming constructions. Many people don't know that in China's 1966 to 1976 cultural revolution many of the relics were destroyed and most things you see in China are replicas. Pingyao seemed to have missed some of the money pouring through Beijing in that the streets were not sealed in tarmac and the low rise built housing still existed everywhere. Though the people had some affluence in that the moped and electric bicycle were popular so was the donkey hauling carts of coal here and there.

Pingyao shocked by the revelation good quality beer could be had for 1.5 RMB for a 1-litre bottle, which pleased us no end. We had a brief look at the old city walls went ooh taking a few photos with Rick pretend busking for a few hours and me generally attempting to pull the local talent unsuccessfully. I was pleasantly surprised also that there was noticeably less spitting. While in Beijing I had had to adapt skills like the agents from The Matrix the odd ptoo was here and there. We started drinking early. Nothing much happened here bar Rick and I going into a café and him calling me in to look at a sign which said "no shitting in the toilet" which gave us a chuckle again more on this later.

I returned to Beijing with 3 more days to spare and decided to go and see the memorial to Chairman Mao. Foreigners aren't supposed to see Mao's body and they only give you a ticket if you are a citizen.

The people of China generally respect Mao. Even though he has killed more people through his policies and executions than every dictator on earth added together throughout history. Low estimates of 30 million and high estimates at the other end of the scale being 90 million as a result of his policies and decisions. However Mao was fairly savvy in that he hooked onto the general dislike of foreigners. In that the people really did have reasons to complain in historical terms, not least the opium wars where Britain exported opium fought two wars over it and took their land. Most insulting were the three uneven treaties that opened up the great middle kingdom to even more exploitation by foreigners. Mao was celebrated to make China for the Chinese. Much like T.E Lawrence to make Arabia for the Arabs, and was cheered greatly for giving them the boot. I wondered if the people who cheered him would have cheered so loudly and vehemently if they realised that so many people would die. However even the PRC government today states that his decisions were 70% good and 30% absurd. If you are interested Jung Chaing's Wild Swans and Mao also by Jung Chaing and Jon Halliday are an excellent read about this, which goes against the official versions and are thus banned in China. However this part of the world you might find uneasy reading it is generally normal for enormous numbers of people to die. The sites of Stalin's *gulags* (even the one he was sent to himself) lay a few hundred miles to the north, where the road of bones is. Millions died building that. In 230BC Qin-Shi-Huiang unified China for the first time and sent millions to die building the first version of the Great Wall of China. 1700 years of regular warfare killed hundreds of thousands. Then sometime in the 13th century the Ming dynasty built it as we see it today. General Zhu Yuanzhang sent hundreds of thousands of people to die building the Great Wall. Legend has it is that the wall is like the road of bones, for every 1ft cost the life of a builder. Life in this part of the world is was and remains cheap.

An American wanted to go see Mao. The guard was surprised that a foreigner really did want to see Mao. The guard had to make up an RMB price, which he kept upping to see what he could get away with before letting him in.

Security was tight and I was searched 3 times on my way in and it was a painfully long 3-hour wait to see Mao that might have been the plastic version in the crystal coffin for all of 15 seconds. Everybody filed into the room in absolute silence and paid their respects.

My most prominent memory of this is not of seeing Mao but all the people interacting with each other in the queue. Where thirsty people would pass RMB notes or coins down the line to a seller, and bottles of water snacks or leaflets would be passed back along the line. It was also completely spoilt by the tourist tat shop once you got out of the mausoleum, which sold all sorts of tacky goods. Mao watches, pencils, key rings anything that had a big enough space to put Mao's picture on it was sold you had to think what Chairman Mao would have thought of this if his corpse wasn't strapped down it might be spinning. Outside he probably would not have recognised Beijing at all with all its cosmetic surgery that had been done to it. It was as if Beijing had received a botox treatment, face-lift, boob job and chemical peel to tart it up. In the memorial hall though there was an even worse scam earlier on in that people would rush to one side and buy a 2 RMB bunch of plastic flowers encased in plastic wrap. It seemed to me that they would 'sell' these flowers to visitors to put at the foot of Mao's coffin and at the end of the day pick them up and put them back at the shop, as the flowers didn't seem particularly genuine.

Next up I went to see the free military museum the shot down American U2 spy plane resides here and to see the history of the world according to the communist government. Mindful that the victors always write history though it is important that anybody who cannot contradict your version of history is dead before you start making revisionist history.

Japan made a massive gaffe about this a few years back when they re-wrote the children's textbooks to deny certain things had happened in China during the occupation of Manchuria. I followed a Cantonese-speaking tour guide sliding in unnoticed and she said this is the mossee powerful handgun in the world. She then walked up to the next hand gun in a glass case and said this is the also the mossee powerful hand gun in the world. There were at least 200 guns lined up in the museum and I had a feeling she would state that each one would be the most powerful hand gun in the world. I spent a few hours wandering around looking at the propaganda that clearly had no effect on me.

Though when I walked out past the most powerful handgun in the world woman I couldn't help thinking that the KMT leader Chen Kai Shek was evil. Japan was evil the USA was the great Satan and China was a democratic free country. This lasted until the next beer and an Internet terminal.

Though contrary to what a lot of people say China isn't as unfree as western media sources and the perception makes it out to be. I'd logged on the Internet to update family of my location and could access most things I wanted including the 4th of June incident (the Tiananmen massacres), facebook and youtube. The great firewall of China, actually called project golden shield does not work as advertised. A cop even sat next to me and updated his facebook account without batting an eye. Maybe the PRC government should ask for a refund. I certainly would. It appeared that ALL Internet cafés had accounts with proxy services so the Internet was pretty much like you would find in other countries. Though there are two levels of Internet in China these days the more open version and the one everybody else gets. An expensive one all the expats use paying $50 a month to use and see anything they want or the cheaper version probably because expats in China generally don't care or are taking advantage of the situation themselves to be too worried about such things.

Though many things in China remained taboo. It reminded me of the UK in the 1980s where people in my hazy memories would even skirt around perfectly normal bodily functions.

"I'm going for a number one dear, please could you wait for a moment."

Or for the hip trendy yuppies of the city.

"Toilet? What's that I'm on dialysis." In Han Chinese society that makes up 92% of the people in China an example was that in the hutong I was staying. In this Hutong (which means narrow street) every other shop was a sex shop. But pretended in a very thinly disguised manner. They would pretend not to be a sex shop, selling all sorts of trashy junk at the front with the odd shelf devoted to things you might find in an Amsterdam back street. With shops selling whips, rubber dolls, spiky underwear, masks, gags all sorts. And lots of risqué lingerie, which did an awfully decent impression of a spider's web and would have left nothing to the imagination. People would walk in and the shopkeeper be a gasp at such a product being on their shelves but decide to make a quick profit from it anyway and sell it. But it didn't end there in that the buyer would walk away and come back and would 'find' a brown package outside the shop.

I often wonder what Chinese factory workers think of people where the goods that they produce end up going to. Absolutely everything is made in China these days. You go into a supermarket and it would probably be easier to make a list of the things not made in China. The last things I recalled from the UK was pulling open a Christmas cracker and finding a fake bar of chocolate that was in reality a disguised water squirt gun. As a worker in a Chinese factory you would probably think that's a bit strange but it's a novelty they must be stupid to buy this rubbish, though it comes in a Christmas cracker so it was less direct buying.

What I wondered was how they thought about the sex toys that they manufactured how they would react to being put in a factory that produced large rubber cocks or blow up dolls, probably those western folk are mighty weird.

Though I digress, regarding freedom ironically I logged onto the BCF and they were all talking about censorship in China and that a person in China would never see the BCF. I had a look without using the proxy and it was clean though for some reason it wouldn't post. They wrote about state controlled media and how that Chinese people were being lied to, and yet the UK media virtually tells the same lies and yet somehow it becomes true. I had a chuckle when the TV news commented about the BBC being a state controlled media source, which it pretty much is. I chatted to a random man in the hostel about this and they felt that they were free, in that they could clearly see progress going on roads, bridges flats being built and that our society was little different to what we see in the UK. The only noticeable difference they said was that they didn't go through the motions of voting which changed absolutely nothing. I suppose there were some advantages of dictatorship the long-term view is taken rather than just constantly worrying about public perceptions. "We are the last sovereign country in the world; I can make profit own things without government interference isn't that true freedom?" he said.

I'll tell you a story, in 2008 the a company sold tainted milk which ended up killing some babies and making many people ill, the chief executives were shot and the CEO sent to life in prison with hard labour. In the UK they would be issued a small fine.

The stories about Chinese government informants are also rubbish. You get 100s of people all over the place wearing red armbands saying security service. In reality these are all old people who sit around playing chess, drinking beer and doing illegal things themselves like spitting or hawking fake goods blatantly. When they see a real police officer or internal security department employee coming all of a sudden they hide all their own illegal things and become officious in looking for criminals as if there was some sort of manhunt going on. In return for them volunteering the government gets to say how many security forces they have and the old people get a bung now and again.

295

I had a walk to scout out Wangfujin street which looked like a high street in New York it was so modern and commercialised. David Beckham, Tiger Woods and athletes I had never heard of stared at me from giant posters and TV screens dotted around promoting various running shoes and sporting goods it felt soulless. The prices of everything there were from Europe too.

By complete accident en-route back to Qianmen I bumped into a girl called SQ that translates into small bridge. SQ and myself a year ago had a short lightening relationship in Hong Kong in the vein of Eagle eye Cherry's save tonight. However we had parted company at the end of a wonderful 2-week holiday in Hong Kong. She phoned me and said she was going back to Beijing in the middle of 2008. We had known each other for years but we were always in the wrong place 9000 miles apart and nothing was ever really suggested but we had remained good friends with each of us not taking the next step. I am the king of coincidence. In 2008 I met an acquaintance where we took the same ferry out to Santander. He went east I went south. 5 days later we happened to be riding along the same stretch of road in Benidorm. What are the odds of that with 499,542-km2 land and a complicated road network where we were on a back road at the same time in the same place? We caught up on what we had been doing the past year but she had to go and we didn't exchange contact details as I expect I will never see her again. It was a pleasant meeting but we had clearly moved on from each other. Almost like when you meet friends who are no longer friends you make small idle talk out of politeness.

The next two days there was nothing to do as I had seen everything, the vampire girl had lost interest in me and the hostel was empty. This is where I met Ollie, the Dutchman and the Aussie. This started out slowly with general chat about life the universe and everything. Ollie was coming through Beijing to spend a year teaching English and learning mandarin in China and had stopped off until his train left in 2 days and was in the hostel café to drown his sorrows as his GF had dumped him. The Aussie was going off to Mongolia on the train the next morning and like me had been stuck in Beijing friendless and generally spent time drinking in the bar.

The Dutchman was recently divorced after not being able to get on with his ex-wife and decided just for the hell of it to drive his car across Russia. He set fire to it in the Gobi desert walking across the border into China and taking a bus to Beijing. The best piece of advice I could give him was an old saying I had stored for 12 years in the back of my mind purposely for such an occasion:

"It doesn't matter if she is ugly as Sin, as when you are poking the fire you aren't looking at the mantelpiece." I stated. He shot me down of course by saying it's not always about poking the fire. He was essentially flash packing (flashy backpacking) his way around the world for a year to try to enjoy himself again as it had been a very messy split. By the end of the evening we had become a fairly large group attracting some Germans who could only say hello. A Japanese guy who didn't speak 2 Korean guys and 2 Israelis a far right and far lefty Israeli who couldn't stop arguing about it.

We spent the next 2 days doing very little and spending time drinking going to Karaoke bars where myself and Ollie who could speak Mandarin (well less me more him) quite well pulled off a tear jerking rendition of the Chinese song Bloodstained glory... there wasn't a dry eye in the house. Though this was less to do with our angelic voices or a stellar performance. No much more to do with the fact that this song has been so carefully written by PRC propagandists so it tugs at the heart strings unsurprisingly it had taken 4 years to write.

We eventually ending up in a massage / sauna place a completely vanilla massage / sauna place sewer mind. In the middle of the massage the power went off and Ollie's wallet went missing and the girl also vanished when the power came back on. He started going nuts shouting accusations about as to his wallet being stolen. He turned a bright shade of red when it turned out to have dropped under the bed thankfully they didn't understand his English very well (I hope). For once a massage had gone well no brutality a sexy girl in white trousers and white T-shirt gave a nice gentle relaxing massage and smiled sweetly. It was nice instead of the usual get your elbows and knees dug in submission hold type massages I've had previously.

We managed to get kicked out of several all you can eat places as we ate too much not counting on a bunch of backpackers who had been on the road for nearly half a year, we ate like savages. We found ourselves in karaoke bars. We found ourselves even in an ice cream shop so incredibly drunken the shopkeepers had to keep rushing out and pulling our faces out of the giant ice creams in case we drown in them.

Most memorable was when Ollie decided to go into a sex shop as a joke and managed to fill a shopping cart with an Hispanic queen model dolls which printed on the side of the box said 'life like skin, an inviting vibrating anus and realistic vagina with realistic moaning sounds' though I suppose they could make a realistic female doll for bikers with realistic moans.

"Me bum hurts."

"Don't go so fast."

"The state of me hair."

"Buy a car."

"I don't like camping."

"Are we nearly there yet?" Ollie then proceeded to ask the man in perfect mandarin if he could try it out before he could buy it. The shopkeeper a gasp at what was happening looked at me in a saucer eyed fashion as if demanding an explanation from me and booted us out.

In a haze of taxi rides neon lights and unfamiliar faces I found myself with a killer hangover on the hostel bed I hadn't been in for the last 2 days and promptly fell asleep for once.

We or rather I was woken by shouting and screaming. Lots of shouting and screaming. I opened the door and popped my head out just in time to be hit by a grubby plastic basin, which was just as well really as it woke me up and alerted me to dangerous flying objects. More people had opened their doors now and popped their heads round the door as the shouting got more and more intense louder and more things being screamed. It was early morning so I wanted to go for my early morning pee to relive myself of all the beer I had sampled last night but the two cleaning ladies were fighting and started beating each other with cleaning tools. A plunger, a horribly stained scrubbing brushes all sorts. This prevented me from entering the toilet area and with last night's beer wanting to come out virtually unchanged into a urinal I just stood and watched thinking it would be all over shortly. The staff of the hostel seemed to be clearly embarrassed at the incident saying sorry, sorry, and sorry for this. While the guests staying just watched this little drama unfold. It came to a head when they were wrestling each other and one of the cleaning ladies floored the other one grabbed a handful of shit out of convenient bucket of shit and rubbed it into the face of the other cleaning lady. Who screamed getting it in her eyes and mouth and started crying and screaming in horror at this and it seemed to be all over, in a gross kind of way.

The guesthouse staff were still saying sorry and helping the woman off the ground. When she sprang up grabbed the bucket of shit (why were there buckets of shit everywhere?) and threw the contents towards the woman walking away.... Into the hall where everybody had poked their heads round the doors I saw this coming a mile off and ducked the blanket of shit which went everywhere and some of it into the ceiling fan. Which was thankfully switched off where it went EVERYWHERE, onto the walls, the ceiling the staff and the there was screaming by mostly girls who had been curious to see what was going on and had been watching sleepy eyed and unprepared for flying objects. Which caused gagging and mass vomiting which in turn caused more gagging and vomiting I quickly packed my bag (another argument for packing ultra light) and checked out as today was the day I left Beijing I said goodbye to the Israelis for the experience and went to get a taxi to the train station.

After telling this story to a Beijing resident at the train station while waiting I discovered that there is a regulation for toilets that do not flush (and the ones at the hostel did not flush properly) you are not supposed to shit in the toilet as this blocks the toilets, and sewers. Much like Korea and Russia where used bog roll is

298

not flushed away but put in a bin beside the toilet. Thus there is some poor bloke whose job it is to collect shit and cart it away and presumably the bucket of shit was for collection, and I used to think my job was bad.

On getting home I discovered a book called NSITT ~ no shitting in the toilet which confirmed this story. The train station is a misnomer though as Beijing is so massive it has 4 train stations. Unfortunately Beijing was under lock down for some reason there were no buses, no metro system and no taxis, walking hurriedly to the station another rickshaw driver nearly hit me and offered me a ride.

"How much?" I asked.

"Ersh," he responded. I hopped on and so did another bloke who sat sideways on the armrest. I immediately realised this was a HUGE mistake. Although there are fenced off cycle lanes for bicycles my driver was reluctant to use them and dodged in and out through the cycle lanes onto the main road. Cars zipping left and right honking their horns until we had to cross a road a big one. An 8-lane road never really fazes me as long as you have the ability to get away quickly to escape. The arc de' triumph in Paris for example is a 13 entry roundabout with 10 lanes with a slippery cobbled street and is no problem on a motorbike. Unfortunately we were on a barely quarter of a horsepower electric bike overloaded with the rickshaw me and another guy along for the ride. My driver who I was questioning the sanity of or the possibility he had a death wish stopped right in the middle of the cross roads, turned back to face me and said ok, ok, no problem! As I watched cars zip by inches from the box I was sitting in, when he saw a gap which didn't look like a gap to me he pushed his little red button and the rickshaw juddered unpleasantly and slowly accelerated. I noticed we'd lost the passenger on the armrest and we were accelerating a bit faster and onto a dedicated concrete tunnel sort of cycle path and into the courtyard of the train station another dodged bullet there.

45: STRANGERS ON A TRAIN

From outside as I approached Beijing west train station a huge blob appeared out of the smog a gigantic pagoda atop a gigantic concrete box that was the train station. It didn't look so big last time, but then I left at night last time to Pingyao. I arrived with an hour to spare plenty of time and was unable to find the international departure gate. The train station only really had two gates for departures anyway so I was quick to find that destination Hong Kong did not leave from these gates. Reunification in 1997 didn't really extend to border formalities and Hong Kong is a separate country by virtue of the S.A.R (special administrative region) like Macau, which is the other one. I made several laps of the train station it provided me with no clues as to my departure gate and the state fetid air with 10000s of people created an infernal amount of heat added to the fact that 9999 of those people were smoking made it worse. I had another look at the boards that had proved so useful to me going to Pingyao and nothing saying Hong Kong again. 45 minutes left and I was in a slight panic about this and finally asked people showing them my ticket and they pointed to upstairs. Where lo and behold a door where immigration for international departures left much to my relief I wondered if questions would be asked about why I had a 90 day double entry visa and barely stayed for a third of it. Though all visas cost the same anyway so I got the most I could at the embassy in UB.

They have to sell snacks / food and things on the platform, they have to. They did sell and quite a lot of other food but just not on this platform, and it was straight through immigration to the train. The T97 'express' to Hong Kong. Why was I on a train? Since flying to Hong Kong was actually cheaper whereas a flight to Hong Kong costs 500 RMB. The train cost 507RMB (about £50 compared to £57).

I suppose it's because a flight is completely single serving the idea that was bounded around in the book/film fight club. You get on have a snack and there you are. While a train is the more romantic notion sort of like dreams of the orient express whereby you would sit and play chess over a glass of wine with your fellow passengers. Though the orient express is actually a rusted hulk of a train dumped in Turkey somewhere sometime during the 1970s. All of the additional time involved with a train allows you to get to know the people you are travelling in greater detail and therefore they are most definitely not single serving. Though for a 1200-mile train ride it was a bargain, mile for mile it cost less than the Tube in

London, or the metro link in Manchester. Though it is not fair to compare it to the tube in London which mile for mile is more expensive than the defunct Concorde.

In effect I had traversed Siberia and, the route through Siberia was either near the road or near the Trans Siberian railway. As you will know in previous chapters camping out there was rough, between cities the distances were immense and hence you generally had to spend time camped out near the railway or the road. I would sometimes look out of my tent or rather hear the Tran Siberia and think the people travelling on those trains were luckier than me as I'd had a few nights thinking what am I doing here? A train would allow me to see it from the other side I suppose and the dull thud of the wheels against the gaps in the track had become sort of a soothing tone to my ears.

Ollie had told me two nights prior to look for a girl named Holly and eyes were peeled to look out for this Holly who couldn't be missed. He just said look out for a girl with great tits and Holly was supposed to be the 'romance of the train', that was the plan anyway. In that of all forms of transport bus / airplane / car / motorbike / camel / horse a train or maybe a boat is the only real way you can get some romancing done without causing too much of a stir.

Getting on the train was simple enough, and the train was primed for Chinese efficiency i.e. a place which would have seated 3 people tops or maybe 4 if the aisle was included had 6 beds crammed into that space with a couple of steel fold out steps to clamber your way to the top almost like a child's climbing frame you might have found in a park 10-15 years ago. It was somewhat cosy even for Asia. Packed isn't really the right word for it, as this by no stretch of the imagination was packed no sir. Packed is either the Hong Kong or Tokyo metro during the morning or evening rush home. Quite often you will see photos even videos of the metro systems in Asia. Pleasant mannered people will stand on the platforms to push (read cram) more people on board than the train car has capacity for. No matter how full the train already is more people can get onboard, there are plenty of photos and videos of that.

What there is less of are videos and pictures of the conditions INSIDE the train carriages during these busy periods. If anybody could raise their arm to raise a camera they would get a picture of the inside. But the real reason was because if those pictures and videos of the busy periods inside the carriages got out into the real world the UN would make a beeline for the HQ of the metro company and make a UN indictment against them for crimes against humanity. Cattle en-route to the abattoir get more space than people do on Asian metro systems though Seoul was a notable exception, perhaps it is because there are so many alternative routes and the distance between stops is walk able and the buses exceptionally efficient is a factor in this.

The first impressions the train kind of remind me of retirement in a way, in that you are trapped with nothing particular to do other and the pressure of time keeping is removed from you. You think should I read this book now or later, or should I get a cup of tea or some noodles or eat hmm what should I do today, bar maybe the regular swaying on the tracks and all the people around you. Though when the other passengers who would share my compartment came in it all of a sudden seemed cosier than I would like. Though thankfully this train was a sleeper train trains in China for anything more than 8 hours have hard and soft sleeper compartments. I had heard horror stories of train journeys from other people where there were no sleeper cars and it was just seats such as the forth class cars on the Trans Siberia railway. But china had improved its trains an awful lot the bad stories generally revolved around India though this again may have changed.

My sister had a few years ago backpacking in India and spent a horrible time on a train where bribery was normal where guards would take your ticket and demand you buy another one as you conveniently had the wrong ticket each and every time. This would happen time and again at each stop.

In fact Doug on one of our drunken nights in Mongolia had told me a tale of woe on an Indian train. Where he bought the ticket days in advance and set down his backpack on a hard wooden seat in a crowded carriage and promptly fell asleep. He awoke suddenly and the train had stopped and was completely devoid of people with shouting and heavy footsteps coming down the corridor he promptly shat his pants. When a man with a rifle came into his car the guard said tickets please! Punched his ticket and moved on. Apparently in India this happens a lot Doug said as he travelled by train an awful lot as he was virtually retired and time meant very little to him. What had actually happened is that all the people on the train had no tickets and when the train stopped for a ticket inspection they promptly scarpered into the wilderness next to the train track alas I digress.

I didn't want to be retired so soon and turned to the young boy sat opposite me on the lowest bunk. It turned out he was going to Hong Kong after visiting his grandparents in Tianjin and had been there just as I was leaving. I seemed woefully under prepared for this trip too (what's new?). His parents unloaded an enormous amount of food for a 26-hour train ride. Two chickens, which looked like they had been run over by a van. Some meaty long thin sausages and enough fruit to make Carmen Miranda jealous.

His sister promptly walked in and plonked herself next to me and joined in the mini interrogation. It started as an interrogation anyway until it turned into virtual hero worship. She was one of those dizzy happy shiny people whom the cynicism and crap of the world just flow over her and do not affect her a rare breed.

Asian people by enlarge are not that adventurous. Too many of them buy into the bullshit of getting good grades at school, college then university to get a good job and be a sort of home boy/girl. Then to get married and settle down to buy stuff and produce more children who go to school and get good grades. The idea of adventure to a person in Hong Kong is to go to Lamma Island for a weekend, Lamma island being a two hour ferry ride from Hong Kong Island and that is only two hours as the ferry is painfully slow, though there are of course exceptions in that it's not everybody's cup of tea. As Doug put it well we've got to have some people who stay behind and work to keep our currencies strong don't we and of course people to buy travel books like this to help weary adventurers recoup their funds and live vicariously through our experiences.

Though this might be something to do with the low number of days off people get in Asia as well. Two weeks is quite standard in Hong Kong, Taiwan, Korea and Japan (though in Mainland China people are mandated a week off alone for the founding day of the PRC, Mao's birthday and all sorts of bank holidays that the government won't budge on). But people do not take the two weeks they only take one to show loyalty to their companies seems a silly situation if you ask me. Overworked tired staff most certainly do not perform as well as refreshed rested staff, seems like a false dichotomy to be honest. I suppose a trek like my own which was coming to an end in a little under 25 hours would not be possible in a week. Even the fastest people around the world on a motorbike take 2-3 weeks of constant riding to circumnavigate the planet. I do however respect their indomitable nature though that they will try and try and try even if they fail they will pick themselves up dust themselves off and try again. It made a refreshing change to moaning.

Before I went off on that little tangent I was saying I didn't want to be retired so quickly so I went to explore the train a bit. The train was about 17 cars long with a dining car at the end and soft sleepers and deluxe super soft sleepers right near the restaurant car. It was ironic that the lower class passengers had western style sit down toilets while the soft sleepers and up got the squat type toilets. I did wonder though who paid for those kinds of things as they were much more expensive than a flight, and by my working if you cram 6 people into the same space the train company will make so much more money. Though they did have one luxury the hard sleepers didn't have showers I later found out that deluxe super soft sleepers have their own toilets. I see a terrible disadvantage of this in that if you make a mess in the toilet the person sharing it with you automatically knows it must have been you. No use attempting the old it was like that when I found it. Hmm I seem a bit obsessed about toilets on this trip of mine. I appear to talk about them in each chapter. I assume this is because other than sleeping, which you generally don't notice because you are asleep using a toilet is where you are most vulnerable and most aware of your vulnerability.

Alas I got to the dining car as I found nothing to hold my interest in the passenger cars, the entertainment system on the train did fire up which consisted of Beijing opera being played over a crackly PA system. Lucky for me I found an off switch thing and turned it off much to the relief of everybody in the car. As we pulled out of Beijing passing thousands of people tenements and houses the city soon faded away after an hour to be replaced by endless fields. Which is when I got bored of the view and decided to explore. Here I found Jonathan a Scottish Canadian (if that makes any sense) who agreed to meet me down in the dining car for beers in an hour. I also found Holly a short time later squeezing past me. Ollie was right in Beijing she did have fantastic tits. She questioned me.

"Oh wow how do you know my name how did you recognise me?" Which was a bit silly. We ploughed into the dining car a couple hours later only to be confronted with San Miguel beer that everybody hates. And to boot the beer was warm.

We discussed life the universe and everything i.e. mainly sex while Holly told me her side of the Holly and Ollie story. It turned out he dumped her and she kept trying to pump me for information as to our couple of days together in Beijing where we literally painted the town red. My attempt at romance here was killed stone dead in that Holly had met Ollie previously which was the reason for him not appearing in the café the next day for even more nefarious drinking activities. She was uncertain what to do. They had been travelling together for 4 months seeing each other day in day out 24 hours a day and had gotten sick of each other's company. Yet separated for a few days seemed to realise they missed each other. She was very confused as what to do and attempted to get myself and Jonathan to help her make this choice I didn't help at all though as I motioned it was her choice and hers alone.

The dining car staff generally abused us; they gave us rubbish food, over charged us and kept telling us to leave the dining car. Granted the chicken peanuts were good but everything else was terrible. This was a Hong Kong owned train not a China owned train. In that China owned companies things are supposed to be better as people want to keep their jobs hence a Big Mac should you try one in Beijing will be superior to that of one in Hong Kong. We felt the same thing was happening here in that since it was a Hong Kong owned train the staff generally didn't care. We did however drink the bar dry even though they were disgusting warm beers and Holly produced a set of hardcore pornographic playing cards where we played poker with cards that had poking on them. This shocked the reserved staff, as this was not your untactful page 3 this was the hard stuff with men with animalistic features and where the au naturelé look was in fashion at the time. This did actually make me wonder what is considered hard-core porn these days. TV producers had been pushing the boundaries for decades. In that once the ball started rolling it was impossible to stop. It started out unnoticed in the 1950s with the odd swear word here and there provoking rage directed at points of view or what ever they had in the 1950s. Then an exposed buttock here and there. And a nipple, which would have infuriated people of the time. Then a harsher swear word and *two* buttocks not always necessary from the same person, then graven images of bear bottomed teenagers swearing in the presence of nuns…. Then nuns in their underwear…. Then naked nuns… then naked nuns with strap on phallus type objects engaged in an orgy, then naked *dead* nuns decapitated on live TV after performing a satanic ritual orgy. As we scarcely notice as we sit on our sofas barely batting an eyelid.

Though porn the 2 dimensional replacement for something somebody can't get in 3d is completely illegal in China one of those things punishable by death like so many things. In China but probably like everything else generally ignored.

We were told to shut the fuck up when we realised we had been making our own entertainment till 2am when we were told to order noodles or tea or get lost. So we ordered noodles and tea and at 3am departed and agreed to meet for breakfast. Breakfast turned out to be horrid cup noodles and drinking the fridge dry of a strangely addictive herbal tea. Life the universe and everything had already been discussed and Jonathan started to tell me all about Nepal that I should go there. My plan had been to fly out to Nepal get a bike and ride it home through India, Pakistan, Iran and Turkey to get home.

A Frenchman overheard me and ever offered me his XT200 that he had left in a shed in Kathmandu. I very nearly took him up on his offer and he told me to think about it on the slow train ride down to Hong Kong. Unfortunately there was a paperwork issue the old Carnet-de-passage. Getting it on a bike you own in the UK is difficult. Getting a carnet on a bike that you do even not own while out of the country is even more difficult. I would have to leave this to another day. Jonathan told me he had done something similar he'd bought a Royal Enfield 350 and spent a month riding around in the Jungle around goat tracks getting horrendous food poisoning that ended up with him shivering in a hot semi tropical jungle of Nepal. I think I'd had enough of riding for a little while anyway. I'd had enough of food poisoning enough of people who were interesting but could not communicate with. Most of all I was running low on money, which wouldn't have made it, back home. I thought another time maybe, strangely the if not now when motivation I used on myself didn't work here. I thought it was time to be on my way home.

46: HONG KONG THE FINISH LINE.

Hong Kong had always been the finish line of my trip Kowloon the notorious Chungking Mansions was the actual finish line, the rooftop of block A. Although Chungking mansions looks like a gigantic monolithic block it is built like many plazas in Hong Kong where there are three floors of shopping where it is almost open plan with 6 tower blocks jutting out towards the sky. It looks like a big single monolith because block A covers the entire Nathan road façade. While to the north the Holiday Inn completely blocks this side while another side is hemmed in giving the illusion that it is just a gigantic cube. Developers would have loved a cube. Cubes like I had seen in Russia far too often. As it would have given them maximum space for their grand designs i.e. more retail space more flats more of everything. Although this effect is lost as towers all around it make the mansions look insignificant though still over 4000 people call the Mansions their home.

Built in 1971 the near 40-year-old building is considered a hot bed of crime and a firetrap. This place only really came into the limelight in 1995 when a film called Chungking Express made by director Wong Kar Wai was released. Otherwise this place would just be another slum and thus nothing special. A mere 150 metres down the road is another mansion the Mirador. It is considerably less famous due to nobody making a film called Mirador Express. The Irony is that Chungking express the entire second half was filmed on Hong Kong Island nowhere near the mansions, and that the first part generally showed the mansions as a bad place of drug smuggling and violent crime. I do wonder if the mansion was a clean and organised place if it would be so famous I suppose not in that if it was it would blend seamlessly into the 1001 other clean organised malls that make up Hong Kong's commercial districts. I wonder how much of an impact "uptown plaza express" would have made. Though Chungking express was not a commercial success it gained a cult following only afterwards.

Busan was the finish of the XT part of the trip, but Hong Kong was the terminus finito nowhere else to go. There had not been enough time at the start of my trip to organise any farther movement to South East Asia and no Carnet to go south.

As the train creaked past Shenzhen down to Lo Wu. I had effectively entered Hong Kong territory. A painfully slow trek down the old KCR (Kowloon Canton Railway now part of the MTR) down to Hung Hom. The finish line was tantalising close enough that I could taste the spicy Indian snacks found almost exclusively in the Chungking Mansions. The immigration in Hong Kong is fast and slick taking me all of 12 seconds to enter and clear immigration. The computerised entry system even welcomes you in is a nice touch it may just be a couple of lines of computer code and a couple of pre-recorded words maybe all it is but when the border control says.

"Hello Welcome Home!" It is a nice little touch compared to the UK where the immigration officers look at you suspiciously and don't say a word other than next. Or even worse the ones who want to know where you've been. Who you've been with where you stayed and a million intricate and probing questions as an abuse of their power to make you feel ten inches tall. Imagine if immigration were how I wanted it to be in the UK, i.e. a strong handshake perhaps even a hug from the customs officer who then proceeds to say in a cheery voice, people would feel welcome as if they belonged.

"Welcome home lad, lookin' good son good to have you back!"

Chungking mansions is one of my favourite places in Hong Kong, if I ever move to Hong Kong I can have a taste of Birmingham by visiting this extremely cosmopolitan area around Nathan road in proximity to the mansions. My dad effectively calls Chungking mansions affectionately as "a shit hole," It suddenly occurred to me that on my trip I had seen a virtual monoculture punctuated by the odd backpacker here and there. Even in Seoul that was supposed to be highly cosmopolitan I hadn't seen many black or Indian people at all. The last of which I had seen were in a petrol station en-route to Dover.

Hong Kong north of Lion Rock considered the Northern territories (once the PRC took control in 1997) or New Territories previously the colonial name. You only ever see Chinese people it feels uniform, dull and almost bland. The Mansions are a stark contrast to this. They are good place to hang out and hide actually as you rarely see Chinese people in the Mansions. It's almost a mini city a world apart from the Golden Mile of Nathan Road and Hong Kong just outside. An Iconic landmark, which contains the ghosts of the Kowloon walled city. Walled city was, destroyed in 1994 when the PRC and British government finally agreed after 50 years of negotiation. The walled city was a model functioning anarchic society, if that makes any sense. The walled city was proof that the Hobson's choice of law and order and the bad things that comes with that or chaos were the only choices was not real.

The walled city in Hong Kong is gone now and all that remains is a small piece in Kowloon Park where the city used to be. Although I romanticise about the place it can be an utter dump though. Open sewers, backed up toilets that have not been

307

flushed since Hong Kong was British (1997). Though it stands out as defiance against what many people in Hong Kong would consider as decent normal society, it's ugly it's rotten but almost all the culture in Hong Kong is contained within its imposing walls. It's iconic almost like the statue of liberty is to people who migrated to the US in the 1800s the Mansions perhaps serves the same purpose.

With Jonathan in tow for a couple nights on the town, we said goodbye to Holly and stepped onto the metro. One stop to the Mansions, in my memory I remember it almost in slow motion climbing the stairs at Tsim Shar Tsui exit E1 and entering the day light of Hong Kong for the first time and the blistering heat causing a deluge of sweat which didn't evaporate due to the humidity. Places never look the same as they do in the night. In the cold hard light of the day, or in our case the bracingly hot sunlight of the day, Nathan road looked decidedly decayed and rotten. The last time I was here I left at night where the neon signs burned holes in your retina. All of the noise and the electric heat and the pulse of the city vanishes during the day and as such Nathan road effectively looked like a slum, which is partially is. The Neon lights ironically the symbolism of modern urban nightlife, glowing seductively in all sorts of garish colours but contains nothing but gas. Passing under the archway of the Mansion entrance a hustler who had refined his sales technique instead of the usual droll lines of.

"You want suit? Tailor made very cheap!"

"You want Rolex? Good bargain!"

"Telephone card sir?" For some reason Hong Kong people do not use Skype. More often asked at the Mansion entrance however was the favourite of touts all over

"Guesthouse, cheap very cheap, you come now please?" he said.

"Welcome to Chungking Mansion can I help you?"

"No thanks I'm great."

"No problems have a good day." There were even some touts who had refined their sales technique to immediately disarm you of any hostility who would Japanese you, i.e. they would start by apologising for hassling you and would suggest a hostel or a guesthouse in the mansions and would kindly take us there. Normally touts I don't particularly like being hustled by them but this made me feel as if I had come home.

It almost bought a tear to my eye. The sights the sounds the smells all a feast for the senses, something I had not seen since Istanbul. Nepali music mixed with Hindi music mixed with modern pop. A hundred different alien languages spoken literally rubbing shoulders with hundreds of people. The smell of kebabs, Indian snacks samosas deep fried onions the rancid toilets and rotting food, people praying on the ground hundreds of shops, happy faces, sad faces, angry faces, indifference.

The almost laissez faire nature of it all money changing hands under tables in envelopes it was oxymoronic in that it was virtually controlled chaos. On the 1st floor the Kebab shop owner greeted me and called me by name. He even remembered my favourite shami kebabs, what a way to end the trip even the shops back home which I've visited 1000 times don't remember my orders or my name. All of the above and for a hundred reasons more is why I like this place I like this place a lot, I know that if I were to ever make the move to Hong Kong that I would visit this place regularly.

Checking into Taiwan guesthouse abandoning our luggage in the room we made for the roof just in time to catch the sunset over Hong Kong. I had finally made it. I had crossed two continents overland unassisted passed through 19 countries en-route to be here and it was a perfect moment to have crossed the finish line. Enjoying a cool beer watching the sunset Jonathan and me went our separate ways for a few hours as I had two promises to fulfil. Those who have followed my blog of my trip must think I am utterly stupid / brave / mad (delete as appropriate) to have continued when disaster pain, injury and life threatening events occurred. I had always said.

I MUST NOT FAIL; I WILL NOT FAIL

This mentality emblazoned on my mind. When family and friends pleaded with me to come back home I kept on going. Part of the reason for this was a feeling that if I turned back I would be a failure. Another part would be I would never know what it would feel like to have done a complete trip.

In my experience of work I often saw people who would often say things such as 'if only,' I had a fear of becoming one of them. I could imagine in five, ten twenty or even just next week sitting at an office desk starring out of the window thinking "If only."

I still had one last thing to do a private matter, which was one of the main motivators of this trip. Suffice to say this reason is private as I said before everybody has some secret to keep and I am no different and therefore it will remain so. Suffice to say that this matter epitomised the adage that life is short, not dissimilar to that of the ancients who would parade the desiccated bodies of their elders to remind them that life is short and all things are fleeting.

After all this was finished I jumped on a bus to take me back to TST. The bus to Tung Chung arrived quickly and the MTR into Kowloon was just as smooth and slick. A warm a sense of achievement something that few people would ever do a milestone in my life had been planted. I stepped across the platform onto the Tseun Wan MTR line changed over to the Hong Kong Island Line and stepped out into Causeway bay. A short walk that felt like a dream and a quick ride to the 16th floor of a nearby building. I unlocked the door and stepped in quietly and sat on the cool leather sofa for a while careful not to wake anybody up. The faint hum of the air conditioning in one of the rooms the only noise above the background din of the city. I failed in this regard though as I heard somebody stirring turn on the lights and their soft footsteps approach me from behind.

Surprised and rubbing her eyes still half asleep, she gave me quick hug from behind a peck on the cheek and slumped half asleep into my lap she asked.

"Where have you been? You look terrible!" As I lifted her up and moved her to her bed sitting to one side while she slipped under the covers:

I said to her softly "I'd like to tell you a story."

EPILOGUE

I spent some time in China before coming back just to extend the trip out a little bit more, just to extend the escape from reality just a little bit more, but there is an old saying.

"All good things"

Eventually most of us bar perhaps Doug and Richard have to come back one day and if my life was just one constant journey. A constant travel I suppose that would one day perhaps grow boring. Almost like being suddenly thrust into the deep end of a pool you sink or swim. Everyday life afterwards hasn't lost its routine in fact from seeing the world out there everything seems more ordinary and restricted than before I left. It is as if I am watching the world on a monitor screen seeing everything around me is an artificial reality almost as if there is something deeply wrong with the world.

On my trip there was only one goal to ride and the most complex decision I made on a daily basis was where to ride. What to eat and where to sleep sometimes not even having to make these decisions. Day after day riding, eating, sleeping and the odd bit of maintenance put into that and this was a nice carefree routine. The future was what happened in the next hour or so and all that mattered immediately was the carefree present.

The question I ask myself is now what? It seems as if there is some sort of void in my life like a black hole almost, I wake up and get out of my soft warm bed that I did not have out there and consider what needs to be done today and slide exactly into route almost exactly as before I left.

My sister came out to see me in Hong Kong before I came home and after I came back she noticed I had slid back into my old ways, from being chilled, relaxed and hopeful about the future I slid back into my niche. This doesn't mean I regret going on this trip far from it, but as the old Sheffield based pop group Pulp once said:

"Something changed"

All I see around me galls me and it seems that there is just so much unnecessary froth to our society in the UK, people work chasing non existent dreams as the television betrays them, thinking they will all grow up to be actors famous or rock stars. So much to the extent that people have an artificial world built around them and fear to leave this. The most trivial things that upset people's world seem

311

pointless such as the TV change over from analogue to digital. As I sit in a café-hearing people complain as if this is the most important thing in the world. I have had this feeling before. Alberto in Spain an Italian who was the happiest man I had ever seen. He had nothing worked a dead end job but nothing really bothered him and he seemed truly happy. In that I had witnessed hundreds of people through my trip like that and it all just seemed that our society it was I don't know sick? That it was wrong that people spent their lives lining the pockets of others.

I have to force myself into grudging acceptance of the things I see around me, I spent time with friends, and engaged in catharsis of my bike trip by writing this very book. My re-integration into society back to reality. The real world integration has been slow but bit-by-bit what I built up out there who I am and who I became diminishes which is incredibly sad really but who I am out there is not who I am back home I suppose.

The me who was formed out there however not been totally destroyed as I can still think back to the hundreds of people I met. Their faces, their voices, the places I saw, nothing can take this away from me and they will remain a milestone in my life until the day that I die and become dust to be returned to the earth.

I have always considered dreams to be a double edged sword in that you spend your time dreaming about them which helps us pass the drudgery of each day, but what we often fail to address is what happens when you achieve your dreams? What then? What do you dream about from then on?

Perhaps, the next one?...........Now there's a plan

Leon K Pang 2009

XT600 gets an overhaul

Minor repair (starter relay) on the XT600E at Calais port facility

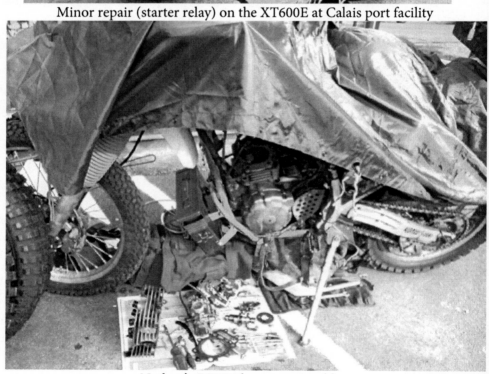

Nathan's DR350 has some troubles

Turkish Mechanics, Left Eruzium, Right 'The Master' Trabzon

Terry on the road towards Trabzon

Bike cop in Batumi, on his XJ900 with bald tyres.

Roman & Mechanics in Volgograd

Africa Twin Pilot Serge lends a hand

Russian Billiards, I could never get the hang of this game.

Tomoro from Japan on his SR500

Lars and Lars after the bad bit towards Irkutsk

Walter (right) and Tony about to Leave Irkutsk, Stass says goodbye

Baikanour Bike Club in Irkutsk

Andreas and Claudia about to leave for Mongolia

Exhausted en-route to Mongolia

Oasis Café Ulaan Baator, Claudia's F800 in the shed

A nomad tending to his animals

Typical *ger* camp Mongolia.

Altan Ulrag plays at Ik Mongol, Doug and Rosa from Hamburg

An accidental picture of Sukebaator Square.

The XT exchanged for 4 legs

Tereji Town centre

Simon, Ingrid and Andi at countryside Nadeem festival

Nadeem festival in Ulaan Baatar stadium opening ceremony

Middle of Nowhere depressing signs

2165KM till the next town!

Amur Highway

Kim, Kim and Choi

A nice campsite on the Amur for a change, the Koreans have done one down the track between the trees.

Tyre repairman David in Tynda

End of the Amur highway at last beautiful tarmac!

Vladivostok at last!

Zarubino

Seoul

(Above) One of the many ancient city gates in Seoul

Hongdae Nightlife

Kim and 'fake' Jesus at a nightclub Hongdae.

Shooting range down town Seoul.

A typical courier bike in Seoul notice the extra side stand

Namsan Park those are padlocks secured to the fence

Namsan Park the safest wall on Seoul messages of forever love.

Simon and Park while travelling on the Seoul Metro.

Chungking Mansions, Nathan Road Hong Kong.

Jonathan on the roof of Block A Chungking Mansions

Lightning Source UK Ltd.
Milton Keynes UK
22 November 2010

163249UK00002B/81/P